Engaging
Cinema

Engaging
Cinema

AN INTRODUCTION TO FILM STUDIES

BILL NICHOLS

W. W. NORTON & COMPANY, INC.

Independent and Employee-Owned

New York | London

W. W. Norton & Company has been independent since its founding in 1923, when William Warder Norton and Mary D. Herter Norton first published lectures delivered at the People's Institute, the adult education division of New York City's Cooper Union. The firm soon expanded its program beyond the Institute, publishing books by celebrated academics from America and abroad. By midcentury, the two major pillars of Norton's publishing program—trade books and college texts—were firmly established. In the 1950s, the Norton family transferred control of the company to its employees, and today—with a staff of four hundred and a comparable number of trade, college, and professional titles published each year—W. W. Norton & Company stands as the largest and oldest publishing house owned wholly by its employees.

Book design by Chris Welch
Art direction by Lissi Sigillo
Copyediting by Jodi Beder
Composition by Roberta Flechner
Manufacturing by LSC Harrisonburg
Production manager: Benjamin Reynolds
Drawn art by Dragonfly Media Group

ISBN: 978-0-393-93491-5

W. W. Norton & Company, Inc.
500 Fifth Avenue, New York, N.Y. 10110-0017
www.wwnorton.com

W. W. Norton & Company Ltd.
15 Carlisle Street, London W1D 3BS

8 9 0

To Bob Rosen, through the
decades and across many miles,
an inspiring colleague and an
indispensable friend

Contents in Brief

Contents

Part II   The Social Context

To the Instructor
(and the Curious Student)

Film is central to the representation of values and beliefs, customs and practices in modern culture. As a society, we unite through the bond of shared values or divide along the fault lines of disputed beliefs. What brings a social group together? How do groups acquire power or experience its absence? How does any group represent itself or respond to the representations of others? What role do stereotypes, hierarchy, power, and desire play in the circulation of images? Answers to these questions demand that such qualities be linked to the specific social and historical context in which they arise as well as to the formal qualities of cinematic representation. *Engaging Cinema* devotes itself to demonstrating how linkages between a social and a formal context yield distinct insights.

The original, founding assumptions of film studies were three: (1) film is an art; its aesthetic features are paramount; (2) viewers enter into a transcendental realm of appreciation divorced from social and historical specificity, and (3) all well-trained viewers respond in similar ways to the aesthetic power of a great film. These assumptions lead to an emphasis on formal techniques such as editing, lighting, camera, and sound, which texts usually present on a chapter-by-chapter basis.

When it was first published, David Bordwell and Kristin Thompson's *Film Art* gave the discipline the tool it needed to earn a place in the humanities in the 1970s. Through a multitude of editions, this comprehensive and valuable book has grown more and more thorough, more and more complex, but it has never shifted its primary focus from the aesthetic and formal qualities of film.

Other introductory books have followed suit, attempting, in some cases, to add a greater degree of reference to social and political issues, but retaining the core assumption that the study of film revolves around an appreciation of film's aesthetic techniques. These elaborations and refinements conform to what Thomas Kuhn, in his great work *The Structure of Scientific Revolutions*, termed "normal science." Normal science takes an existing paradigm and fleshes out its many implications and consequences. It does not result in what he termed a "paradigm shift," in which basic assumptions are questioned and an entirely new way of seeing things arises. Such a paradigm shift took place in film some time ago, roughly in step with the rise of the women's movement, but our introductory textbooks have failed to incorporate it into their basic design.

Engaging Cinema reverses the assumptions that founded film studies as a discipline in the 1970s. It offers, for the first time, an introductory text that responds to the paradigm shift that has swept the humanities, including film studies, during the last twenty to thirty years. *Engaging Cinema*, like our discipline today, adopts three alternative assumptions: (1) film's social implications are paramount even though the cinema relies on aesthetic means to convey these implications affectively; (2) viewers respond to films in direct relation to their actual social and historical situation; as a result, the perceived significance or greatness of a film will vary with time and place; and (3) different viewers and groups of viewers in the same time and place interpret any film, including great films, in different, but understandable, ways.

The organization of this book reflects this paradigm shift, with its stress on the linkage between formal technique and social impact, with chapters that take up film as a language, the constraints and opportunities any formal or social system affords, the rhetorical power of documentaries, the social function of genre films, the cultural value of narrative storytelling, the differences between realism, modernism, and postmodernism, and issues of ideology, ethnicity, masculinity, and feminism, among others.

Instead of creating a divide between "content analysis" and "formal analysis," *Engaging Cinema* seeks to demonstrate how these approaches can be fused into a single, comprehensive framework that respects both the formal art and the social power of cinema. The book seeks to provide film instructors and those who use films in history, sociology, media studies, ethnic studies, women's studies, and other areas with a resource that directly addresses the social significance of cinema. *Engaging Cinema* places films within the formal context of the medium but always relates this to the broader social context in which films circulate.

Engaging Cinema champions, and strives to demonstrate, the value of a dual formal-social analysis. The power of film stems from the art of film but, ironically, this art, studied in isolation, loses its social power. Most film scholars join the two in their own research and in the advanced courses they teach. There is no reason to postpone to advanced levels the study of film in social contexts that makes the most sense of its genuine power. There is no need to isolate formal elements from their social content. Film scholarship has clearly shifted to address questions of historical representation, ethnicity, gender, and class alongside issues of film aesthetics and appreciation. This book seeks to integrate these two divergent concerns at the introductory level so that the split between aesthetics and content diminishes.

This approach enables students who are majoring in film to engage from the outset with questions of film's social significance. For those students who may not take any additional film courses, *Engaging Cinema* surveys the key ways in which film has figured as an important social as well as aesthetic force. Such students will not leave with a mistakenly narrow perception of what film studies is all about. They will have a range of tools to help think about the impact of film in their own lives and the lives of others. Students in other disciplines will also gain a greater sense of how film studies draws on and contributes to concepts and debates in a variety of fields from history, literature, and art history to sociology, anthropology, ethnic studies, and gender studies. No discipline is an island, and the many achievements in film studies demonstrate that point vividly.

Engaging Cinema also seeks to achieve this integration in an affordable format. Textbooks have become behemoths, commanding extraordinary prices that almost guarantee students will have to resell them at the end of a course. Their very price makes them, ironically, disposable, as does the relentless churn of new editions. *Engaging Cinema* sidesteps this problem partly by eliminating the expense of acquiring and reproducing still images. Perhaps unique among introductory film texts, *Engaging Cinema* offers no images—either frame reproductions or publicity stills.

An introductory film text without photos? Can this be possible? I believe it can be, for multiple reasons. Film stills accompanied the first film textbooks as an unquestioned necessity. And, in the 1970s, they were. University courses relied on 16 and 35mm film rentals to teach film. Few campuses possessed projectors that could freeze-frame a film print. Few courses could screen a film more than twice. Essays had to be written to a great degree from memory and from notes, and even published books contained factual errors as a result. Visual reminders were thus an important part of any book on film.

Since the 1980s, the situation has changed dramatically. First videotapes, then laserdiscs, then DVDs, and now the Internet all make films and film images readily available. Every film professor has access to a vast repertoire of images, clips, and films to show and discuss. Every film student can find work to view and review readily. This is one of the great facts of contemporary film distribution and exhibition.

Engaging Cinema does provide close analysis of specific scenes in specific films, but it leaves it up to the instructor to select visual materials that best convey concepts and questions posed here. The book does not presuppose a common curriculum and does not seek to impose one. Many films are referred to and quite a number receive detailed discussion, but the points being made could be made with other films as well. *Engaging Cinema* at once offers an economic solution to the costly problem of the modern textbook, and turns greater discretionary latitude over to the instructor. The result is a book that no longer necessitates immediate resale for most students. If these assumptions about what will fit the needs of film instructors today prove incorrect, future editions may well contain still images. By choosing to do without them in this first edition, *Engaging Cinema* is both distinct in content—stressing the social aspects of cinema over formal ones—and distinct in form—leaving the choice of illustrations to the student and instructor. Those differences separate it from all other introductory textbooks and give instructors a clear and distinct choice in how to introduce film to a new generation of students.

Acknowledgments

Without Eugenia Clarke and Catherine Soussloff this book never would have come into being. Throughout its long gestation, it has drawn its inspiration, and many of its ideas, from my former wife and my stepdaughter.

More than any other single person, the greatest debt I have is to all the colleagues and students with whom I have engaged in either the teaching or conception of introductory film courses. Such efforts began at Queen's University, Kingston, Ontario, where the introductory course was always taught by senior faculty, including myself for over ten years, and provided a genuine foundation to all of the department's endeavors. It was there that I became convinced that an introductory course was not merely a preliminary or secondary endeavor but a fundamental and crucial aspect of any film program's overall sense of shared purpose.

That said, a number of individuals have made direct and invaluable contributions to the shape of this book. Kris Fallon read and commented on earlier drafts of many chapters, some still present and some since eliminated or absorbed elsewhere. Kevin Esch provided chapter-by-chapter feedback on an earlier draft of the entire book. My Introduction to Graduate Studies seminar students Fall 2007 read and critiqued almost all the chapters of the book. These individuals— Julia Barbosa, Whitney Borup, Derek Domike, Michael Endlger, Keith Francher, David Gray, Katherine Hughes, Jonathan Hutchings, Miyo Inoue, Scott Knopf, Don Lewis, Jose Nevarez, Christina Polito, Taylor Quist, Jenny Rowland, Kyungsook Suh, and Justin Vaccaro— provided an invaluable jolt of objective insight into the limitations of the penultimate draft of the book.

David Gray also served as an assistant in the final preparation of the book. His feedback and detail-oriented attentiveness proved indispensable.

W. W. Norton & Company solicited feedback from individuals who teach introductory film courses at various institutions. Their feedback on earlier drafts generated a great deal of additional reflection and invariably led to improvement in the overall shape of the manuscript. Many limitations and weaknesses came to light even as the core strength of the book became more apparent through the direct comparisons readers made between this text and other introductory textbooks. Although they were anonymous to me during the revision process, I am glad to have the opportunity now to join my publisher in thanking them by name: Dudley Andrew (Yale University), Dennis Bingham (Indiana University–Purdue University, Indianapolis), Hisham M. Bizri (University of Minnesota–Twin Cities), Katrina G. Boyd (University of Oklahoma), Arthur Knight (College of William & Mary), Kecia McBride (Ball State University), Stuart Noel (Georgia Perimeter College), Tasha G. Oren (University of Wisconsin–Milwaukee), Tom Powers (Illinois State University), Chris Robe (Florida Atlantic University), Matthew Sewell (Minnesota State University–Mankato), and Paul David Young (Vanderbilt University).

Many of my colleagues at San Francisco State University have contributed to the book as well, sometimes unwittingly simply by dint of
their comments and observations on films and filmmakers over the
years. Pat Ferrero, Jennifer Hammett, Karen Holmes, Pat Jackson,
Aaron Kerner, Jim Kitses, Jenny Lau, Randy Rutsky, and Greta Snider
all contributed in one way or another to the final shape of the book.
Randy Rutsky also offered specific feedback on the discussion of modernism and postmodernism.

In a similar spirit, there is no one with whom I have taken greater
pleasure in the discussion of films in all contexts from film theory and
film history to film production and film distribution, in fact, in reference to everything cinematic and much that extends beyond it, than
Bob Rosen. We met in the 1960s, on a cross-country "share a ride" car
trip to Stanford University, where he was a grad student in history
and I a beginning medical student. Some years and a few career
changes later I first managed to bring Bob to UCLA as a graduate
instructor for a seminar that we, the first cohort of Ph.D. students,
had proposed. I left not too long after to take up my first appoint-
ment at Queen's University, but Bob remained to become head of the
UCLA Archive, chair of the Film Department, and eventually dean of
the School of Film, Theater, and Television. Throughout all that
time—the course of my career, in effect—he has been a great source
of knowledge, insight, and inspiration, as well as friendship. We came
to film with a shared sense of its social value, and now, some decades
later, key elements of that common vision have found their way
between the covers of a book.

At Norton, Pete Simon proved a great editor: clear and sharp in his
observations, steadfast in his commitment to the project, patient in
the evolution of the book through several drafts, and bold in his imaginative conception of an introductory film text without illustrations.
As discussed in the prefatory comments, "To the Instructor (and the
Curious Student)," the disciplinary paradigm shift that guides the con-

ceptual structure of the book parallels a similar shift in the availability of films for viewing and study. It was Pete Simon who first realized
that this offered us an opportunity to rethink the basic layout, as well
as the content, of an introductory film book. Jodi Beder provided as
thorough and astute a revision of the final manuscript as I have ever
received at the copyediting stage. It is far better book because of her
vigilant and adept hand.

The errors and omissions, of course, are mine.

Engaging
Cinema

Introduction

SOME BASIC ISSUES
AND CONCEPTS

The Appeal of the Cinema

Moving images never fail to fascinate. From the ordinary moments of family life captured in home movies to the spectacular adventures of Luke Skywalker, from the struggles of victims of Hurricane Katrina to the thrill of men walking on the moon, and from the immersive experience of an IMAX movie to the simultaneity of real-time interaction on a cell phone, moving images possess an irresistible allure. There is an art to all this: the most memorable experiences result from considerable artistic skill, but there is more to this than art alone. Seeing motion and hearing sounds where no living creature actually exists—on two-dimensional screens of all types and sizes—defies logic. The experience is a form of enchantment. Whether the classic cinema of the old-time movie palace or a streaming podcast on the Web, the power of the cinema resides in this quality. Examining the uses and implications of this enchantment forms the focus of this book.

Why we find moving images fascinating may, ultimately, defy rational explanation, but, we may still ask, to what uses has this fascination been put? What types of relationship do we have with moving images? What specific techniques contribute to the power of images to tell stories, recount histories, invent characters, confront issues, and provide pleasure? How does a given social, technological, or historical context offer opportunities but also impose constraints? What lessons, learned in the early days of cinema, continue to inform the most cutting edge work of today? Why is storytelling such an integral part of almost all moviegoing experience, and what underlying narrative principles are at work, whether in a five-minute animated cartoon like *Duck Amuck* (1953, Chuck Jones), the Paris Hilton YouTube channel, or a three-hour epic like *Lawrence of Arabia* (1962, David Lean, UK)?

The commercial means devoted to the circulation of moving images change with time. New technologies, new materials, new forms of production, distribution, and exhibition all come into play, opening up new opportunities and setting new limitations. 35mm nitrate film stock, for example, widely used until the 1940s, was highly flammable, readily bursting into flames if it jammed in the early film projectors, whose source of light came from the intensely hot glow created by a current jumping across a gap just inches from the film. A feature film on nitrate also had the bulk and weight of a small trunk. Offsetting all this was the gloriously rich, detailed image nitrate film made possible. It is no wonder that this dangerous substance has given way to LED and plasma displays that now approach the quality of nitrate itself and to digital storage devices with almost no weight at all.

The average viewer now has an enormous range of options when it comes to deciding how and where to see movies and other forms of moving image. This freedom comes with a trade-off in the immersive power of the experience and (at least for now, in the case of the Internet and hand-held devices) in the overall quality of sound and image. But while we may bemoan the loss of traditional movie viewing, less nostalgic and more enterprising spirits see that all media constantly evolve; that their future growth depends on exploiting fresh opportunities and overcoming limitations. In that sense the cinema has never been more vital than it is today.

Engaging Cinema as a Subject of Study

Why study film? What is the goal of such study? There was a time when the same questions were asked about contemporary English literature (at the turn of the twentieth century), when such study was unheard of and literature meant the Greek and Latin classics. The answer given most often is that film, like contemporary literature, represents the most artistically resourceful use of a given language, in this case, an audiovisual language. Great films are the modern vernacular equivalent of the ancient classics, embodiments of the human capacity to imagine and create in a commonly understood language. Great art represents the highest use of the creative spirit and provides a uniquely aesthetic experience. What others have attained in poetry, prose fiction, music, theater, ballet, and opera, filmmakers now attain with the tools and techniques of cinema.

Introductory studies of the art of the cinema stress the expressive techniques that are most crucial to artistic achievement: editing, sound design, cinematography, screenwriting, and so on. Aesthetic experience, usually defined as a form of experience that has no functional purpose other than to please, and that does not, therefore, provide the kind of usefulness we expect from a telephone, automobile, or item of clothing, becomes the ultimate measure of cinematic quality. By learning more about the artistic aspects of how a film gets made, we come to appreciate the complex choices and subtle differences that separate the exceptional from the pedestrian.

But while aesthetics, technique, and skill matter tremendously, these are not the qualities that attract most viewers to the cinema. What stands out as truly fascinating about movies is that they animate a series of still images. They appear to restore life itself to mere images taken from life. The fascination of moving images is something we may now take for granted, but it remains at the heart of the movies' power to enchant. They bring what happened once, before a camera, back to life, before a spectator. The cinema can document events with great fidelity; it can, for example, slow down motion so much that what would otherwise be invisible suddenly becomes remarkably clear. From home movies to global simulcasts, from historical interpretation to political mobilization, from humorous distraction to dramatic immersion, and from detached observation to spine-chilling involvement, moving images do much more than please aesthetically. Aesthetic achievement is just one criterion of significance.

Nothing argued here disputes the centrality of aesthetics. Quite the contrary. The power of moving images may often have little to do with aesthetics per se, but aesthetics are important in intensifying that power. The careful use of formal techniques is what makes moving images so memorable. *Engaging Cinema* demonstrates how various uses of cinema have emotional, intellectual, and ideological impact precisely because most films carry an aesthetic punch.

Aesthetic experience usually involves an encounter with the unexpected. Until we saw it, we did not imagine a world quite like the one of *Shrek* (Andrew Adamson and Vicky Jenson, 2001) or *Little Miss Sunshine* (Jonathan Dayton and Valarie Faris, 2006); nor had we as sharp an image of Nazism or the Ku Klux Klan as the ones that emerge from *Triumph of the Will* (Leni Riefenstahl, 1935, Germany) or *The Birth of a Nation* (D.W. Griffith, 1915). Choices are made, images presented, scenes and situations developed that take us in unexpected directions. It may be a matter of cutting back and forth between simultaneous events to telling effect in *The Birth of a Nation*, or seeing a family's young daughter demonstrate her show biz talents by performing bawdy, over-the-top vaudeville routines that her granddad just happens to think are totally appropriate in *Little Miss Sunshine*. Aesthetic achievement often goes unnoticed as the effortless grace that lets a story unfold as if it were simply telling itself, but it can also flash up in the form of something highly unconventional: an unusual or unprecedented way of using the medium of film, or a fresh, unanticipated view of social reality. Subsequent chapters will examine how formal innovation and social insight go hand in hand.

Movies are also fun, whether classics like *Gone with the Wind* (Victor Fleming, 1939) or a download of a friend's trip to Europe. Fun has an aesthetic dimension to it, but it is not necessary to identify the techniques, degree of innovation, or storytelling conventions involved in order to experience it. Fun is the by-product of letting go, enjoying oneself, and putting aside larger thoughts and concerns, at least for the moment. Fun can also have implications and consequences; it can relate to aesthetic pleasure and social issues. While carefully tying film to these contextual issues is far from a prerequisite for enjoyment, the context of technique and history adds resonance to any film, and placing it in this context gives us a much greater understanding of what draws us to the movies.

Movies contribute to a sense of belonging. That is, viewing movies creates the opportunity to participate in different forms of social activity, from going to a drive-in theater to watching a DVD at home with friends. Movies bring a range of people together, provide them with a common experience, and create a reference point around which to build shared values and beliefs. Adopting fashions, gestures, and dialogue from movies, debating a film's merits or meaning, comparing preferences of genres, directors, or stars—all these activities contribute to a sense of belonging and the building of community.

Movies also deliver a powerful emotional impact distinct from the impact of other media. This, too, relates to the ability of moving images to bring situations and events back to life on a screen as well as to aesthetics. The representation of sex and violence has been a topic for public debate since the beginnings of cinema in the nineteenth century, not simply because sex and violence provide thematic content, but because their visual representation has an extremely visceral, exciting or appalling, arousing or repellant, affect on viewers. Are movies a social danger? The power of graphic, visual depictions to affect behavior, stimulate the imagination, set a cultural standard, or undermine existing values can prove a danger as well as a virtue. The affective power of moving images raises considerable concern when what they depict is at all controversial.

Relying on the power of moving images and recorded sound, the cinema creates a vivid sense of what it feels like to be someone else: perhaps a former movie star living on past glories (in *Sunset Boulevard* [Billy Wilder, 1950]), a principled but confused sports agent (in *Jerry Maguire* [Cameron Crowe, 1996]), a resolute and resourceful gunfighter (in *Unforgiven* [Clint Eastwood, 1992]), or a young girl who escapes an oppressive reality through fantasy (*Pan's Labyrinth* [Guillermo del Toro, 2006, Spain/Mexico/U.S.]). Films convey what it feels like to enter into a particular world in a compelling, immersive way, be it the world revolving around a mysterious, elusive woman (in *Vertigo* [Alfred Hitchcock, 1958]) or the world of armed combat on a grand scale (in *Saving Private Ryan* [Steven Spielberg, 1998]). Cinematic engagement is not just intellectual or observational. It unmistakably involves sensation, feeling, and emotion as well.

For some the fascination of the cinema lies primarily in its visceral power. Action films, horror films, thrillers, melodramas, disaster movies, science fiction, and, of course, the entire adult movie industry thrive on marketing films that stimulate the senses. Like a roller coaster ride, such films generate bodily responses that are the opposite of classic aesthetic repose; they arouse sensation or desire far more than identification and empathy. Many critics of the treatment of sex and violence in the cinema consign such work to a lowly status, labeling it sensationalism, pandering, titillation, and exploitation, claiming that it is not art.

Engaging Cinema acknowledges that this type of labeling takes place. It tries to understand it as a social phenomenon without endorsing or judging it. To some extent, this hierarchy of aesthetic vs. sensational films, high culture vs. popular culture, refers to differences of class, social status, and taste. It also refers to **ideology**—the ways in which a certain image of one's place in the world becomes internalized and then functions as a guide to proper conduct in a given social context. Is the image gleaned from an opera like *The Magic Flute* more appropriate than the one promoted by a movie like *I Spit on Your Grave* (Meir Zarchi, 1978)? Is *Psycho* (Alfred Hitchcock, 1960) as serious an exploration of mental pathology as Dostoyevsky's *Crime and Punishment*? Should *Glory* (Edward Zwick, 1989) be studied in high schools alongside *The Red Badge of Courage*? To what degree are such debates purely questions of aesthetic value and to what extent are they functions of different ideologies about the role of art, culture, and the mass media? Proponents of many ideologies want to have a shaping influence on the kind of images made available; one ideology may dominate, but alternatives invariably contend. These forces come to bear on film production and viewing in the form of constraints and, simultaneously, opportunities. All these facets of the place of film in society receive extended attention in later chapters.

Whether designed to engage us by highly visceral or more traditionally aesthetic means, films frequently appeal because they give us tangible images of things that would otherwise not be visible. The great *Why We Fight* (Frank Capra and Anatole Litvak, 1943–45) series of films, for example, explained to new military recruits why the United States chose to enter World War II, what was at stake, and what could happen if we failed to win. Recruits could say "I see (why we have to fight)" and carry with them an internal image of what that actually meant. Fiction films like *The Birth of a Nation* and *Gone with the Wind* render an imaginative reconstruction of what happened in a time before movie cameras. They can portray the behind-the-scenes manipulations that led to the television quiz show scandals of the 1950s (in *Quiz Show* [Robert Redford, 1994]) or the deals and double-crosses that allowed real-life life mobster Frank Lucas (Denzel Washington) to become the king of heroin trafficking in the United States (in *American Gangster* [Ridley Scott, 2007]). Films give us entry into worlds we would not otherwise be able to enter, even those of fantasy and science fiction, and in a vivid and emotionally absorbing manner that is unique to the cinema.

Cinematic Worlds and Their Relation to the Historical World

MICROCOSMS AND METAPHORS

The cinema, in sum, enchants for multiple reasons. Much more than a record or chronicle, a document or treatise, it has an immersive dimension that engages our senses and emotions. It offers imaginative engagement with constructed worlds that draw us into a microcosm resembling the world we already know but that is now shaped and patterned in distinctive ways. By sharing the experiences of the characters that live on screen, a hero, a family, or a small group of characters, we enter into microcosms that bear strong resemblances to aspects of the historical world itself.

In this regard, the cinema shares a tendency toward metaphor with novels and plays. It tells stories that imply things about the world around us. Like parables, films often seem to say one thing but simultaneously hint at something else unsaid or unstated. How can metaphorical or allegorical levels of a film be understood, and what are the formal properties that make such layering possible? What are the social implications of the commentary these metaphors suggest? If *Double Indemnity* (Billy Wilder, 1944), a classic film noir of seduction, betrayal, and murder, suggests that the world is a dangerous, precarious place, *Star Wars* (George Lucas, 1977) suggests that the world is a great testing ground for heroism and valor where good ultimately triumphs over evil. Why such views arise at different times, how they

relate to different attitudes toward society or to different political perspectives, are all questions pursued in Part II, "The Social Context"
(chapters 5–11).

METAPHOR AND ALLEGORY

Metaphors are figures of speech in which one thing stands for another.
"He pounced on his clients," metaphorically likens an individual to a
lion or other predator. **Allegory** is a sustained narrative in which the
characters and situations stand for more general qualities or states. A
character on a quest for an elusive, spiritual truth that involves numerous obstacles and trials may be an allegorical representation of all
Christians whose search for communion with God involves temptations
and setbacks. When a film conveys what it feels like to live in a particular kind of world, it is offering a vicarious experience that may be analogous to various aspects of everyday life. This oblique form of reference,
common to almost all fiction films, makes film viewing into a metaphorical or allegorical experience.

Because of its indirect or metaphorical qualities, the cinema prompts
reflection. Films get us thinking about their thematic concerns, about
what kind of comment they are making about the world we already
know, but viewers seldom agree with one another entirely. What does
a film mean? Does a violent film like *Goodfellas* (Martin Scorsese, 1990)
serve to criticize the tendency toward violence in American society, or
does it demonstrate the necessity to live by a code of violence in a social
context that knows no real alternative? Is *Psycho* about what makes a
killer kill, or about the desire of audiences to experience the sense of
danger, and excitement, such a killer stirs up? Does the director, Alfred
Hitchcock, want us to reflect on the power of the cinema to create a
bond between viewers and killers? What ethical issues arise regarding
the filmmaker's, or film viewers', responsibility? How do we feel about

rooting for the killer, when Marion's car stops sinking into the swamp, for example? How graphic can scenes of violence be and still be acceptable? Such questions, which *Psycho* posed for many viewers in forceful terms for the first time, have become staples of debate about *Psycho*'s gory successors like *The Texas Chainsaw Massacre* (Tobe Hooper, 1974), *Untraceable* (Gregory Hoblit, 2008), and *Saw* (James Wan, 2004). These questions and the pursuit of their answers are part of what makes the thoughtful engagement with film so rewarding.

CONSTRUCTING CINEMATIC WORLDS

THE FORMAL CONTEXT How do cinematic worlds come into being? They are clearly more than a heap of sounds and images thrown together. Much effort goes into their creation. This effort collects its reward when viewers enter into, imaginatively inhabit, collectively reemerge from, and critically reflect on what they have experienced during their encounter with a cinematic world. Time and space take on new qualities. In the course of a few hours, a film may tell an entire life history, as *Gandhi* (Richard Attenborough, 1982) and *Malcolm X* (Spike Lee, 1992) do. The story time, in these cases, spans decades but the film's running time is just a couple of hours. A story may loop back and forth in time, as *Pulp Fiction* (Quentin Tarantino, 1994), *Babel* (Alejandro González Iñárritu, 2006, U.S./Mexico), and *Before the Devil Knows You're Dead* (Sidney Lumet, 2008, U.S./UK) all do, or tell its story backwards, as *Memento* (Christopher Nolan, 2000) and *Irreversible* (Gaspar Noé, France, 2002) do. Characters can readily vault from one physical location to another in the split second between shots. Physical reality, rendered in such rich detail, suddenly appears to have no material presence at all.

Broadly speaking, a film relies on two primary sources for its shape: a formal context and a social context. The formal context involves medium-specific qualities such as technology (lighting options, special effects, characteristics of digital cameras, and so on). Expressive techniques such as editing and sound design, and their history; genre conventions and exemplary films within a genre; actors and their strengths and weaknesses, and principles of narrative structure: all are key aspects of the formal context to which every film belongs.

The filmmaker's challenge is to create a world viewers want to inhabit. Is it plausible on its own terms, even if, in relation to everyday reality, it possesses the unrealistic or bizarre qualities as *The Wizard of Oz* does? Most viewers engage with the film wholeheartedly, partly because of rather than despite the bizarre secret world that the very down–to-earth Dorothy discovers. The tangible surface of a film stems from countless decisions about acting, composition, lighting, costumes, editing, and so on, is what engages viewers. It is the shape and tone of what we actually see and hear. If the formal surface of a film lacks plausibility or appeal, the social issues it may refer to metaphorically are not likely to sustain viewer interest for very long. The look of a painting, the flow of a novel, and the shape of a film all accomplish the same thing: they produce the viewer's immediate experience of a distinct world. Pondering its significance follows from active engagement with form.

Although every film is unique and every cinematic world different from every other, similarities quickly emerge. The formal context includes a vast repository of stylistic alternatives. Of particular importance are the familiar large categories into which individual films fall. These categories include genres (melodrama, thriller, gangster), national cinemas (French, Australian, Japanese), avant-garde or experimental film, animation, and documentary, as well as the broad stylistic categories of realism, modernism, and postmodernism. How a film relates to other films has consequences for what an audience will anticipate or expect from it, what formal conventions are likely to appear, what counts as innovative uses of technique or convention, and what types of social issues may arise.

THE SOCIAL CONTEXT The social context involves social and historical problems, conflicts, issues, and contradictions that provide a story's
thematic focus. This level of a film is often referred to as its content,
as opposed to its form, but the form itself has considerable bearing
on how viewers experience and understand the content of a film, as
this book will demonstrate throughout. The social context turns our
attention beyond aesthetics and film technique to issues that are not
specific to the film medium but, instead, characteristic of the times
and culture in which a film appears.

The theme of revenge may occur in a novel, play, or film, for example. Nothing about revenge is uniquely cinematic, although specific
ways of representing it are. Creasy (Denzel Washington) seeks
revenge in *Man on Fire* (Tony Scott, 2004) just as much as Hamlet
does in *Hamlet*, but the ways and means of representing the need for
revenge differ as much as theater differs from film. Questions that
deal with the representation of men and women; the qualities of a
hero, or antihero; the appeal of evil; the nature of community, of social
belonging and exclusion; the treatment of ethnic minorities and the
issues of prejudice and stereotyping; a film's political perspective, be
it progressive or conservative—these questions all refer to the broader
social context that surrounds any given film. They take on a specific
manifestation thanks to form. Grappling with the relationship
between form and content is part of the fundamental appeal of the
cinema.

Fritz Lang's *Metropolis* (1927), a triumph of sophisticated aesthetics and German expressionist style, asks how to keep social conflict in
check so that a complex urban space can flourish under the rule of
one man, whereas *There's Something about Mary* (Bobby and Peter Far-
relly, 1998) asks how contending suitors can win the hand of an attractive young woman. *There's Something about Mary* pursues its theme
with a broadside of tasteless but also hilarious jokes. The hilarity of
There's Something about Mary, like the solemnity of *Metropolis*, derives

from formal, or aesthetic, accomplishment, but the appeal and value of both films depends on their ability to tap into social issues that resonate with a general public: they speak to concerns and issues that already exist in society. Both films pose questions about masculinity, courtship, and love, but they do so in radically distinct ways. Broad social topics like these open up a vast gamut of possibilities. The exploration of how to address such topics in a film proves an inexhaustible source of fascination.

THE FORMAL AND SOCIAL CONTEXTS ESTABLISH CONSTRAINTS AND OPPORTUNITIES Every context sets up limitations or constraints—a low-budget movie cannot afford to pay for a top-rated star; a film shot on location will gain an aura of authenticity but the quality of the sound recording may be worse than if it had been shot on a soundstage. Every context also opens up opportunities—a low-budget movie can take risks that a big-budget film might be unwilling to try; a film shot on location can catch events as they happen rather than rely on reenactments. *The Blair Witch Project* (Daniel Myrick and Eduardo Sánchez, 1999) turned poor sound recording into a plus, for example: it helped "authenticate" the footage as the only record of what happened to the hapless trio of would-be filmmakers who had the misfortune of encountering the Blair Witch. It helped lend a documentary aura to the fictional world created by the film.

Much resourcefulness goes into minimizing constraints and maximizing opportunities. Success will depend, in part, on familiarity with the formal context for a given film. If it is a science fiction film or a documentary, for example, does the film make fresh use of conventions established in previous work or does it simply, perhaps unwittingly, recycle them? Viewers may find that the imaginative use of lighting options, color, or special effects allow a thematic issue to take on greater complexity. *Collateral* (Michael Mann, 2004), for example, uses richly saturated nighttime shots of Los Angeles, a city often caught in dusty, pale hues, to impart a dense, romantic luster to the environment. This choice increases the mounting tension between a good-natured cab driver and a merciless hit man. *The Matrix* (Andy and Larry Wachowski, 1999) utilizes a technique that goes back to the nineteenth century and the still photography of Edward Muybridge to allow characters to battle in a complex, slow-motion ballet that standard motion picture cameras could not capture. The innovative use of this technology required computers to carry Muybridge's use of dozens of still cameras to a new level. The achievement allowed the film to represent Neo's (Keanu Reeves) death-defying struggle to confront the true nature of reality in a compelling, visceral way.

When Billy Wilder made *Sabrina* in 1954, he wanted to suggest that Humphrey Bogart and Audrey Hepburn made love together, but the Production Code, which ruled on film content, banned any such reference, since their characters were unmarried and Bogart was several decades older. (Wilder wanted to hint at a sexual encounter by having Bogart's maid find a hairpin in his bed rather than present anything of an explicit nature.) This restriction on content is a social constraint, imposed by the film industry. Be it a genre convention, budgetary limitation, or moral standard, every filmmaking context establishes constraints as well as opportunities.

In Iranian films, men and women cannot touch at all. This constraint has not prevented Iranian cinema from flourishing over the last two decades. Filmmakers often find ways to circumvent constraints. *Baran* (Majid Majidi, 2001, Iran), for example, tells the story of a young man who falls in love with a woman who poses as another male construction-site worker to help her family. He can't approach her lest he compromise her masquerade; he must watch and woo her from a distance, guaranteeing suspense for the viewer and compliance with the Iranian censors. Films seen outside their social context, like musical notes or words treated in isolation, lack the density and complexity that an actual social content creates.

The Filmmaker's Perspective on the Constructed Cinematic World

ACCESS TO CINEMATIC WORLDS COMES FILTERED BY THE FILMMAKER'S PERSPECTIVE

Film worlds seem autonomous and complete. Rick's café in *Casablanca* (Michael Curtiz, 1942), Xanadu in *Citizen Kane* (Orson Welles, 1941), Mount Doom in *The Lord of the Rings* trilogy (Peter Jackson, 2001–2003, New Zealand/U.S.) belong to story worlds that pulse with a life and vitality all their own. It is important to remember, though, that these worlds are the product of a creative process and that they are seen and represented from the distinct point of view of their creator. In this sense they are not autonomous and self-sufficient at all. Everything that happens—everything characters do and the audience sees—follows from decisions made by the filmmaker. Opening credits and prologues often make this point, as they do so dramatically in *Star Wars*, for example, where George Lucas takes pains to link his tale to the heroic myths of old. But once the written prologue has rolled, this story, like most others, takes on a life of its own.

The audience's view of any film world comes filtered through the social attitude, political perspective, and aesthetic sensibility of that world's maker. Viewers cannot stroll through these cinematic worlds at their own pace, along a route of their own choosing. Computer-based interactive narratives enhance the degree to which such choice becomes possible, but even here the choices must first be mapped out by others. Every encounter with a cinematic world is more like a guided tour, and every tour guide, or filmmaker, has her own perspective on the film world she displays for us. Viewers need not accept the filmmaker's perspective, but they cannot escape it either. The everyday world may exhibit criminality and athletic achievement, business maneuverings and lonely misfits, car chases and romantic interludes, scheming connivers and total innocents, individuals full of humor and grace, folly and mischief. A film world may contain many of these things, but they always arrive selectively, with a filmmaker's tone, perspective, and point of view attached to them.

The tone or point of view adopted toward what audiences see is often unique: no one makes films or sees the world quite the way Alfred Hitchcock, David Lynch, or Jean-Luc Godard does. On the other hand, just as films congregate into categories due to the similarities they share, the perspectives of filmmakers share common qualities as well. These qualities may include romantic, comic, humane, cynical, or ironic social attitudes, reactionary or radical political perspectives. A filmmaker's perspective may be informed by gender, be it male chauvinist, strongly feminist, gay or lesbian, or by ethnicity, as in the case of directors like Spike Lee, Euzhan Palcy, Ousmane Sembene, or Mira Nair. Chapters 9–11 take up the question of the filmmaker's perspective in much greater detail.

PREJUDICE AND PRIVILEGE FROM TWO DISTINCT PERSPECTIVES

The centrality of the filmmaker's perspective looms dramatically in a comparison of two films that gave vivid representation to major social issues: D.W. Griffith's 1915 denunciation of the Civil War and Reconstruction as an attempt to dismantle the Old South and its entire way of life, *The Birth of a Nation*, and Steven Spielberg's 1993 tribute to the courage of one man who saved Jews destined for destruction in the Nazi death camps during World War II, *Schindler's List*. The directors' feelings are very strong in both cases, making the perspectives from which they tell their stories more pronounced than usual. Griffith clearly laments the death of the Old South with its racial hierarchy and agrarian economy based on slavery. Spielberg clearly despises the gross inhumanity of the Nazis' "final solution" with its call for the eradication of all European Jewry.

PLOT SUMMARY OF *THE BIRTH OF A NATION*

The film takes place before, during, and after the Civil War. The fate of two families (the Stonemans and the Camerons) forms the crux of the film. In the North, Austin Stoneman, the father, is a prominent abolitionist politician. Elsie (Lillian Gish), Austin's vivacious daughter, falls in love with Ben Cameron, a member of the Southern Cameron family, during the Civil War. Stoneman has a political protégé, the mulatto (mixed race) Silas Lynch. Central to the Cameron family, in the South, are Ben, the son, and the two daughters, Flora (Mae Marsh) and Margaret. All of the principal actors are white: those playing blacks don blackface to do so.

The Civil War flings the two families onto the opposing sides, but North and South fight with valor. President Lincoln's assassination, however, upsets the postwar apple cart: unprincipled opportunists from the North, including Silas Lynch, invade the South and collude with freed slaves to run wild, turning the law into a travesty. Southern white women become the targets of sexual lust. Gus, a freed slave, pursues Flora Cameron, who chooses to leap to her death from a cliff rather than succumb to sexual violation. When rampaging black troops surround the Cameron parents and daughter Margaret in a remote cabin, the father stands ready to kill his daughter rather than let her fall into their hands.

Ben, deeply distressed at the chaos in his beloved South, has an inspiration. Calling upon kindred spirits and donning white robes to hide their identity from the corrupt law, Ben creates the Ku Klux Klan. The Klan rises from the ashes of war and the treachery of the opportunists. Ben and his companions ride to the rescue of Elsie, whom Silas Lynch has forcibly captured and plans to marry despite her love for Ben, and of the rest of the Cameron family trapped in the remote cabin. The Klan succeeds. They soon restore order by forcibly preventing blacks from voting. Austin Stoneman stands chastised for his misplaced trust in Silas Lynch, anarchy comes to an end, and Ben and Elsie's happy reunion signifies the restoration of one great nation under white rule.

PLOT SUMMARY OF *SCHINDLER'S LIST*

Oskar Schindler (Liam Neeson) is an enterprising German in Krakow, Poland, who sees the Nazis' rise to power as a business opportunity. Using bravado and formidable social skills he befriends the local Nazi leaders. Soon he is setting up a business to manufacture kitchenware for the Nazi army. To make sure he can outsmart the Nazis, he recruits an experienced, no-questions-asked accountant from the Jewish ghetto, Itzhak Stern (Ben Kingsley).

Schindler realizes he can increase his profits if he uses Jews for his labor force. He begins recruiting Jews from the Krakow ghetto created by the Nazis rather than using Poles whom he would have to pay (a salary for Jews would be a waste of money from the Nazi point of view.)

Tensions mount when the Nazis build a forced labor camp, herd the Jews into it, and liquidate the ghetto. Schindler watches the liquidation and begins to realize the depth of the evil with which he is collaborating. He must pay more bribes, especially to the new commander of the camp, Amon Goeth (Ralph Fiennes), to get the Jews working for him out of the camp and into his factory. Goeth proves a monster: he happily shoots Jews in the camp at random. Despite numerous obstacles Schindler manages to keep the Jews together and essentially safe.

As the war turns against the Nazis, Schindler creates a list of all the Jewish workers he wants to evacuate to Czechoslovakia. He confronts more crises, especially the mistaken transport of the women to Auschwitz instead of his factory. His funds are exhausted as the war draws to a close. With the German surrender, he flees, fearing his public persona as a Nazi party member, war profiteer, and employer of slave labor will outweigh the extraordinary rescue of the workers on his list. Titles explain that his later business ventures failed and that he died in Israel. The final scene takes place at his grave, where survivors from Schindler's list place stones to commemorate his heroism.

Controversial or galvanizing as the themes of these two films are, they offer no guarantee of popular success. In fact, Griffith's theme is completely out of touch with prevailing sentiment today, a fact that causes some film scholars to squirm as they defend the film's artistic achievements despite its repugnant politics. There is no reason, however, not to assess films within their formal context one way and in their social context another way.

In its time *The Birth of a Nation* was far less out of touch with contemporary values and beliefs than it is today. American society remained strikingly divided racially in the early twentieth century, despite the Emancipation Proclamation of 1863. Racially discriminatory practices, whether against descendants of African slaves or immigrants from Asia, were commonplace. The Chinese Exclusion Act, in effect under different guises from 1882 to 1943, barred most Chinese citizens from entry and made it next to impossible for Chinese already in the United States to assimilate into the larger culture. The idea of white or Aryan racial superiority, championed just a decade after the release of *The Birth of a Nation* by Adolf Hitler in his venomous book, *Mein Kampf*, had many adherents. Anti-Semitism and the Nazi policy of racial genocide capitalized on long festering biases and converted them into a campaign of mass extermination.

By the time of *Schindler's List*, racist and anti-Semitic views no longer had the protection of the law; they had clearly become the beliefs of a fringe minority. Both directors, in this sense, were in step with the dominant social currents of their time. They also confronted the fundamental issue of racial privilege and ethnic prejudice directly. What, then, might a comparison of the two films reveal about how cinematic worlds always derive from the perspective of their maker? What characters do, or don't do, what we see happen, or don't see happen, how situations and events are represented in concrete ways all reveal aspects of the director's perspective.

When it comes to racial or ethnic prejudice, Griffith and Spielberg are as different as night and day. Griffith's sympathies were entirely with the genteel traditions of the Old South, and slavery was considered a necessary, justifiable part of that tradition. Spielberg's sympathies are entirely with the victims and opponents of the Nazi's ethnic hatred; in his view, anti-Semitism is a virulent disease that corrupts its perpetrators as it destroys its victims.

At the same time, the two directors reveal their distinct perspectives by means of how they address very similar aspects of the worlds they create: family, manhood, womanhood, good and evil, heroes and villains. In fact, both films exhibit strongly melodramatic qualities such as heightened emotion, clear-cut forces of good and evil, and a focus on the family as a microcosm of the larger social world.

Griffith is often described as a pioneer of narrative filmmaking techniques, and his formal achievements rank among the most impressive of the early cinema. Spielberg, like countless other directors, has clearly learned from what Griffith did and puts the lessons learned to uses of his own. Spielberg, like Griffith, places a premium on building suspense in many scenes. Both directors rely on cutting between simultaneous actions to heighten suspense. Whereas Griffith cut between damsels in distress and the Ku Klux Klan riding to the rescue, Spielberg cuts between a group of Jewish women being herded into a mass shower—or is it a gas chamber?—and Schindler's desperate efforts to rescue them. Whereas Griffith ends with a sentimental coda in which a Jesus-like figure hovers over peace-loving mankind, Spielberg ends with an emotional coda in which Jewish survivors place stones on Schindler's gravestone.

Both Griffith and Spielberg have an extraordinary feel for pacing; they both maintain a lively rhythm to their three-hour-plus films. Both also make claims of historical authenticity for what they depict, Griffith by citing books, including one by President Woodrow Wilson, and by staging scenes to resemble well-known paintings of the same events, Spielberg by adopting black and white photography, and, at times, a handheld camera to imitate qualities associated with documentaries from World War II. How they claim authenticity differs, but both share a desire to root their melodramatic story in a historically verifiable reality.

These similarities and differences demonstrate why it is vital to both acknowledge a formal context and distinguish it from a social one. Acknowledge because it is through a director's craft that a film attains its emotional, affective power. Distinguish because the same formal techniques can be used for very different social purposes. To say that these two films make brilliant use of crosscutting between simultaneous events acknowledges the artistry of both films but says nothing of their social attitude or political perspective. One social issue, such as prejudice, allows for multiple perspectives and various formal treatments. Racism can be defended, compellingly, in the case of Griffith, or denounced, conclusively, in the case of Spielberg. A filmmaker's perspective hinges on the concrete uses of form to tackle specific questions of content.

The Viewer's Challenge to Respond and Interpret: Formal-Social Analysis

Films, from *The Birth of a Nation* to *Schindler's List* and from *Titanic* (James Cameron, 1997) to *Wall-E* (Andrew Stanton, 2008) please, move, distract, provoke, challenge, amuse, inspire, enrage, and entertain us. To understand these responses calls for interpretation, often in written form. (The last chapter discusses writing about film in detail.) Reflecting on the experience of watching a film affords an opportunity to contextualize the experience, to find comparisons and similarities with other experiences, to evaluate its worth, to explore implications, question assumptions, and to support or challenge other views of the same experience.

Formally, a sci-fi film invites comparison with other sci-fi films. Crosscutting in one film invites comparison with crosscutting in other films. Socially, a sci-fi film invites discussion of its vision of the future and the uses of technology: is it utopian or dystopian; is society moving toward redemption or doom? Is crosscutting used to create emotional identification with the villain, the hero, or both? Does the use of film technique undercut our established values or reinforce them? Questions like these occur throughout the book. Although they take many forms in relation to the vast array of films, and film worlds, that exist, the core questions boil down to two:

1) Formally: In what ways does a film alter, subvert, or transform existing conventions innovatively? Alternatively, if a film primarily recycles existing conventions, are they used effectively to engage the audience? Films that recycle existing conventions may hold considerable appeal; their formal qualities may lie more in the exemplary use of existing conventions than in pioneering new ones. A formally conventional film can be extremely exciting thanks to excellent execution, and a formally daring film can be painfully dull due to inept handling. No absolute value attaches to innovative or conventional work; each case calls for assessment on its individual merits. Exploring this question calls for some knowledge of film techniques (discussed in Chapter 1) and of previous, related films so that informed comparisons can be made.

2) Socially: In what ways does a film present a perspective on the historical world that is fresh and unexpected? Does it lead viewers to see aspects of social reality in a new way or does it reinforce pre-existing points of view? Does a film support the status quo or call for change, and how does it do so? Does it resolve the social conflicts it raises in thought-provoking ways or mechanically? A film that upholds the status quo can have as much appeal as one that doesn't. No absolute value attaches to efforts to transform, or

maintain, the status quo. The coherence, plausibility, and insightfulness of each film in terms of its relation to the surrounding social context calls for individual assessment.

This book advocates combining formal and social analysis into one practice that remains mindful of both these crucial components of film.

Viewers will not agree in their assessments of these aspects of a film. Individuals and groups bring various assumptions and expectations, different life experiences, and distinct sensitivities to a film. These skew responses in different directions. Most films, as metaphorical statements about the world around them, also possess an inherent ambiguity. Because they say what they mean indirectly, by means of their perspective on and representation of a distinct cinematic world, room for different interpretations, stressing different aspects or qualities of a film, always exists. This is part of what makes interpretation or criticism engaging: what others see and understand can enrich what we see and understand ourselves. The following chapters survey the concepts and techniques that go into understanding the cinema formally and socially.

Part I

1

FILM AS A LANGUAGE

Film Is a Visual Language

E very language makes communication possible by means of symbols or signs. While we usually think of languages based on words, films rely on images. These images can be put together in almost any way. Even if they do not seem to make sense, viewers routinely find meaning in their juxtaposition. Films such as Godfrey Reggio's *Koyaanisqatsi* (1982), for example, bring together images from a vast array of locations around the world. *Koyaanisqatsi* is an eloquent plea for harmony between man and nature. There is no commentary or dialogue at all, no main characters, no plot in the usual sense, and the only sound is Philip Glass's mesmerizing music. Yet the film makes sense to most viewers. It does not necessarily mean the same thing to everyone, nor do viewers necessarily agree on the merits of the film, but almost all viewers agree that there is a formal pattern and a consistent structure that conveys expressive meaning.

The patterns of organization that operate most frequently in films and that viewers expect to encounter are **conventions**, a customary way of doing things, rather than grammatical rules. (All words that appear in **bold** are explained in the text and listed in the Glossary.) These basically function as guidelines for selecting certain types of images (shots of domestic space in melodramas and of landscape in westerns, for example) and for arranging them into scenes (an **establishing shot** to reveal the overall space of a scene followed by a closeup of the hero, for example). The selection and arrangement of sounds and images are the two activities that build a film from isolated shots.

Film conventions, including genre conventions, vary over time and with the type of film under consideration, but among the most universal are those that create **continuity**. **Continuity** includes all the ways of organizing shots so that the transition from one shot to the next does not jar the viewer. Something occurs in the first shot—the character looks in a particular direction, for example—and this motivates or justifies a cut or edit to another shot, most likely to what the character sees. In other cases, a musical soundtrack continues smoothly beneath a series of shots. The music creates a sense of continuity even if the images come from diverse sources, as in the case of *Koyaanisqatsi*. Many conventions govern the creation of continuity and are discussed further below.

Films use images to convey emotional impact, express various states of mind, tell a story, or present an argument. The reliance on conventions to achieve these ends helps explain film's universal appeal. Viewers can draw on their experience of previous films and on their experience of interpreting what they see in the world around them. If there is subtlety and complexity involved in understanding films, it involves grasping the nuances made possible by a range of different, often competing conventions and interpreting the metaphorical implications of what we see. A slightly raised eyebrow; exactly when a shot cuts to another; the angle from which the camera views a scene; the insertion of a sudden sound, the placement of the actors in relation to each other—these are the small things that distinguish one film from another and that challenge the viewer's interpretive skills.

The Semiotics of Film

THE BASIC UNIT OF CINEMATIC
COMMUNICATION: THE SIGN

Anyone communicating in film or other audiovisual forms like television or Internet websites needs to be familiar with the basic elements of film language. Spectators need a comparable familiarity to understand and interpret what they see. This basic knowledge is a prerequisite for all film communication, not just those instances that are artistically or aesthetically remarkable. The artistic use of film language is but one possible use. The art of cinematic expression receives consideration at many points in this book, but it is not the exclusive focus.

Whatever use is intended, all films rely on the basic building block of the **sign**. The study of communication, be it verbal or nonverbal, visual or aural, is called **semiotics**. Semiotics defines a **sign** as the smallest meaningful unit of communication. Words are only one of many kinds of sign. In film, each shot functions as a sign. In fact, within each shot, there may well be a variety of signs mixed together: the scowl on the hero's face; the smug look of superiority on the villain's; the scruffy suit worn by the hero that signifies his ethic of hard work for low pay; the very elegant suit worn by the villain that signifies his preference for the easy life, regardless of whom he might hurt in getting it. *American Gangster* (Ridley Scott, 2007), for example, dresses drug kingpin Frank Lucas (Denzel Washington) in professional, understated attire but presents Richie Roberts (Russell Crowe)—the cop who brings him down—in cheap, scruffy clothes, as if to say that impressive appearances are deceptive and unimpressive ones a sign of genuine principles.

Because viewers usually recognize what an image represents quite quickly, it may seem as if the meaning is already in the image; the viewer simply notes it. This, however, is incorrect. What an image represents, or signifies, is not in the image but in the beholder. The spectator instantly attaches a **signified**, the meaning of a given image, to the **signifier**, the thing seen or heard. The **signifier** is what is materially presented to the viewer. The **signified** is the meaning the viewer supplies to it. Together they form a **sign**. To recognize an image of an apple as an apple requires that the viewer already have in her mind an idea of what an apple looks like. A visual signifier, a photo of an apple, can then instantly have the proper signified attached to it.

Without prior knowledge, a word or image is meaningless. "Demit" may look like a word, but is it? A trip to the dictionary will tell us it means "to resign." With this signified attached "demit" becomes a meaningful set of letters, a word. A shot of a shadowy figure moving down a narrow alleyway may look like a person, but is it? Perhaps it is the shadow of a moving object; maybe it is important to the story but maybe not. A gap suddenly opens up between the signifier and the signified. The felt need to supply a signified intensifies. If the shadow is of a person, who is it and what is she doing? If the viewer recognizes the shadowy figure as the heroine, it's likely that the shot will now become meaningful: perhaps the viewer realizes that the heroine wants to warn the hero of danger or that she is, in fact, about to betray him, depending on what is already known about the story.

The strict separation between materially present signifiers and assigned meanings or signifieds has three important implications:

1) The image as signifier, and its relationship to any accompanying sounds, is the raw material with which the filmmaker works. The image is comparable to the painter's paint or the musician's notes. The options sketched out below in relation to the expressive, persuasive, and poetic techniques of the cinema catalogue ways in which a filmmaker can shape images, or sounds, to convey just the right tone, feeling, and meaning.

2) Despite this shaping effort, the viewer must still assign meaning to the image and its relationship to any accompanying sounds. A

shadowy face may be shot that way to suggest untrustworthiness, but it remains up to the viewer to interpret the specific look of the image as meaningful.

3) A film signifier will not mean the same thing to every viewer. A shot that includes the American flag in the background will carry different meanings for a highly patriotic American and an anti-American foreigner. A violent fight between hero and villain may signify bravery and skill for one viewer and a resort to crude brutality for another. These variations cannot be fully controlled by the filmmaker. By the same token, they help account for the fact that a range of different, valid interpretations exist for the same film.

Alfred Hitchcock stages the dramatic climax to his film *North by Northwest* (1959) on the faces of the four American presidents carved into Mount Rushmore. In doing so, he presents a set of signifiers that mean different things to different viewers. Some may simply recognize it as a dangerous site, since the hero (Cary Grant) and heroine (Eva Marie Saint) could fall off the rock at any moment. Some will recognize that faces are carved into the stone and that the heroes are on the brow of one of the faces, just above the nose. Others will recognize that the faces are famous American presidents (George Washington, Abraham Lincoln, Thomas Jefferson, and Theodore Roosevelt). Some may recognize the irony of the hero battling villains who are involved in espionage against the United States on the faces of four presidents who helped define the United States as a nation. Yet others will recognize an element of humor in a deadly fight taking place on the face of a president. Finally, some will recognize that the scene is strikingly similar to the climax of another Hitchcock film, *Saboteur* (1942), in which the hero confronts the villain atop the Statue of Liberty. The image or signifier, in other words, offers extra rewards for those who bring familiarity with its social and formal context. Such viewers draw more meaning from the scene because they can assign more signifieds to the images presented.

In most cases, the viewer is familiar with common signifiers (clothing, cars, guns, etc.) and their possible meanings before seeing them in a film. This is why silent cinema was called a universal language: it relied on viewers' familiarity with visual signs. Almost all viewers recognize a film shot of a hat as a hat. They might well be able to infer things about its wearer as well from the type of hat and how it is worn. Similarly, viewers recognize something about a character's social status from her clothing, expressions, gestures, and actions. They might also recognize the actor playing the character. Part of the pleasure of seeing a silent short by Charlie Chaplin such as *Easy Street* (1917) or *The Immigrant* (1917) comes from recognizing the character of the tramp that Chaplin had begun to develop as his primary screen persona.

THE SIGN AND ITS REFERENT

Most cinematic signifiers possess a **referent**. The referent is what a sign refers to outside the language in which it appears. A photo of a hat is a signifier and the viewer's response, "This is a hat," generates the signified, but the **referent** would be the actual hat used in the photo. This referent, the hat, exists in physical reality. Almost all photographic images, but not all computer-generated images, have a referent. A viewer, for example, may recognize that the specially equipped car driven by James Bond is an Aston Martin. The actual car is the referent. It exists outside the world of the movie and the language of cinema. But this particular car now functions as a signifier. The viewer recognizes that the Aston Martin signifies what a Volkswagen would not (wealth, driving prowess, sophistication). In terms of signifieds, this particular car reinforces Bond's image as someone adept with technical gadgetry, his skill at daredevil maneuvers, and his sophisticated taste in luxury goods. The diagrams in Figure 1.1 show the relations of the different parts of the sign and how any communication involves selecting specific signs from a repertoire of available signs and then assembling the selected signs into a meaningful sequence.

IMAGES AS A SIGN SYSTEM

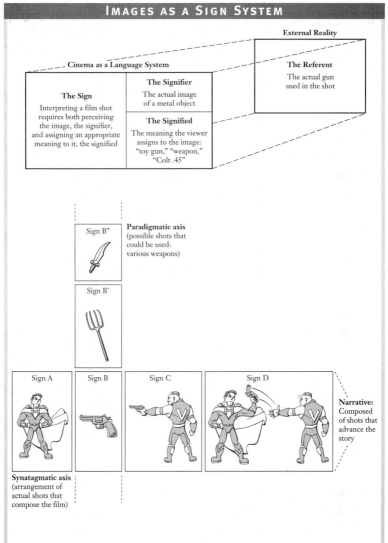

A filmmaker chooses each shot from a set of possible shots that work in a given context. Here the shot is of a gun, but shots of a knife, pitchfork, whip, sword, rope, or other weapons would also work. The sum of the available choices exists on the **paradigmatic axis**. This amounts to all the choices that work in a given context: one is chosen and the others are not.

IMAGES AS A SIGN SYSTEM (CONTINUED)

Similarly, each sign couples with other signs to form a chain. In the sequence represented in Figure 1.1, a shot of the hero cuts to a shot of a gun pointed at him and then to a shot of the villain. The **syntagmatic axis** consists of the actual arrangement of the chosen signs: the hero, gun, villain, and the hero's action. This axis unfolds over time. The paradigmatic axis is sometimes called the metaphoric axis and the syntagmatic the metonymic. In any language, the selection of one sign from a range of possible signs and the arrangement of these choices into a series are the two steps that allow communication to occur.

The Expressive, Persuasive, and Poetic Uses of Film Technique

Filmmakers expend considerable effort to shape the images they shoot. They place the camera with great care. They select camera lenses and arrange the lighting to fit the needs of the story. Actors play specific parts or agreements are struck with non-actors. The director may start, stop, and repeat a specific shot as many as twenty, thirty, eighty times. A scene may be shot from a multitude of angles, which then requires intricate lighting and, later, editing, including the introduction of music and sound effects, to assemble it into the most effective form for a given purpose. These expressive elaborations move a film from being "mere film," or just a factual document, however valuable such a document might be as evidence, to something that reveals the attitude, perspective, or point of view of its maker. Expressive techniques create an emotional impact on the viewer.

Style involves the particular way a filmmaker makes use of cinematic signifiers. It also refers to broad categories like realism to which many works belong. Style is always medium specific. Film style involves the way a filmmaker selects and arranges images, together with any accompanying sounds. This means more than choosing to film a face, say; it becomes a question of how to film a face. Is it shot from above, or below? Is it in color or in black and white? With bright light from nearby or dim light from further away? Every shot raises questions like these. The filmmaker chooses one option from the paradigmatic range of choices available and then arranges these choices into syntagmatic scenes, sequences, and, ultimately, entire films.

Although it may seem to be merely the backdrop for the action, the natural or built environment is not simply documented in films but can also carry metaphorical meanings. In the classic Japanese film *Woman of the Dunes* (Hiroshi Teshigahara, 1964), about a man who stumbles upon a modest house at the foot of huge sand dunes and cannot escape it, and in *The Crowd* (1928), King Vidor's remarkable silent film study of urban alienation, both the looming sand dunes and the huge office act as signifiers of isolation and of the power of invisible, almost inexplicable forces. They provide a visible stand-in for what cannot be shown (power, dominance, hierarchy, and so on). As such, the images have not only real life referents but important signifieds. They allow the thematic concerns of the films to find visual expression.

For a film to fulfill an expressive, persuasive, or poetic purpose it must utilize signifiers that convey the desired feelings, tones, and attitudes effectively. A character may be a cruel monster; to make this quality evident one director may choose to have him do something truly heinous, such as torture female captives in his prison-basement as serial killer "Buffalo Bill" does in *The Silence of the Lambs* (Jonathan Demme, 1991). Another director, with the same goal, may have the monstrous character compel an honorable, loving person to do something unforgivably cruel. In *Sophie's Choice* (Alan Pakula, 1982), for example, the greatest horror of Sophie's (Meryl Streep's) deportation to a Nazi concentration camp is not physical violence, but the calm, clinical command of the doctor assessing new arrivals. He tells her she must choose which of her two children will go to the left with her and which to the right and certain doom. He forces her to act as an accomplice in the murder of her own child. Expressivity, persuasiveness, and poetic effect amounts to a question of how a filmmaker represents her own conception of the world to an audience.

To be as adept as possible, a filmmaker must be familiar with the repertoire of choices available as a result of technology and tradition. James Cameron could not have shot the masses of passengers tumbling across the decks of the Titanic as effectively or safely as he did, for example, without the use of **computer-generated images** (**CGI**) that placed lifelike figures created on a computer onto the deck of the sinking ship in *Titanic* (1997). CGI does not photograph objects but creates them from software; it offers a huge range of options for creating entirely fabricated images, or altering images that have real-world referents.

An attentive viewer must also be familiar with this repertoire of choices a director faces to recognize her decisions as choices rather than as simply the product of the camera's mechanical ability to record images. The following sections review the most important expressive techniques. Each topic is treated in a brief manner with primary attention to those techniques that are most often important when looking at film in a social context.

The Expressive, Persuasive, and Poetic Techniques Available in Film

EDITING

Editing is the primary means of building a syntagmatic chain of shots and scenes into a complete film. Each edit terminates one shot and begins another. Edits allow filmmakers to create relationships across different times and spaces that would not otherwise be possible. Every edit also introduces the possibility of deception (just as a person is about to be hit, the film might cut to a shot from a different angle as the character recoils, eliminating the need to actually hit the actor or to fake the blow in a single shot).

Sometimes considered an alternative to editing, **long takes** are shots that are noticeably more extended than usual: the viewer gains the most obvious plot information from the shot but the shot lingers, or things continue to happen without a cut occurring. Some directors favor long takes to allow action to occur in real time; it demonstrates that no deception took place in staging the action. The documentary film *Grizzly Man* (Werner Herzog, 2005) contains numerous shots made by the film's protagonist, Timothy Treadwell, in which he and wild Alaskan bears share the same frame, and therefore the same time and space in reality. No form of editing could convey the same sense of Treadwell's extended proximity to the creatures that will ultimately kill him. *Time Code* (Mike Figgis, 2000) and *Russian Ark* (Alexander Sokurov, 2002, Russia/Germany) are two films that consist only of one take (of four simultaneous long takes that are projected together in separate quadrants of the screen in *Time Code*, and of one continuous journey through the Winter Palace in St. Petersburg in *Russian Ark)*. Both films immerse the viewer in the experience of one continuous segment of time.

Editing has a distinct history and set of traditions in cinema. The techniques needed to edit moving images, with or without accompanying sound, developed as film became a new medium of communication. These techniques now serve as a template for television, video, and digital forms of moving image making. One basic choice is between **continuity** and **discontinuity editing**. The latter covers all of the alternatives to continuity editing, including **montage editing,** which brings individual shots together to generate a shock, strange juxtaposition, or a new idea. Montage is discussed further below.

CONTINUITY EDITING Continuity editing is the standard form of editing. It creates a smooth sense of flow so that the story takes priority over the mechanics of storytelling. Viewers do not notice most of the edits; attention goes to the characters and actions, situations and events that take place in the story, be it fictional or nonfictional. Some of the main elements of continuity editing are described below.

MATCH **Match editing** means that some element of one shot is carried over to the next shot to smooth the transition. Matches using movement are among the most common, but other choices include matching the position of an object in the frame. A person's hand reaches out to open a door. A cut or edit may shift to a **close-up** that isolates the hand in the screen, larger than life until it turns the doorknob. The next cut may place the viewer on the other side of the door in another close-up as the doorknob turns. The cut from the hand reaching out to the close-up of the hand continuing forward and from the hand turning the doorknob on one side of the door to the same turning motion on the other side are examples of **match action**.

Many choices complicate the apparent simplicity of matched action. How much of the action should be included in the first shot relative to the second? How much should the camera position change between shots? Attention to lighting and matched **screen direction**—ensuring that the lighting intensity matches from shot to shot, that shadows fall the same way, and that movement toward the right in one shot is also toward the right in the next shot—is also important. (**Screen direction** is the onscreen direction in which characters are looking.) While these aspects of match are virtually taken for granted by the spectator, on a set they may require rearranging lights or repositioning objects to produce a seamless match.

A **graphic match** tries to guide the viewer through the transition from one shot to the next by making the two images similar in appearance. If a table is in the left corner of the screen in one shot, a graphic match may cut to another shot where a different object is also in the left corner of the shot. A close-up of one character who is centered squarely in the middle of the frame might be followed by another shot with another character squarely centered. In *No Country for Old Men* (Ethan and Joel Coen, 2007), the merciless villain, Anton Chigurh (Javier Bardem), frequently occupies the center of the frame, whereas Ed Bell (Tommy Lee Jones) and Llewelyn Moss (Josh Brolin) commonly appear close to the sides of the frame. This pattern reinforces the sense that Chigurh represents evil as an unstoppable, superhuman force capable of taking control of every situation he encounters.

A standard practice is for a director to shoot **coverage** for a scene in a **master shot** that positions the camera at sufficient distance from the actors to cover all their movements and gestures. (Shooting **coverage** gives the editor options in case more specific shots do not work out.) The master shot is different from an **establishing shot**, which provides an overview of the scene, often locating the action in a larger context. The first shot in *Psycho* (Alfred Hitchcock, 1960), for example, pans across the Phoenix, Arizona, skyline until the camera moves inside a hotel room window. It is too distant from what takes place in the hotel room to serve as a master shot—we don't see the main characters at all—although it is an effective establishing shot.

Beyond the master shot, other shots of the same scene provide for dramatic tension or variation. **Over-the-shoulder shots** (discussed below) locate the two principal characters in relation to each other by filming over each character's shoulder in succession. **Inserts** or **cutaways** are separate shots that are inserted into scenes, normally closer shots of objects that can be shot at an entirely different time or place, and then inserted or cut into the scene at the appropriate point. The close-up of Marion's sandwich, a cut-away that comes when Sam says she didn't seem to be very hungry, may well have been shot days after the **principal photography**, the shooting that involves the main characters themselves. Shots of what a character sees in a **point-of-view shot** are often produced by the same method rather than asking a highly paid actor to wait while a close-up is made of a relatively inexpensive **prop** (an object provided for use in the film such as a gun, photograph, or piece of clothing).

Eyeline match involves having one character look in the direction of another character even if that second character is not in the shot. This type of match is commonly employed in over-the-shoulder shots. The actor's gaze, to the right side of the screen, say (this is referred to as looking **screen right**), creates an imaginary line between the actor in the shot and the actor outside the shot. Later the other actor looks **screen left**, that is, toward the first actor. By editing these shots together, an eyeline match will be achieved.

Screen direction is quite important in cases such as this. If the first character looks to the right, the second character needs to look to the left to achieve match. If both characters look off screen to the right, they will appear to be looking at someone or something else and not at each other. Over-the-shoulder shots achieve eyeline match by shooting the first actor over the left shoulder of the second actor and the right shoulder of the first actor, or vice versa. To shoot over the left shoulder of both actors would create the impression that both are looking screen left at something else. Both choices are possible. In a film, though, whether characters actually seem to be looking at each other or both seem to be looking at something else depends on screen direction, since that is the cue used by the audience to understand the scene.

POINT-OF-VIEW SHOTS Point-of-view shots normally involve eyeline matches. They show us what a character sees from her vantage point. The camera's perspective matches the character's. By getting us to share a character's visual perspective, such shots frequently increase our emotional identification with the character.

A classic version of point of view involves three shots:

1) A character looks **off-screen**, that is, he looks toward something outside the frame.
2) A second shot reveals what he sees. Suppose he looked screen left at a woman who is across the street; the second shot may be a **medium shot** that makes it appear that we see the woman from a few feet away. This violates the assumption that the camera takes the literal place of the character who looked across the street in the first shot, but it is not distracting: it allows the viewer to get a better look at the woman he sees. It exhibits a form of **psychological realism**: the shot represents how the person is singled out and magnified in importance in the character's mind.
3) A third shot presents the man who looked off-screen again to show his reaction to what he has just seen. Surprise, anger, excitement— these and other emotions might play across his face and bring the point-of-view construction to a close.

A vivid example of point of view and how it can engage the viewer occurs in *Psycho* when Norman removes a painting in his office parlor. He exposes a small hole in the wall and then looks through it to see Marion Crane preparing for a shower. We then see Norman's (somewhat ambiguous) reaction. The shot constitutes a classic A/B/A' point-of-view figure, where A represents Norman, B is what he sees, and A' is his reaction to what he sees. That Marion is unaware of Norman's gaze removes the possibility of an exchange of looks. The viewer realizes that Norman is behaving voyeuristically, a likely sign of deviance and, perhaps, danger. Even so, the viewer shares Norman's literal point of view. This may create discomfort. Hitchcock often maneuvers the viewer into identifying with characters who are unsavory, or worse. This point-of-view figure thus creates moral tension and builds suspense as well as drawing the viewer into the world of the characters.

SHOT/REVERSE SHOTS AND OVER-THE-SHOULDER SHOTS Both of these editing patterns achieve continuity by matching eyeline and screen direction. They are valuable in scenes with dialogue between two characters. They can be considered variations of the point-of-view shot because the audience sees characters from positions close to those occupied by other characters. In the case of shot/reverse shots and over-the-shoulder shots, though, the audience follows an interaction from two different positions. Whether the audience identifies with one character more than the other will likely depend on the characters' roles in the story, whether one is the hero and the other a supporting character, or one the hero and one the villain, for example. In the **shot/reverse shot** pattern, one of the characters talks to the other, who is off-screen. The next shot reverses the view and shows the other person talking to the first person, who is now off-screen. In **over-the-shoulder shots**, both characters are visible and the camera alternates shooting from over the shoulder of each one.

In both cases, it is also usually important that the shots conform to the **180-degree rule.** This rule, actually a convention that can be violated, states that if an imaginary line is drawn between the two characters and treated as if it were the diameter of a circle surrounding the two characters, all of the shots should be taken from one side of that line. This allows each character to remain on the same side of the screen, which, in turn, minimizes any possible confusion on the part of the audience as cuts occur. The 180-degree rule is therefore one more convention for the creation of continuity. The figure below illustrates how it works in a specific situation.

THE 180-DEGREE RULE

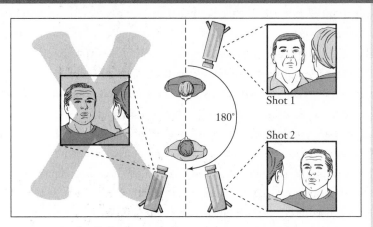

The dotted line divides the space around Clint and Joe into two 180° zones. The "180-degree rule" (actually a convention) states that all shot/reverse shots or over-the-shoulder shots should be made in one of the two zones only. Shot 1 shows Clint from over Joe's shoulder. Clint occupies screen left. Shot 2 shows Joe responding to Clint. Clint is still on screen left and Joe remains on screen right in both shots. In the shot on the left Joe jumps from screen right to screen left. By breaking the rule, the shot on the left makes it seem that Joe has suddenly changed position, potentially confusing the viewer.

PARALLEL OR CROSSCUT EDITING Finally, there are larger editing patterns than those between individual shots. These would include **parallel editing** or **crosscutting**, in which the film cuts back and forth between two different actions: one person fleeing and another in pursuit, for example. This technique was refined in the 1910s, particularly by D. W. Griffith. Alternating between two parallel events can be a highly dramatic device. If a film cuts between a couple riding along a road in a car and a train hurtling down its track, the viewer begins to anticipate impending danger. Suspense rises as the audience

sees the couple approach the railroad crossing, unaware of the onrushing train. By the 1920s this had become such a cliché that some films
mocked it. *The Red Lily* (Fred Niblo, 1924), a typical silent film about
ill-fated lovers, contains a scene where, after a suspenseful buildup,
the car passes quite safely across the railroad tracks as the driver con-
verses nonchalantly with his sweetheart, the speeding train passing
just behind them.

MISMATCH **Mismatch** occurs when there is a lack of continuity
between shots. For example, a character with earrings may lack earrings in the very next shot, or a character whose dinner jacket is but-
toned in one shot may have it unbuttoned in the following shot. Such
lapses disrupt continuity but may be valued in montage editing.

An important form of mismatch is the **jump cut,** in which the shift
from one shot to the next fails to maintain smooth continuity in space
or time. In a jump cut, a character on the left of the screen may "jump"
to the right side of the screen in the next shot. Violating the 180-
degree rule produces jump cuts. Jean-Luc Godard used jump cuts frequently in his first feature film, *Breathless* (*À bout de souffle*, 1960,
France), to convey a sense of nervous energy and unpredictability.
Michel (Jean-Paul Belmondo) and Patricia (Jean Seberg) move around
her apartment without the aid of match action. Instead Michel suddenly "jumps" from sitting on the bed to standing by the closet
between shots. This type of edit produces a confused feeling in the
viewer, one that Godard judged appropriate to the psychological state
of Michel, who has killed a policeman and is on the run.

FLASHBACKS AND FLASH FORWARDS Similar to but significantly
different from a mismatch is the **flashback** or **flash forward**. In this
case, the disparity between shots is not accidental but is a result of
jumping back or forward in time; the director normally goes to some
pains to make the jump in time and space intelligible, motivated by
memory or anticipation on the part of a character. Mainstream films
usually signal these jumps carefully in order to maintain continuity,

using devices such as nostalgic music, a slow camera movement in toward the eyes of a character as she recalls the past, or dialogue that cues the spectator to an impending shift in time or space. *Easy Rider* (Dennis Hopper, 1969) used quick flashes of images from later in the film in several scenes to signal flash forwards in an abrupt and disorienting way. This served the film's thematic point of questioning the success of the two men's journey across America.

DISCONTINUITY AND MONTAGE EDITING While continuity, well executed, is largely transparent and will go unnoticed by viewers, discontinuity and montage editing styles are much more apparent and draw attention to themselves. **Discontinuity editing** is a more inclusive concept than montage. It refers to jarring leaps between shots in some avant-garde films such as *Un chien andalou* (literally *Andalusian Dog*, but the French title is normally used; Luis Buñuel and Salvador Dali, 1929, France) or *Meshes of the Afternoon* (Maya Deren and Alexander Hammid, 1943) as well as the mysterious, inexplicable edits that occur in European art cinema, MTV-style videos, and other non-Hollywood films. In the early surrealist film *Un chien andalou*, Buñuel and Dali used editing to make coherence and intelligibility impossible. The filmmakers wanted to replicate a dreamlike state in which anything could happen. A man is attracted to a woman in an apartment. The film then cuts to a shot of the man dragging a piano and two priests, among other things, across the floor. These objects suddenly appear without any narrative explanation. *Un chien andalou* abounds in mysterious juxtapositions and contrasts like this one. It resembles a dream more than everyday reality.

Discontinuity editing has also been quite central to the work of other avant-garde filmmakers such as Peter Kubelka's *Unsere Afrikareise* (*Our Trip to Africa*, 1966, Austria), a film made from footage shot of an African safari but used to challenge the very idea of a safari, or Sadie Benning's *It Wasn't Love* (1992) and *Girl Power* (1993), films that explore Benning's sexual desires and lesbian identity. Discontinuity editing is also used widely in MTV-style music videos, where the song imparts a sense of continuity to a dizzying array of images that violate almost all the conventions of continuity editing—much as the Phillip Glass score does in *Koyaanisqatsi*.

Montage editing techniques were advanced by the silent Soviet cinema and by Sergei Eisenstein in particular. Although Eisenstein told coherent stories in all his films, he placed far less value on continuity between shots than on contrast and conflict within and between shots. Montage, as Eisenstein described it, sought to induce the spectator to connect two dissimilar shots emotionally, intellectually, or politically in order to make associations that might not otherwise be apparent. For him, such editing achieved a Marxist analysis of social reality by visually exposing contradictions between various forces and conditions such as the conflict between owners and workers.

Montage editing drew on currents within the modernist art movement, which is discussed in greater detail in Chapter 5. Modernism often favored jarring juxtapositions over harmonious wholes. Artists might combine newspaper clippings, paper clips, and oil paint in a single painting, or present a portrait from multiple perspectives as the cubists did repeatedly. Sergei Eisenstein, an extremely well-read young man, who had already begun a career in the theater, carried ideas like these to the cinema. His proposals parallel those of Bertolt Brecht, who created a strongly political but entertaining theater (discussed further in Chapter 8). Eisenstein rejected the conventions of continuity editing in favor of montage that made smooth transitions in time and space secondary to vivid contrasts in values and actions.

In *October* (1928, Soviet Union), Eisenstein's film about the Soviet Revolution of 1917 that brought the Bolsheviks to power, he presents a shot of the interim leader, Kerensky, a socialist but not a Bolshevik, ascending a staircase in the royal palace. Because Kerensky did not support the Bolsheviks, as Lenin's Communist party was called, Eisenstein did not want to present him in a favorable light. (Lenin would eventually replace Kerensky as leader of the government.) Therefore, Eisenstein cuts from the shot of Kerensky, decked out in all his military regalia, to a shot of a peacock. The peacock is not on the staircase or in the palace; it does not belong to the same historical world as Kerensky at all. But Eisenstein inserts this shot to make a political point: Kerensky acts like a peacock. He values the trappings of power more than the liberation of the common man. This metaphorical attack on Kerensky has a higher priority for Eisenstein than maintaining the appearance of spatial and temporal continuity within the story world.

Editorial inserts like that of the peacock are generally known as **extra-diegetic inserts**. **Diegesis** is a Greek word that means narrative or story; in film the term used to describe the story world occupied by the characters. Musical scores, intertitles, commentary by a narrator, and shots such as this one of a peacock are called **extra-diegetic** because they don't belong to the same world as the characters, who normally remain completely unaware of them. Extra-diegetic material helps establish the filmmaker's distinct attitude or perspective toward the story world.

Within the conventions of Hollywood cinema, **montage sequences** typically refer to an assembly of shots that mark the passage of time or the unfolding of a process. A montage sequence in *Blonde Venus* (Josef von Sternberg, 1932) shows the main character's (Marlene Dietrich) rise from poverty and outlaw status to become a top nightclub celebrity through a series of shots of various marquees, flashing lights, and a continuous, upbeat music track. The montage masks the very forms of conflict and struggle that Eisenstein's concept of montage made vivid: her rise turns into an apparently effortless migration toward larger and flashier billboards, increased adulation, and critical acclaim, not unlike the conventional tale of the Hollywood star's inevitable rise to fame. A similar montage occurs in *Raging Bull* (Martin Scorsese, 1980) as Jake

LaMotta (Robert De Niro) advances through the boxing ranks by winning one fight after another. The shots showcase his rise with a montage of powerful punches and sudden knockouts. Montage sequences like these almost invariably mask more complex social processes. Michael Moore received criticism for summarizing U.S. military intervention in a host of other countries from Guatemala to Iraq in just such a montage in *Fahrenheit 9/11* (2004). It made for a succinct, powerful summary, but left some viewers feeling as if all of the reasons for debate about these interventions had been cast aside.

CINEMATOGRAPHY

Classic cinematography shares many qualities with photography, videography, and digital cinematography. The basic principles carry over from one medium or technology to the next, but adjustments must be made for the particular qualities that distinguish each medium such as the light sensitivity of the recording medium, the fidelity of color reproduction, and **resolution**—the maximum degree of detail captured. Cinematography involves making choices: between types of shot, types of lenses, and camera movement. Lighting will be taken up as a separate category, but it clearly goes hand in hand with these three aspects of how filmmakers use the camera expressively.

TYPES OF CAMERA SHOT Given the centrality of individual characters to most stories, it is little wonder that camera shots are characterized according to how they represent the body, from shots that locate the figure in a larger context to shots that isolate body parts. A **long shot** renders the central characters as small figures relative to their surroundings. Charlie Chaplin ended most of his films with a long shot of his Tramp character walking down a road away from the camera. The long shot differs from the **long take**, which includes any type of shot that continues for an extended time, and the **establishing shot**, which is often a long shot but is always the first shot of a scene. A long shot can occur at any point in a scene, not only at the beginning.

A **medium long shot** begins to isolate one or more figures. The body is visible from the ankles or knees up. Such a shot is also known as a **plan américain,** from the French. Very early films preferred to show the full body rather than cut off the feet or lower leg, lest the viewer become puzzled about missing body parts, but a preference for tighter shots that drew more attention to the face eventually prevailed. **Medium shots** present the human figure from the waist up, and **medium close shots** do so from mid-chest up. In these shots, the person or persons photographed dominate the screen. (A **medium two shot** shows two people from the waist up.) These are very common and serve as visual workhorses in most films.

Close-ups fill the screen with an object or figure of significance, typically the face, but the shot is also used for important objects such as a key, knife, or letter. The shot leaves no doubt where the viewer's attention should be directed. Such shots draw attention to details, quite often the facial expression and eyes of a character. Some filmmakers refuse to use the close-up. In films such as *Play Time* (1967, France/Italy), French comedian and director Jacques Tati used a repertoire of shots that come no closer to the characters than a medium shot, and the majority do not even come that close. Other films, like Sergio Leone's spaghetti western *The Good, the Bad and the Ugly* (1966, Italy/Spain/West Germany), rely almost entirely on the close-up. Leone constructs numerous scenes from cuts between close-ups and choker shots of his principal characters as they confront one another, face down threats, scheme, or engage in deadly shoot-outs.

Choker or **extreme close-ups** present only part of the face or an object. They often fill the screen with a mouth, an ear, or a pair of eyes—the organs of perception and expression. Such shots can be flattering or unflattering. In Frederick Wiseman's classic documentary,

High School (1968), choker close-ups of the teachers tend to make them appear somewhat sinister and threatening, whereas the students, shot mostly in wider shots, appear more open and receptive. The famous bathroom murder scene in *Psycho* ends with a choker shot of the victim's eye in which the camera begins to rotate as if to imitate the water that is swirling down the shower drain. This shot also rhymes—it has a similar visual quality and occupies a complementary position in the story—with the choker shot of Norman Bates's eye as he gazes through a peephole in his office into the motel room of Marion Crane. The camera's gradual approach to a subject creates a dramatic buildup, equivalent to a musical crescendo; it can culminate in a close-up, which is its visual payoff.

CAMERA LENSES Camera lenses come in different **focal lengths**, measured in millimeters (mm), and apertures (**f-stops** are a measure of how large the **aperture**, or the lens opening through which the light passes, is). The aperture of the lens and the shutter speed of the camera determine how much light enters the camera. Movie cameras, whether they record on film, videotape, or a digital chip, normally operate at a fixed rate of 24 frames per second for film and 30 frames per second for television. Therefore, the speed of the lens—its maximum aperture, or f-stop—has great importance. The maximum and minimum apertures of the lens set limits on the movie camera's ability to function in very dim or very bright conditions. The "speed" of the lens is a measure of the maximum aperture possible and therefore does not involve physical motion, whereas shutter speed is a measure of how long it takes the shutter to open and close. Since the shutter opens and closes either 24 or 30 times per second and is therefore fixed, it is the speed of the lens, the maximum amount of light it can admit, that becomes more crucial. The sensitivity of the recording medium—film, videotape, or digital cells—also becomes crucial. All else being equal, a more sensitive medium allows filming in dimmer light.

Still and movie cameras possess an aperture ring that can be enlarged to admit more light or tightened to admit less. Many consumer cameras do this automatically, but a motion picture camera operator sets the f-stop or aperture and the focus manually to maintain maximum creative control of the image. A high f-stop number such as f-16 or f-22 indicates a small aperture, whereas a low f-stop number such as f-1.4 or f-2 indicates a large aperture, which will admit more light. A lens with a maximum aperture of f-2 will be faster than a lens with a maximum aperture of f-4: it can collect more light and be used in a dimmer situation. Similarly, a lens with a minimum aperture of f-32 can admit less light than a lens with a minimum opening of f-16. This makes it more useful in a very bright situation. The aperture is also used to control **depth of field,** the span of distance from the camera over which the image remains in sharp focus. All lenses possess greater depth of field at their smallest apertures and the least depth as their largest apertures. A **wide-angle lens** will also have greater depth of field than a **telephoto lens** at a given f-stop.

Focal length measures the distance from the lens to the recording material in the camera needed to bring the image into focus. Longer focal lengths require physically longer lenses to allow the image to come to a sharp focus on the surface of the film, videotape, or digital chip receptors. The greater the focal length, the narrower the **field of view.** A **telephoto lens** brings a narrow slice of the field of vision in front of the camera into close, detailed view, appearing closer than it would seem to the naked human eye. A **wide-angle lens** has a short focal length and captures a wide field of vision. The terms are relative, but they pivot around the focal length of a **normal lens** that renders the relationships between figures in depth much as they appear to the human eye. The different effects these three types of lens have on the representation of space, and therefore, on the viewer's perception of space, are summarized in Table 1.1. Depending on the expressive effect desired, a director will choose the focal length that best achieves

Table 1.1 The Characteristics of Different Focal Length Lenses (for a 35mm camera)

	Wide-Angle Lens	Normal Lens	Telephoto Lens
Typical Focal Length	25mm	50mm	250mm
Coverage	Wide angle of vision, covers a large horizontal or vertical area.	Angle of vision is similar to the human eye.	Narrow angle of vision, covers a relatively small horizontal or vertical area.
Depth of Field	Considerable. Often possible to have objects from 1–2 feet to infinity in sharp focus.	Moderate. Can often have objects in focus from 8–10 feet to infinity in sharp focus.	Restricted. May only bring objects over a certain range into focus, sometimes a matter of only a few feet. Objects closer or further away will be blurred.
Distortion of the Image	Objects very close to the camera appear to bow outward; they seem bloated or unnaturally large. The gap between objects that are at different distances from the camera is increased. Increased sense of depth of field.	Spatial relations resemble those of normal human perception	Objects very close to the camera will usually be out of focus. The gap between objects at different distances from the camera seems reduced. Reduced sense of depth of field.
Stability of Image	Very stable; camera can move slightly without having significant effect.	Less stable. Hand-held shots can be a bit blurry.	Unstable. Effect of hand-held shots or sudden camera movements will be considerable, making image shake or blur noticeably.
Motion toward or away from Lens	Exaggerated, more vivid, faster. Objects increase size in the frame rapidly as they approach the camera.	Similar to perception by the human eye.	Diminished, less vivid, slower. Objects increase size in the frame slowly as they approach the camera.

the intended result. The values are for a 35mm camera, one that records its images on 35mm film. A 16mm camera uses lenses that possess focal lengths approximately half as great, since they are producing images on a film frame that is almost half as large.

Any lens can be **racked** to bring objects at different distances from the camera into focus. **Rack focus** is the practice of shifting from one plane of focus to another rapidly during a shot. A common use of it is to hold focus on a character near the camera until that character leaves the frame and then to **rack focus** to another character or object at a different distance from the camera and therefore initially out of focus. **Soft-focus cinematography** is the use of a special lens, gauze, or filmy substance (like Vaseline) to produce a slightly out-of-focus or soft, diffuse look to the image. It is a flattering form of cinematography and is frequently used to shoot the faces of female stars at moments to emphasize their beauty or sexual allure. In *The Diving Bell and the Butterfly* (*Le scaphandre et le papillon*, Julian Schnabel, 2007, France/U.S.) a soft, blurry focus, particularly at the start of the film, simulates the way the main character sees the world around him after he has had a stroke and comes out of a coma. The cinematography creates a powerful sense of the subjective quality to vision and of vision's dependence on the normal functioning of the eye and brain to represent the world in a well-formed image.

CAMERA MOVEMENT A camera can be fixed in place, on a tripod or hand-held, but it can also be put in motion. In the **tracking shot** the camera is moved from place to place while filming continuously. The camera can be hand-held, often using the **steadicam** harness, which absorbs the jerkiness of human movement, or mounted on a **dolly,** a wheeled platform. The **dolly** can also be mounted on **tracks,** similar to small-gauge railroad tracks, which assures smoothness of motion.

A stunning example of camera movement occurs at the opening of Jean-Luc Godard's *Contempt* (*Le mépris*, 1963, France/Italy). We see a movie scene being shot at the famous Italian movie studio, Cinecittà. A camera crew pulls a 35mm camera along a track until they stop, and the camera operator **tilts** down to focus on the camera that records this very view, appearing, therefore, to look directly at the audience. Godard uses two cameras throughout the scene: the one we see being pulled along, and another, unseen camera, toward which the camera we see turns at the end of the shot. As it does so, it then seems to be looking at us, since our point of view is determined by this unseen camera. Godard uses the shot to draw attention to the act of filming itself. It reminds the viewer that the camera is normally invisible and ignores the viewer's own location beyond the frame. Godard's camera approaches the viewer, much as the train approached the film audience in the Lumières' film *Arrival of a Train at La Ciotat* (Auguste and Louis Lumière, 1896, France), and breaks the illusion of a diegetic or story world by tilting down as if it spots the viewer watching from her theater seat. This type of reflexive device frequently occurs in Godard's films to break the illusion of an autonomous story world. A **tilt** is a vertical movement of the camera; it tilts up or down. A **pan** is a horizontal movement, the camera scanning left or right, and a **Dutch tilt** is a shift of the entire camera off its vertical-horizontal axis so that it the entire camera tilts to the left or right, producing an image no longer perpendicular to the ground.)

An alternative form of movement is optical rather than physical. **Zoom shots** traverse space but do so by changing the focal length of the **zoom lens** rather than moving the camera. As a camera operator increases the focal length of the lens, distant objects are magnified and appear to be brought closer. Unlike in a **tracking shot,** the perspective also changes, since the **lens** effectively shifts from a **wide-angle lens**, with an exaggerated sense of depth, to a **telephoto lens**, with a diminished sense of depth. A **zoom shot**, therefore, does not correspond as closely to normal human perception as a tracking shot; it can be used to convey a subjective or impressionistic view of a scene.

Lighting

Lighting is a subtle part of filmmaking. Even though film stocks and digital cameras respond to a wide spectrum of lighting levels, light still has to fall within a given range for the image to approximate what the naked eye would see under the same circumstances. Variations in the amount and quality of this light will have significant effects on the tone and emotional impact of a scene. In most cases whatever efforts are made to alter the available light wind up disguised so that the light appears to come from natural sources. Considerable effort, though, goes into achieving this effect, from eliminating the ceiling of a set to place lights above the characters to setting up high-intensity floodlights outside a window to give the appearance of natural light entering a room.

Few feature films are made that rely solely on natural light, even when they are shot on location. Terrence Malick's films, including *Days of Heaven* (1978), *The Thin Red Line* (1998), and *The New World* (2005), take place primarily on location, but the soft, warm light that bathes almost every scene is a result of filming during the "magic hour" just after sunrise and just before sunset, as well as the addition of various lights, reflectors, gauzes, and filters to even out and soften the available sunlight. A great many contemporary documentaries, from *The Thin Blue Line* (Errol Morris, 1988), about a murder case in Texas, to *The Last Days* (James Moll, 1998), about five Hungarian Jews who survived the Holocaust, rely on carefully lit interviews that simulate the flattering light seen in portraiture. In many cases the cinematographer will add **fill light**, described below, to soften or eliminate shadows and to reduce the overall contrast between bright and dark portions of the frame.

The predominant form of lighting is **high key lighting**. High key lighting involves using a variety of light sources so that everything in the frame is uniformly well lit. The light is bright throughout the frame, with few shadows, and a minimum of contrast in the lighting values throughout the scene. Three primary light sources occupy different locations:

1) The **key light** is typically above and to the side of the main character(s). It is the strongest source of light on the set and casts some shadows.

2) The **fill light** is typically placed lower and to the opposite side of the main characters. It is a weaker light but is adequate to fill in most or all of the key light's shadows.

3) The **back light** is placed behind a main character, out of view. It serves to cast something of a halo around the head or figure of the character (most noticeably when shining through the character's hair): it differentiates the character from her surroundings and makes her stand out in the frame. This subtle effect functions to draw a soft outline around the character, separating her from the background, attracting the viewer's eye, and reinforcing the character's centrality to the story. **Backlighting**, like the placement of characters in the frame and an emphasis on their dialogue relative to other sounds, discreetly serves to draw the viewer's attention to the actors who are at the center of the film.

Low key lighting is a less common paradigmatic choice but also a more dramatic one. With low key lighting, only parts of the frame, if any, are well lit; shadows are plentiful, contrasts vivid, and the human figure may blend into the surrounding darkness and shadow (little or no backlighting). This style was highly popular in **film noir** (literally, "black film," because the films seem so darkly lit), a cycle of postwar films that used minimal lighting and left many dramatic shadows. They were, in fact, often shot at night with only enough key light to identify the main characters. Their emotional tone was also dark, exploring themes of seduction, betrayal, and murder. Low key lighting also finds use in other genres such as sci-fi films like *Alien* (Ridley

Scott, 1979, UK/U.S.) or *Blade Runner* (Ridley Scott, 1982). In low key lighting, a key light is used to illuminate a portion of the scene or even just a portion of a character. It is more often a **spotlight** than a **floodlight**, selecting discrete portions of the frame for illumination (a **spotlight** is sharply focused on a limited area; a **floodlight** covers a larger area more diffusely). A fill light may be used only in moderation to highlight specific details within the scene, or not at all. Back light may be omitted. Alternatively, the back light may be treated more expressively as a **rim** or **kick light**. In this case, it will cast a harsh, silhouetting light that catches only part of a face or figure. A **rim** or **kick light** may replace the **key light** entirely to leave most of a character in shadows and only partially illuminate him with light that comes from the side or rear.

Animation can produce striking lighting effects as well. Richard Linklater's *A Scanner Darkly* (2006) uses established actors (Keanu Reeves, Robert Downey, Jr., Winona Ryder, Woody Harrelson) to provide the template for the film's animated images. The film presents a convoluted plot involving paranoid delusions and corporate machinations. Much of what the characters say and do follows from drug-induced states. The visual style has echoes of low key lighting and film noir to it, especially in the extreme use of sharp contrasts between the levels of light falling across the characters' faces. Normally, film will capture the different shadings of light and shadow as a subtle gradient. But Linklater divides the characters' faces into clearly differentiated swaths of shading. A face may have three or four zones of different light intensity playing across it. They are never stable but shift and pulse as if the light levels were constantly flickering. Each zone is a monotone, with no differentiation of shading inside it at all. The shift in the intensity of the light occurs all at once at the boundary with the next zone. The effect is quite eerie. It renders faces in an unnatural way and heightens the strange, unstable quality of the world the characters inhabit.

Mise-en-scène: COMPOSITION OF THE IMAGE

Mise-en-scène is a French term that means "put in the scene." The term derives from theatrical use, where it refers to all the elements of stage design (walls, windows, furniture, props, and so on). In cinema the term refers to the arrangement of what appears in front of the camera. It can include set design, lighting, costumes, props, character placement, and movement. As with the creative aspects of lighting, these efforts often go unnoticed. Characters seem to move across the screen based on the nature of their interactions rather than in response to what the director decides should occur. To have a character walk across a room to a bookshelf and wind up flush against the right-hand margin of the frame, however casual it may appear, requires planning and rehearsal. Most of John Cassavetes' films, such as *Shadows* (1959) or *Faces* (1968), adopt a sense of life caught on the run among characters who interact freely and spontaneously, but this style only emerges on screen in a compelling form as a result of considerable rehearsal. The cinematography is subordinated to character action, but character action is rehearsed to allow the camera to capture it effectively. Films by Alfred Hitchcock, such as *Psycho* or *Vertigo* (1958), give less sense of free-wheeling characters who move at whim. The characters are but one element among many in carefully composed images. This, too, requires considerable planning and rehearsal, but here the character is made more subordinate to the camera than the camera to the character.

The placement of characters is particularly important. While the director has complete freedom to place characters as she wishes, it quickly becomes apparent that there are conventions that normally determine their position. This is true even in animated films. An animated film has no real-world referent other than the cartoon images created for the film itself. It is therefore possible to organize the composition of the frame in any way whatsoever. But animators do not normally exercise this freedom any more than painters do. They depict their characters and the relations between characters using the same familiar forms of composition and character placement found in painting, photography, and live-action films. These forms provide pleasing arrangements and fulfill the needs of the narrative to advance the story efficiently.

The animated feature *The Incredibles* (Brad Bird, 2004) makes this clear. The characters fill the frame to provide balanced, pleasing arrangements that also give indications about the nature of their relationships to one another. The arrangement of characters stresses the formal nature of the pattern they create in space (a taller character in the middle of the frame with shorter characters to either side, for example, creates a pleasing, triangular shape) or the social nature of their interaction (one character looms over another to issue a threat). The main characters are normally the best lit, they occupy the foreground and remain in focus, and the camera follows their movements. A single character is usually placed near but not exactly at the center of the frame. When there are two characters, which produces a **two shot** (two people present in the same frame), they are located near the center of the frame. Eyeline match maintains their relationship when the film reverts to **one shots**, showing one character only.

Another paradigmatic choice, similar to high and low key lighting, is between **open** and **closed frames.** Any shot that gives the sense that it is part of a much wider field of potential action rather than an enclosed, formally balanced composition yields an **open frame.** What is inside the frame seems to be an arbitrarily isolated portion of a larger field. Lila's walk up toward Mrs. Bates's house is an **open frame** where the landscape seems to extend well beyond the somewhat arbitrary frame of the shot. War documentaries typically have an open frame. The visible image represents a limited slice of a much larger field of battle that extends well beyond what the camera can see.

Conversely, a shot that gives the sense that it is entirely self-sufficient and composed to represent a specific world where action takes place inside the boundaries of the shot yields a **closed frame**. What goes on inside the frame seems separated from the space around it. Television sit-coms that are located almost exclusively in the living room or other shared space for a group of characters, from *Ozzie and Harriet* in the 1950s to *Curb Your Enthusiasm* in the 2000s, invariably opt for a closed frame. In *Psycho*, the shots of Sam and Norman (as Sam tries to distract Norman so that Lila can slip up to the house) use the walls of the office, the eyeline match between the two men, and their placement on opposing sides of the reception counter to produce the sense of a **closed frame**.

Vivid examples of closed frames occur in Rainer Werner Fassbinder's *Ali: Fear Eats the Soul* (*Angst essen Seele auf*, 1974, West Germany). The characters seem trapped inside frames inside the frame. Fassbinder appears to make do with the physical realities of specific spaces—staircase banisters, doorways, corridors and so forth—as if the sense of entrapment could not be otherwise, but, in fact, the composition is carefully designed to accentuate this effect. It creates a thematic stress on the role of an oppressive environment in the characters' lives.

Another important aspect of *mise-en-scène* or composition is the relation between **foreground** and **background**. Early cinema preferred to arrange characters in a line at the same distance from the camera, but by the 1910s, depth—relative to the camera—had come into use. Action in the foreground and action in the background now occurred in the same shot, inviting the spectator to shift attention between different planes of the shot. **Deep focus cinematography**, which keeps objects at different distances from the camera in focus, relies on wide-angle lenses, deploying a large amount of light to permit the use of a small aperture with increased depth of field, and fast film stocks to explore foreground/background relationships for dramatic purposes. Digital cameras are very sensitive to light and can also achieve considerable depth of field.

Orson Welles used **deep focus cinematography** extensively in *Citizen Kane* (1941) to bring multiple planes of the image into play. In the scene in which Susan Alexander lies in bed dying from a drug overdose and Kane pounds on the door to her room, the camera views her from near her bed table. A medicine bottle with a skull and cross-bones symbol on it occupies the foreground of the shot, giving us important information visually. Susan is unconscious in her bed, lit only by fill light, and Kane is heard in the deep background, off-screen, pounding on her door. The sound of his pounding, although it originates in the depth of the shot, is loud, made prominent to represent the dramatic tension in the scene. His significance is stressed by the clear proximity between the bottle of poison and Susan, in the foreground, and the door to the room, in the deep background. His entry may save Susan's life, and the spatial relationship stresses that he is, at this point, at some considerable distance from her, both physically and metaphorically.

Finally, an important aspect of *mise-en-scène* involves the space outside the frame, known as **off-screen space**. **Visual** or **aural cues** activate the viewer's awareness of the space beyond the frame. The pounding on the door in *Citizen Kane* as Charles tries to enter his wife's bedroom, coupled with the viewer's sight of a door in the depth of the shot, activates awareness of the space on the other side of the door. Often a character looks at something off-screen, or a sound originates off-screen, triggering the viewer's awareness of off-screen space. This can be very effective for building suspense, since the viewer becomes aware of something that cannot be seen. "What is it?" the viewer may ask, and by postponing an answer to that question, the filmmaker builds suspense.

Common techniques for activating off-screen space include:

- Off-screen looks by a character (human, animal, cyborg, etc.), including point-of-view shots. An off-screen look gives a sense of asymmetry or imbalance to the image, as if more space should be included.

- Off-screen sound that is diegetic (part of the characters' story world, so that they can respond to it, unlike musical accompaniment to the film, which is usually extra-diegetic, not part of the story world).
- Motion toward off-screen space by an object or character.
- An object or character that occupies both on- and off-screen space, such as a person only partially visible in the frame.
- Windows, curtains, screens, walls, and doors—these structures mark a boundary, and the other side of the boundary, if it is off-screen, can be activated, as in the example of Kane pounding on Susan's door in *Citizen Kane*.
- An open frame shooting style, which makes the intrusion of objects or people from off-screen more likely.

Off-screen space exists above, below, behind, to the left and right sides and in front of the screen. Any of these spaces can be activated and drawn into the development of the film. Surround sound systems make this option all the more attractive to filmmakers and engaging for audiences.

SOUND

Sound is as crucial as image in conveying meaning. Silent films, for that reason, were seldom truly silent. Musicians, from a single piano player to a full orchestra, provided accompaniment to the film. Some silent films have had new musical accompaniments created for them, which contribute enormously to the overall impact of the film. The Alloy Orchestra's accompaniment for *The Man with a Movie Camera* (Dziga Vertov, 1929, Soviet Union) is an extraordinary tour de force; it adds vibrancy and drama to Vertov's portrait of a day in the life of Moscow's citizens.

Film sound can be **diegetic** or **extra-diegetic**. **Diegetic sound** appears to originate in the story world or diegesis. Traffic noise in a scene shot on a street is diegetic sound. Like extra-diegetic sound, diegetic sound can be manipulated to serve the dramatic and emotional needs of the story. Traffic sounds might be faded out as the characters begin a serious conversation to make it easier to hear them, or it might be faded up, made louder, to suggest that the characters, in the thick of a dispute, are not listening to each other.

Characters may speak dialogue in **sync**, that is, synchronized to a shot of them saying it. Achieving sync is not an easy matter, but contemporary filmmaking equipment, be it film, video, or digital, takes much of the difficulty out of the process. Characters can also speak in **voice-off**, from beyond the frame, off-screen. A character who goes into a second room and is no longer on screen but continues to talk to a character in the room where the camera remains, is heard speaking **voice-off**.

Most **extra-diegetic sound** comments on the story world and belongs to the narration—the process of storytelling—rather than to the narrative—the story that is told. It is an important way in which the filmmaker conveys an attitude or perspective on the story world. Itzhak Perlman's violin playing through much of *Schindler's List* (Steven Spielberg, 1993) conveys a rich, respectful tone, underlining director Spielberg's desire to memorialize this particular story from the Holocaust. Commentary that arrives from **extra-diegetic** space, that is, from outside the story world, is **voice-over commentary**. Voice-over can be spoken by a character who offers her thoughts to the audience, in the manner of a soliloquy or monologue that is unheard by other characters, or it can be offered by a narrator who is not part of the story world at all. Voice-over is a common feature of many documentaries.

Subjective sound renders sound as a character hears it rather than as an objective auditor would hear it. A shriek that turns into a train whistle, for example, might serve as a sound bridge between a murder and the killer's escape by train, but a railroad whistle that turns into a shriek might signify the way a guilt-ridden killer hears such a whistle as the shriek of his victim. Music can also serve a subjective purpose. The eerie, vibrating tones of the theramin, an early electronic instrument that produced notes when its player passed her hands through an open space, was a staple of sci-fi and horror films in the 1950s. It created a haunting, other-worldly impression that served these genres well.

VIEWING TECHNOLOGIES

How spectators view moving images has considerable impact on the nature of the experience and its impact. Home viewing on a traditional television offers sound and image quality far below that of a modern motion picture theater or a **high definition (HD)** digital television broadcast. Traditional television sets offer 525 lines of resolution, but high definition more than doubles the resolution. High definition produces images with almost as much detail as 35mm film. Moviegoing has traditionally served as a social ritual, a form of collective activity known as "going to the movies." Newer technologies, especially digital forms of image delivery such as computers, PDAs (personal digital assistants), and cell phones, have created a form of social networking in which individuals view material separately but share it widely, often in real time. Digital viewing and sharing allows for a high degree of interactivity that adds another level of complexity, but the basic techniques described in this chapter remain of central importance.

Home viewing may also mean that the viewer will see films shortened or otherwise edited for television. A film that originally had an R rating (limiting its audience to adults and those accompanied by an adult) might be edited by a broadcaster to convert it to the equivalent of a PG-13 rating (allowing anyone to view it but urging parents to use caution for those under 13), thereby making it more suitable for a home environment.

A DVD release may differ from the theatrical release of the same film. Lengthening or shortening of the film with the addition or deletion of individual scenes commonly occurs. A **director's cut** is a new release of the film that has the full approval of the director. The theatrical release may represent the **studio cut**, the version whose final form was determined by executives at the film studio that funded or distributed the film. Whoever possesses the right of **final cut** has the power to make the ultimate decision about the final shape of a film. Directors seek it, but studios, who put up the money, usually retain the right of final cut. The DVD market makes it possible to release both cuts and let viewers compare the two.

A vivid example of the difference between the theatrical release and the director's cut can be seen in Ridley Scott's *Blade Runner*. In theaters the film ended with the two main characters fleeing the city by driving through a verdant countryside, radically different in appearance from the urban jungle where the rest of the film has occurred. The director's cut eliminates this apparently too happy ending. Scott's director's cut also eliminates Deckard's (Harrison Ford's) voice-over narration throughout the film. To add to the variety of choices, Scott returned to the film again after more than two decades to reedit it one final time in what is, for now, the third and ultimate final cut.

The multiplication of versions of *Blade Runner* reminds us that the integrity of a given version of a film may be disputed by parties with a vested interest in it, and that with DVDs, profit can be made by marketing multiple versions. In addition, many films are reedited for release in countries where certain references may be less easily understood. Entire scenes may be cut out as too obscure or eliminated to secure a more favorable rating. In other cases, films survive only in partial or previously altered versions. Sergei Eisenstein's *Que viva Mexico* (Sergei Eisenstein and Grigori Aleksandrov, 1932, U.S./Mexico) and his *Bezhin Meadow* (1937, Soviet Union) are prime examples of such films: Upton Sinclair, his chief financial backer for *Que viva Mexico*, and the Soviet government, which funded *Bezhin Meadow*, disapproved of the direction in which Eisenstein took the projects and prevented their completion. Eisenstein never made a final edit in either case, and only some of the footage survives from both films. Only incomplete versions, not authorized by Eisenstein, exist today.

Film viewing in theaters, or on television, computer, and other screens, involves two other important qualities of the film image: the **presence-in-absence** of what the camera photographed and the experience of **apparent motion**. Every frame of a film strip is a still image, but when these frames are projected successively, at 24 frames per second, the eye perceives movement rather than slight shifts or jumps in position from one frame to the next. Apparent motion brought the world to the screen in a "living" form, surpassing the realism of still photography. Apparent motion, together with the absent presence of the actor, distinguish film from the other performing arts. **Presence-in-absence** refers to the phenomenon by which the photographic image represents in a realistic way a referent, an object or person, that is no longer physically present. The spectator knows that the image's referent is no longer present, but it appears to be. We see the ghosts of actual flesh-and-blood figures.

The larger-than-life quality of the motion picture image, coupled with the absent presence of its figures, exerts a peculiar power to fascinate. It encourages forms of **identification,** or emotional and psychological involvement, with characters, and with the stars who play them. It differs from identification in dance, opera, and theater, where the living performer shares the same time and space as the spectator. It also differs from painting or photography by virtue of the addition of movement. Filmmakers often make considerable use of the identificatory possibilities of cinema to draw the viewer into the world of the characters and into the filmmaker's or a character's perspective on this world.

Over time the projected image has taken on different shapes. The Academy of Motion Picture Arts and Sciences set the initial standard at a width-to-height ratio of 4:3 in 1932 to accommodate optical sound at the side of the 35mm film strip. This image was 1.33 times wider than high. The current Academy standard is 1.85: the image is 1.85 times wider than high, yielding more of a wide-screen effect. The 1950s saw the development of even wider screen ratios, up to 2.35:1, such as Cinemascope and VistaVision, when the sheer size of the image was considered an important selling point as television became increasingly popular. Since television remained at the older Academy ratio of 1.33 until the recent introduction of "letterbox" formats, any wide-screen film image had to be cut down to display film on the narrower television screen. This was done by an electronic **pan and scan** process that selected what appeared to be the most important part of an image (bodies and faces, for example) and cropped or eliminated the rest. This often led to a serious distortion of the original *mise-en-scène*, or composition, of the image.

In chapters 2 through 4 we will examine how film language and the expressive techniques associated with it take on different characteristics in the three main categories of cinematic communication: poetic or avant-garde experiments with form, rhetorical or documentary efforts to speak about the world in which we live, and narrative forms of storytelling.

2

FORMS OF CINEMATIC
ENGAGEMENT AND THE
AVANT-GARDE FILM

Cinematic Worlds

The notion of cinematic worlds puts representation on somewhat more elaborate footing than the idea of a one-to-one correspondence between, say, an image (signifier) of a knife, a referent (an actual knife), and a meaning (signified) such as "murder weapon" or "cutlery." Within a complete film, a shot of a knife becomes part of a broad spectrum of actions and gestures, situations and events, motives and desires. Every film envisions a world of its own with its own spatial and temporal dimensions, its own distinct forms of activity and thematic concerns. These worlds often bear similarity to the world in which we live, and they frequently bear similarity to each other, as genre films make clear.

A world is a vast, complex place, full of ambiguity and significance. When we encounter a new world, as we do with almost every film, the experience calls for understanding and interpretation. Different people will take interest in different aspects of a newly discovered world, ask different questions about it, and come to different conclusions. This is why the concept of formal and social analysis, a dual interpretation, discussed in Chapter 1, proves so useful. As a tool, it encourages viewers to explore the complexity of a given film from their own particular perspective. What is formally conventional and what innovative? What is socially distorted and what revelatory? These questions can be put to any film.

Films may not only *represent* physical reality, be it people or landscapes, but also *embody* (give palpable form to) or *exemplify* (provide a vivid model for) what it feels like to encounter a certain kind of world. They can do these things all at the same time. Confronting the mystery of something present (a word or image) standing for something absent involves us in intense fascination with worlds that not only represent a way of understanding the existing world but give embodied, exemplary form to alternative worlds. The enchantment of Dorothy in the Land of Oz in *The Wizard of Oz* (Victor Fleming, 1939), the machinations of Michael Corleone in *The Godfather* (Francis Ford Coppola, 1972), or the sense of doomed romance that builds throughout *Titanic* (James Cameron, 1997) invite different forms of engagement just as they embody distinctly different worlds.

Audiences do not, in other words, come away from their encounter with a cinematic world—be it the world of *The Battleship Potemkin* (Sergei Eisenstein, 1925, Soviet Union) or *Bowling for Columbine* (Michael Moore, 2002, Canada/U.S./Germany), *The Seventh Seal* (Ingmar Bergman, 1957, Sweden) or *The Passion of Christ* (Mel Gibson, 2004)—with the same understanding and experience. Every film meets different needs and produces different interpretations. Imagined worlds, like the basic act of representation itself, arise for many reasons:

1) To give free play to the imagination, as *Aliens* (James Cameron, 1986) or *Across the Universe* (Julie Taymor, 2007) do with their extraordinary flights of fancy in outer space or in a world populated by the music of the Beatles. Similarly, *Blue Velvet* (David Lynch, 1986) and *Boys Don't Cry* (Kimberly Pierce, 1999) give

visible form to the directors' imaginative understanding of sexual desire and the impact of social taboos. Every film is an adventure into a world seen from a distinct perspective.

2) To gain a feeling of magical control or power over the existing world, as *Mr. Smith Goes to Washington* (Frank Capra, 1939) or *Pan's Labyrinth* (*El laberinto del fauno*, Guillermo del Toro, 2006, Spain/Mexico/U.S.) do with their tales of individual triumph over government bureaucracies, political machines, and criminal conniving. In films, we can identify with characters who overcome obstacles and exemplify admirable qualities.

3) To join individuals together in participatory rituals of aesthetic and ideological significance, as midnight movies that enjoy cult status such as *The Rocky Horror Picture Show* (Jim Sharman, 1975, UK/U.S.) or *Night of the Living Dead* (George A. Romero, 1968) do with their bizarre tales of a Transylvanian, transsexual doctor and his houseguests or of a small group of people fending off attacks by the undead.

4) To represent, embody, or exemplify possible ways of seeing and being in the world itself, as *A Scanner Darkly* (Richard Linklater, 2006) and *The Diving Bell and the Butterfly* (Julian Schnabel, 2007, France/U.S.) do with their highly innovative ways of representing human perception. From *A Trip to the Moon* (Georges Méliès, France), made in 1902, to *The March of the Penguins* (Luc Jacquet, France) in 2005, the cinema shows us the world around us with fresh, revealing eyes.

5) To propose a particular political or ideological way of seeing the world. From *The Birth of a Nation* (D. W. Griffith, 1915) to *Malcolm X* (Spike Lee, 1992) and from *Triumph of the Will* (Leni Riefenstahl, 1935, Germany) to *Fahrenheit 9/11* (Michael Moore, 2004), some films take explicit stands on issues or demonstrate a clear political perspective. As viewers, we must then decide how to respond to such representations in relation to our own lives, values, and beliefs.

PARTICIPATING IN CINEMATIC WORLDS

The experience of cinematic worlds involves at least three common categories of participation:

1) *Emotional investment*, ranging from intense identification with or attraction to characters and their relationships to ironic detachment, comic distance, or visceral loathing. The very rhythms and tonalities of a film can also exert an affective attraction, or repulsion, that contributes to our overall emotional investment.

2) *Intellectual engagement*, which makes us search for patterns and attempt to make sense of what we see using our knowledge of film language and its expressive techniques, formal conventions, and social implications.

3) *Ideological involvement*, which can run from the wholehearted adoption to the vehement rejection of the attitude the filmmaker takes toward the world she places before us as well as the acceptance or rejection of the specific political perspective the filmmaker champions (not all films adopt a specific political perspective).

These forms of participation locate viewers in a realm of conflicting, even contradictory worlds that represent society in all its complexity. The interpretations viewers make of these worlds and the filmmaker's attitude toward them lead to journeys through territory both familiar and strange. Are we like James Dean in *Rebel Without a Cause* (Nicholas Ray, 1955), agonizing over the difficult passage to manhood in a dysfunctional family, or are we like the young Ali Le Point in *The Battle of Algiers* (Gillo Pontecorvo, 1966, Italy/Algeria), willingly and purposefully sacrificing ourselves for a larger political cause (the struggle for independence from France in colonial Algeria, in Ali's case)? Are we detached yet all-knowing like the omniscient voice-over commentators of classic documentaries such as the *Why We Fight* (Frank Capra and Anatole Litvak, 1943-1945) series of films (on

American involvement in World War II), or are we like the self-questioning filmmakers Jill Godmilow in *Far from Poland* (1984) (about the Solidarity movement in Poland as it challenges Communist rule) and Ross McElwee in *Sherman's March* (1986) (as he travels through the South in search of a partner), who pose far more questions than answers? What aspects of these works hint at the filmmaker's own point of view or attitude toward the world created—from the clear admiration conveyed by *The Battle of Algiers* for its doomed revolutionary heroes to the intense self-doubt of Ross McElwee in *Sherman's March* about his hopes for romance in the modern-day South?

The viewer does not passively receive a film. From the outset viewers must assign signifieds to shots, scenes, sounds and images, and construct a coherent whole, a distinct world seen from a specific perspective. This activity is neither wholly cognitive (it is not purely a rational, problem-solving exercise) nor wholly affective (it is not simply an emotional, sensation-generating experience). The audience's engagement with a film combines aspects of both these ways of being and knowing: the audience perceives formal patterns and social conflicts cognitively during a process that engages them affectively. Surely this is one of the qualities that make cinema such a powerful, compelling force. Not solely based on reason—though not indifferent to it either; not solely based on emotion—though hardly bereft of feeling; cinema opens up worlds we enter with body and soul, thought and feeling, reason and empathy, logic and desire.

The maps we chart of this complex territory must acknowledge that our relation to films includes emotional investments, intellectual engagement, and, often, ideological involvement in subtle and powerful ways. This complex relation stems from our response to a basic quality of cinema: its ability to construct complex worlds that fascinate and intrigue from sounds and images fashioned into signifiers. The process of understanding cinematic signs is both simple—almost everyone can understand movies—and complex—the basic working parts of a sign and the degree of creative effort in creating it are not always apparent. Because the avant-garde cinema takes up this issue of the complexity of the cinematic signifier most directly, it forms the primary subject matter of this chapter.

The Relation of Cinematic Signs to Power and Desire

The peculiar quality of a signifier to both *stand alone* like any other material thing and to *stand for* something not materially present gives languages, including film, a power and a fascination mere physical reality lacks. Unlike a kick or a rifle shot, representations do not produce results or effects in direct proportion to their physical force. Their impact may not be immediate; their consequences cannot be fully predicted, nor can their affect be readily measured. They produce results indirectly, in relation to their ability to engage their audience.

We always desire what we do not have. Desire is the longing for something absent or unavailable. Language, including film, is one way to give expression to our desires. All languages have the ability to give expression to hopes and dreams, yearnings and fantasies. Desire lives through images, which give us a mental picture of the things we want to obtain. Images nourish desire. Images offer us the power to regain and celebrate, to possess and extol what we might not otherwise possess. The very act of converting desires into images and giving them the shape of a completed film can be a source of pleasure, and power, of its own.

Film proposes ways of seeing and being in the world. Every film moves us to take up or reject the perspectives and attitudes it proposes. Films urge us to embrace experiments with form, strategies of persuasion, and the pleasures of storytelling. Many desires can be pursued and many forms of power demonstrated by the language of cinema.

These pursuits of pleasure and demonstrations of power take place in specific historical situations: filmmakers and audiences meet each other in particular times and places. In almost all cases, there is a purpose to the communication, as the ancient Greeks recognized in their own reflections on language. Their categories, constructed over 2000 years ago, continue to be useful today.

The Three Domains of Language and the Different Purposes They Serve

In ancient times, the Greeks divided forms of symbolic communication into three broad categories according to the purpose each served. The categories all presuppose an audience and the goal of engaging that audience in one way or another. For each category different conventions governed what made for a coherent, pleasing, or effective effort. These conventions rely on different principles and evoke different forms of engagement. The three categories are:

1) Reason, which relies on logical procedures
2) Aesthetics, which relies on the conventions of either
   a) poetic form, or
   b) narrative structure
3) Persuasion, which relies on rhetorical strategies

Collectively, logic, aesthetics (poetics and narrative), and rhetoric constitute the total universe of symbolic communication. They describe how someone communicates in order to reason with, provide pleasure for, or persuade an audience. They remain pertinent today even though entirely new media such as film, television, and the Internet add to the forms of symbolic communication available. Logical reasoning is seldom the primary purpose of art or entertainment (although it can play a very important supporting role). It therefore does not receive extended treatment here. Rhetoric corresponds most closely to the persuasive goals of many documentary films. They are the focus of Chapter 3. Poetics and narrative lead to the well-developed domains of avant-garde and narrative film respectively. Each receives examination in its own chapter, the avant-garde here and narrative in Chapter 4. Avant-garde or experimental film, narrative fiction, and documentary nonfiction, in fact, are the three prime examples of how the original Greek domains of language apply to film even though they are not direct equivalents: avant-garde films, for example, may include elements of logic and aspects of storytelling but they also give great emphasis to the poetic qualities of film language.

The Six Forms of Emphasis

The three basic categories of symbolic communication are not mutually exclusive. A single film can serve more than one purpose and bring together more than one set of conventions. Aspects of logic or reason are also involved in almost any communication to avoid contradiction and error. In fact, as many as six different emphases can occur in a single message or film regardless of whether its primary purpose is logical, poetic, narrative, or rhetorical. These emphases are:

1) Expressive: an emphasis on the feelings, tone, or point of view of the filmmaker. This quality conveys the filmmaker's attitude toward the world she presents and, in some cases, the filmmaker's political perspective. As discussed in Chapter 1, extra-diegetic music is often a signifier of the filmmaker's attitude or perspective on an aspect of the world she places before us.

2) Persuasive: an emphasis on moving or persuading the listener or

viewer. This quality is found in many documentaries as well as in advertising and political campaign messages. It is the domain for which rhetorical principles provide the most useful guidance.

3) Poetic: an emphasis on the form of the film itself. This quality is prominent in written poetry, rap music, most avant-garde films, and poetic documentaries. In most documentary nonfiction, the poetic element is subordinate to the effort to provide access to the historical world that exists outside the film. In narrative fiction, the poetic element remains important (a well-told story invariably has a pleasing form), but it usually becomes secondary to creating a vivid sense of what the characters that populate the film's world experience and do.

4) Referential: an emphasis on some aspect of the world outside the film itself. This quality is strong in most documentary films and is also a prominent feature of news reporting, advertising, informational films, and many fiction films that have a basis in real events or true stories. The neorealist films from postwar Italy, for example, give a vivid sense of what it felt like to live in the aftermath of a devastating war. A strongly referential purpose often draws attention away from the film's form (its poetic quality) and places it on social or historical issues external to the film.

5) Meta-communicative: an emphasis on the nature of the film itself. "This film is a true story," for example, is a meta-communicative statement. It clarifies what kind of film a film is but is not necessarily poetic. Meta-communication is seldom the dominant aspect of a film. The opening credits and, for studio-produced films, the studio's logo—a roaring lion for MGM, an image of Columbia for Columbia Pictures, a revolving globe for Universal—are, in part, meta-communications telling us that the film is a feature fiction film from a major Hollywood studio. Voice-over commentary in documentary is often referential but it can also be meta-communicative. John Huston, the director of *The Battle of*

San Pietro (1945), tells us that the film represents a true account of the fighting that occurred as Allied troops advanced northward in Italy near the end of World War II. From his initial statement we can safely assume the film is a documentary.

6) Phatic: an emphasis on maintaining contact between filmmaker and viewer or between characters. This quality is also seldom the primary purpose of a film, but it can serve a valuable role. In conversation, we use verbal "fillers" such as "um," "hmmm," and "yeah" to indicate that we want to remain engaged in the conversation even though we do not have anything to say at the moment. Similarly, a film may include descriptive passages that do not advance the overall argument or story very much but do serve to stress the filmmaker's desire to remain in touch with the viewer. The opening shots of *Dr. Strangelove* (Stanley Kubrick, 1964, UK), which show a military bomber being refueled in mid-flight, or the long shots of the city of Boston in *The Departed* (Martin Scorsese, 2006, U.S./Hong Kong) serve to set the scene and put the filmmaker in touch with the audience more than to develop character or advance the action. If such moments were to be filled with a blank screen, the viewer might well wonder if the filmmaker remained committed to the encounter at hand.

The ability to combine these emphases adds to the complexity of symbolic communication. They can readily be mixed together as a film sets out to achieve its goals, sometimes poetically, sometimes expressively, sometimes eager to maintain a sense of connection more than convey information. In fact, the transfer of information is but one, often minor part of the communication. Every language serves many purposes, and the six emphases described here are frequently more crucial to the understanding and interpretation of a film than more factual matters. The distinctive qualities of avant-garde film will make this even more apparent.

The Avant-Garde Cinema and Poetic Discourse

Purpose

A poetic emphasis dominates films by the avant-garde. The goals of poetic work contrast sharply with the goals of logical discourse. Whereas logical discourse conveys information and presents the truth of a matter objectively, poetic works seek to create aesthetic patterns and speak to the heart of a matter subjectively. Poetic film draws attention to its form as much as or more than to what it refers to externally. The impact of poetic work is more expressive and emotional than rational. Clearly, there are poetic elements in narrative fiction and documentaries, especially those documentaries that describe forms and patterns that the filmmaker finds in the world, such as the passing of a summer shower in Joris Ivens's beautiful portrait of such a moment, *Rain* (1929, Netherlands), the daily rhythms of an urban metropolis in Walter Ruttman's great montage of urban life over 24 hours, *Berlin: Symphony of a Great City* (1927, Germany), the large-scale changes that modernity has etched into the environment in Godfrey Reggio's stunning tour of global transformations, *Koyaanisqatsi* (1982), or the astonishing and constantly shifting patterns of birds and landscape in *The March of the Penguins*. The primary home of poetic form, however, is the avant-garde.

Poetic films often deliberately make cuts more visible so that the rhythm they create is more fully experienced by the viewer. Logical argument has little importance in avant-garde film; often the logic of dreams replaces waking logic. These films do not attempt to tell stories that appear to tell themselves, with events simply unfolding before the viewer; and they limit character development in favor of an organizing structure built around formal elements such as color, light, rhythm, and repetition.

Poetic discourse may nonetheless have an ideological dimension. In fact, avant-garde work frequently urges us to see the world in a fresh light, and that light may illuminate social and political issues as well as form, pattern, or rhythm in the abstract. The poetic documentary *Koyaanisqatsi*, for example, stresses the imbalance that modernization produces between man and machine, society and nature, through the juxtaposition of its images, without any voice-over commentary.

Luis Buñuel's avant-garde masterpiece, *L'age d'or* (sometimes referred to as *The Golden Age*, 1930, France), is a poetic reverie with a structure somewhere between a narrative and a nightmare. It launches a savage attack on bourgeois values of propriety and decency and works to undermine our faith in the civic institutions of society, especially the church. The characters and events are fabricated, but they lack the coherence of a conventional narrative. Buñuel sets out to violate cinematic as well as social conventions. In the opening scene, for example, Buñuel adopts a dry, didactic tone to present information about scorpions, but the film veers in a totally different direction as we follow different characters in different places who have only a metaphorical link, if any, to the information about scorpions. Narrative, poetic, and documentary conventions are mixed together into a unique and sacrilegious stew.

In one scene, for example, the central characters start to make wild, passionate love, rolling around on the ground in ecstasy, even though they are in formal attire and surrounded by a large number of onlookers at a social gathering. The couple's well-dressed appearance is a signifier of their bourgeois status, whereas their animal-like lust strips away the veneer of propriety. Underneath the fancy appearances lurks a carnal lust that "good taste" and "etiquette" want to keep from public view. Putting lust front and center becomes Buñuel's way to skewer the conventions of polite society. His work has something of a literary counterpart in the equally scandalous writings of the Marquis de Sade, who celebrated unbridled lust in the face of a sanctimonious establishment. Buñuel adapts this aristocratic tradition of scorn for a class that had to buy its position in society and twists it into a more politically motivated attack on all forms of hypocrisy. For Buñuel, self-delusion and immorality flourished among the aristocracy as much as the bourgeoisie. Both groups engaged in elaborate rituals of pretense that masked the cruder, harsher aspects of life and their own desires and machinations. For Buñuel, a Spaniard steeped in the Catholic tradition, the church becomes a favorite target for its promises of "pie in the sky" in the face of poverty on earth. But he has no less contempt for the bourgeoisie itself.

Kenneth Anger's great homage to male passions, *Scorpio Rising* (1964), is a classic example of avant-garde filmmaking. It invents a world populated with motorcyclists whose fetishistic devotion to their bikes is synchronized to a series of popular songs. Its use of a pop music soundtrack has since been imitated by scores of feature films. *Scorpio Rising* both celebrates the outlaw status of the bikers and hints at a strongly **homoerotic** dimension to this world. (**Homoeroticism** involves same-sex attraction, whether associated with physical contact or the indirect expression of sexually charged feelings.) Without voice-over or dialogue, it relies on tunes such as "Blue Velvet" to convey the emotional involvement Anger wants viewers to develop with these young men and their bikes. It evokes poetically, rather than documenting, what it might feel like to enter a world of motorcycles and leather, pagan rituals and flirtations with death. As an avant-garde film, *Scorpio Rising* draws attention to its own formal structure more than to its referential sources in reality or the strength of its narrative tale. Each of the pop songs that make up the soundtrack is like a stanza in an extended love poem to this imagined world of motorcycles and men.

Maya Deren's *Meshes of the Afternoon* (Maya Deren and Alexander Hammid, 1943) also creates a highly subjective experience in which we explore the multiple perceptions and personalities of a woman as she confronts an everyday world turned dramatically askew. Again, without dialogue or voice-over, originally shot as a silent film, *Meshes* stresses the ambiguity of its poetic, dreamlike sequence of scenes.

In one scene, Deren, who plays the main character in the film herself, returns home and enters her living room. The room looks normal at first, but it soon takes on an eerie undertone. Things aren't what they seem. At one point, as she sits in a chair she sees multiple versions of herself occupying the same space. She is still in the chair, but other images of herself appear in different parts of the room. The shots possess a formal elegance and enigmatic structure so that their meaning remains obscure. Are they real or merely fantasies? Why does she see or imagine them, and what do they signify? Do the other personas see her as she sees them? There is no clear sign of recognition on the part of the other figures, although they look in her direction. Does this lack of recognition call her existence into question, or is the sequence a way to give visual representation to a character's other selves that normally remain out of sight but lurk within her own psyche? Deren gives no answer to such questions.

The film offers an experience more than an argument or tidy story. It suggests what it might feel like to be a woman, alone in a house, vulnerable to anxiety, and yet capable of confronting its most threatening features with calm purpose. The film ends ambiguously as the central character escapes the confines of her ominous, unstable home only to reappear as a lifeless figure on the shore. Made over fifty years ago, *Meshes of the Afternoon* remains one of the most important films of the American avant-garde.

Key Elements

Avant-garde films, poetic documentaries, and some narrative fictions explore questions of form. Ideological implications may follow, but the most distinctive aspect of poetic film is its stress on form. The form of the work, which continuity editing in fiction and stress on an external referent in documentary deemphasize, takes on primary importance. Ernie Gehr's *Serene Velocity* (1970), for example, films a view of a corridor, with the filmmaker systematically cutting between shots taken with a telephoto lens and shots taken with a wide-angle lens in an accelerating pattern. The result is less the objective transmission of information about corridors or a story about characters in a corridor and more a subjective experience of depth of field, editing, and rhythm that happens to use a corridor as its material basis.

Fiction films often create a sense of what it feels like to experience a different sort of world—of spontaneously singing and dancing in *Singin' in the Rain* (Stanley Donen and Gene Kelly, 1952), of the complex, ambiguous search for the meaning of a man's life in *Citizen Kane* (Orson Welles, 1941), of the prodigious effort to conform to what counts as normal in a fascist society in *The Conformist* (*Il conformista*, Bernardo Bertolucci, 1970, Italy/France/West Germany), of the toll it takes on a man to run a criminal empire but act as if he is a normal, respectable father and citizen in *The Godfather*. These forms of experience revolve around the interactions of characters among themselves and with their surroundings.

Poetic films frequently explore what it feels like to experience qualities of cinema as such. The worlds made possible by the cinematic medium itself often serve as the focal point for the viewer's experience of the film. *Serene Velocity*, for example, explores the experience of viewing a scene through alternating lenses. *The Flicker* (Tony Conrad, 1965) explores the experience of flicker, as the film screen reflects pulsating intervals of light and darkness (something filmmakers usually take pains to eliminate or minimize even though it is a basic part of film projection). *Ray Gun Virus* (Paul Sharits, 1966) demonstrates what it feels like to watch a series of single-color frames as they flicker past over a fourteen-minute period.

In a movie that includes a meta-communicative statement about feature fiction films, Martin Arnold's *Pièce touchée* (1989, Austria) takes

an eighteen-second segment from *The Human Jungle* (Joseph Newman, 1954), a standard fifties drama, and subjects it to various forms
of optical printing that slow the action and give a sense of what lies
behind, unsaid and unseen, the most routine of viewing experiences.
In this case the experience involves watching a man enter a room and
kiss his wife; slowed down and repeated, these originally minor actions
take on much larger, more primal dimensions, with undertones of
threat and violence lurking in the frame. Arnold's new, poetic editing
rhythm alters our perception of the type of daily routine most films
use simply to establish their social setting. A perfunctory moment that
simply gets the scene started in the original story becomes an elaborate, prolonged ritual that begins to feel as if it could go on for a very
long time. Arnold turns a simple greeting into a form of indefinite,
somewhat menacing ritual as the film loops back over the same
motions repeatedly.

As poetic works, all these films offer the viewer a heightened awareness of the very form and structure of cinema. Like paintings that
emphasize brushstrokes or the flatness of a canvas, these works remind
the viewer of the material basis for signification in film and related
audiovisual media—sounds and images that pass across a screen.

Stan Brakhage's *The Machine of Eden* (1970) is one of many films by
this great filmmaker that reflect on birth and creation, life and death.
Its images possess a lyrical beauty and invite the viewer to imagine
what the world of Eden, before the Fall, might have been like. Like
all films, *The Machine of Eden* unfolds over time; as it does so, the
images gradually amount to a recreation of an edenic world. Brakhage
said that these images are something like what a child might see, and
there is little reason to doubt that the child is, in part, Brakhage himself. He had a remarkable capacity to see the world anew and to revel
in the sheer physical wonder of light itself.

In *Mothlight* (1963), Brakhage taped the wings of moths that had
flown into a light and died to a strip of film, then re-photographed it

and used this strip as his raw material. There is a vivid sense that the image's usual **indexical** relationship to its referent—the object the image refers to, a collection of moth wings in this case—became the focal point of Brakhage's meditation on the cinema and death. He said that just as the moths perish as a result of the irresistible allure of the light, so he, too, suffered, financially and physically, from his own fascination with light and his obsessive need to make films that did not find a mass audience. *Mothlight* is a eulogy to lives lost, the art that can honor them, and the role of vision and light in the creation of poetic form.

STYLE

Poetic films adopt a wide range of styles. They are the type of work least beholden to the conventions of **realism**. (**Realism**, discussed in more detail in Chapter 5, constructs a cinematic world that bears strong resemblance to the world with which viewers are already familiar. Realism also includes a process of storytelling that typically passes unnoticed by means of techniques such as continuity editing.) In poetic film there is often little pretense that what we see resembles the world we already know. The force of the filmmaker's distinctive vision and formal preoccupations give considerable shape to what appears on the screen. Continuity editing is seldom a guiding principle. Poetic films may jump from one place to another, one character to another, and one object to another. They find their coherence in the patterns created from such jumps and in other departures from convention.

Guy Maddin's *Brand upon the Brain!* (2006, U.S./Canada), a postmodern blend of German expressionism, black and white silent movie style, melodramatic conventions about repressed family secrets, and a murder mystery subplot that includes the discovery of strange holes in the heads of the orphans living in a bizarre island orphanage run by the filmmaker's mother, affirms the power of avant-garde film to conjure up fantastic worlds and delirious obsessions. The elements of narrative seem to be little more than a tease, or a weak glue straining to hold the wild flights of Maddin's imagination together. Such a film is experienced more than it is understood, and the experience can be exhilarating as we discover, once again, a fascination born of images that give life to worlds never before encountered.

The various artistic movements associated with modernism in the early part of the twentieth century contributed to the growth of a poetic, avant-garde cinema. Surrealism and Dada, constructivism and expressionism (discussed further in Chapter 5), were all large-scale stylistic movements that broke with realist conventions to explore interior states and alternative realities in new and unexpected ways. *Un chien andalou* (Luis Buñuel and Salvador Dali, 1929, France), for example, grew out of the filmmakers' surrealist interests. Like similar works in other media, it attempts to convey what it feels like to experience a dream. Things do not make sense in the usual way, even though the film exerts considerable fascination. There are patterns and motifs, but not a consistent story or clear-cut theme.

One important element found in many avant-garde films is **collage**. A favorite device of many modernist artists, **collage** involves mixing together various elements from different sources or media to create a new effect. Photo-collage involves combining different photographic images into a single new image. The result may be satirical or humorous, or it may result in a distortion of reality by, for example, placing together in the same place two people who had never actually met. Collage can include mixing different raw materials together: adding cigarette butts or newspaper clippings to a painting, for example, or taping dead moths to a strip of film, as in Brakhage's *Mothlight*. In Russia, during the heyday of the Soviet silent cinema, the collage principle grew into the theory of montage championed by Sergei Eisenstein (discussed in Chapter 6). In the avant-garde, collage became an important device for finding new meanings in existing films.

Avant-garde filmmakers have often made use of **found footage:** footage that was originally shot for another purpose, whether portions of a finished film, such as the scene from *The Human Jungle* used in Arnold's *Pièce touchée*, or footage that was never used in a film. *The Atomic Cafe* (Jayne Loader and Kevin and Pierce Rafferty, 1982) is a collage of 1950s civil defense films produced to prepare the public for nuclear attack. Cutting them together to emphasize their paranoid and often silly proposals for how to survive nuclear attack, *The Atomic Cafe* adopts a satirical and richly humorous attitude or perspective on material that was, originally, utterly serious.

Craig Baldwin and Bruce Conner are two filmmakers famous for their collages of **found footage.** Baldwin splices together a wide array of footage to support an argument as far-fetched and wide-ranging as the footage itself: in *Tribulation 99: Alien Anomalies under America* (1992) U.S. interventions in Latin America seem to result, in some strange way, from alien invaders who inhabit former atomic bomb test sites. The loony quality of the conspiracy that the film exposes takes on the dimensions of a satire of conspiracy thinking itself. Collage proves a perfect vehicle with which to imitate the dizzy conglomeration of facts and fantasies that seem to lie at the paranoid heart of highly elaborated conspiracy theories.

Bruce Conner's earlier work is not quite so vivid a satire of conspiracy, but it, too, mixes a wide array of found footage—from softcore nudie photographs to atomic bomb explosions and cartoons—to create a compelling sense of what it feels like to be caught in the grip of a fevered imagination. In *Cosmic Ray* (1962), instead of a voice-over commentary, Conner utilizes the famous Ray Charles song "What'd I Say" to give a haunting quality to the collage of disparate images. Lyrics such as "Tell you I feel all right (make me feel all right)," when combined with nude images and atomic explosions, gain a deeply disturbing and ironic quality, in which nothing seems quite all right. The exuberance of the song is matched by the exuberance of what seems to be an end-of-the-world scenario of visual non sequiturs (cartoon characters and nuclear destruction). *The Atomic Cafe, Tribulation 99,* and *Cosmic Ray* all use a collage style to highlight what the filmmakers perceive as a disturbing tendency in American society to wish away unpleasantness. None of the films claim to represent a factually accurate portrait of society; instead, they give a striking sense of what it would feel like to inhabit a nightmare version of our everyday reality.

INTERPRETIVE GOALS

Like dreams, poetic films invite interpretation but evade understanding. They stimulate intellectual engagement. They also require empathetic understanding on their own terms and conditions. Since these films seldom make an argument, attempt to arrive at a known truth, or tell a straightforward story, their impact is more oblique than works that adhere to logical, rhetorical, or narrative form, but this impact can be quite profound or disturbing. The viewer's social assumptions and viewing expectations may be thrown into question. Poetic films are works that are meant *to be* rather than *to mean*, which is another way of saying that the experience and impact of the actual work, qualities highly dependent on form, take precedence over thematic interpretation.

Many poetic or avant-garde films invite criticism that locates them in a formal context. This formal context helps explain the conventions each film adopts, challenges, or subverts, the alternative forms of perception it invites, and the implications these choices have for the development of the art of film. Such criticism often pays close attention to the form and structure of the film, even at the level of examining individual shots and the patterns they form. The metaphorical relationship between a story world and the actual world becomes secondary to the experiential relationship between the viewer and the screen. Watching a flickering succession of black and white

images that has no external referent, no linkage to anything other than
the presence of black frames of film followed by white frames of film,
requires attention to what this specific experience feels like and what
it suggests about how we can understand the nature and process of
film projection itself.

In other cases, such as *L'age d'or*, *Pièce touchée*, *Meshes of the Afternoon*, *Tribulation 99*, *Cosmic Ray*, and *The Atomic Cafe*, the critic needs
to couple an examination of formal innovation to an understanding of
what social conventions or shared values and beliefs the film subjects
to scrutiny. Unlike a traditional documentary, an avant-garde film seldom states its case directly. It may idealize the biker world of danger,
death, and lurking sexual attractions found in *Scorpio Rising*, for example, without trying to celebrate the nature of troubled adolescence,
of the male fascination with machines and speed, or even of homoeroticism as a distinct form of desire.

The critic has to infer much of the filmmaker's attitude or point of
view. The main means of doing so is by paying close attention to the
formal organization of the work and the effect it has on the viewer.
The humor and outrageous claims that pop up throughout *Tribulation
99* make it clear, for example, that the filmmaker does not intend to
endorse the conspiracy claims he brings together through a dizzying
array of clips but to present them as if he were photographing a nightmare: what we see and hear is incredibly bizarre and fundamentally
illogical, but we see and hear with the clarity of someone who is not
caught up in the very fantasy the film describes.

When it comes to the question of how to interpret these works,
we might even speak of two avant-gardes:

1) The formal avant-garde that is primarily concerned with the
   nature of the cinematic signifier, the basic raw material of sound
   and image. Films like *Mothlight*, *Wavelength* (Michael Snow, 1967,
   Canada/U.S.), or *Serene Velocity* possess little or no referent exter-

nal to the cinema. They draw our attention to properties of cinema and the nature of perception. Their internal rhymes and tones become of primary importance.

2) The political avant-garde that concerns itself with social reality and seeks to reveal aspects of this reality in formally innovative ways. Films like *Meshes of the Afternoon*, *L'age d'or*, *Tribulation 99*, *Human Remains* (Jay Rosenblatt, 1998), and *The Maelstrom* (Péter Forgács, 1997, Hungary) possess a social or historical referent that figures significantly into their overall goal. They draw our attention to how what already seems familiar can be seen from a fresh perspective. The validity and quality of their insights becomes of considerable importance. Assessing these insights and placing them within a larger context can then serve as an important part of the critic's task.

The process of applying the dual analysis of formal-social interpretation proves extremely valuable in relation to both of these avant-gardes. Formal innovations can be situated within a larger social context involving other arts and changing social conditions, and political engagement can be understood in terms of its use of fresh, cinematic techniques. In both cases, criticism can attempt to identify the formal conventions that remain in place as well as the ones that are transformed, and also to identify the degree to which the film's political perspective sees the world in a fresh light or a customary one.

Examples

Michael Snow's *Wavelength* consists of a single, forty-five-minute take that slowly zooms in from a wide-angle shot of an empty loft space to a close-up of a calendar on the opposite wall. One could rightfully say that the film is "about" the zoom shot, the long take, duration, and the experience of time and space. Although there are a few hints of a narrative story (at one point the camera reveals a body on the floor but without granting it any special attention—the zoom continues without any hesitation or shift of focus), *Wavelength* reverses the usual balance between the forward momentum of the plot and the descriptive lingering of the camera. The camera assumes an autonomous power to gaze according to its own rhythm, no longer beholden to characters, actions, or events. The passage of the zoom shot through space takes precedence over what this movement does to advance a story. *Wavelength* is about the experience of time freed from its usual connection to storytelling.

David Rimmer's *Variations on a Cellophane Wrapper* (1970, Canada) consists of a single short loop of found footage of a woman factory worker unfurling a giant sheet of cellophane, which repeats for nine minutes. Rather than using exact repetitions, though, Rimmer introduces variations involving contrast, colorization, and music that spark numerous allusions, including reference to manual labor, the representation of women in film, and the delicate veneer of images cast on a screen that defines filmmaking itself. As the woman unfolds the sheet of cellophane like a bedsheet, it billows upward to fill the frame. This action can be seen as an analogy to the way in which individual frames of celluloid, the physical material housing movie images, fill the movie screen one after another. *Variations on a Cellophane Wrapper* most emphatically functions as a poetic form of visual experience asking viewers to reflect on what it feels like to see and hear sheets of film being unfurled and spread before them.

Su Friedrich's *The Ties That Bind* (1985), by contrast, mixes a poetic reworking of found footage of her family's home movies with more argumentative and narrative strategies. The resulting film reflects her adult understanding of her childhood experience. Sound, which in *Cellophane Wrapper* is largely in the form of music and shifts increasingly toward the electronic, here takes the form primarily of speech, mainly that of Friedrich herself commenting on aspects of the home movies and what they mean to her. The final result is a thorough mixture of the poetic, narrative, and rhetorical (with an implicit critique of the traditional, patriarchal family structure) that demonstrates how film-makers merge avant-garde, documentary, and narrative techniques in a single film.

The Ties That Bind, though, remains primarily experimental in its form. It draws considerable attention to the way in which it imagina-tively reworks home movies so that what was once personal and pri-vate, of interest to few beyond immediate family members, takes on fascination for a wider audience. Friedrich's comments about her home movie footage are analytical and questioning. They allude to the darker side of family life and the ways in which she experienced the power and control of her father as a child. Sequences often have a nar-rative ring to them as Friedrich retains a sense of the everyday events that played out in the original footage: bathing, swimming, and so on. As in *Pièce touchée*, through this complex reworking of previously shot film the viewer comes to understand what lies hidden, unseen and unspoken, beneath what at first appear to be innocuous images of daily life.

In *The Ties That Bind*, a referent remains for each image, often a his-torical referent of some importance, namely some aspect of Friedrich's own childhood. It is nonetheless reworked and modified so that new signifieds become associated with the original signifiers. Shots of Friedrich swimming as a child serve as signifiers with an original signi-fied of family fun and childhood recreation, but her comments add other, darker signifieds of her feelings of patriarchal power and expec-tations for which she had to perform to gain approval. This is an impor-tant version of the collage principle that is of considerable importance to a number of contemporary artists. Emile de Antonio's history of the Vietnam War, *In the Year of the Pig* (1968), told as the war raged and with a voice radically different from the U.S. government's, assembled a vast array of found footage to argue that the conflict in Vietnam was more a civil war than an attempt at Communist domination (by China), and that American intervention was therefore not justifiable. His thesis is clearly open to debate, but the point here is that, as with many other recent works, it was made largely with footage that had already been shot by others, often for quite different purposes from those of de Antonio.

An extremely vivid example of this tendency to recycle previous footage for a new purpose is the work of the Hungarian filmmaker Péter Forgács. Forgács has taken home movies initially shot in various parts of Europe during the 1930s, '40s, and '50s and turned them into poetic chronicles of European social history. In *The Bartos Family* (1988, Hungary), *Free Fall* (1996, Hungary), and *The Maelstrom*, three of his most outstanding films, Forgács draws on the home movies of one European Jew, using the footage of family and friends to examine the fate of European Jews in general as Hitler came to power in Germany, began World War II, and implemented the notorious "Final Solution" that had as its goal the eradication of European Jewry itself. Forgács adds minimal voice-over commentary to his re-edited version of these home movies. He does add titles, music, freeze-frames, tinting, slow motion, and, in *Free Fall*, a slow, dirge-like incantation in which various anti-Semitic laws are intoned. Meanwhile, each film follows the chronology of one family's routine activities. Gradually, however, the mounting forces of war and hate overwhelm their private worlds and personal pleasures. Family members find themselves unwittingly drawn into the horrible maelstrom of the Holocaust. Their home movies become inadvertent testimony to the fate that befell them.

The viewer is highly aware of the horrors awaiting these individuals. The films produce a profound sense of irony and suspense as we see people go about their lives unable to foretell what lies in store. We know what they do not know; we want to warn, help, or protect them—to no avail. The effect is not to offer a sweeping overview of

European history or the causes of World War II, as the much earlier *Why We Fight* series had done from various found footage sources of its own, but to create a poetic, affective impression of what it felt like to attempt to maintain a sense of integrity and normalcy in the face of the terrible onslaught of the Nazi party's genocidal policies.

Similar efforts to return to the past and to forge new responses and new meanings from found footage are also central to Jay Rosenblatt's *Human Remains*, which fabricates personal diary-like commentaries for five twentieth-century dictators; Marlon Fuentes's *Bontoc Eulogy* (1995, U.S./Philippines), which reconstructs the fate of the film-maker's grandfather, who was brought to the St. Louis World's Fair of 1904 as part of a fabricated Filipino village; Leandro Katz's *El día que me quieras* (1997, Argentina), which retraces the circumstances that led to the famous photograph of Che Guevara after he was captured and killed in Bolivia; and Michael Rappaport's *Rock Hudson's Home Movies* (1992), which recycles footage from Hudson's films to discover a consistent homosexual subtext. These films take up a wide variety of topics but share a desire to reveal hidden or suppressed meanings in preexisting images that may at first appear banal or quaint.

Human Remains portrays the private lives of Mao Zedong, Adolf Hitler, General Francisco Franco, Benito Mussolini, and Joseph Stalin. Rosenblatt chose footage that showed them dressed informally and in private, or he cropped images to eliminate governmental and military trappings from the shot. To these images he added a scripted first-person voice-over commentary, purportedly the words of the dictators, in which each revealed some of his personal ailments, food preferences, and sexual habits. The result is an unsettling personalization, in which men usually considered inhuman monsters become mere humans, with foibles like anyone else. And yet, as in the films of Péter Forgács, the viewer cannot help but bring her own knowledge and memory to bear. This creates a powerful tension between the apparently quaint idiosyncrasies of these men and the off-screen horrors and atrocities associated with them. Their monstrosity no longer belongs to a realm apart, but is resituated squarely within the morally ambiguous realm of human possibility.

In *Bontoc Eulogy* Fuentes paints a nightmarish picture of the 1904 World's Fair that is very different from the romantic view of it in the musical *Meet Me in St. Louis* (Vincente Minnelli, 1944). In this quest to understand the fate of his grandfather, who was lured from the Philippines, along with scores of other Filipino men, to serve as fair exhibits, the filmmaker recycles found footage of the fairgrounds that shows men like his grandfather performing traditional rituals and conducting the business of everyday life in a makeshift village. On display in this artificial setting, the men take the place of animals in a zoo. Fuentes is well aware that the scientific spirit of anthropological knowledge used to rationalize the Filipino exhibit belongs to an earlier historical moment, and yet its disturbing effects linger. He cannot determine with certainty what became of his grandfather, and so he resorts to fictional techniques to create an imaginative, wishful story of resistance and subversion. By seamlessly blending documentary and fictional techniques with found footage, Fuentes challenges assumptions the viewer may have about historical facts and about those people and events that fall outside the official record. The film becomes a provocative reworking of history and memory that attests to the power of the past to haunt the present.

El día que me quieras does something similar in relation to one of the most famous images of revolutionary fervor from the 1960s: the photograph of the dead Che Guevara lying on a slab in a nondescript laundry room surrounded by Bolivian military figures. Guevara, one of Fidel Castro's closest allies, left Cuba in 1965 to launch a peasant revolution in Bolivia. Two years later, a Bolivian military unit captured and killed Guevara and his band of followers, but he lives on as an icon of a romantic, revolutionary ideal, thanks in large part to the reverential photograph of his dead body.

The artist and filmmaker Leandro Katz revisits the photograph, using it and other pictures taken by the photographer Freddy Alborta to reexamine Che's death and legacy. It becomes clear that the photo was not a hastily taken shot that just happened to become an icon. Alborta himself speaks of how he quickly realized that he had entered an extraordinary historical moment and that the dead Che, with his open eyes and forceful gaze, retained the luminous power of a natural leader even in death. He captured these qualities with a photograph that paralleled the classic Lamentation, Christ removed from the cross, portrayed in many classic paintings. Katz mixes an array of found footage with imaginative, romanticized images of peasantry from the region where Che died to give a sense of what it must have felt like to experience the moment as the photographer experienced it: like the European Jews in Forgács's films, with no knowledge of the future but with an uncanny sense that something of great importance had just taken place. His fantasy images of peasants marching across grassy fields carrying red banners contrast sharply with the harsh black and white photos of the dead Che. The combination gives the film a haunting, rueful, but also strongly affirmative tone.

Finally, *Rock Hudson's Home Movies* adopts a playful but provocative tone as it reexamines Rock Hudson's numerous films to discover a subtext of homoerotic desire. Hudson was a leading man and major star during the 1950s in films such as *Magnificent Obsession* (Douglas Sirk, 1954), *All That Heaven Allows* (Douglas Sirk, 1955), *Written on the Wind* (Douglas Sirk, 1956), and *Pillow Talk* (Michael Gordon, 1959). His good looks and solid build made him a natural lady's man, although he was, in fact, gay. This was a secret in the 1950s. It only became publicly known when Hudson admitted his homosexuality in 1985, just months before dying of AIDS. Mark Rappaport culls through the found footage of Hudson's films, adding commentary and juxtaposing scenes so that a homoerotic **subtext** begins to appear. (A **subtext** is an unstated or implicit theme or message that is not readily apparent but that may nonetheless register and have an impact on a viewer.)

Rappaport finds that the physical gestures of the male characters in Hudson's films and the dialogue, glances, and gazes between them are not the neutral or simply plot-driven devices they appear to be, but carry a sexual charge his reediting and commentary bring to the surface. A playful element enters into the film in Rappaport's almost wishful effort to find a sexual subtext in almost every gesture and a double entendre in almost every line of dialogue. For example, when Doris Day innocently asks Hudson, "Why can't you get married?" the question takes on a much loaded significance as a result of the new context in which Rappaport places such remarks.

Beneath the humor, *Rock Hudson's Home Movies* also raises an important question about how repressive social codes force certain forms of human behavior into disguised forms that only careful, purposeful analysis can retroactively make visible. Like the other filmmakers, Rappaport is keenly interested in using avant-garde techniques that dwell on the found fragment and its aesthetic manipulation, the recycling of images, and unexpected juxtapositions to pose questions about how we can represent and understand the past.

These works from the political avant-garde enter into the social arena of historical interpretation in a more direct way than the more strictly formal works of the avant-garde. With their reference to actual events and people, political avant-garde films provide a useful transition to the documentary tradition within which some of these same films are often included.

3

DOCUMENTARY FILM

Purpose

PERSUASIVENESS AS A GOAL OF DOCUMENTARY

Documentary films address the historical world itself rather than construct an imaginary or fictional world. They typically seek to engage the viewer in relation to some aspect of the world in which we live. Rather than inviting engagement with the poetic form of the work itself, as most avant-garde films do, documentaries invite engagement with their respresentation of the historical world. This is a matter of emphasis rather than either/or alternatives, and many documentaries make frequent use of poetic and narrative storytelling techniques as well as rhetorical ones.

A reliance on rhetorical principles, though, characterizes most documentaries. Even when a documentary is distinctly poetic in form, a rhetorical emphasis turns attention toward the viewer and her view of the world. The form of the work draws less attention than its perspective on the world. Documentaries seek to engage the viewer persuasively by emotional or persuasive means. Like the classic art of oratory, rhetorical film discourse serves to move or affect, persuade or convince the audience. Persuasiveness is not necessarily identical to persuasion: a documentary may move viewers or arouse feelings more than persuade them of the soundness of a specific argument. Documentaries are therefore not necessarily argumentative, didactic, or propagandistic. These forms exists but are only a small fraction of contemporary documentaries. Films such as *Sherman's March* (Ross McElwee, 1986), about the filmmaker's quest for a romantic partner as he journeys through the American South, *Wild Parrots of Telegraph Hill* (Judy Irving, 2003), about an eccentric and endearing man who befriends a unique flock of wild parrots in San Francisco, and even *Waltz with Bashir* (Ari Folman, 2008), about what it was like to be an Israeli soldier during the 1982 invasion of Lebanon, an experience conveyed almost entirely by animation, do not make literal arguments. They draw us into a particular perspective on the world and invite us to experience the world in a distinct way. Engaging the viewer in a distinct perspective emotionally or persuading the viewer of a particular perspective intellectually go hand in hand in documentary, even though different films vary the balance between these two goals. Both goals take precedence over the narrative emphasis on telling an engaging story or the avant-garde stress on the form of the work itself.

When persuasion regarding a particular issue is the goal, reason is a very valuable tool. Reason or logic carries a discussion from premises through well-reasoned arguments to a conclusion. However, often there is no clear-cut solution to a real-life problem, and logic alone cannot persuade. In this case, the premises or assumptions that lead individuals to take up different positions may derive from values and beliefs. Here, rhetoric takes priority over pure logic. This is the case for most forms of social conflict: different individuals and groups uphold different values and beliefs, have different perspectives on issues, and adopt different views on how to deal with them. Rhetoric provides the means for presenting a particular point of view persuasively.

For rhetorical purposes the appearance of logic may do the job as well as actual logic. This is not a defect, since strict logic is not entirely persuasive. It is important, however, to recognize its use. In *Sicko* (2007), for example, Michael Moore brings a group of 9/11 responders with medical problems stemming from their efforts to rescue others to Cuba. He finds a clinic where they receive extraordinary, free medical care. This visit serves to prove that Cuba has a splendid health care system, and further, that if a poor underdeveloped country can have such a system, so can the United States. A viewer may be moved to believe what Moore implies through this segment of the film (it has the potential to be, in fact, correct), but it has the form of a faulty **syllogism**. (**Syllogisms** are ways to state premises and draw a conclusion; some are valid but some only appear valid. "Dogs have four legs; Fido is a dog; therefore he has four legs" is valid, but "Fido is a dog; Fido has spots on his legs; therefore all dogs have spots on their legs" is faulty. A characteristic of one dog may not be true of all dogs.) In *Sicko*, Moore argues in effect that a given Cuban clinic is wonderful, and therefore all Cuban clinics are wonderful, and if all Cuban clinics are wonderful, then they are a great model for American health clinics. If he stated this in a sentence, the flaws would be more apparent: are all Cuban clinics as good as this one? Can the system be readily transferred to another country? Are there deficiencies that the treatment of this one group of patients fails to expose?

The visit to Cuba has considerable rhetorical power. It is, in fact, a classic use of rhetoric and is perfectly acceptable as rhetoric. Understanding how it functions in these terms will help the viewer come to her own conclusion about its ultimate effectiveness. It will convince some viewers, and if it does not convince everyone, it may still succeed in making a compelling case that opponents of Moore must now rebut. He has put his opponents on the defensive, and all through a faulty syllogism. This is a common effect of rhetoric. It is used across the political spectrum.

In rhetoric, anecdotal, impressionistic, and selective "proofs" are relied upon instead of strictly logical reasoning or purely narrative storytelling. The anecdotes, impressions, or proofs may, in fact, be true, but most important for rhetorical discourse is that they convey the impression of truthfulness. Numerous television advertisements use terms like "greater sheen" and "radiant complexion," "powerful engine" and "outperforms other cars." The actual measurement of such qualities is left vague, but they are usually coupled to images that suggest something an audience will find desirable, such as a model with beautiful hair, or an automobile blazing across empty roads in a bucolic setting. It remains open to question whether the model's appearance is a direct result of the use of the product advertised, or the car's performance is an honest measure of its capability relative to similar cars, but a powerful impression has been created all the same. Similar, and not necessarily dishonest, strategies are at work in documentary. The seemingly neutral, non-polemical *Monterey Pop* (D. A. Pennebaker, 1968), a great observational documentary, portrays Janis Joplin, Grace Slick, Jimi Hendrix, Otis Redding, and the other musical stars of this stunning concert in situations that foreground their exceptional talents, not their complex and sometimes dysfunctional personal lives. This is fundamentally a rhetorical decision that leads to building respectful, appreciative portraits of individuals that someone else might wish to portray far less sympathetically.

Historically, documentaries have been associated with social issues. The 1930s saw numerous documentaries emerge that tackled pressing issues, usually to promote policies and perspectives favored by the governments. *The Plow That Broke the Plains* (Pare Lorentz, 1936), for example, shows how the American dust bowl, which covered a huge swath of the Midwest and West, was restored to fertile productivity through government-sponsored acts of conservation in the 1930s. First the film shows scenes of drought, dust, and erosion, land gone fallow, and farms abandoned. Then it shows the results of new techniques of water conservation, crop rotation, and animal husbandry. The result: productive land, once again fertile and bountiful. But are the images of desolation truly from the American Midwest in the early 1930s? Are they typical of what this area looked like on the whole or are they worst-case examples?

The images present evidence of what was there before the camera, but whether the camera took the images in the Midwest or in the Gobi Desert, whether they were shots of hard-to-find areas, completely uncharacteristic of the plains as a whole, or glaring examples of a massive problem, cannot be determined from the images or film alone. The images have a powerful impact, but their ultimate validity must be determined by other forms of investigation. This is not to argue against the need for conservation in the 1930s as promoted by *The Plow That Broke the Plains*, since there is abundant confirming evidence from others sources that the film's argument is, in fact, correct, and the images truly representative, but only to point out that the argument is not the airtight piece of reasoning it purports to be. That the film's factual claims can be amply authenticated by cross-checking with external sources only adds to its rhetorical persuasiveness.

More than a written policy paper or even a descriptive piece of journalism, *The Plow That Broke the Plains* also gives a vivid sense of what it might feel like to encounter a devastated swath of land that once served as a prodigious breadbasket. It embodies and exemplifies what drought looks like—what the land that suffers it and the faces who must endure it look like. It fulfills its persuasive purpose by mobilizing the resources of film to provide a unique sense of what something physically remote from most urban audiences was like and what might be done to alter it. It is in this sense affective and argumentative, emotional and logical. Like most documentaries, the purpose of the film is not to provide documents and evidence as such but to shape a documentary experience that uses such material to make a moving, affective case from a particular perspective.

PERSUASION AND GOVERNMENT POLICY

The Plow That Broke the Plains embodies a clearly liberal political perspective in which the film presents the federal government as the proper agent to address a natural disaster. A similarly liberal but hard-hitting indictment of the federal government for failing to honor the call to address a natural disaster and help individuals, communities, and even an entire region regain solid footing runs through Spike Lee's *When the Levees Broke* (2006), a four-hour study of the Hurricane Katrina disaster of 2005 in New Orleans and the surrounding region. While *The Plow That Broke the Plains* relies entirely on a voice-over commentary, Lee utilizes interviews. He finds individuals who make vividly clear that the failure of government agencies at every level was as profoundly traumatic as the original hurricane. What the Roosevelt administration wanted to do on a massive scale in the 1930s, the Bush administration was unable to do on almost any scale at all in the 2000s, according to the film.

The Plow That Broke the Plains excludes the voices of victims of drought and poor soil conservation from the soundtrack and from most of the image track as well. This was not unusual for the 1930s, when capturing **sync sound** on location was extremely difficult and very costly. (**Sync** or **synchronous sound** is produced by recording the sound and image simultaneously. Before 1960 or so, documentaries relied heavily on voice-over commentary, music, and sound effects that could be added after the silent images had been edited together.) Reliance on a voice-over commentary also fits with an ideology that grants the filmmaker the authority to speak for others, make their case for them, and mobilize an audience to action. By the 1960s this approach had become less popular as changes in technology made it possible to record the words of people in their own environments. Filmmakers soon discovered that many people could speak with passion and eloquence in front of a camera and that they brought their own distinct sensibilities to bear in a way that a voice-over narrator could not duplicate.

Spike Lee stresses the heroic nature of the people he interviewed. Instead of seeking out striking images that speak for themselves as evidence of disaster, Lee sought out citizens who speak in their own voices about what they experienced firsthand. Shot in carefully lit situations, against neutral but flattering backgrounds, his subjects look as if they are posing for portraits. Lee clearly evokes the aura of the portrait painting tradition, which began as a way to immortalize the lives of saints, religious leaders, royalty, and wealthy patrons, in order to lend comparable nobility to these victims of a hurricane.

In contrast to the closed-frame portraits of his interviewees, an open-frame aesthetic prevails in the footage Lee includes of President Bush and Vice President Cheney visiting the region. They are caught on the spur of the moment, as ordinary figures in a far from ordinary landscape. The shots are found footage, obtained from television coverage of the event (such footage has become a crucial ingredient in many documentaries on topical events). They do not flatter their subjects but instead convey a sense of what spontaneously happened in front of the camera, even if what happened may have actually been staged by White House operatives for filming. The contrast between the two types of shots functions as a clear signifier of where Lee's own sympathies lie. When his interview subjects say the government did nothing, there is no corresponding response from the highest figures in the government. They appear to go about their photo opportunities and press conferences oblivious to the criticism of the people Lee assembles. This contrast in shooting style functions as an example of how a documentary filmmaker can convey an attitude or political perspective without recourse to spoken commentary or to the rigors of logical analysis: the framing of individuals does not necessarily correspond to the validity of what they say or do. It does, however, color their appearance in a subtly persuasive way.

In both *The Plow That Broke the Plains* and *When the Levees Broke*, the absence of a collective voice speaking for the dispossessed is striking. Both films make clear how deeply individuals can suffer from natural disasters, but neither film finds a community-based or indigenous organization to channel this suffering into collective action. In this sense, neither film can be said to exhibit a radical political perspective that demands a major change in the existing social order. As victims, individuals await the aid they need. In *Plow* the government provides it. In Spike Lee's film, the government largely abandons them to fend as best they can.

Key Elements

THE INDEXICAL QUALITY OF THE FILM IMAGE

THE INDEXICAL IMAGE AS AN APPARENT COPY OF REALITY The photographic image commonly bears a strict correspondence to what it represents. It is said to have an **indexical relationship** to its referent. That is to say, normal photographic lenses and film or digital storage devices preserve the appearance and proportions of what they photograph in extremely precise ways. Medical imaging depends on this indexical quality to obtain X-rays, MRIs, and CAT scans that provide an accurate picture of the body's interior. Unlike a painting or drawing, which may bear only a loose resemblance to its referent, if any, a film image, like medical images, bears a very precise one. This quality is true of fiction films as well as nonfiction. In fiction, the indexical relationship allows the image to faithfully replicate what the director has chosen and often expressly designed to film. In documentary the indexical relationship allows the image to represent a specific aspect of the historical world with great accuracy.

The cinematic image makes what once appeared elsewhere reappear before the viewer as if the original referent were once again present. To see Johnny Depp in *Pirates of the Caribbean: Dead Man's Chest* (Gore Verbinski, 2006) or Clark Gable in *Gone with the Wind* (Victor Fleming, 1939) is not only to recognize a particular actor at a particular point in his career but to behold an image that matches his appearance at the time of filming to an extraordinary degree. The appearance of Depp or Gable may be altered by makeup and costume, but both the altered and the unaltered physical features of their face and body are represented with a faithfulness that exceeds the grasp of all but the most exacting of drawings or paintings.

Indexicality gives the cinema a distinct sense of magic and wonder. This is the quality behind accounts of audiences who fled from their seats when a train rushed toward them in the Lumière brothers' film, *Arrival of a Train at La Ciotat* (Auguste and Louis Lumière, France), shown in 1895. The train moved diagonally across the screen and into the foreground of the shot, growing in size, as if the actual train were about to hurtle off the screen and plunge into the theater. The shot's vivid impact on early audiences suggests the enormous power of such lifelike representations. Things come back to life and once again move. This remarkable quality contributes to film's ability to generate evidence of what the world beyond is really like and what happens in it. Indexicality contributes strongly to the aesthetics of realism, which is discussed further in Chapter 5.

THE INDEXICAL IMAGE AND THE QUESTION OF EVIDENCE The indexical quality of the image has additional significance in the documentary film. When images from the historical world are assembled into a film, they often serve an evidentiary function. War photographs, surveillance footage, and medical images commonly possess a high degree of evidentiary value. They are understood to represent what occurred or what was the case (an explosion, crime, or wound, for example).

A vivid example is the videotape shot by George Holliday, an individual who happened to have a video camera and to see the beating of a Los Angeles motorist, Rodney King, by the police in 1991. His footage turned up on numerous news shows across the country and beyond as evidence of police brutality toward African American men. Because it possessed an indexical relationship to what took place, it seemed to offer conclusive proof that the police beat and kicked Mr. King repeatedly while he lay on the ground struggling to escape their blows.

The meaning of evidence, however, remains a matter of interpretation, of what signifieds get attached, even to indexical signifiers. The prosecution at the trial of the police officers interpreted Mr. King's physical movements as self-defense; the defense lawyers called it a potential attack. Similarly, the prosecution interpreted the indexical images of the officers' blows as excessive, unprofessional violence but the defense lawyers described them as self-defense. In some cases, discrepant interpretations can be resolved by further investigation and evidence, as they were here when a second trial found the officers guilty of civil rights violations and sentenced them to jail, but in other cases no such clear-cut resolution proves possible. Evidentiary images do not offer proof of their own meaning. Meaning depends on interpretation. These interpretations will almost certainly vary, depending on the skills, background, and motives of the interpreter.

THE THREE C'S OF PERSUASIVE DISCOURSE

A documentary often begins with a problem, explores its complexity and implications, and arrives at a solution. These solutions are a function of specific values and beliefs, which the film sets out to support. Values and beliefs, in turn, function within an ideological context. They are the principles that guide conduct in accord with a certain way of viewing the world. In this sense, ideology is not the pejorative thing it is sometimes made out to be but a necessary quality that gives a political, social, or spiritual perspective its purchase in the hearts and minds of people. Documentaries can contribute to efforts to uphold the dominant ideology of any given moment or they can work to contest, alter, or subvert it. To do either, they must be persuasive—capable of garnering belief for the solution or perspective they propose. To be persuasive, they typically have recourse to the three basic principles of rhetorical proof that were first described by rhetorical authorities of antiquity such as Quintillian, Horace, and Aristotle.

The three principles used by rhetorical discourse focus on each of the three key elements to any communication: author, text, audience, *or* speaker, message, recipient. To be effective a documentary sets out to do three things: (1) establish the credibility of the filmmaker, (2) provide a convincing set of arguments, and (3) achieve a compelling form of presentation.

The "Three C's" of rhetoric—credible, convincing, compelling—were first discussed by Aristotle in his writings on rhetoric, but they remain as crucial today as they were then. The media and techniques may change but the strategies remain the same. It is important to note that the "Three C's" aim for an emotional, affective result: a credible, convincing, and compelling case may or may not be scientifically true, socially beneficial, or politically wise, but it can be successful if it is believed. The ultimate wisdom or value of a given position is of no concern rhetorically. Questions of value and use are decided elsewhere in realms such as ethics, religion, politics, social policy, and public debate. Rhetoric serves to make a case persuasively, not to decide its ultimate merit.

In the Year of the Pig (Emile de Antonio, 1968) provides a vivid example of the use of classic rhetorical principles in cinematic form. This film presents a counter-history to the Vietnam War that is seriously at odds with the official story of the war advanced by the Johnson administration in the mid-1960s. Filmmaker Emile de Antonio tries to establish his credibility by avoiding a polemical, one-sided argument that would make the film seem a simple case of advocacy for a specific point of view. De Antonio, in fact, minimizes interviews with antiwar activists. He does so not because he disagrees with them—he seems to agree to a very high degree—but because he also recognizes that the credibility of the film's claims will increase if its analysis comes from individuals not already identified as partisans. Such individuals can dispute the government's argument that the war is a war against Communist aggression that threatens to engulf all of Southeast Asia without making the viewer feel that she is only hearing the prepackaged views of the radical left. Hence he relies on scholars of Vietnamese history, respected journalists, foreign observers who are not caught up in domestic American politics, and U.S. senators such as Senator Thurston Morton (R-Kentucky) to provide factual information more than to present predetermined positions and judgments. In other words, de Antonio not only avoids becoming a mirror for views already widely articulated on the American left, he withholds the moral judgments and political denunciations that often accompany those views. Although the film has a clear point of view, de Antonio leaves the final judgment up to the viewer as much as possible. The film's credibility rises as it strikes this more detached tone, as if it were perhaps even more objective than it actually is.

De Antonio not only tries to establish his own credibility, he also sets out to build a convincing case. He does so by developing an historical argument that puts events within the context of a struggle for national liberation in which Ho Chi Minh, the leader of the North Vietnamese, is widely regarded as the country's foremost patriot. He turns to archival footage of Ho Chi Minh meeting with French officials during the days of French colonialism, footage that clearly shows Ho as the national leader de Antonio claims him to be. He uses interviews with journalists and scholars to support the claim verbally. By using multiple sources he gives the impression that the view he wants to present is a widely held if not unanimous one. It runs contrary to the U.S. government's portrayal of Ho Chi Minh as a puppet or stooge of the Chinese Communists who are more interested in global domination than the independence of Vietnam. But de Antonio again lets the viewer assess the information he provides. Part of what makes the film convincing is that it avoids a polemical attack on U.S. government assertions and simply presents an alternative interpretation of Ho's background, motives, and goals that the viewer, once again, must assess on her own.

Finally, de Antonio sets out to make his argument compelling. Here is where he needs to appeal to the emotional responsiveness of his audience. He includes footage of a Vietnamese Buddhist monk burning himself to death in a Saigon street as a protest against American involvement. He has footage of the destruction of villages and the terrified looks of Vietnamese peasants rousted from their homes by American soldiers. Such images evoke alarm and sympathy by their very nature. They do not readily fit into the official version of a war against an external Communist threat but stress the bloody cost of a war that seems directed at the Vietnamese civilian population far more than at any opposing army.

Similarly, found footage of a U.S. GI who has written "Make War Not Love" on his helmet, an interview with an officer who praises his men as "a bloody good bunch of killers," and a portion of a television interview with General Curtis LeMay in which he speaks of bombing all of Vietnam until it is turned into a giant parking lot, undercut the high moral tone used to justify the war officially. The war effort is made to appear to bring out the worst in the American character rather than the best. Such footage does not prove that the war was or was not justified, but it does generate a level of emotional investment to accompany the intellectual engagement and ideological involvement that de Antonio desires. It may provoke outrage among some viewers that a few bad apples are used to place the entire war effort in a negative light—such footage is analogous to Michael Moore's visit

to Cuba in *Sicko*: it may be an accurate representation of a specific situation or what a given individual says, but, as a false syllogism, it is not
necessarily proof of any larger claims. For others these comments
offer proof that the high-minded rhetoric of official press conferences
does not tell the whole story.

De Antonio proves a cunning orator. He does not try to bludgeon
his audience into accepting a fully formed argument or siding with him
in a quixotic battle against the power of the U.S. government. Instead
he tries to (1) establish a credible presence through his choice of
sources, (2) build a convincing case by giving ample evidence for an
alternative interpretation of the war, and (3) have a compelling effect
by showing both the suffering inflicted on those the U.S. wants to help
and the callousness of some of those responsible for doing the helping.
De Antonio does not seek to produce converts to an alternative position directly so much as to stimulate thought and provoke debate.

In the Year of the Pig nonetheless has weaknesses as well. The lack of
any acknowledgment that Communism played a formative role in the
tactics and policies of the North Vietnamese is such a weakness. The
stress on the civil war aspect of the film can be justified from many perspectives, but it does not necessarily mean that the North Vietnamese
did not draw support from outside the country, just as the South Vietnamese drew considerable support from the United States. Ho Chi
Minh and his opponents may have taken support from where they
could get it and still valued independence more than foreign allegiance.
The emphasis on the war as a civil war at the expense of acknowledging external sources of support makes it seem as if de Antonio has sim-
plified his argument at the expense of historical complexity. The formal
eloquence and argumentative sophistication of his case presents a fresh
view of the war, while the sleights of hand that eliminate some of the
complexity prove a limitation.

This issue of sleight-of-hand simplification comes to a head in
the films of Michael Moore. The scientific truth, social benefit, and

political wisdom of *Roger and Me* (1989), *Bowling for Columbine* (2002, Canada/U.S./Germany), *Fahrenheit 9/11* (2004), and *Sicko* are clearly open to debate. This, however, is part of their appeal. Moore is a filmmaker whose credibility hinges on being not so much an authority who knows what's best for his audience or what's true, as an average Joe who happens to be very, very persistent, and more than a bit irreverent, and humorous. He pokes fun at those who claim to know what's best or right, and he creates credibility as "one of us": someone who lacks officially certified legitimacy but wants to get to the bottom of things all the same.

This ploy does not work for all viewers. Some see him as a troublemaker who will use specious arguing and manipulated evidence to make his case. The fact that Moore is able to make this type of controversy part and parcel of his public persona has clearly contributed to his success as a filmmaker: his disarming simplemindedness can be highly appealing to some—a sign of his credibility as an average Joe, and offensive to others—a sign of his willingness to oversimplify or distort complex issues. This disparity, which usually hinges on the viewer's preexisting values and beliefs or ideologies, becomes an important point of debate and a great marketing tool for Michael Moore himself.

Of course, not all documentaries engage major political issues. Some, as noted in the discussion of the avant-garde, are more poetic than polemical. Some describe processes, profile individuals, or adopt a comic tone. Some, such as Errol Morris's *The Thin Blue Line* (1988), investigate questions of guilt or innocence in a particular case, leaving broader questions of social justice to the side. The film takes the form of an investigation of the murder of a Texas policeman. One man, Randall Adams, sits in jail, condemned to death for the crime. Another man, David Harris, who was with Adams at the time of the murder, remains free. Through a series of interviews with the two men and others involved in the case, Morris gradually leads the viewer to realize that the wrong man is in jail.

Morris builds credibility by adopting a low-key, nonconfrontational style in his interviews. He makes his case convincing by including, near the conclusion, a close-up shot of a tape recorder playing as we hear David Harris make a striking confession that the wrong man was convicted of the crime. And he makes his overall case compelling by adopting a film noir style of low key lighting, ominous landscapes, and eccentric, perhaps duplicitous characters that engages the viewer emotionally as well as cognitively in a tale of an innocent man trapped in a web of deadly machinations.

THE SIX MODES OF DOCUMENTARY FILM

The majority of documentary films adopt one of the following modes of organization. Each mode involves a set of conventions for representing reality. The fact that there is more than one mode strongly suggests that the representation of reality is not an objective, cut-and-dried affair. Although there may be only one historical world, and even if certain facts about it can be agreed upon as objectively true, the ways of seeing and representing that world, like the ways of interpreting it, vary considerably. These modes can be mixed and matched in any film, even if one mode tends to dominate. The choice of mode helps locate a given documentary within a larger formal context.

EXPOSITORY The expository mode has served as the most common way of representing reality since the beginnings of the documentary film in the 1930s. It also prevails in television news and journalism, political campaign messages, and most audiovisual advertising. The expository mode of direct address involves the use of a voice that speaks to the viewer directly. This voice may be an unseen **voice of God**, who delivers commentary on behalf of the film and is external to the events depicted, or a visible **voice of authority**, someone who is both seen and heard, such as a television reporter, anchorperson, or the filmmaker. (Michael Moore is the best-known example.) Unlike an interview subject who represents her own point of view, such an expository voice, whether the voice of God or the voice of authority, represents the viewpoint of the filmmaker. It is not one voice among many but a guiding voice. It takes the viewer through the material covered.

Expository documentaries receive much of their organizing structure from what the guiding voice says. This means that the images often serve to illustrate what is said and can be quite eclectic, coming from different times and places but always serving to advance the overall argument. Continuity editing gives way to evidentiary editing, which presents the best possible visible evidence rather than giving the appearance of a smooth continuum of time and space between shots.

The *Why We Fight* (Frank Capra and Anatole Litvak, 1943-1945) series, for example, recruits the actor Walter Huston as the voice of God to speak for the film's perspective. At the time, the narrator, Walter Huston, was most familiar for his role as the main character in *Dodsworth* (William Wyler, 1936), a down-to-earth businessman who must come to terms with the sophistication of the Europeans he encounters on a holiday trip with his wife. Huston was the perfect choice for the unassuming, straight-talking narrator who strove to tell draftees why the United States had to go to war against the Axis powers. The images that help demonstrate his argument that World War II is a battle between a free world and a slave world come from a rich amalgam of Hollywood fiction films, captured enemy newsreels, enemy propaganda films, and battlefront footage shot by Allied forces. This hodgepodge of material would appear quite incoherent if it were not for Huston's commentary, which ties the images together in the service of an argument to support American participation in the war.

POETIC The poetic mode is a major link between the documentary and the avant-garde film. It stresses form or pattern over an explicit argument, even though it may well have an implicit perspective on some aspect of the historical world. Rhetoric as a spoken, oratorical activity, carried forward into documentary by voice of God and voice of authority commentary, cedes pride of place to a poetic rendering of the world, even though poetic documentary may still address real social issues. Werner Herzog's film *Wodaabe: Herdsmen of the Sun* (1989, France/West Germany) is a highly poetic, mesmerizing portrait of this African tribe. Herzog gives particular attention to the courtship rituals that feature the male members of the tribe donning elaborate and stunning costumes, applying considerable makeup to create striking facial designs, and dancing to impress, and woo, the female onlookers. Its coherence and compelling quality derive largely from the rituals of dance and music, which replace speech as a kind of organizational glue. The selection and arrangement of the images gradually build a vivid sense of what it feels like to enter a world in which gender roles reverse but courtship and romance retain their vital importance.

In another film, *Lessons of Darkness* (1992, France/Germany), Herzog presents the spectacle of hundreds of oil wells fiercely burning in Kuwait after Iraqi troops set them ablaze before their retreat back toward Baghdad in the first Gulf War. There is no commentary, no interviews, and no clear-cut view on the war or these images of destruction. Seen from a detached, poetic perspective, the images take on a strange, haunting beauty. Herzog's poeticism, though, reminds us that war and carnage often have an aesthetic allure, especially when seen from a distance, like the aerial footage of these oil fields, and, similarly, telephoto images of nuclear test blasts. Allied with the political avant-garde, Herzog's film couples formal beauty with a real-world referent.

The poetic mode, like the expository mode, breaks with continuity editing to build patterns that simulate the look and feel of real-world activities and processes. Bert Haanstra's classic film *Glass* (1958, Netherlands) celebrates the extraordinary work of artisanal glass-blowers in his native Holland, and contrasts their work with the industrial production of glass items, by stressing the complex dexterity and sensitivity of the blowers as they shape blobs of molten glass into striking forms. The film celebrates the visual beauty of the objects the artisans produce. The film lacks any verbal commentary: the skill and craft of the artisans speaks for itself. An expository film on the same subject might include a voice-over commentary describing the glass-blowing process and asserting what *Glass* attempts to demonstrate: that the result of this process is work of extraordinary beauty.

OBSERVATIONAL Whereas the first two modes sacrifice the principles of continuity editing to create alternative patterns and forms, the observational mode, sometimes referred to as direct cinema, returns to a fiction-like stress on the continuity of time and space. Utilizing new lightweight equipment that allowed filmmakers to record **synchronous sound** on location readily for the first time, the pioneers of this mode in the late 1950s and early 1960s sought to capture the unfolding duration of what took place in front of the camera. Expository and poetic films, by contrast, often build up their impact by assembling fragments rather than simply observing an action or event unfold.

Observational filmmakers like Frederick Wiseman, Richard Leacock, D. A. Pennebaker, and Albert and David Maysles have chosen to exert minimal influence over what takes place in front of the camera. They avoid interviews, voice-over, even, in many cases, extra-diegetic music or montage-style editing. They seek out events likely to occur in the form they do whether a camera is present or not, such as the campaigning of senators John F. Kennedy and Hubert Humphrey for the Democratic presidential nomination of 1960 in Drew Associates' *Primary* (Robert Drew, 1960), or the routine activities of students and teachers in Frederick Wiseman's *High School*

(1968). These films give a vivid sense of what it feels like to share the specific world of particular individuals at a given moment in time. The sense of immediacy and access to specific, telling moments in the lives of individuals has proven a great strength of the observational mode just as its inability to convey a broader, historical picture is something of a liability.

In fact, the emergence of carefully delineated portraits of individuals is one of the strengths of this method. The viewer gains a clear sense of the different styles of Humphrey and Kennedy in *Primary* and discovers a complex if still enigmatic Bob Dylan in the behind-the-scenes portrait of him that emerges from D. A. Pennebaker's *Dont Look Back* (1967). Pennebaker accompanied Dylan on his tour of England in 1965 but never interviewed him. He unobtrusively follows Dylan as he relaxes between concerts, performs, and gives interviews. Observing rather than participating in the interview process, Pennebaker lets us see how Dylan prods many of his interviewers, testing whether they have done any homework at all before asking him probing and sometimes personal questions. Like Pennebaker, Dylan refuses to play the usual interview game. The film allows us to see how this fits within a larger picture of Dylan that emerges strictly from observing him.

PARTICIPATORY This mode—sometimes referred to as interactive documentary or *cinema verité*, a term coined by Jean Rouch and Edgar Morin during the making of *Chronicle of a Summer* (France) in 1961—arose at the same time as the observational mode. It, too, relies on recording synchronous sound and building scenes that have a strong sense of internal continuity. While in the observational mode events unfold as if the filmmaker were not there, the participatory filmmaker becomes an openly integral part of what happens in front of the camera. Interviews, which only occur because a camera is present, are a staple of participatory films. The filmmaker interacts with subjects—

probing, questioning, challenging, perhaps even provoking. He may actively participate not only in eliciting comments but also in affecting or even provoking what social actors—documentary subjects—do. The film becomes a record of the interactions of subjects and filmmaker. This is why Jean Rouch, who had a strong anthropological background, called this approach *cinema verité*: in French the term means film truth, and for Rouch, it meant the truth that arises specifically from the interaction of filmmaker and subject. Such a truth could only exist on film or, now, on video or digital recording media.

Rouch's own pioneering film, made with the sociologist Edgar Morin, *Chronicle of a Summer*, involved interacting with six different individuals in Paris over the summer of 1960. In one memorable scene, Rouch asks an African student in Paris if he knows what the numbers tattooed on a French woman's wrist mean. "No," he says, and the camera continues to roll as the woman, Marceline Loridan, explains that this was the number assigned to her in a Nazi concentration camp. This extraordinary exchange only occurs because Rouch instigates it. It is a form of film truth that vividly reveals the potency of this mode.

Similar moments occur in Claude Lanzmann's extremely powerful account of the Holocaust, *Shoah* (1985, France). Lanzmann overturned the traditional form of historical documentaries that coupled archival footage to present-day interviews when he made *Shoah*. He refused to include any archival footage, claiming that it only perpetuated the atrocity it represented. Instead he engaged in intense, sometimes provocative interviews with survivors, bystanders, and perpetrators. His interview style is, at times, aggressive. Unlike observational filmmakers, Lanzmann is a felt presence in the interviews, pushing subjects to speak.

In an interview with a barber, Abraham Bomba, Lanzmann urges Bomba to describe what it was like to cut the hair of prisoners before they were sent to the gas chamber. Bomba is very reluctant to relive

a traumatic past, but Lanzmann sets him in a barbershop that Lanzmann rented for the occasion and prods Bomba until he reveals this
traumatic memory of his Holocaust experience. As Lanzmann prods,
their exchange goes like this:

> BOMBA: I can't. It's too horrible. Please.
> LANZMANN: We have to do it. You know it.
> BOMBA: I won't be able to do it.
> LANZMANN: You have to do it. I know it's very hard. I know
>   and I apologize.
> BOMBA: Don't make me go on, please.
> LANZMANN: Please. We must go on.

Lanzmann interviews a wide variety of people. He can be cajoling,
hostile, empathetic or judgmental, depending on the situation, but
seems consistently driven by a desire to obtain each person's fullest,
most revealing comments about her experience.

Unlike the Democratic primary race that forms the backdrop for
the observational *Primary*, nothing in *Shoah* would have occurred had
the film not been made. (It consists entirely of interviews.) The interviews bring into being a rich, emotionally involving, intellectually
engaging, and politically charged understanding of what happened in
the past. The viewer can see in the gestures and expressions, the hes-
itations, equivocations, and outbursts of emotion among interviewees
that the Holocaust is not a thing consigned to the past. It persists,
both mentally in memory and physically in its ability to produce bodily effects such as tears, shudders, stammering, and an averted gaze.
These effects—be they of equivocation and denial or remembrance
and sorrow—are strikingly visible. They are etched into the faces and
voices of all those Lanzmann interviews.

In other participatory films, filmmakers opt to combine interviews
with footage that illustrates what the speaker refers to. This is one

version of the compilation film where found footage is compiled and used to tell a story or make an argument from the filmmaker's point of view. The interviews, rather than an off-screen commentator, provide, thanks to skillful editing, the overall line of thought or argument. The archival or found footage provides the substantiation, or at least rhetorically appears to do so. The assembled footage isn't chosen so much to produce an aesthetic effect, though, as was common in modernist avant-garde work, as to support a specific historical interpretation or account. It documents how things were; but it is also, importantly, a moving image of how things were, in two senses: as a literal moving image, restoring animation and, hence, life to the past, and as an image that moves, chosen for its emotional impact, its ability to move us affectively.

Films built from a string of interviews coupled to archival footage from the past have become the dominant mode for recounting historical events. When a voice-over commentary dominates over the interviews, the film falls into the expository mode, but ever since de Antonio's *In the Year of the Pig*, one of the first films to make full use of this version of the participatory mode, filmmakers have painted compelling historical portraits without recourse to a guiding commentary. The participatory documentary relies on the information that follows from the filmmaker's interaction with people; the argumentative thread stems from a wide range of interviews edited together without any voice-over commentary at all.

Connie Field's *The Life and Times of Rosie the Riveter* (1980), for example, tells the story of how women were urged to take up the jobs left behind by men who joined the military during World War II and then asked to give them up again when the men returned. It couples interviews with a rich array of archival footage. There is no voice-over narration. The film is discussed further in Chapter 11. Stephanie Black's *Life and Debt* (2001) explores the impact of the global economic policies of the IMF (International Monetary Fund) and World

Bank on Jamaica through a string of interviews with local farmers, political leaders, and bank officials. They describe the results from different vantage points, but all of them, thanks to the editing, support Black's perspective that the policies proved disastrous. The local economy collapsed in the face of foreign competition. This film also has no voice-over narration.

REFLEXIVE The concept of the **reflexive** mode is somewhat more abstract than the other modes. Like meta-communicative statements, it draws attention to the type of film a documentary is. It makes the viewer aware of the conventions, the expectations and assumptions that usually go unspoken. It stimulates reflection on the viewing process and how it differs from viewing a fiction film. The filmmaker may interact with her subjects, and may include interviews, but even these may be done reflexively, that is, with an eye to prompting the viewer to think about the normal conventions that govern interviews.

Trinh Minh Ha's *Surname Viet Given Name Nam* (1989) begins with a series of interviews with women in postwar Vietnam who talk about their experiences after the end of the war. The great promise of a revolutionary transformation in Vietnamese culture to accompany the unification of North and South Vietnam was not fulfilled. Patriarchal assumptions went unchallenged. (**Patriarchy** refers to a social system in which social and domestic power resides with males, notably with the senior male member of a family group, the patriarch.) The content of the interviews goes unchallenged by the filmmaker, but not the structure of the interview. Later in the film, the viewer learns that the "interviews" were not shot in Vietnam at all and that the women live in California, not Vietnam. In fact, they are reciting statements that the filmmaker has drawn from a book by a journalist about the experience of women in postwar Vietnam. Normally, on-screen interviews give a documentary authenticity: people testify to what they experienced directly and do so in their own words. These, however, were not spontaneous interviews, but scripted reenactments in which Trinh's interviewees recite the words of others. The result throws the presumed authenticity of the interview structure into question. The film reflexively exposes the assumption that the subject represents herself and is not giving a rehearsed performance, that the location is what it appears to be, and so on.

Often considered the first reflexive documentary, Dziga Vertov's portrait of life in post-revolutionary Moscow, *The Man with a Movie Camera* (1929, Soviet Union), is a vividly poetic celebration of a day in the life of the city. Running through the film are direct references to the filmmaking process itself. Rather than pretend that the camera just catches what occurs effortlessly, Vertov takes pains to show the viewer how much work, often vigorous and risky work, goes into getting the shots we see. The film shows the cameraman, for example, lying down on a railroad track to get a shot of an onrushing train. Will he be annihilated by the onrushing train? No! The train roars past and the intrepid cameraman pops up to go on to his next shot.

Later, the film freezes a shot of a horse and carriage and then shows • us this frame on an editing table as the editor views it and cuts it into the film. We now see that a shot that simply appears in the film is actually culled from dozens of other contending shots (on the paradigmatic axis). This feat involves the intense efforts of an editor, who must catalogue and then choose among all the available shots. These reflexive gestures reminded contemporary viewers in the 1920s that art is a form of physical labor, similar to the efforts of the workers and peasants celebrated by the revolution. The final film does not just appear on the screen but arises from an extended process of collaborative effort. The reflexive element not only draws attention to what kind of film *The Man with a Movie Camera* is (it shows how the cameraman documents things) but also directs attention to how much it, although a work of art, is also part and parcel of the ordinary labor process that the Soviet Revolution valued over and above the ability of some to profit from the work of others. By reflexively showing the process of making the film, Vertov indirectly demonstrates his support for what the revolution set out to achieve.

PERFORMATIVE If the reflexive mode stresses intellectual engagement with aspects of the filmmaking experience, the performative mode stresses emotional involvement with what it is like to witness a particular kind of experience. Performative documentaries rely less heavily on commentary to convey information than on form to convey emotion. They may well imply, therefore, that knowledge of the world is incomplete without a sense of affective engagement to complement intellectual comprehension. This gives them an affinity with fiction films. But they share with other documentaries the mission to address aspects of the historical world directly.

Night and Fog (Alain Resnais, 1955, France), for example, covers the same historical subject as *Shoah*. But *Night and Fog* relies on a voice-over commentary to sketch out the broad historical outlines of the event, along with found footage of the concentration camps, mainly footage shot by Allied forces when they liberated the camps. At first it appears to be an expository documentary, but a performative dimension soon enters in. The commentary is not abstract and anonymous. It was, in fact, written by a camp survivor, Jean Cayrol, and it has a strongly personal, anecdotal quality. It stresses memory over history: what should we remember of a catastrophe and why? It invites an emotional response as well as cognitive understanding. It shows the atrocities that took place, but confesses that it is impossible to speak about them coherently and does not try to do so. Instead, it questions the viewer in so many words: "How are we to understand acts of barbarity? What are we to make of them?" The film as a whole displays a performative desire to make the viewer feel what it might be like to have to remember something traumatic and to use this memory as a vital tool in the present to prevent a recurrence of the original catastrophe.

The world consists of more than facts and information. Performative documentary stresses the affective dimension to lived experience. Perhaps for this reason it has been often been used for autobiography and for films by members of ethnic minorities. For those who experience discrimination or prejudice because of their group affiliation, the felt hurt of this experience takes on a palpable reality of its own. The sense of a shared oppressive experience, for example, was crucial to the rise of the feminist movement in the 1960s and '70s. Things that had been rationalized as "Just the way it is," such as deference to men, lower pay for comparable work, shouldering the burden of most of the housework and childrearing as well as working for a wage, became open to question. The experience of oppressive conditions sparked political organization.

Many performative documentaries locate the roots of political activism in a history of shared oppression that becomes a unifying rather than a divisive agent. Unlike a political tract, films such as *Tongues Untied* (Marlon Riggs, 1990), about the experience of being a black gay male (discussed further in Chapter 10), *The Body Beautiful* (Ngozi Onwurah, 1991, UK), about a daughter's efforts to come to terms with her mother's deformed body after she undergoes a mastectomy, and *Silverlake Life* (Peter Friedman and Tom Joslin, 1993), about the wrenching experience of living with and, ultimately, dying of AIDS, do not propose solutions or seek to galvanize action. They seek instead to draw us into an affective, experiential engagement with what it feels like to encounter the world from a specific perspective and in a particular time and place. The performative mode demonstrates the great expressive power of the documentary form to do more than convey information or mount an argument. Like fiction films, documentaries can be a source of deeply felt and long remembered emotional experiences.

Agnes Varda's stunning film *The Gleaners and I* (2000, France) explores the world of gleaners, those who scavenge for what others leave behind. This practice derives from an old agricultural tradition, but Varda sees it as a metaphor for many forms of modern scavenging and for cinema itself. She gleans images from her travels and marvels at their power to enchant. Her images derive from the historical world rather than a fictional world of her own design and are, in this sense, too, gleaned. Varda conveys a sense of wonder and appreciation more than she informs about a little known activity, although both impulses are at work.

Gleaners thrive on what others find superfluous; they find value and use where others do not. Varda's infectious fascination with gleaning stems from her ability to see things anew, to see new possibilities where others do not, and to value the lives and activity of those who share a kindred spirit. When she "captures" a truck by framing it with her hand, or when she finds a clock with no hands and values it for its surreal beauty, Varda celebrates a performative emphasis on the expressive over the informative. The film, which is part essay, part diary, and part documentary, possesses a gentle, meditative touch but nonetheless confronts the serious issues of aging, impermanence, fragility and beauty. *The Gleaners and I* exudes a quiet joy, a vivid sign of its performative power.

Style

Rhetorical style ranges from plain to ornate. Documentary films and other works that rely upon rhetorical strategies can be straightforward or overblown. The choice of what style to use is a question of what is fitting for the subject and purpose, which classic rhetoricians called **decorum**. Whereas we now think of decorum as an ultra-refined form of behavior, in film rhetoric the term signifies the choices of style most fitting to a particular occasion. As the occasion changes, so does decorum. The opening of Leni Riefenstahl's *Triumph of the Will* (1935, Germany), for example, about the major 1934 Nazi rally in Nuremberg, is full of pomp and exaggeration. Several explanatory titles appear as portentous music engulfs the viewer. The titles describe Germany's humiliating defeat in World War I and the long years of suffering that followed. But now there is a path forward, and the man who leads the way is the man the film will soon introduce. His plane emerges from a sky of billowing clouds, and lands, allowing him to step onto the German soil of Nuremberg: Adolf Hitler has arrived. The overblown quality is part and parcel of what the Nazi party saw as an effective, hence decorous, strategy of turning politics into aesthetics, of making a political rally into a spectacle. Leni Riefenstahl proved a master of creating cinematic spectacle in such a context.

Michael Moore's form of decorum is just the opposite. His films extol the virtues of the plain-talking, straight-acting Everyman who just happens to want to get to the bottom of things and can do so in a remarkably inventive way, without any need for glory or celebrity for himself (at least within his films' terms, but not necessarily in terms of how the media then represent him). Moore's film appearance is not wrapped in pomp and ceremony meant to legitimize his stature and heroism. The folksy image reverberates with an American tradition and mythology of the populist hero who neither comes from a privileged background nor seeks personal gain. He is just one of us, or so his films' sense of decorum would have us believe.

In terms of decorum, a plain, not very sophisticated style might work extremely well in a given situation. Hemingway probably ushered in the matter-of-fact, emotionally restrained style of commentary that many documentaries in the 1930s and '40s adopted. The tone of John Huston, as writer, director, and narrator of *The Battle of San Pietro* (1945), is very dry and laconic. This film, on the aftermath and human consequences of war, contains none of the strident urgency that belonged to the far more inflammatory commentary of his father, Walter Huston, in the *Why We Fight* series of films. The film's goal is not to motivate the United States to go to war, as it was for the *Why We Fight* films, but to commemorate the heroism and losses of those who waged war on behalf of their fellow countrymen. The low-key, almost solemn tone seems entirely appropriate to the goal.

In rhetorical terms, decorum and eloquence are simply the properties of persuasive discourse when it works. A crude or hyperbolic style, like a blunt or hysterical style, is not necessarily a defect if such styles work. The fiction film *8 Mile* (Curtis Hanson, 2002, U.S./Germany) demonstrates this point by stressing the great difficulty Eminem's semi-autobiographical character has in performing rap in public when he has to put down other performers. Politeness becomes a handicap. What works, the form of speech that possesses the greatest decorum, is raw, bold, witty, and cutting toward its intended victim. Achieving decorum in this case means giving up courtesy and politeness in order to adopt a combative form of speech fitting to the occasion.

A personal, non-authoritative tone has become a commonplace of documentary film in recent years. In many cases, this effect is achieved by the filmmaker providing his own commentary. The filmmaker provides a personal perspective on the events we see, in work ranging from Mark Rappaport's *Rock Hudson's Home Movies* (1992) and Péter Forgács's *Free Fall* (1996, Hungary) to Nick Broomfield's often self-congratulatory investigative films such as *Aileen Wuornos: The Selling of a Serial Killer* (1992, UK), about a woman convicted of murdering a series of men. (*Monster* [Patty Jenkins, 2003, U.S./Germany] tells the same story as a fiction film, with Charlize Theron playing Aileen Wuornos.) Like the more famous example of Michael Moore, these filmmakers prefer to speak in their own voice and to insist on the personal nature of their filmmaking efforts, even if they also adopt a documentary form that conveys the aura of an objective, omniscient perspective. Their work, in fact, is one important reason why the idea of **objectivity** in documentary has come to be seen as a red herring, more important to certain forms of journalism than it is to the persuasive and expressive goals of most documentaries.

OBJECTIVITY AND DOCUMENTARY FILM

Objectivity is a term in the sciences for the detachment of the experimenter from the experiment and the replicable, verifiable nature of the results, but it is a more complicated term in the humanities. In the study of nature, objectivity requires adherence to scientific procedure. Facts must be true, results must be verified. Controls, such as giving one population of test subjects a drug and another population a placebo, isolate one variable and measure its effect. Double-blind controls mean that those conducting the experiment do not know which members of the overall population receive the drug and which receive the placebo. Verifiability means that anyone else versed in the correct procedures should achieve essentially the same results. For one team of researchers to find a drug effective against migraine headaches and another team to find no effect at all suggests that objective results have not been attained.

The matter is more complicated in the humanities, where the subject of study is humanity itself. The investigator, be it a filmmaker, historian, or philosopher, is part of the very object of study. What proves valuable is less the ability to perform verifiable experiments on other humans (this can be done, particularly in medicine, science, and the social sciences, but ethical safeguards become a necessity to protect subjects from inhumane treatment) than the quality of insight that one person achieves. There is little reason to assume that this insight stems from objectivity in the scientific sense of the word, although it may well involve detachment, contemplation, and an interpretative process that values arguing from evidence more than proclaiming opinions.

Filmmakers see the world from a distinct, personal perspective; historians offer their own interpretation of past events; philosophers develop their own systems of thought. Are such activities objective? It would be more accurate to say that they are inevitably subjective even if they must adhere to certain institutional standards such as citing

OBJECTIVITY AND DOCUMENTARY FILM (CONTINUED)

sources in history or avoiding the creation of composite (fictitious) characters in journalism. The explanatory, interpretative, or expressive power of a documentary usually takes precedence over questions of objectivity, especially if a purely objective assessment of an issue is not possible in the first place. What objective measure can there be of the value of the lost lives documented, and lamented, in *the Battle of San Pietro*? What objective measure can there be of how much it hurts to experience discrimination as gay, or black, or both—an experience to which *Tongues Untied* gives eloquent expression? In documentary as an expressive form of communication, feeling and emotion carry more weight than objectivity in a scientific sense.

Interpretative Goals

A common goal of documentary criticism is to gauge the extent to which the film succeeds in persuading its audience. A dual formal-social analysis, looking for both strengths and weaknesses, can focus attention on what a documentary does that is formally innovative or conventional, and socially revealing or manipulative. Manipulation or distortion is often a question of looking for what is omitted, suppressed, minimized, or perhaps taken out of context.

The persuasive dimension to rhetoric encourages the audience to trust the credibility, reliability, and authenticity of what the films claim to be the case or propose as a way of seeing and understanding a situation. Analysis often seeks to uncover the precise formal or stylistic means by which a film achieves, or fails to achieve, persuasiveness, how credibility is earned, convincingness demonstrated, and compellingness achieved. Reliability and authenticity, for example, almost always depend on external verification. Interpretation may then turn to external sources to judge whether the credibility is genuinely achieved, convincingness soundly demonstrated, compellingness honestly and ethically earned.

Documentary has many strategies for attaining its ends. Critics who are aware of these strategies can analyze how they are applied and judge whether the application is valid. Convincingness regarding past events, for example, can often be enhanced by the use of reenactments or by the use of archival, historical footage. Numerous films combine historical footage with interviews of individuals who know about or participated in past events. What they tell their audience about what really happened can then be made to appear all the more authentic by combining it with historic footage that supports their point of view. Whether archival footage comes from the time and place asserted, whether reenactments, if used, capture the essence of a past event effectively without passing themselves off as historical footage per se, and whether individual accounts jibe with other known sources of information, are all important questions for the critic of documentary films.

Critical analysis can also be an important way of adding credence to a documentary by exploring the ramifications of its perspective. Such analysis fleshes out what the film implies and makes its point even more explicit. Early commentary on Alain Resnais's *Night and Fog* stressed its enormous value as an educational tool. Such commentary stimulated further screenings and even gave rise to proposals, such as one made in postwar Germany, that it be made mandatory viewing for schoolchildren. More formal analysis of how the film achieved its powerful effects and altered documentary tradition did not occur until some time later.

Examples

NANOOK OF THE NORTH

Nanook of the North (Robert Flaherty, 1922) focuses on the exploits of one Eskimo, Nanook, and his extended family. The film is strongly narrative in its tale of Nanook's struggle to survive. It could almost be a western about settlers attempting to tame an untamed land (untamed from a settler's perspective rather than a Native American's). But it is also regarded as a pioneering film that helped establish the form of the documentary by being shot entirely on location in 1922, with non-actors, in order to represent the traditional ways of Eskimo, or Inuit, life.

In Flaherty's vision of the world, character is measured not by the speeches and pageantry of *Triumph of the Will*, but by the ability to survive and provide basic necessities for others in a harsh environment. Flaherty adopts a highly observational style, as if we are looking in on a world that unfolds without his intervention. He sets out to convince the viewer that Nanook is a fine provider by demonstrating his prowess at hunting walrus, harpooning seals, and building igloos. He makes a compelling case by involving us empathetically, via camera angle and editing, in Nanook's activities. In a long take, the viewer sits, watches, and waits as Nanook sits above a hole he has cut in the ice, waiting for a seal to appear for a breath of air. At that moment, he will hurl his spear into the hole and bring food home to his family.

Critical analysis can complicate the picture by examining whether the events depicted were as uncontrolled by Flaherty as they seem. Flaherty himself admits to staging some scenes. For example, to show life inside the igloo, he built a cut-away version with one wall removed so that there was sufficient light to film. He argued that this only allowed him to capture the typical more effectively. Later critics and scholars, though, have demonstrated how Flaherty staged an entire world of pre-contact Eskimo culture that had, in fact, almost entirely vanished by the time he came to film in 1922. Flaherty had to recreate hunting methods (rifles had become common by the 1920s), family structures (the Inuit formerly traveled in extended family units rather than in a nuclear family like the one Flaherty shows), and housing (igloos had given way to wood-framed cabins).

These forms of interference or transformation undercut the credibility Flaherty's observational style tries to establish. He is, in effect, documenting a reality he first created in order to document, even though he did so with scrupulous attention to factual details. This line of analysis clearly depends on knowledge external to the film; it measures how well the film compares to general knowledge about the subject Flaherty chose to represent. A follow-up question would then be, why did Flaherty make the changes if they put his credibility at risk? What was he attempting to achieve that required this sleight of hand? Did he want to lend a documentary aura to something that was at least partly a product of his own way of seeing things?

NANOOK OF THE NORTH AND ETHNOCENTRISM

Ethnocentrism refers to the tendency to rank one's own cultural values over those of another culture. Imperialist conquest and colonial settlement had many long-term benefits for the conquerors and settlers, but it also had many negative consequences for its victims, the native peoples who were considered inferior. An ethnocentric attitude justified colonial policies, since the colonial powers considered themselves superior to the colonized peoples.

Nanook of the North is not a film of **ethnographic** intention. (**Ethnography** is that part of anthropology devoted to the descriptive study of other cultures; ethnographic film is the visual version of written ethnographic accounts.) Flaherty wanted to make a feature film that would attract an audience, and considered his work neither documentary nor ethnography. But he did belong to an historical period in which it was

NANOOK OF THE NORTH AND ETHNOCENTRISM (CONTINUED)

common to regard native people as less civilized or an earlier, more primitive version of what was to become modern civilization. The image Flaherty offers of Nanook is at once ennobling—Nanook is an adept hunter and a charming screen character—and disturbing—he is a romanticized version of the Inuit hunter as Flaherty wanted to imagine him. Flaherty did not seem to have any reservations about modifying reality, staging aspects of the seal hunt he appears to observe or telling us Nanook and his family are on the brink of starvation even though Flaherty is there with plenty of provisions. These distortions helped him to create the ennobling image he sought. The result is a complex, ambiguous portrait by virtue of the ethnocentric ideology that mixed admiration with condescension. For many viewers, admiration triumphs over condescension in *Nanook* but the complexity is no doubt part of what has made it a much discussed film.

TRIUMPH OF THE WILL

Another film often considered a documentary classic, *Triumph of the Will*, begins with a problem—how to restore German national pride? It then offers a solution: Adolf Hitler and his Nazi party program. Here there is no question of how Hitler will rise to power, or how he will carry out his plans. The film is devoted to presenting Hitler as a full-blown political leader worthy of the highest praise, praise that Riefenstahl offers through the nonverbal means of camera angles, editing, and music rather than through direct address of any kind.

In this sense, *Triumph of the Will* is strictly observational (after the initial written scroll of text that sets the scene) but hardly objective. There is no voice-over commentary and no interviews. Much of what the film viewer sees could have been seen by a participant or onlooker, although the specific position of the camera is often privileged—it ascends giant columns, accompanies the Führer's motorcade, tracks past long lines of assembled troops—and the final result is highly edited into a cadenced, almost rhapsodic piece of ceremonial rhetoric. Hitler is the man and the National Socialists the party of the future. Hitler's own agenda is clearly a reactionary one, returning to medieval myths and folklore for much of its message, but Riefenstahl takes a highly romantic attitude toward this political perspective: she idolizes Hitler as a dynamic leader more than she scrutinizes his policies and programs.

These strategies attempt to establish the credibility of the film as an honest account of an actual event. The extent to which Leni Riefenstahl, the director, worked with the Nazi party organizers to ensure that her cameras caught events just so, and the extent to which actual events were carefully choreographed to maximize their visual impact, with Riefenstahl collaborating in their preparation, remains hidden beneath the film's claim to be a record of an undoctored, real event. It was, on the contrary, one of the first large-scale political events expressly staged as a spectacle for dissemination by the mass media—cinema in this case; more typically today, the medium is television.

A dual formal-social interpretation of the film encounters challenges similar to those presented by *The Birth of a Nation* (D. W. Griffith, 1915), with its praise for the Ku Klux Klan: draw attention to the many achievements in film technique that make both films works of art, but also examine the specific ways in which the films' form contributes to conveying a particularly disturbing political perspective. Both aspects deserve attention to complete the analysis: the innovative use of formal technique can be readily acknowledged and the reactionary political perspective carefully examined. That the former contributes to how the latter is rendered in a convincing, compelling manner brings form and content into a common frame. Rather than simply praising or condemning the film, such analysis strives to understand and interpret the effect this film had in a given historical context because of rather than despite its formal accomplishments.

4

STORYTELLING AND NARRATIVE FICTION FILM

Storytelling as a Universal Phenomenon

Narrative is the great storytelling device that occurs around the world. The universality of stories—about the past, present, and future; about characters, real and imaginary—suggests that narratives play a vital role, probably multiple roles, in the construction of any social reality. As discussed in Chapter 2, storytelling serves many purposes: (1) to give free rein to the imagination; (2) to recount the past, explore the present, and invent the future; (3) to exert a magical power over what might otherwise seem an intractable reality; (4) to evoke moods and feelings in an affective way; (5) to give visible shape to models for and alternatives to a given social order; and, (6) to embody or promote a particular political position or ideological perspective. By these means, narrative can give imaginative form to the ways in which real social conflicts and contradictions that trouble a given culture might find resolution. By having characters do what actual people do, or what people wish they could do, or fear others might do, narrative can convey a sense of magic or power. Stories allow entry into a world similar to the existing world but with freedom from the implications and consequences that occur in real life. This freedom to explore implications and consequences in an imaginative way spells out the ideological and utopian qualities of storytelling.

Not all films use narrative in the same way. Broad stylistic differences arise. Chapter 5 discusses the three main stylistic tendencies of the twentieth century: realism (and its relation to fantasy), modernism and postmodernism. Here, at the outset, it will be important to note at least one significant difference between familiar **genre films** and a somewhat less familiar art cinema. (**Genre films** share thematic and stylistic features that become known as conventions, such as shoot-outs in westerns, betrayal in film noir, or episodes of song and dance in musicals. These conventions establish a set of constraints and opportunities that individual films explore in distinct ways.)

Mainstream Films and the Art Cinema: Some Fundamental Differences

The study of narrative brings us to the commercial heart of the cinema. Fictional storytelling is where the great Hollywood studio system has asserted its dominance around the globe since the 1920s. This form of storytelling, based on principles of realism and genres, is often considered the true core of cinema. It is the type of filmmaking with which people are most familiar. The avant-garde and documentary forms, central to understanding the range and complexity of filmmaking possibilities, do not generate the kind of industrial power base that fictional storytelling does. They are not as widely familiar to most viewers, and they lack the extraordinary range of publicity from studio trailers, posters and websites, fan and gossip magazines, talk shows and interviews, and lavish award ceremonies such as the Oscars that cast their spotlight on the industry as a whole.

Avant-garde, documentary, Third World film, and art cinema may seem to be terms of marginalization, as if those kinds of film don't count the way mainstream movies count. Mainstream, popular, genre, or Hollywood films identify the primary form of filmmaking, while the other terms refer to subordinate, secondary, or minor forms. Filmmakers who work in other forms and places are well aware that economically and socially mainstream cinema is the dominant cinema; and they sometimes pursue their filmmaking goals in reaction to the tendencies of mainstream cinema they wish to reject or change.

On the other hand, mainstream cinema does not enjoy a privileged position in terms of its aesthetic merits or its social significance; it is just one of the many forms that the aesthetics and politics of film take. This is why this book surveys the avant-garde and documentary film traditions first: they offer a broader conceptual framework in which to understand the power and appeal of narrative film. In every case, economic clout, vast publicity, and widespread popularity do not necessarily translate into aesthetic achievement or social significance— nor do they translate into aesthetic inferiority and social irrelevance. Such judgments need to be made at the level of individual films.

For the most part we will refer to "mainstream films" as the works most familiar to us, and use a variety of terms to characterize alternatives to it. The art cinema is among the most important of these alternatives.

Art cinema is a cinema of interiority (mental states) and style more than of exteriority (physical action) and plot. Art cinema originates with the stylistic movements of the 1920s, '30s, and '40s such as the Soviet silent cinema, German **expressionism**, and Italian **neorealism**. It enjoyed a major renaissance in the postwar years as a host of major directors made their mark in Europe, from Michelangelo Antonioni and Federico Fellini to Ingmar Bergman and Jean-Luc Godard. The inner thoughts and feelings of characters take precedence over dramatic action, making for generally slower, more ambiguous results.

Table 4.1 Basic Differences between Mainstream and Art Cinema

Mainstream Cinema	Art Cinema
Examples: *Birth of a Nation, Gone with the Wind, Psycho, The Searchers, Star Wars, Titanic, Oceans 11, The Matrix, Mr. and Mrs. Smith, Pirates of the Caribbean, Charlie Wilson's War, No Country for Old Men*	Examples: *Umberto D, The 400 Blows, The Conformist, 8½, L'avventura, Last Year at Marienbad, The Sacrifice, Shadows, Breaking the Waves, Talk to Her, The Lives of Others, 4 Months, 3 Weeks and 2 Days*
Linear plot in which each action sets up and leads to subsequent actions.	Episodic plot in which actions may be secondary to impressions, attitudes, or states of mind.
Scenes follow one another in a way that suggests causality. Each action functions as the cause of later actions or events.	Chance plays a large role. Events seem to occur without clear-cut causes. Feelings and the exploration of consequences loom larger than causality.
Style is relatively unnoticeable (via continuity editing); stress is on the behavior of main characters, physical actions, and dramatic situations.	Style is relatively noticeable; stress is on inner states of mind of main characters, emotional responses, and a general tone or atmosphere.
The world in which the action occurs, the diegesis, has a coherence and plausibility to it.	The world of the characters may be incoherent or fragmented so that links between characters, situations, or events may be difficult to determine.
Achieving a goal preoccupies characters; obstacles in reaching the goal play a key role in engaging the audience.	Doubt, anxiety, or uncertainty may preoccupy the characters; goals are often secondary to exploring a troubled state of mind.
The ending provides resolution or closure to the initial problem.	The ending may be arbitrary, with issues and feelings still in the air; open-ended.

The challenges facing central characters in the art cinema, unlike those in the standard genre film, seldom revolve around doing things that require cunning, prowess, and athleticism. Art cinema explores many forms and levels of problems, many of which seem existential in their nature, such as alienation or loneliness, and are therefore less amenable to clear-cut resolution. Many of the events come filtered through the perception and consciousness of the characters rather than through a neutral, observing camera that simply allows the tale to unfold and the characters to act. The individual style of art cinema directors is often highly distinctive, since it does not depend on the conventions of genre films.

A good example of how art cinema treats character conflict occurs in Jean-Luc Godard's beautiful film, *Contempt* (1963, France/Italy). Godard explores how a single gesture ends up destroying a marriage. Paul (Michel Piccoli), a writer, agrees to do the script for a film of *The Odyssey*. His wife, Camille (Brigitte Bardot), worries he kowtows too much to the producer, Jeremy Prokosch (Jack Palance). He alienates her by letting Prokosch drive her home in his hot red sports car despite her clear desire that he not allow it to happen. A significant portion of the film then unfolds in the couple's apartment. This exceptionally long scene chronicles the ways in which their relationship begins to unravel. Neither can stop it, and neither can help themselves from furthering the breakup. Godard locates much of the narrative middle of his film in this one time and place; he adroitly captures what it feels like to experience the collapse of love and trust over the course of a single afternoon.

The characters' interactions in *Contempt* are not broad, vigorous ones like chases or physical fights. They are small exchanges that matter greatly to each of them. Each event adds to our understanding of the characters; each event poses a challenge. How Paul and Camille acquit themselves becomes a measure of their character. In a subtle, emotionally rich film like *Contempt*, narrative suspense and questions of what will happen next are of secondary importance; what is happening now, what levels of meaning and reaction are taking place, what each look, gesture, or statement reveals about the characters, these are the central questions as the viewer engages with this particular world.

Key Narrative Elements

BEGINNINGS, MIDDLES, AND ENDS

Narratives incorporate a beginning, middle, and end, usually in that order. *Pulp Fiction* (Quentin Tarantino, 1994) is a good example of a variation on this truism. Viewers have no reason to doubt that the opening scene of *Pulp Fiction* is where the story begins, but much later they realize that the earliest chronological event actually takes place in the middle of the story. This is also true of *Tell No One* (*Ne le dis à personne*, Guillaume Canet, 2006, France) and *The Edge of Heaven* (*Auf der anderen Seite*, Fatih Akim, 2007, Germany/Turkey/Italy), two recent European films.

The beginning typically launches the story by identifying a problem, conflict, or lack, establishing a situation that will pose an issue in need of resolution. *The Graduate* (Mike Nichols, 1967), for example, begins with Ben Braddock staring into the distance with a blank expression as he is transported through the Los Angeles airport. The viewer soon realizes that the issue raised at the start involves what kind of future Ben can make for himself now that he has graduated from college but lacks plans or any clear ambition. *Singin' in the Rain* (Stanley Donen and Gene Kelly, 1952) begins, over the first several scenes, with dual issues: Don's encounter with a chorus girl, Kathy Selden, whom he pines to meet again, and how to cope with the coming of sound to Hollywood. *Psycho* (Alfred Hitchcock, 1960) begins with a documentary-like panning shot of the Phoenix, Arizona skyline and then passes effortlessly through one window to enter the hotel room where Sam and Marion are discussing their problem: they want to be married but Sam still needs to get a divorce, and to get a divorce he needs money. The issues of legitimate and illegitimate relationships, of money and marriage, will become central to the events that follow.

The ending typically rounds out a story by resolving the initial problem, conflict, or lack. Ben finds a purpose for his life in his successful pursuit of Elaine Robinson. Romance and talking pictures both achieve success by the end of *Singin' in the Rain*. At the end of *Psycho*, a psychiatrist explains the twisted mind and bizarre behavior of a motel manager who has destroyed Sam and Marion's plans. The resolution provided by the ending allows the viewer to reflect back over the previous events and see how they have led to this particular conclusion when, for much of the film, resolution seemed uncertain. The final revelation of what the word "Rosebud" stands for in *Citizen Kane* (Orson Welles, 1941), for example, invites the viewer to reflect on how each of the characters missed an important dimension to Kane's personality.

The ending of a film not only resolves the personal or social problems that arise at the outset; in many cases, it also gives visual expression to the sense of closure. Orson Welles's *Touch of Evil* (1958), for example, begins with an extraordinary long take of several minutes as the camera follows a car from the Mexican to the American side of the border. Near the end of the shot the camera lingers on Vargas (Charlton Heston), a Mexican detective, and his wife, Susan (Janet Leigh), as the car continues to drive away off-screen. Vargas and Susan embrace and are about to kiss when, suddenly, there is a giant explosion. The explosion interrupts their kiss. It is not until the end of the film that they reunite and consummate their kiss. The completion of the kiss announces the restoration of the couple (Susan had been kidnapped) and also marks the resolution to their hardships. The film uses a visual signifier (the conclusion of the kiss) to convey the sense of an ending. A similar movement creates symmetry between the opening

and ending of *Citizen Kane* as the camera rises over the fence bounding the Xanadu estate at the start of the film and then descends back
over the fence at the conclusion.

The middle of a narrative constitutes the bulk of the story and is
typically organized in an arc of ascending and descending action that
pivots around some form of climactic moment in the realist stories that
are the staple of Hollywood cinema. Characters typically confront
challenges on the way to resolving the issue that drives them. Other
characters then function either as obstacles, impeding their progress,
or as helpers, aiding their progress. *Singin' in the Rain* takes the viewer
through numerous complications that arise involving characters who
prove to be obstacles to success, like Lina Lamont, the jealous star of
limited talent who tries to block Kathy's ascendance, or helpers, like
Cosmo, who gives pep talks to Don and comes up with bright ideas.
The middle is where hope encounters dilemmas, plans go awry, suspense rises, and obstacles must be overcome.

Art cinema moves away from realism and genre conventions. In this
case the middle may be more heavily devoted to exploring the ramifications and complexities of a given situation. The main character may
experience a crisis, but this may be subjective or internal, rather than
something that involves physical feats or external actions in relation
to other characters. In *The Conformist* (Bernardo Bertolucci, 1970,
Italy/France/West Germany), for example, the middle revolves around
Marcello Clerici's crisis of conscience as he attempts to create an
impression of normalcy that requires him to commit abnormal, even
abominable acts, such as assassinating his former professor. *The Conformist* explores the emotional and psychological complexity of a situation that pushes the main character toward the brink of instability
rather than following a relatively stable character through a series of
actions, challenges, and obstacles.

This pattern is also quite common in American independent films
such as John Cassavetes' great pioneering film, *Shadows* (1959), which

follows a set of characters over a stretch of time as they struggle with personal demons and interpersonal relationships. Little happens in terms of action. The middle of the film seems to loop back over similar situations of misunderstandings, thwarted desires, unfulfilled ambitions, and empty distractions among its principal characters. The sense of a distinct world with recurring patterns and problems slowly builds and takes on considerable complexity. A noticeable absence of action and adventure, together with stress on how characters interact with others to explore emotional issues and psychological problems, gives the American independent film, like the art film, a tone and style distinct from most Hollywood cinema.

In the middle, the narrative works its way toward an ending, often with a mixture of revelation and suspense that surrounds the central characters. Narratives therefore typically possess a sequential arrangement of events that achieve closure. Suspense—uncertainty about the outcome of a situation—works to sustain the viewer's engagement. **Suspense** is a key difference between storytelling and logical discourse. Reason seeks the simplest, clearest, shortest path to the solution of a problem. Narration, on the other hand, looks for ways to postpone or delay the resolution so that the psychology of characters, the complexity of situations, and the suspense of not knowing what will happen next gain intensity. This produces an affective quality, a feeling of what a given world or way of being is like and what it feels like to live within it.

Many expressive techniques—from the use of sound to composition within the frame—produce suspense. Editing, for example, often generates suspense. A character's attention turns to something off-screen, perhaps near the position of the camera. The film might withhold a **reverse shot**, which could reveal a character watching from off-screen. (The **reverse shot** shows what could be seen if the camera angle were reversed 180 degrees, often showing another character.) The viewer continues to see the first character from what appears to be the point of view of another character but without knowing who that character is. The viewer's concern for the visible character and curiosity about the invisible character increase. An off-screen sound, a creaking stair, for example, can warn of a danger that may not be revealed for some time as suspense mounts.

Parallel editing almost always creates suspense. In this case, the film cuts from one sequence of actions to another, related sequence of action. In *Psycho*, Marion's sister explores Norman Bates's home while Sam tries to distract Norman by talking to him in the motel parlor. The two lines of parallel action converge when Norman realizes the deception, escapes from Sam, and rushes off to confront Lila. The confrontation not only brings the two lines of action together but helps resolve the entire film. Films with many central characters whose stories converge, such as *Nashville* (Robert Altman, 1975), *Magnolia* (Paul Thomas Anderson, 1999), *Crash* (Paul Haggis, 2004, U.S./Germany), and *Babel* (Alejandro González Iñárritu, 2006, France/U.S./Mexico), or the prototypical *The Birth of a Nation* (D. W. Griffith, 1915), rely on parallel editing to cut between not two but numerous sequences of action. Rather than stressing suspense, this tactic moves the viewer from a state of confusion about the various parallel stories to an eventual realization of how the stories and characters relate to one another.

STYLE, PLOT, AND THE FILMMAKER'S SOCIAL ATTITUDE

Every narrative combines a **plot**—the sequence of situations and events as they unfold chronologically on the screen—and a **style**—the particular cinematic techniques used to present these situations and events. The plot is what is most often summarized or distilled as the content of a film: a woman steals some money and has to face the consequences (*Psycho*); a son is drawn into the family's criminal business but wants to become a respected businessman (*The Godfather* [Francis Ford Coppola, 1972]). The same plot can be told in a wide range of media, but style is medium-specific: "Boy meets, loses, and wins girl" is a plot that could be told as a novel, play, or film, but the stylistic devices available to make it "novelistic," "theatrical," or "cinematic" are different for each medium. The expressive techniques specific to film were discussed in Chapter 1.

Style signals the mark of an author who has created a world from a particular perspective and told a story in a distinct way. Unlike the plot, which can be told in many ways, the style represents an individual filmmaker's idiosyncratic way of seeing things. Through style the viewer senses the filmmaker's attitude toward the story, its characters and world. Jean-Luc Godard once said that a story told in long shots is a comedy and that the same story told in close-ups is a tragedy. The first produces detachment, the second fosters involvement. Critics have consistently praised Roberto Rossellini and Vittorio De Sica, two of the most important neorealist directors, for their compassion toward their characters, their hesitation to pass judgment, and their acceptance of human foibles. This praise refers to a style that observed events unfolding without edits, music, or lighting that might have condemned one character and praised another. For this reason, critics have also termed the style humanistic. Jean-Luc Godard, on the other hand, creates characters who present positions, take stances, act out dilemmas in a self-conscious way, and remain elusive in terms of their interior states of mind. In his style, which has been termed essayistic, detached, or philosophic, compassion for characters as symbols of the human spirit diminishes.

Plots, what we usually mean by content, fall into various categories, especially in genre films: how individual resourcefulness overcomes danger stemming from a mysterious or supernatural force in horror films, for example, or the tensions within family life that bring about vivid emotional conflict and wrenching personal sacrifice in melodrama. One of the most common plot devices across all Hollywood film genres is the parallel or dual plot: the hero must achieve a goal that requires him to undertake a journey or quest while also trying to preserve or establish a romantic relationship. *Gone with the Wind* (Victor Fleming, 1939) hangs its four-hour, two-part story on the vicissitudes of Scarlett O'Hara's efforts to survive the Civil War and to find an ideal mate. She survives, but finding the ideal mate proves elusive. In *No Country for Old Men* (Ethan and Joel Coen, 2007), the parallel plotting involves Llewellyn's efforts to elude the murderous Chigurh and Sheriff Ed Bell's efforts to find him. Neither succeeds, and their parallel stories never converge. The ending is not happy. These innovations represent ways in which the Coen brothers adapt and rejuvenate genre conventions in their film.

Stylistic Schools: How Films Share Similar Stylistic Features

Despite the complex array of stylistic choices every filmmaker must make, narrative films exhibit considerable commonality. At a micro level, this is often true for directors: their overall body of work exhibits common preoccupations and stylistic features. But stylistic commonality also occurs at much more macro levels. The largest of these levels or categories, realism, is discussed in Chapter 5. The chapter surveys a number of other commonalities.

FILM MOVEMENTS, HISTORICAL PERIODS, AND NATIONAL CINEMAS

Differences among film movements, historical periods, and national cinemas also generate a range of narrative styles. Movements arise at different times and places for complex reasons that involve both formal and social factors. German expressionist film, for example, drew on the formal model established by expressionist painting in the 1900s

and 1910s. Socially, it responded to the sense of psychological disorientation produced by Germany's defeat in World War I and the rampant runaway inflation of the 1920s. A once powerful country now
faced an uncertain future. Expressionist films focus on disturbed psychological states, highly distorted environments, physical entrapment,
and sinister machinations that engulf the innocent. *The Cabinet of Dr.
Caligari* (Robert Wiene, 1920, Germany) epitomizes the expressionist movement, with its tale of a mad doctor and his somnambulant
assistant who wreak havoc in a town characterized by bizarre angles,
jagged shadows, and irregular walls (shot entirely on a studio set). The
film's expressionist style caught the pessimistic, doomed mode of the
country perfectly.

Historical **periodization** is another way to identify stylistic clusters.
(**Periodization** involves identifying specific time spans during which
consistencies prevail and between which differences emerge or transformations occur.) Different periods tend to share an emphasis on similar qualities. Studio films from the 1920s and early '30s often displayed
a lack of depth to the image, whereas by the 1940s the aesthetic use
of depth of field had become increasingly common. Observational documentaries flourished in the 1960s and '70s and almost defined what
it meant to make a documentary, at least in the United States. The fly-
on-the-wall quality of looking in on contemporaneous events as they
unfold in front of the camera marked the documentary of the 1960s
as vividly as voice-over narration and the skillful assembly of evidentiary images marked the documentary of the 1930s and '40s. French
cinema of the 1930s possessed a poetic, impressionistic quality, which,
in the 1940s, yielded to a more theatrical and literary model, the model
against which the French New Wave directors subsequently rebelled
with their anarchic, looser style. The **French New Wave** took shape
at the end of the 1950s and beginning of the 1960s with the first films
of Jean-Luc Godard, François Truffaut, Claude Chabrol, and others.
Their films broke sharply with the poetic and literary traditions to cel-

ebrate a raw immediacy and to pay overt tribute to American genre films by largely neglected directors like Sam Fuller, Nicholas Ray, and Phil Karlson.

Delineating historical periods for study can lead to the discovery of stylistic commonalities as well as of shared social concerns that relate to that particular moment. It is often by identifying periods when transformations occur that a previous period of consistency becomes more evident. The question of what factors combine to bring about a transition from one period to another can also prove a rich area of inquiry. A more formulaic and stylistically conservative mode of film-making, socialist realism, for example, followed the heyday of the great Soviet films of the silent era. Rather than simply noting this shift, exploring how and why it occurred can yield valuable insights into how aesthetic sensibilities adapt to different social environments and how different social environments create opportunities for some approaches and impose constraints on others.

National cinemas, as the example of German expressionism suggests, are also a source of stylistic differences. Some qualities of American cinema in general—dynamic characters, efficient editing to propel the story forward, brilliant staging of action to maximize its impact, ingenious use of special effects, the centrality of the star system—correlate to an aesthetic that values bold characterization, vivid problems, and a high-velocity style of engagement with the viewer. That such qualities may correlate with aspects of American culture is a virtual certainty, but the specifics of how this correlation takes place, what doubts or subversions may get raised about the value of these qualities, requires more careful analysis than generalizations about national character or a national culture can support. Comparative studies of national cinemas will also make clear that what seems like a natural and obvious way to make movies in one context does not necessarily apply in another. Bollywood films, for example, although hugely popular in India and clearly modeled on many aspects of Hollywood cinema, also depart from it significantly, most notably in the potpourri quality of most of the films: they contain an amalgam of drama, action, melodrama, and musical numbers that seem wildly incongruous to most American viewers.

INDIVIDUAL STYLE AND THE AUTEUR THEORY

Individual style distinguishes the work of one director from that of others, even if they work in the same genre, period, movement, or national cinema. The world of Ridley Scott, for example (*Blade Runner* [1982], *Thelma and Louise* [1991], *Gladiator* [2000], and *American Gangster* [2007]), is a boldly stylized, visually dense, thematically vivid world of sharp conflicts and intense struggles, whereas the world of Hal Hartley (*Trust* [1990, UK/U.S.], *Flirt* [1995, U.S./Germany/Japan], *Henry Fool* [1997], and *The Unbelievable Truth* [1989]) is a casually designed, visually loose, thematically ambiguous world of everyday events and unexpected, often ironic complications.

Thelma and Louise creates a visual world of heightened emotion and stylized action. The women's reply to a male chauvinist truck driver isn't to have a discussion with him: it is to shoot at his truck until it explodes in flames. Scott stages the action so that the women become vivid, heroic icons, clearly set off against their environment, acting boldly, standing defiantly. By contrast, Hal Hartley locates his characters in an environment that subsumes them. They coexist with furniture and decorations and do not seem to command extraordinary attention. Their dialogue is more elliptical than decisive, turning the same points over and over. Hartley's characters explore their situations as if any change would be a surprise, whereas Scott's characters explore their situations knowing that change is inevitable. The visual style of the two filmmakers differs, but each conveys the filmmaker's distinct social attitude toward the world he constructs.

The individual style of directors has been taken up most actively under the banner of the **auteur theory**. More a matter of emphasis than a true theory, **auteur theory** began with French critics who saw recurrent patterns and themes in the work of Hollywood directors whom other critics regarded as highly competent journeymen carrying out a wide variety of assignments in different genres. The discovery of underlying themes and consistent stylistic tendencies among films in different genres by the same director became evidence that some studio directors qualified as artists: they pursued personal preoccupations and developed an individual style. Among the directors championed by auteur theory were John Ford (*Stagecoach* [1939], *The Searchers* [1956]), Howard Hawks (*Only Angels Have Wings* [1939], *Bringing Up Baby* [1938]), Anthony Mann (*Man of the West* [1958], *T-Men* [1947]), and Nicholas Ray (*In a Lonely Place* [1950], *Rebel without a Cause* [1955]).

Alfred Hitchcock is another director the auteurists championed, less for his popularity and brilliant creation of suspense than for the deeper implications of that suspense for the viewer. Auteur critics pointed out that the suspense usually revolves around issues of guilt and punishment, anxiety and conscience, as well as the more conventional plot devices of danger and escape. Characters are put to the test morally as well as physically, and by getting the audience to identify with characters who commit criminal or evil deeds, as Hitchcock does in *Psycho*, *Marnie* (1964), and *Strangers on a Train* (1951), he puts the audience to a moral test as well. The result is a set of thematic preoccupations and a distinctive individual style that goes beyond his own clever self-promotion as "the Master of Suspense."

In one scene of Hitchcock's *Psycho*, for example, Norman attempts to dispose of incriminating evidence (an automobile). Marion's death implicates Norman and his mother. But point-of-view editing leads the viewer to identify with Norman's visual point of view. Hitchcock subtly draws the viewer into an alliance with Norman: we, too, hope the car will disappear despite the injustice that may result. Hitchcock frequently uses point-of-view shots to create identification with characters whose actions might be readily condemned from an objective perspective. Hitchcock encourages the viewer to root for the character, despite moral objections that might arise. This becomes part of his films' allure. By such means, Hitchcock established a distinct niche within the genres of suspense, thriller, and horror films.

In contrast to Hitchcock, in films such as *Stranger than Paradise* (1984, U.S./West Germany), *Mystery Train* (1989), and *Dead Man* (1995, U.S./Germany), Jim Jarmusch builds a world with minimal suspense using long takes, seemingly mundane dialogue, protracted scenes with "dead time" in which nothing of great importance occurs, and **fades to black** between scenes to increase the sense of separation and lack of a strong dramatic arc to the story. (A **fade** is a gradual elimination of light from a shot so that the image becomes darker. A **fade to black** eventually eliminates all light so that the screen becomes black.) Jarmusch does not invite audience identification with characters and the morality of their actions to any significant degree. The viewer observes the characters go about their lives with a sense of emotional detachment but with a strong sense of curiosity about the eccentricity and offbeat sensibilities they possess. They do not typically belong to the middle-class world Hitchcock's work focuses on, but to marginal and ethnic **subcultures** that seem to possess their own rhythm, perspective, and sensibility. (A **subculture** is a distinct cultural group living within a larger society. The Beats of the 1950s and the hippies of the 1960s were two subcultures based on a rejection of the norms of middle-class, American life. Different religious and ethnic groups that form a minority within the larger society often have a subculture of their own.) Within a given subculture, prevailing values and beliefs may be at odds with those of the larger society, often leading to various forms of conflict.

Interpretative Goals

The many purposes of storytelling invite different forms of interpretative engagement. One aspect of interpretation acknowledges that a film is not exclusively an analytic or an emotional experience. Films fuse emotional, intellectual, and ideological elements to produce a unique form of encounter. What does it feel like to enter into an imaginary world presented from a particular point of view or perspective? What is the filmmaker's perspective or attitude toward the world and characters we see? How does the viewer's understanding of things change as the fictive world of a narrative film grows in complexity over the course of a film? What does it feel like to embark on a perilous journey to cast an ominous ring into a fiery cauldron in *The Lord of the Rings* trilogy (Peter Jackson, 2001-2003, New Zealand/U.S.), or to experience the world as a heartbroken but tough-skinned lover now trying to start his life all over again in a remote corner of the world in *Casablanca* (Michael Curtiz, 1942)?

Broadly speaking, the interpretation of narrative films lends itself to a dual formal-social analysis. Usually one of these two emphases predominates but reference to the other contributes to the richness of the interpretation. The use of a dual analysis that asks both what does a film do that is conventional and what does it do that is innovative in formal terms and what does it do that is distorting or manipulative relative to social reality versus what does it do that is revelatory has considerable value. Films are seldom monolithic in their effect. Being aware of both expressive technique and social implications helps the critic respond to the full complexity of a given work. Some of the main subdivisions of a formal-social analysis include the following emphases.

Exploring the Formal Context

THE MODE OF PRODUCTION AND THE NATION-STATE AS FORMAL CONTEXTS The mode of production (**artisanal**, industrial, or in-between) can serve as the focus of investigation in terms of its formal structure and qualities. (**Artisanal production** occurs outside the context of a full-blown film industry. A filmmaker or the producer of a film marshals the resources to make one film and then does the same thing again for the next film, using a mix of funding sources. Artisanal filmmaking receives further discussion in Chapter 6.) A formal study of the studio system itself might differentiate the grittier, down-to-earth tone of Warner Brothers films in the 1930s and '40s from the glossier, more escapist films of MGM during this same period.

A production company or producer can exert an influence not only on production values and content but on style and tone as well. Jerry Bruckheimer, for example, is famous for his emphasis on non-stop action films such as the *Pirates of the Caribbean* series (Gore Verbinski, 2003–2007), *Black Hawk Down* (Ridley Scott, 2001), *Gone in 60 Seconds* (Dominic Sena, 2000), and *Armageddon* (Michael Bay, 1998), in which character development is secondary to highly orchestrated, spectacular action. He clearly plays a large role in shaping the tone and pace of the films he produces regardless of the cast or the director. Producer Ismail Merchant, on the other hand, worked closely with director James Ivory to create a series of tasteful period costume films that dwelled on the psychological complexity of cross-cultural encounters rather than action and adventure, such as *Jefferson in Paris* (1995), *The White Countess* (2005, UK/U.S./Germany/China), and *Howards End* (1992, UK).

Governments, in their role as defenders and promoters of national culture, can also play an important role in shaping the mode of production, as Chapter 6 demonstrates in greater detail. In exchange for subsidies and incentives, a government may establish guidelines that have an impact on the style of films made under its sponsorship. It may expressly try to define ways in which a film should exemplify national qualities.

Canada, for example, uses a point system that requires a fixed number of points before a film is considered Canadian and eligible for financial incentives (one or two points go for **above-the-line** personnel: a Canadian producer, director, editor, or star each adds points). Foreign investors soon discovered they could gain tax advantages by hiring Canadians to make films that had nothing to do with Canada as such. This approach provoked considerable debate, since it brought a great deal of film production to Canada but did not necessarily enrich the repertoire of films that addressed Canadian themes and issues. This debate tied into broader, long-standing debates about the distinctiveness of Canadian identity in relation to the United States, especially outside the French-speaking province of Quebec.

FILM HISTORY AS A FORMAL SYSTEM   Examining the formal context for any given film also involves situating it in relation to other films. In contrast to the films-in-history approach that stresses the social context of a film's production, this approach examines the history of film itself. How has cinema changed over time? Any student of film as a medium will want to learn about its development, just as students of the novel or symphony want to know more about how these forms have altered over time. What role, for example, do technological innovations, creative individuals, institutional structures, and audience expectations play in the changing nature of film form?

The introduction of sound in 1928 made a rich array of new aesthetic innovations possible. A key debate revolved around whether sound should be **contrapuntal**, adding informational or emotional qualities that elaborated or commented on the visual image, or **synchronous**, emphasizing in a more unadulterated way what characters said and what sounds arose at the actual moment of shooting the scene.

Sergei Eisenstein was a strong advocate of contrapuntal sound. He argued that synchronous sound was simply redundant and demonstrated little creative control by the director. Hollywood films, however, quickly adopted sync sound and reserved contrapuntal effects for the music track. Here sound could amplify the emotional tone of a scene or, sometimes, undercut the solemnity of characters in a comedy or the grandeur of spectacles in parodies like *Spaceballs* (Mel Brooks, 1987).

Changes in form, style, and structure unveil new possibilities for the medium. Italian **neorealism**, for example, clearly arose from the historical ashes of Italy's defeat at the end of World War II, but also from the desire to construct a different kind of narrative, one that focused on everyday life and "little people" who endured hardship outside the spotlight reserved for public figures and historic events. Films like *Umberto D* (Vittorio De Sica, 1952, Italy), *Rome, Open City* (Roberto Rossellini, 1945, Italy), *Paisà* (Roberto Rossellini, 1946, Italy), *Bicycle Thieves* (Vittorio De Sica, 1948, Italy), and *La terra trema* (Luchino Visconti, 1948, Italy), with their location shooting, non-actors, and low-key, quotidian events, broke with the tradition of the polished studio film.

Neorealist directors generally composed the image in an extremely simple fashion; the events were those that a passerby might have glimpsed. The tormented, interior states of mind that took visual form in German expressionism is nowhere to be found. Interior distress only played out in the physical gestures and facial expressions of characters, who maintained a predominantly stoic attitude toward their hardships and tried to make the best of things.

Umberto D epitomizes many neorealist qualities. It tells the story of an elderly gentleman who strives to maintain his dignity despite his loss of financial security. His pension is not enough to pay the rent. His struggle to maintain appearances is at times comical, at times desperate. The director, Vittorio De Sica, captures much of the complex human dynamic that flows between characters who cannot acknowledge the full range of their emotional and economic needs. De Sica shoots in lingering long takes and utilizes deep focus. The relation of character to environment is thereby given considerable stress.

The humanist tone or attitude of the neorealist directors like De Sica had considerable influence on world cinema. **Humanism** stresses the common bonds of love, trust, labor, hopes and dreams that can bind people to a common destiny. Humanism divorces this compassionate view from any explicit religious doctrine—it is a secular view of the world—although the spiritual qualities of tolerance, charity, and forgiveness are often quite pronounced. It can be thought of as the opposite of a cynical, ironic, or satirical attitude.

Neorealism, in short, developed a distinct style that broke with narrative conventions and created a fresh, revelatory view of life as it is lived. On the other side of the interpretative coin, critics have noted that elements of sentimentality often crept in as well—through melodramatic music and the frequent use of children to elicit emotional responses more forcefully. Their example gave inspiration to similar approaches elsewhere, from the French New Wave of the late 1950s to the American independent cinema of the 1980s. Formal film histories stress these shifts in narrative structure and emphasize them over socio-political factors that also contributed to the shift.

The dominant model of film history itself changes with time. For a long time the standard history told of an early period of fumbling efforts to figure out how to use this new moving picture invention that finally jelled into the narrative fiction film in the 1910s, epitomized by D.W. Griffith's *The Birth of a Nation*. More recent studies, however, have described early cinema as a complex, multifaceted endeavor in its own right. It had different assumptions and conventions from present-day mainstream films, and therefore a logic and coherence all its own.

Many early short films, for example, functioned as demonstrations more than as stories: they sought to show distinct, strange, or unusual things without any desire to formulate a story about what was shown.

Whether it was a coronation or a battle, a foot race or life on urban streets, these films brought the wonders of the world, large and small, to an audience that had never seen anything quite like this before. They fulfilled their own, distinct goals quite well rather than serving solely as the spawning ground for narrative film.

AUTEURS AND GENRES FROM A FORMAL PERSPECTIVE Interpretative goals can also involve questions of directors, or auteurs, and genres. From the point of view of auteur theory, key questions involve identifying the thematic preoccupations and stylistic consistencies that characterize an auteur's work. Authorship derives from an analysis of the film itself rather than from biographical or autobiographical background information or from the director's statements about intentions. For the auteur critic, Alfred Hitchcock holds less interest for his personal biography and how it may reveal aspects of British or American culture. Instead his films are revered for the way in which they consistently treat issues of mistaken identity, the innocent man accused of a crime who is compelled to prove his innocence, a fascination with women as alluring figures who threaten male autonomy, and a rich exploration of the moral ambiguity that point-of-view shots can generate.

Genre criticism looks at films in relation to the various genres as formal systems of conventions and expectations. (Genre film is the subject of Chapter 7.) Criticism may try to identify the distinct formal qualities that characterize a genre or to single out exceptional examples of a given genre. Interpretations may ask what a genre is, what films belong to it, how and why it arose, what formal conventions distinguish it, or how individual films adapt these conventions in innovative ways. Frequently, genre study couples with auteur study, since many of the auteurs of American cinema, such as John Ford, Preston Sturges, Vincente Minelli, Martin Scorsese, Todd Haynes, the Coen brothers, and Ridley Scott, work in established genres but inflect them with their own distinctive thematic preoccupations and stylistic traits.

Sometimes, the critical perspective on a filmmaker's status as an auteur changes over time. For example, early film histories considered Howard Hawks a noteworthy studio director. He made a long series of terrific films that enjoyed popular acclaim over several decades. Among them were *Twentieth Century* (1934), *Bringing Up Baby*, *His Girl Friday* (1940), *To Have and Have Not* (1944), *The Big Sleep* (1946), *Red River* (1948), *Monkey Business* (1952), *Gentlemen Prefer Blondes* (1953), and *Rio Bravo* (1959). He gave the studios, and the audience, what they wanted. But he was not considered an artist or auteur of the same caliber as a Jean Renoir or Sergei Eisenstein. His overall output of films lacked the type of stylistic and thematic consistency found among the great auteurs of the cinema.

French critics of the 1950s took a different view. They argued that there were indeed consistencies, even preoccupations, in the Hawksian universe, and that these were not trivial. His narrative plots frequently involved a band of men who had to test their manhood by confronting danger with a stoic manner and a cool hand. Panic, fear, insecurity, doubt, almost any emotion at all, apart from unquestioning loyalty to the group, was anathema. Hawks's style was as unassuming, straightforward, and workmanlike as his characters. It belonged not simply to realism but to a Hemingway-like world of stoic men and resilient women.

In a groundbreaking essay on Hawks, Jacques Rivette, who went on to become a French New Wave director in the 1960s, compared what seemed to be a frivolous comedy, *Monkey Business*, about a professor who reverts to infantile behavior thanks to a magic potion, with Josef von Sternberg's great classic, *The Blue Angel* (*Der blaue Engel*, 1930, Germany), a comparison designed to goad those who were automatically dismissive of Hollywood entertainment into a reconsideration. Rivette asserted that "The measure of Hawks's films is intelligence, but a *pragmatic* intelligence, applied directly to the physical world, an intelligence which takes its efficacy from the precise viewpoint of a profession or from some form of human activity at grips with the universe and anxious for conquest. Marlowe in *The Big Sleep* practices a profession just as a scientist or a flier does."

It remained for another critic, Robin Wood, to point out that Hawks's comedies were the inverse of his dramas. In the dramas men strove to prove that they were "good enough" in terms of the professional codes of conduct that governed male conduct. Dean Martin had to sober up and become a straight-shooting deputy again when Wayne needed him, for example, in *Rio Bravo*. But in the comedies, men lose their bearings; the all-male group is nowhere to be seen; women emerge as discombobulating forces—nowhere more vividly than in the figure of Marilyn Monroe in *Monkey Business* or in the daffy, uncontrollable eccentric played by Katherine Hepburn in *Bringing Up Baby*. The flip side of a rugged, professional masculinity, it turns out, is reversion to a primitive, infantile state in which men become the unwitting playmates of impulsive, carefree women who run circles around them.

EXPLORING THE SOCIAL CONTEXT

Interpretations that stress the social context can extend across a wide range of approaches. These approaches acknowledge the integral relationship of form to content so that reference to formal qualities as well as social issues informs the criticism. Understanding how expressive cinematic techniques give distinct representation to social issues and conflicts and engage the viewer effectively allows a discussion of the social context to remain sensitive to film as a unique medium with its own expressive techniques. Such approaches avoid a concentration on plot at the expense of style or form.

Narrative films give abstract issues (poverty, greed, loyalty, miscommunication, evil) concrete form. No one can film greed, evil, or loyalty as such—they are generalized concepts or abstractions represented succinctly by words—but a good filmmaker can find a concrete situation that will embody what a particular form of greed, evil, or loyalty looks like when acted out by specific characters. This allows viewers to gain a visceral experience of what these abstract qualities feel like in concrete instances. Questions arise. Does this involvement foster a social attitude or political perspective toward what happens? How does it relate to the historical moment when the film was made or the time in which the film is set? Does it achieve resolution in a plausible or implausible way? In terms of a dual formal-social analysis, a viewer may decide that a film identifies real, pressing issues in a fresh, insightful way but resolves them in an unrealistic or implausible way? Both the insight into the issue and the sleight of hand involved in its resolution merit discussion.

IDEOLOGICAL INTERPRETATION   Over and over in this book, we will explore the ideological dimension of narrative. Through this endeavor we attempt to better understand the ways in which a narrative or type of narrative—a western, say, or a film noir— proposes an imaginary or mythic solution to an actual problem. Does the resolution the narrative achieves come at the cost of magically making problems "go away"—for the story—when they continue to persist in reality? And even if the resolution involves sleight of hand, does it still provide an imaginative way to address real social problems, which, in turn, can have a bearing on how audiences perceive and confront actual problems? Ideological criticism has considerable importance in relation to questions of gender and ethnicity. The representation of women and minority group members often raises issues of stereotyping. Critical analysis can involve identifying any distortions or misrepresentations that occur, examining what function these distortions play in the narrative, and perhaps balancing them against other aspects of the film. A stereotype may, for example, serve to indicate how a character perceives women or a minority group rather than how the filmmaker does. The director may signal that his attitude toward the stereotype differs from that of the character.

In *Charlie Wilson's War* (Mike Nichols, 2007, U.S./Germany), the opening scene has Charlie Wilson in a hot tub with several stereotypical Playboy Bunny–type women: blond, fun-loving, ill-informed, but very attractive. They are the type of women Charlie enjoys spending time with, but Mike Nichols, the director, makes it clear that they are not the only type of women he will meet and that Joann Herring (Julia Roberts), a smart, aggressive, powerful woman who knows what she wants and how to get it, is a far more challenging character for him. The stereotypical image of women with which the film begins is vigorously counterbalanced by a strong, intriguing woman who proves crucial to Charlie's own development as a character. The filmmaker provides his own critique of the stereotypical image of women that he includes but does not endorse.

SYMPTOMATIC INTERPRETATION   Another related approach is to give attention to the ways in which a story serves as a symptom of common social tensions or conflicts. The film explores a concrete situation, but may stand for or be a symptom of a more widespread or deep-rooted problem. The film may not overtly address larger issues like masculinity, patriotism, or paranoia, but it nonetheless might demonstrate how they erupt at a local level, in specific characters, just as a patient might display headaches, upset stomach, and fever as signs of an underlying medical condition. The patient, or film, cannot say why they have these symptoms. They do not consciously set out to produce or display them, and they can't control them. The interpretive goal then is to identify what the symptoms refer to. Identifying symptoms is less a question of proving one and only one cause for a given form of behavior than of finding associations that can be plausibly traced to the larger social context while also being firmly anchored in the actual actions and events represented in the film.

Consider Arthur Penn's western, *The Left-Handed Gun* (1958), from a script by Gore Vidal. This film added a layer of neurotic disturbance to the image of the western hero. William Bonney (Paul Newman) is a teenager eager to please and to avenge the murder of his patrician benefactor, a rancher with a kind heart and gentle way. Bonney displays an attraction to violence and death that makes him impatient with the normal course of justice, but he also remains unaware of these darker currents inside himself. He throws the world around him into turmoil, compelling Pat Garrett, a man who regards Bonney as a son, to confront him in a fatal showdown. Bonney's behavior is clearly symptomatic of dangerous tendencies at an individual level; more open to debate is the extent to which Penn, and Vidal, are calling the tradition of the western hero itself into question. Are they suggesting through Bonney's destructive ways that this tradition is itself symptomatic of a masculine disorder that confuses vigilante-style violence with social justice?

NATIONAL CINEMAS   One of the most frequently examined aspects of the social context is the nation-state. The critic might ask, for example, how does the film fit within the framework of a national cinema and national history? This approach was applied to the discussion of *The Birth of a Nation* in the Introduction and of *The Cabinet of Dr. Caligari* in this chapter. In what ways does a given film share qualities and preoccupations with other films from the same time and place, for example, Britain in the 1950s or Germany in the 1970s?

To take one example, *The Holy Mountain* (*Der heilige Berg*, Arnold Fanck, 1926, Germany) was one of several "mountain films" that appeared in Germany during the 1920s. It was in this genre that Leni Riefenstahl made a name for herself as an actress. She played bold but innocent characters who were magically drawn to the mountains. Critics like Siegfried Kracauer, in his classic study, *From Caligari to Hitler*, linked this cycle of films to a social movement in which middle-class

Germans, especially males, celebrated the rugged outdoor world and the mountain terrain in particular as an escape from the bureaucratic and social regimentation of a society in the midst of a major economic depression. The mountains provided an escape that could purify the soul and reaffirm the spirit. Kracauer and others saw this longing for transcendence and redemption as fertile soil for the growth of extremist movements such as the National Socialist Party, headed by Adolf Hitler. His book examines how the style and structure of various types of German silent films present a vivid feeling of what it was like to live in a period of high national aspirations yoked to limited socioeconomic opportunity. Others have taken up similar questions in relation to periods and topics such as Hollywood films in the era of the Vietnam War or British "kitchen sink" films of working class life and struggle from the 1950s.

FILM IN HISTORY How do films respond to or represent both an historical period—if they are set in the past—and the time of their own making—whether set in the past or not?

Citizen Kane is commonly seen as one of the great accomplishments of cinema, not only for its innovative use of deep focus cinematography, but also for its exploration of the flawed nature of a man of public stature. This was not simply a thematic point, made in dialogue or character behavior, but also embedded in the narrative structure that wove five different stories about Kane into one overlapping and sometimes contradictory portrait. This attempt to construct a biography from fragmented, disparate parts—rather than to pave a single road forward from birth to death—draws on modernist experimentations with form that had begun in the first decades of the twentieth century. It stresses fragmentation over unity, ambiguity over clarity, uncertainty over certainty, mixed motives over unshakable principles.

But *Citizen Kane* owes a debt to its time socially as well as formally: the story of Charles Foster Kane has uncanny parallels with the actual life of William Randolph Hearst, who also founded a media empire and had a mistress (the actress Marion Davies). Screenwriter Herman Mankiewicz and director-screenwriter Orson Welles clearly altered aspects of his life such as Hearst's close relationship to his mother, which, in the film, becomes a relationship of loss and separation, but the parallels were unmistakable at the time of the film's initial release. Further, the story of Kane's life is patched together by Thompson, the reporter for "News on the March," a newsreel in the spirit of the news-reels produced by Henry Luce's rival media empire, Time-Life. These weekly newsreels, in the days before television, covered current events from a conservative perspective and played routinely in movie theaters across the country. One may well have played in the theaters that showed *Citizen Kane* itself in 1941. It is this fictitious news organiza-tion that now sets out to learn the meaning of "Rosebud," Kane's dying word, to produce its own version of Kane's life from the stories told by Kane's friends, mentors, and lovers.

These references to the time when the film was made take on yet fuller significance. Time-Life and the *March of Time* newsreels were the successor to the empire built by William Randolph Hearst. *Citi-zen Kane*, can, from this perspective, be seen as a story about the growth and development of the American news media, beginning with the flamboyant, personality-driven Kane (Hearst) and ending with the anonymous, corporate (Time-Life) team player Thompson. An earlier mode of flamboyant journalism succumbs to a more imper-sonal mode of faceless reporting, and it is this latter mode and its "News on the March" newsreel that gets to tell the story of Kane's life. Locating *Citizen Kane* as a film in history involves exploring and developing these historical links to actual people and events and then assessing what Welles makes of them. (He clearly sides more strongly with Hearst than with Luce.)

When placing a particular film in history, tracing the formal devel-opment of film as an artistic medium becomes secondary to exploring the relationship between films made in a given period and the prevailing social issues of that time. Since the 1980s, for example, the world socioeconomic system has moved beyond the postwar model of competing nation-states divided into a first world of capitalism, a second world of communism, and a third world of developing nations to become one, complex, interlocking global system. The actual mechanisms that guide and control such a system often appear intangible and elusive, more remote and ill-defined than those that structure the nation-state. The individual may seem lost, without a meaningful voice, and subject to unseen but powerful forces whose principles and goals are not obvious. In this case, films of paranoia such as *The Parallax View* (Alan J. Pakula, 1974), *Three Days of the Condor* (Sydney Pollack, 1975), *Videodrome* (David Cronenberg, 1982, Canada), *JFK* (Oliver Stone, 1991), *Syriana* (Stephen Gaghan, 2005), *Babel* (Alejandro González Iñárritu, 2006, France/U.S./Mexico), and *The Manchurian Candidate* (both versions: John Frankenheimer, 1962; Jonathan Demme, 2004) may serve as symptomatic evidence of nebulous but disturbing transformations brought about by economic globalization. A critical analysis might try to identify how these or other films convey a sense of intangible forces that shape events without taking definite shape themselves.

INTERPRETATION AND THE MODE OF PRODUCTION Another social context that invites interpretative effort is the mode of production, the socioeconomic framework in which a film is produced. An artisanal model tends to grant considerable latitude to the director so that a highly idiosyncratic tone or perspective on the subject matter may emerge in the finished film. Films that take more risks formally or politically are also likely to emerge from the artisanal mode of production. Gillo Pontecorvo's classic work of revolutionary struggle, *The Battle of Algiers* (1966, Algeria/Italy), for example, relied exclusively on non-traditional, non-studio funding for its production; its radical politics would not attract mainstream funding.

The institutional context of a film's production can be examined in terms of its general structure, basic assumptions, and underlying goals. The Production Code and the Ratings system, discussed in Chapter 6, demonstrate how the mode of production introduces constraints and limitations. These constraints often become an incentive to find ways to address real issues and conflicts obliquely, in terms of their symptoms and effects, rather than directly. How are innovative forms of filmmaking related to the constraints a filmmaker must contend with? In what ways do constraints actually prevent some topics, themes, or actions from being represented, and what are the consequences of this? The treatment of sexuality and violence in American cinema is a perennial topic of debate in these terms.

AUDIENCES, RECEPTION, AND INTERPRETATION   Another important social context involves the audience. Different audiences, in different places, with different backgrounds and experience, and at different points in time, do not understand the same film the same way. What exactly accounts for these differences, and how might different interpretations be related to specific characteristics of the audience? Carol Clover's *Men, Women and Chainsaws*, for example, took up the question of how teenage men and women understand slasher films differently. Another study asked how audiences could believe in the realism of the television show *Dallas* even though it centered on the highly melodramatic intrigues of the rich and powerful and bore little resemblance to the day-to-day realities of its audience's actual lives. Blaxploitation films raise questions about how black audiences see the characters as positive role models even if the roles possess all of the implausibilities usually associated with action heroes of hyper-masculine prowess and cunning. Though highly exaggerated in these superheroes, these traits had far greater appeal than the traditional stereotypes that denigrated black males in various ways. Most white, mainstream critics dismissed the films as mediocre genre products, but some African American audiences, especially males, ignored the superhero stereotypes, since they could take genuine pleasure from the sight of powerful black characters commanding the movie screen.

Shaft (Gordon Parks, 1971) is generally considered the model for a wave of **blaxploitation films** that featured African American males in the role of the heroic tough guy who defeats an assortment of villains, usually drug dealers, pimps, and mobsters. (A more offbeat version of this genre is *Sweet Sweetback's Baadasssss Song*, also released in 1971.) In the original *Shaft* (two film sequels and a TV series followed), private eye John Shaft (Richard Roundtree) has to rescue the daughter of a gang lord. This provides a perfect pretext for a journey through a criminal underworld in which Shaft must repeatedly display his prowess. It allows for an episodic string of action scenes and for a great deal of masculine posturing. The combination proved enormously popular, especially among black audiences and with young males of various races. Shaft was their hero. For African American audiences he stood up to "the man" (at one point he refers to the "honky government" he has to deal with); he possessed the articulateness and the cool of the classic western hero, the street smarts of the hard-boiled detective, and the sexual magnetism of a James Bond. The exaggerated masculinity that seemed stereotypical to some mattered less to others than the vivid presence of a black male actor dishing out rough justice to anyone who crossed his path. The very different ways in which difference audiences understood and interpreted *Shaft* can be as important a part of the film's effect as its formal structure or its generic borrowings.

THE INTERPRETATION OF SIGNIFICANT ABSENCES One final interpretative tactic that is particularly useful as a way to examine the social context is to ask what a film does *not* address. What is absent in a way that suggests denial or repression rather than omission or irrelevance? Criminals who got away with their crimes, sex outside of marriage, homosexual relationships, miscegenation, and drug use, for example, were all absent from Hollywood films from the 1930s up to the 1950s. These were not accidental omissions or the result of the subject choices of individual directors. The absences stemmed from the standards set by the Production Code (discussed in Chapter 6) that banned many subjects outright. Since these themes were absent, critics might well ignore them; but an analysis could also ask in what ways filmmakers skirted the edges of these topics, or how the Production Code Association (created by the major studios) actually operated in detail, perhaps looking at the internal studio correspondence that surrounded the production of a specific film or set of films.

Examples: *Vertigo* and *Bicycle Thieves*

A classic Hollywood film such as Alfred Hitchcock's *Vertigo* (1958) begins with an initial disturbance: the hero, Scottie Ferguson (James Stewart), cannot successfully apprehend a criminal when he experiences vertigo in the midst of his pursuit. His lack of stable orientation and sense of failure is the initial problem that drives the narrative forward. A shipping magnate hires Scottie to follow his wife, but once again vertigo makes pursuit impossible, and he finds himself unable to prevent her death. Scottie slides into despondency only to be revived when he encounters another woman who resembles the dead wife. His relationship with her plunges him further into dementia and disorientation but ultimately becomes the source of his recovery. The film concludes by resolving its initial lack, with Scottie regaining his stability in psychological as well as moral terms. Women, and Scottie's voyeuristic, obsessive relationship to them, become the means of doing so.

Vertigo adopts a dual plot structure in which courtship simultaneously becomes a means of therapeutic recovery for the hero. Recovery allows him to solve a murder mystery. The film explores sexual politics, voyeurism in particular, and in doing so addresses key issues of desire and the function of women as temptresses and possible sources of salvation (for the troubled male). Hitchcock's style leads viewers to identify with Scottie. His obsession with a woman whose greatest attraction is her resemblance to a dead woman galvanizes him like nothing else. Is this where misguided desire leads—to the brink of necrophilia—and is this the fate of female characters—to be phantoms, ghosts of the dead, in the eyes of male pursuers? Hitchcock leaves the viewer to ponder these questions.

Hitchcock's focus excludes socioeconomic factors to dwell on psychic states of mind as if they arose from a terrain that did not include issues of class or social status. He also presents an all-white world as if this were a natural representation of American society, even though *Vertigo* is set in San Francisco, a principal port for Chinese immigrants and home to a significant Chinatown. A symptomatic analysis might explore the exclusion of ethnic minorities here while recognizing that this film is far from unique in that sense. Such an analysis might also examine the uneven power dynamic between the parties involved. The observer strips the person who is observed and worshipped of her autonomy as an individual. When and why does such a dynamic arise? Is Scottie's voyeurism more characteristic of men than women, and, if so, why? (The concepts of fetishism and voyeurism are discussed further in Chapter 10.)

By contrast, *Bicycle Thieves* makes psychic distress a direct corollary of economic upheaval. (The original title in the United States was *The Bicycle Thief*, in keeping with an American emphasis on the individual hero. The Italian title is more accurately translated as *Bicycle Thieves*. This title helps link Ricci and the man who takes his bike to others like them and to the broader social problems facing postwar Italy.) The beginning establishes the postwar world of Rome (1948) as one of poverty and unemployment. The lack or problem is a collective one, but it finds its dramatic center in the story of one man's effort to provide for his family. De Sica uses long shots to populate the frame with dozens of hungry, dispirited men, each one hoping against hope that he will land a job. The main character, Antonio Ricci, eventually does get a prized job putting up movie posters for American films. For a moment he thinks his worries are over, but he soon learns he must have a bike to do the job. The lack of a bicycle spurs action: he and his wife pawn their bedsheets to get a bike, only to have it stolen by someone even more desperate than he is.

From the outset a disruptive lack (of a job, a bicycle) is built into this realistic portrait of a defeated society. The scenes are shot on location; the performers are not trained actors. Lamberto Maggiorani, who plays Antonio, had been unemployed and was working in a factory when De Sica cast him. Like Allakariallak, the Inuit who took on the role of Nanook in *Nanook of the North* (Robert Flaherty, 1922), with no previous training as an actor Maggiorani draws on his own experience to present a character who serves as a composite or representative character in postwar Italy.

The middle of *Bicycle Thieves* prolongs the story to develop character and heighten suspense. Detours and delays occur. The viewer identifies with Antonio's thwarted desire and becomes emotionally involved in his struggle to succeed. De Sica broadens our sympathies when Antonio finds the thief and his son gets a policeman but they soon discover that the thief is in even worse straits than they are. Ricci loses his one chance to recover his bicycle and keep his job. This experience intensifies the sense of an entire world in which desperation abounds and no public institution has the capacity to restore hope.

The ending refers back to the beginning and in a limited way resolves the disruption or lack that launched the narrative. We find Ricci driven to the point where he commits an act of desperation himself, repeating the crime of the man who stole his bike, but now doing so in full sight of his son, a boy who reveres him as only a son can. The attempted theft fails. In fact, at the end of the film the initial problems all remain, as they did in Italian postwar life for many years. We have seen two men steal bicycles, but neither is depicted as a criminal. Ricci's humiliation in front of his son points to the need for resolution at a broader, more collective level. Individual actions cannot resolve a social problem, and this insight is what allows the film to achieve a bittersweet sense of closure. Bruno and Antonio have deepened their bond, but economic hardship continues to loom large.

The ambiguity of this ending represents the type of complex resolution that is more common in art cinema than in mainstream films. To have the hero fail, let alone experience profound humiliation in front of his son, is a bold step that many filmmakers would hesitate to take. *Bicycle Thieves* converts a search for a physical object into a social portrait and spiritual odyssey. Whereas Scottie's search for a missing woman turns into an interior tale of personal obsession that draws the hero into an intrigue centering on deception and murder, Ricci's search for his missing bicycle turns into a social tale of postwar desperation that pushes his sense of dignity and honor to its limits. The film reveals how something is missing from postwar Italian society, but this lack turns out to be more far-reaching than a single bicycle.

Part II

THE SOCIAL CONTEXT

5

THREE FUNDAMENTAL STYLES: REALISM, MODERNISM, AND POSTMODERNISM

Realism as the Cornerstone of Film Style

Forms and styles change with time, but the times also change. Art inevitably draws from and responds to the historical moment of its creation. This relation between film and its historical context is true not only of realist cinema and Hollywood genres, but also of European art cinema, Third World cinema, the avant-garde, and documentary film. As the discussion of poetics, rhetoric, and narrative also indicated, individual films can belong to multiple stylistic categories. Several of these, from film genres to national cinemas, received consideration in Chapter 4. This chapter looks at the three overarching stylistic schools into which almost all art from the mid-nineteenth to the early twenty-first century falls: realist, modernist, and postmodern. These categories embrace film as much as they do novels, plays, painting, and architecture.

To see art shift from one major stylistic school to another raises the question of why. A basic premise is that major shifts involve both a formal component (the aesthetic possibilities may seem played out or exhausted; a new way of seeing things is called for to reinvigorate the imagination) and a social component (society changes and as it does, the means of representation best equipped to address this change are new ones responsive to the social changes that surround them). Realism, particularly in the novel, for example, arose during the heights of the industrial revolution in the nineteenth century, and gave graphic representation to a new world of commerce, industry, urban growth, and a rising middle class. It supplanted art that focused on imaginary realms of the aristocracy, religion, myth and folklore. **Modernism** arose at the start of the twentieth century as a reaction against both the apparent sacrifice of a high art tradition to commercialism and the collapse of civilization and the social order signaled by the horrific carnage of World War I. (**High art** refers to the traditional arts—painting, sculpture, ballet, opera, and theater—especially as they flourished during the Renaissance and after. High art served the interests of a largely bourgeois and aristocratic audience and received patronage and support from these classes. Modernism often drew on this tradition to distinguish itself from popular culture and the more lower- and middle-class audience it served.) Postmodernism began after World War II. It rejects the high art aura of modernism and celebrates the popular art of the mass media in a way that tends to repeat and recycle previous work. Tradition is cut free from its historical anchorage; individual works float in a relativistic sea of references, citations, and nostalgia. We will examine these tendencies in further detail throughout this chapter.

Two Types of Realism

Considerations of realism can focus on either of two characteristics:

1) Formally, the film presents its story world in an unobtrusive, almost invisible manner so that characters, actions, situations, and

events simply seem to exist on their own. The process of narration, or storytelling, is relatively unnoticeable, and the narrative, or story, receives the bulk of the viewer's attention. Such work is rarely reflexive: it doesn't direct awareness to how it is constructed.

2) Socially, the film conveys a commonsense understanding of everyday reality as most people experience it. The world viewed bears a strong correspondence to aspects of the historical world. Realism in this sense breaks ranks with myths and folktales that tell of extraordinary worlds, magical feats, and remarkable characters. Realism, by contrast, aligns itself with the rising middle class and its public and private struggles; it also turns a fresh light on the working class and issues of poverty, injustice, and crime.

Realism as a self-effacing form of storytelling draws on the general tendency in much art to hide the process of its own making in favor of the impression that the world it represents exists on its own, autonomously. Realist films that nonetheless conjure up fantastic worlds, such as *The Lord of the Rings* trilogy (Peter Jackson, 2001–03, New Zealand/U.S.), adhere to realism in this sense. The film looks nothing like everyday reality, but the story unfolds effortlessly, as if propelled by nothing more than the actions of the characters themselves. Since our own actions seem self-propelled, this contributes a realist quotient to the film. The majority of genre films rely on realism in this sense to endow their imagined worlds with coherence and autonomy. This, in turn, encourages viewers to make an emotional investment in the situations and events, characters and actions that unfold in this unfamiliar space.

Realism as a representation of the everyday devotes the bulk of its attention to the lives of working-class and middle-class people rather than a social elite. This focus is in keeping with the rise of democracy and the spread of capitalism as an economic system in the nineteenth century. It parallels the change in the social system with a style that speaks to the very classes that high art neglected and feudalism subordinated. Self-effacing storytelling is a formal quality of this style (the act of constructing a story is masked by techniques like continuity editing). The stress on a familiar world of everyday activity with its attendant conflicts and dilemmas is a social quality of the narrative (it focuses on aspects of the world that are already familiar to its principal viewers). Some films, sci-fi or horror films, for example, may possess the first quality but not the second; and, as we shall see below, some sci-fi, horror, or other genre films are made in a modernist or postmodernist style. When a film both masks its own storytelling efforts and focuses on the familiar world of everyday activity, it belongs most fully within the domain of realism.

Continuity editing, sync sound, naturalistic lighting, and **method acting**, among other things, all work to convey the impression of worlds that simply unfold before us, so that the viewer is absorbed in the experience of the story world rather than the storytelling. Most dramas, melodramas, and action films, for example, focus on characters who seem to step directly onto the screen from real life, even if their skills or personalities prove exceptional. Critics have praised the realism of films that capture the hopes and dangers, risks and dreams that run through the peaks and valleys of lived experience. Such praise went to William Wyler's hit *Best Years of Our Lives* (1946), about the struggles of three GIs returning home from World War II, and to Steven Spielberg's triumph, *Saving Private Ryan* (1998), about the effort to bring home safely the sole surviving son out of the four brothers who signed up for duty in World War II. Despite differences between these two films, critics and audiences valued both for their realistic portrayal of the pressures, anxieties, and courage that give familiar forms of experience complexity. (Both films received Oscar nominations for Best Picture; *Best Years of Our Lives* won the Oscar for 1946.)

Lumière and Méliès: The Original
Realism/Fantasy Polarity

When film historians looked back to the early days of motion pictures in the 1890s, the short films made by or for the Lumière brothers, Auguste and Louis, seemed to anchor the realist pole of cinema. Films like *The Arrival of a Train at La Ciotat* (1896, France), *Workers Leaving the Factory* (1895, France), or *Hoser Hosed* (1895, France) gave a realist view of familiar activities and events. Meanwhile, another Frenchman, Georges Méliès, presented a fantastic world unlike anything anyone had ever seen before in films such as *A Trip to the Moon* (France), a fanciful tale of space travel in 1902. Both the Lumière and the Méliès films, though, adhered to a relatively invisible process of storytelling to create worlds that seemed to exist independent of the filmmaker's invention.

The Lumières' early films did not yet make great use of continuity editing (the long take or single shot was common), but they were often composed with an awareness of depth—with actions occurring at different distances from the camera. They were also shot to capture the most relevant action gracefully. "Graceful" here refers to how the camera position is not a random choice but reflects an awareness of composition and movement within the frame. For example, in *Workers Leaving the Factory* (*La sortie des usines Lumière*, 1895), they appear to have their "performers," their own workers in this case, move in specific directions at well-chosen angles to the camera, or, in other cases, to carry out particular actions in the center and the foreground of the frame. These choices heighten the naturalness and typicality of the scene without altering their normal everyday behavior so much that it seemed overtly staged or theatrical.

The departure of the workers from their factory has the aura of a Sunday afternoon outing. Everyone is well dressed and some appear aware of the camera. They move in a processional manner, with little lingering, joking, or clustering into less photogenic groups (they all face toward the camera). Although there is the strong sense that this continuous long-take film is a document in the pure sense of the term, there are also lingering suspicions that, as with so much of cinema, there has been a negotiation or collaboration between filmmaker and subject to achieve a desired effect. The basic impression, though, is that this is something a passer-by might well have seen in reality.

On the other hand, Georges Méliès's *Trip to the Moon*, *The Impossible Dinner* (1904, France) and *Little Red Riding Hood* (1901, France) draw the viewer into a clearly fabricated world. The illusion that what viewers see matches what they might see in their everyday world no longer pertains. Manipulations of time and space, action and performance, are overt, but they are not designed to fracture the story world or make the viewer more aware of the filmmaking process. In that sense, his films remain realist. But they invoke commonsense notions of spatial and temporal continuity to produce magic instead of reinforcement for the familiar. The story world appears to come into existence on its own but with magical properties. Méliès gives the viewer an opportunity to take flights of fancy that go beyond what normal perception and everyday life offer, in a world designed to accommodate these flights.

Méliès was nothing if not inventive. A device others immediately understood as a way to record and document aspects of the everyday world was for him a means of inventing a magical reality just as convincingly. Méliès was a genius at realizing that cuts between shots needn't conform to the real-life logic of spatial and temporal continuity but could, instead, perform sleights of hand and other tricks in apparent defiance of everyday expectations. By performing magic with his editing, Méliès was able to make objects disappear and reappear, things jump from one location to another, or to reverse the course of time to restore an earlier state of affairs.

Méliès gave tangible expression to the imagination. His films demonstrated how the cinema makes possible the visible representation of unreal spaces and distorted temporalities. Georges Méliès, from this perspective, anchored the fantasy-oriented pole within a realist tradition. He maintained the illusion of an autonomous story world but made it appear magical instead of natural. It would be the realist pole that science fiction, animation, and full-blown fantasies like *The Lord of the Rings* trilogy or the *Harry Potter* series (Chris Columbus, Alfonso Cuarón, Mike Newell, and David Yates, 2001–07, UK/U.S.) would later populate.

Lumière and realism, Méliès and fantasy—this simple, suggestive dichotomy, therefore, does not quite capture the full range of cinematic possibility, something that would have been impossible to foretell from film's origins. It is little wonder that early film historians thought that the Lumières and Méliès epitomized the limits of film expression: they had not yet considered modernist and postmodernist alternatives.

The realism/fantasy dichotomy is therefore not a direct answer to the question of how the dominant aesthetic conventions of the last two centuries or so find tangible expression in the cinema. Fantasy, as a way of imagining distinctive worlds, goes back far beyond the nineteenth century to Greek myth and innumerable fairy tales. It persists in realist, modernist, and postmodernist incarnations. The fantastic end of the realist spectrum tells us something about the incredible range of work achieved in the first decade after the birth of the cinema, but it is in the history of film's encounter with all three major tendencies— realism, modernism, and postmodernism—that we can witness film's overall stylistic evolution.

HOLLYWOOD REALISM AND THE GENRE FILM

Hollywood realism is of a particular kind. It shares realist characteristics with nineteenth-century novels and plays and belongs to the realist tradition in painting and photography. Hollywood films, especially from the 1920s to the 1980s, almost always remain within the realist tradition in the sense that character motivation and action is readily recognizable, and the storytelling process, with some notable exceptions, does not draw attention to itself so much as work unobtrusively to let an imagined world unfold before us.

Hollywood realism revolves around situations and events that are *plausible* within the terms and conventions of a given kind of world. The world may have fantastic qualities, but plausibility remains a key litmus test. In westerns, for example, we routinely find shoot-outs on the main streets of frontier towns, women who live in hard times but whose hair and costumes look impeccable, and bands of fierce warriors who nonetheless ride in circles around trapped wagon trains until the outnumbered defenders can pick them off. In horror film, we find monsters with a special affinity for women, either to defend or attack them, and in film noir, an abundance of scheming, manipulative characters eager to pull a double cross. In terms of genre conventions all these situations and qualities appear plausible. They may not be an accurate representation of everyday life, or history, but audiences come to regard them as a familiar, plausible representation of situations and events, characters and actions in the kind of world common to a given genre.

John Carpenter's offbeat science fiction film *They Live* (1988), for example, presents everyday reality as an illusion. *They Live* also enables its hero to *see* the illusion. When he puts on special sunglasses he sees traffic signs and billboards, TV shows and magazines as camouflage for a set of subliminal, ideological messages: what they actually say, in bold black and white letters, is "Obey," "Conform," "Consume." All public information reduces to basic imperatives. The film literally exposes a dominant ideology embedded in routine media messages that promotes conformity and consumerism.

They Live exaggerates and distorts everyday reality to make its point, but this does not mean it lacks artistic merit or social significance; the metaphor of sinister and subliminal advertising that it creates remains memorable. And the film belongs squarely in the realist tradition in terms of familiar character types, linear causality, temporal continuity, and spatial coherence. Aspects of its world are fantastic, but continuity editing prevails throughout the film.

Realist representation does not duplicate the world; therefore, the analysis of such films can readily focus on the question of how reality gets altered. Viewers can adopt a dualistic social analysis of suspicion and appreciation regarding what aspects of lived experience become altered or distorted to allow the story to achieve resolution, on the one hand, and what aspects of lived experience are seen from a fresh, revealing perspective, on the other. In a formal context, the same dual analysis would ask what aspects of a film rely on the uncritical adoption of established genre conventions and what aspects represent innovative transformations.

SOCIAL CHARACTERISTICS OF THE REALIST FILM

From a realist perspective, men and women are social animals whose identity arises not in isolation but from active participation in the lives of others. For example, individuals typically share in the practices, values, and beliefs that underpin community. We adopt shared perspectives that foster a sense of belonging. The commonsense tenets of realism—a coherent organization of time and space, the creation of character types with recognizable personalities and needs, a linear narrative of actions, reactions, and results that moves toward the resolution of familiar problems or issues, reliance on highly realistic or utterly fantastic settings for a story world that seems to exist autonomously—attest to this common perspective. These tenets affirm a sense of common cause and enduring community over the alienation and disenchantment of modernist narrative or the irony and cynicism that underlies much of postmodernist art.

Realism, in this sense, fits comfortably with the ideology of the nation-state as a melting pot that produces social unity or an "imaginary community" (rather than an uneasy and perhaps incompatible amalgam of different class, religious, ethnic, and linguistic or cultural groups). In classic Hollywood cinema it is genre films, with their base in a pre-dominantly white, middle-class world, that stand for this all-embracing sense of community. Most genre films suggest that we live in a world beset by identifiable and remediable problems. These problems catalyze the hero to act. Heroes are able do for others what others cannot do for themselves. The world may be threatened from without or from within in westerns (Indians, the environment, greedy cattle barons), science fiction (aliens and marauding colonizers), horror films (monsters and psychopaths), melodramas (disturbed or dysfunctional family members), or comedies (mavericks, oddballs, and dreamers). The triumph or defeat of the central community becomes a key measure of how any realist film locates itself in relation to the dominant culture of its time.

Realism is hardly a rubber stamp for the existing status quo. Its search for conflicts that can be imaginatively modified and, in one way or another, resolved demands that realism address real issues. It does so in a way that makes these issues highly recognizable even when the setting and events are not part of most viewers' everyday lives. For example, in *The Departed* (Martin Scorsese, 2006, U.S./Hong Kong), Billy Costigan's (Leonardo DiCaprio) father was a criminal, but Billy wants to be a cop. The cops want him to be an informer. He must penetrate the crime world he thought he was escaping. A genuine sense of community eludes him. A realist style strengthens the profound feelings of deception and betrayal that he, along with the other central characters, experience. The emotional issues are familiar even though the cop and criminal setting is not part of most peoples' everyday experience.

Anguish is not an uncommon experience: in *Brokeback Mountain* (Ang Lee, 2005, Canada/U.S.) Alma (Michelle Williams) watches with pained disbelief as her husband, Ennis (Heath Ledger), eagerly awaits the arrival of his old buddy and lover, Jack Twist (Jake Gyllenhall). Meanwhile, in *Dreamgirls* (Bill Condon, 2006) Effie White (Jennifer

Hudson) suffers the painful rejection visited on her by the Dreamettes' manager, Curtis Taylor, Jr. (Jamie Foxx), who has decided that her voice and appearance are not conventional enough to cross over to a mainstream (that is, predominantly white) audience.

These three films are far more realist than modernist or postmodern. They examine significant questions involving loss, loyalty, and belonging. They focus on the ways in which the sense of a community may unravel, driving individuals to strive to discover alternatives. Close-ups, point-of-view shots, and continuity editing all serve to boost the intensity of pivotal dramatic moments. Each film also conveys a skeptical view of the health of the surrounding culture's dominant values and beliefs.

Another way to understand the social characteristics of realism is to compare it to the Greek philosopher Plato's allegory of the cave. In his famous allegory, Plato suggested that people live their lives inside a cave, fascinated by a series of sounds and images projected onto a wall from a source behind them. Facing the wall and the images moving across it—not unlike the images that surround Neo as he moves through the apparently real-life matrix in *The Matrix* (Andy and Larry Wachowski, 1999, U.S./Australia)—the average individual mistakes this complex illusion for reality, never turning around to see how such a shared perception is actively produced by the culture as a whole, or to step outside the cave to explore realities of a different order. For Plato, these projected sounds and images are, in fact, a distraction from less visible ideal forms like beauty or truth, which only take material, tangible shape as copies or imitations. Platonic philosophy strove to attain knowledge of the forms that exist apart from or beyond the reality of sensory perception and everyday experience.

Presumably, the shadows cast on the walls of Plato's cave were highly realistic ones, which bolstered their credibility and heightened their dangerous allure as distractions. For some critics and theorists, realism is a representational style that supports the **dominant**

ideology (the values and beliefs that reinforce the status quo). Realism reinforces a commonsense belief that the way things appear to be is the way they are, that individuals rather than collectivities or social forces are the primary source of change, and that the social world possesses a high degree of stability so that problems or conflicts can be identified, addressed, and resolved.

As the discussion of *The Departed, Brokeback Mountain*, and *Dreamgirls* suggests, realism is not entirely devoted to supporting or maintaining the social status quo or the dominant ideology that supports it. This style also conveys the hardship and suffering that may be part of everyday existence. Linking any one style with any one specific ideology or political position is a risky business. To claim that realism serves any one master, be it a dominant ideology (capitalism, democracy, commercialism, ethnocentrism, or any other) or produces any one result (distraction, entertainment, reinforcement of the status quo, and so on) overstates the case. Realism may represent familiar forms of experience in a plausible manner, but it need not endorse the status quo. The discussion of *They Live* demonstrates how a realist genre film can, in fact, present a critique of the existing order of things.

THE MYTHICAL AND THE HISTORICAL

A powerful effect of film realism is that everyday qualities, reinforced by a commonsense understanding of what society is and how it operates, may strike viewers as timeless. Realism can *naturalize* a way of seeing the world or an ideology, so that it no longer appears contingent, constructed, or debatable. Certain values and beliefs and the social practices that embody them come to appear as far beyond human design as nature itself. The nuclear family, for example, which realist dramas and melodramas explore in great detail, may come to feel like a universal attribute of human experience, whereas many cultures value extended families, clans, and kinship systems more than the nuclear family per se.

Dominant ideology commonly offers a mythic as opposed to an historical view of the world. A mythic view sees the social world as a fixed, permanent reality, with values and beliefs that lie beyond question. Values and beliefs appear to derive from timeless principles considered natural and obvious by all. The future shape of society will preserve the values and beliefs that already prevail. Conservative and reactionary political perspectives tend to be mythical in this sense. The dominant ideology of patriarchy, for example, sees male privilege as perfectly natural. It is not something to alter but a foundation stone for the construction of culture. An alternative, feminist ideology regards gender roles as historically variable. This perspective argues that channeling women's talents into functions such as motherhood, to the exclusion of other possibilities available to men, represents an ideology rather than a law of nature, and is, therefore, open to challenge.

A historical view understands the social world as a place populated by contending forces and competing ideologies even if one happens to dominate. The future shape of society derives from the complex process by which social conflicts arise, provoke struggle, and achieve at least partial resolution. Liberal and radical political perspectives tend to be historical in this sense. They question the evocation of timeless principles; they attempt to understand how such principles—such as male privilege (versus female equality), class privilege (versus equal opportunity), ethnic superiority (versus ethnic differences)—arise under certain conditions and serve particular interests.

Realism has the capacity to support either a mythical or an historical view of the world. Rather than a fault, its flexible adaptability to either goal is one of its greatest strengths and sources of appeal: it serves many masters. This is a major reason why realism remains the stylistic mode of choice for filmmakers and artists across the political spectrum.

Modernism

TWO EMPHASES IN MODERNISM

Modernism consciously takes issue with the tenets of realism. The two types of realism—invisible storytelling and representations based on commonsensical assumptions about everyday life—no longer prevail. Instead, modernism exhibits two alternative characteristics:

1) Formally, a very noticeable storytelling process, replacing the effort to make it seem as if the story world possesses an existence of its own. Reliance on collage and montage, discussed below, is a key element in this new emphasis on narration or the storytelling process.

(2) Socially, an exploration of the interior, subjective life of characters, in which characters drift into their own imagined worlds regardless of their surroundings. The individual reality of consciousness, memory, and desire receives a weight equal to or greater than a shared social reality

HISTORICAL BACKGROUND: MODERNISM AND MODERNITY

Modernism was, in many ways, a critique of **modernity**, the conditions of life in the period of late nineteenth- and early twentieth-century capitalism, especially in the urban centers of industrialized nations. **Modernity** referred to the consolidation of capitalism into large, corporate, often international or colonial forms and to the ascendancy of finance capital as a way to control development at one remove from actual production. (This latter quality of control at a remove reaches new heights with the rise of a global economy and postmodernism.) The benefits and defects of the industrial revolution had become apparent by the mid-nineteenth century, when Karl Marx wrote his major works. For some, industrialization had run its course as a dynamic liberator that freed individuals from the rigid hierarchies of feudal, aristocratic society. It not only brought untold fortunes to some and new levels of comfort and convenience to many but had become responsible for urban poverty, human degradation, and a despoiled environment on an unparalleled scale. The enormous carnage of World War I dramatized as no Marxist writings could the realization that a dangerous force was now afoot. The unprecedented magnitude of death and destruction was a direct result of industrial technology used for military ends (poison gas, powerful artillery, highly efficient machine guns, land mines, bomber planes, etc.). Many artists and intellectuals recoiled from the transformations wrought by industrialization and modern warfare.

Modernism questioned the independence and wisdom of the individual. Techniques of fragmentation characterized a world that no longer seemed to have a moral center or a unifying agent of the sort that the heroic central character of realism represented. Fragmentation, disconnection, alienation, and anonymity were in the air. Modernism became the movement that sought a new aesthetic form to convey a new social reality.

As a result modernism rejected many of the conventions of nineteenth-century art: novels did not need to create fully rounded characters; paintings did not need to offer realistic depictions of external reality, and architecture did not need to disguise a building's function with embellishments of form. The international style of architecture, for example, pioneered by Walter Gropius and the Bauhaus architects, stressed basic, unadorned shapes that made the function of the building as factory, office building, museum, or apartment complex self-evident. Like constructivism (discussed below), this style also drew attention to the physical qualities of the actual building materials (slab-like expanses of concrete, exposed girders, and beams of steel) as a promi-nent feature. This form of stripped-down architecture was seen as a kind of honesty or truth-telling about the actual nature of architectural form. Like collage, it drew attention to the structural foundation of a work rather than to the aesthetic elaboration that had traditionally dis-guised this basic quality.

Modernist cinema seeks less to compete with mainstream, Holly-wood-style cinema on its own terms by inventing new genres or stars, for example, than to develop a different conception of narrative form. Like realism, it responds to the social realities of the early twentieth century. As discussed in Chapter 2, the avant-garde, heavily indebted to modernist principles, stressed the poetic dimension of cinema over storytelling. Since the 1920s, avant-garde filmmakers have identified their efforts with various modernist currents such as surrealism, Dada, constructivism, and German expressionism more than with realism. In the period following the Russian Revolution of 1917 and in Europe during the 1950s and '60s, modernism also made a distinct contribu-tion to narrative fiction film. The Soviet period stressed the principle of montage to engage the viewer in a radically new way, whereas the European postwar period stressed the interiority or subjectivity of characters who no longer seemed to belong to a shared social reality.

MAJOR STYLISTIC VARIATIONS WITHIN MODERNISM

Modernist work draws attention to the act of narration and to con-struction of a story world. It gives high priority to **collage** or **montage**, principles that allow unrelated, dissimilar elements to be joined together to form a complex whole. Fragmentation often disrupts the sense of a unified, coherent work, one that obeys the classic unities of time and place or that arrives at a clear sense of resolution. An encounter with fragments in a collage style presses home the idea that the story world is not self-contained and autonomous but the product of many fragments cobbled together, precisely what editing typically does, whether the editing is noticeable or not.

Collage involves combining different types of material in the same work. This technique is a vivid demonstration of fragmentation, since a single painting might contain a cigarette butt, grains of sand, newspaper clippings, and oil paint. Some critics consider Jean-Luc Godard's films collages, given his tendency to draw on a wide variety of disparate source materials—other films both documentary and fiction, interviews, staged interviews, asides to the camera by actors, voice-over commentary by Godard himself, dialogue that is actually extended quotations of other people's work from philosophers to art critics, and so on. **Montage** is a more specifically cinematic technique exemplified by the films of Sergei Eisenstein, discussed further below. He saw individual shots as raw material. The real art, and power, of cinema came from the juxtaposition of these shots to unsettle the viewer and provoke new insights.

Surrealism took collage principles in the direction of the unconscious by rejecting realism and substituting the more bizarre and fantastic principles of dreams. Salvador Dali painted pocket watches drooped over the limb of a tree as if they were made of melted plastic. Luis Buñuel mocked social conventions in ways that challenged the normalcy and obviousness of habit. In *The Phantom of Liberty* (1974, France) he offers a notorious reversal of dining etiquette: participants at a well-heeled dinner party converse around a table, but they sit on toilets. At discreet intervals the members excuse themselves to slip off to a small, tile-paneled dining room where a waiter slips them a tray of food through a slit in the wall. The reversal violates common sense, and maybe decency; it certainly throws the viewer's ability to make assumptions based on past experience into serious jeopardy.

Dada was a small but influential movement at the start of the twentieth century that used shock, strange juxtapositions, and collage to create work that often had a political overtone. The Dadaists rejected the idea of aesthetics as a form of detachment. They believed that art should be a provocation or attack on the status quo and favored shock, disgust, and outrage as visceral responses that could provoke change. Marcel Duchamp, for example, installed a urinal in an art gallery and relabeled it art. Dada was often more overtly political than other modernist movements, but, unlike constructivism, its politics emphasized shock more than any particular alternative to the existing social structure.

Dusan Makavayev's *WR—Mysteries of the Organism* (1971, Yugoslavia/West Germany) presents a biography of Wilhelm Reich, an important but eccentric psychiatrist who linked fascism to repressed sexuality and invented the "orgone box" to capture and channel sexual energy. The film mixes 1960s-style guerrilla street theater with a decapitation (a Russian ice-skater uses the blade of his skate as Luis Buñuel used a razor at the start of *Un chien andalou* [1929, France]— to stylized but gruesome effect). In true Dada fashion, the film sets out to shock and offend more than to entertain or inform.

Constructivism was a movement peculiar to the Soviet Union. It began before the revolution of 1917 and continued, in different forms, after. Constructivism helped pave the way for the great silent films of the Soviet cinema by breaking with realist representation. Form and the physical materiality of objects received prominent attention. New materials such as concrete, steel, and plastic replaced the classic materials of stone and oil paint. Like Dada, constructivism rejected the traditional role of art, which was now seen as a handmaiden to the aristocracy and bourgeoisie, the very classes the revolution had overthrown. Constructivism sought to establish a new way of seeing and organizing reality rather than stressing shock for the sake of shock as Dada did.

Expressionism, which arose in Germany and spread to many countries, gave visual expression to inner, typically conflicted or disturbed states of mind. It emphasized what it feels like to experience emotional turmoil more than it sought out the social causes for this turmoil. Broken or jagged lines, deep shadows, and anguished expressions all spoke to inner, emotional turbulence. Edvard Munch's famous painting *The Scream* is one vivid example of this tendency, but numerous artists adopted it, including filmmakers. Expressionism relies less on fragmentation than on stylistic exaggeration, and it draws less attention to the medium or formal qualities than, say, cubism or constructivism. Expressionism significantly influenced the visual style of American film noir in the postwar period and more recent neo-noir such as *Body Heat* (Lawrence Kasdan, 1981), *L.A. Confidential* (Curtis Hanson, 1997), *The Last Seduction* (John Dahl, 1994), and *Memento* (Christopher Nolan, 2000).

The Cabinet of Dr. Caligari (Robert Wiene, 1920, Germany) was one of the first German films to capture the expressionist spirit in a vivid, successful way. The film's distorted sets and exaggerated acting style create a world compatible with the nightmarish, demented views of a mad doctor, who controls a somnambulant creature, Cesar, who roams the city at night killing innocent victims. Many critics interpreted the film as a symptomatic display of middle-class anxiety in a time of rampant inflation and social instability. It also expresses the fear that authority, represented by the apparently respectable doctor, could become a tool of terror and social control. The filmmakers added a not entirely convincing coda that put Doctor Caligari in charge of a mental hospital where the narrator of this bizarre tale turns out to be a deluded patient. The film leaves many viewers with the vivid sense that all is not well despite the ostensibly happy ending provided by the coda.

CHARACTERISTICS OF MODERNIST STYLE

FRAGMENTATION Modernism stresses the fragmented nature of reality. Techniques of collage and montage give formal expression to this idea. Even the individual may no longer exhibit the qualities of consistency and coherence that realism typically provides. Eruptions of unpredictable urges, displays of uncharacteristic attitudes, a lack of moral compass, and a general inability to demonstrate that consciousness holds the upper hand over unconscious impulses and desires makes the modernist character a more fractured, if not wholly divided, figure than the typical realist hero.

Fragmentation bears a close relationship to Sergei Eisenstein's theories of montage, where new impressions—emotional and cognitive—arise as a result of the juxtaposition of shots that lack the seamless flow achieved by continuity editing. Walter Benjamin, in his seminal essay, "The Work of Art in the Age of Mechanical Reproduction," celebrated the transformative potential of montage this way:

> Our taverns and our metropolitan streets, our offices and furnished rooms, our railroad stations and our factories appeared to have us locked up hopelessly. Then came the film and burst this prison-world asunder by the dynamite of the tenth of a second, so that now, in the midst of its far-flung ruins and debris, we calmly and adventurously go traveling. (*Illuminations*, p. 236)

Fragments draw attention to the surface of things, but their juxtaposition suggests linkages that are not at first apparent. In describing his efforts to make *Battleship Potemkin* (Sergei Eisenstein, 1925, Soviet Union), for example, Eisenstein wrote,

> The shot is a montage *cell*.
>
> Just as cells in their division form a phenomenon of another order, the organism or embryo, so, on the other side of the dialectical leap from the shot, there is montage.
>
> By what, then, is montage characterized, and, consequently, its cell—the shot?
>
> By collision. By the conflict of two pieces in opposition to each other. By conflict. By collision. (*Film Form*, p. 37)

Eisenstein sought to recreate the actual experience of conflict in the collision of one shot against another, one scene against another, over and over, during the course of a film. What did it feel like to think and act in a revolutionary manner? Answering this question meant, for Eisenstein, stressing the emotional impact and conceptual understanding that follow from making new connections rather than accepting the prevailing ones.

The most cited example is the "Odessa Steps" sequence in *Battleship Potemkin*, where Eisenstein crosscuts the attack of the Cossacks on the citizens of Odessa with their flight, on the one hand, and their defense by the rebellious battleship crew, on the other. This is the classic "hero to the rescue of the damsel in distress" narrative, but told without individual heroes or villains and in a thoroughly modernist style. Eisenstein emphasizes groups and classes of people. He cuts from aiming a rifle to the shattering of an eye piece, from shooting a mother to the baby carriage tumbling down the Odessa Steps, from the advance of soldiers to the retreat of the people, and from the Cossacks' bloody attack to the battleship's retaliation. The "thesis" of repressive violence is propelled to another level by the "antithesis" of the people's defiance. The rebel sailors of the Battleship Potemkin achieve a momentary "synthesis" in which repression and resistance yield to a new form of collective solidarity. (These terms—"thesis," "antithesis" and "synthesis"—are classic Marxist concepts and speak to Marx's understanding of society as an arena in which conflicting forces, such as classes, confront each other (thesis/antithesis) and produce an outcome that transforms the original forces. For example, for Marx, Communism would result from the defeat of the ruling class by the working class.) The film, set during the failed revolt of 1905, concludes with the newly forged unity among the people that will eventually, in 1917, prove capable of overthrowing the czar and his feudalistic reign.

FORMALISM Modernist art often engages in a dialogue with its medium, making the brushstrokes of a painting, the flatness of a canvas, the concrete and steel of a building, the presence of words on a page, or disruptions in time and space produced by film editing the subject of the work as much as the external world to which the work refers. This self-referential quality is also known as **formalism**. *The Conformist* (Bernardo Bertolucci, 1970, Italy/France/West Germany), for example, draws attention to its own exaggerated style and disjointed representation of time, even as it also addresses the nature of fascism.

Formalism steers the viewer's attention to the formal processes, usually unnoticed and taken for granted, that construct the story world. Continuity editing, for example, is usually unnoticed, but montage editing is highly noticeable. Such editing can have a political effect, as when Sergei Eisenstein edits between the slaughter of striking workers by the czar's armed Cossacks and the slaughter of cattle in *Strike* (1925, Soviet Union), his first feature film.

Many modernist films stress the fragmentary nature of the shot or scene by editing that throws continuity into disarray. The convolutions that ravel past and present into complex tangles of memory, fantasy, and fact in *The Conformist*, *Hiroshima mon amour* (Alain Resnais, 1959, France/Japan), or *Memories of Underdevelopment* (*Memorias del desarrollo*, Tomás Gutiérrez Alea, 1968, Cuba) overwhelm any sense of a causal, linear progression. Spatially, the coordinates of where actions occur and how they relate to one another may also remain vague or indeterminate. Subjective, inconsistent, often inexplicable motivations drive characters forward in irrational or unexplainable ways. Ambiguity or the sense of a fundamental enigma to existence that no realism can cure often looms as an overriding impression.

HEIGHTENED SUBJECTIVITY Modernism frequently explores the subjective interior of its characters' thoughts and consciousness, without attempting to link them to a fixed reference point in external reality.

Techniques like stream of consciousness, as used by Virginia Woolf or James Joyce, and the strange, dreamlike sequences in surrealist films fracture the sense of a temporal and spatial continuum, they disconnect effects from causes, and they present a mysteriousness to life that reason cannot explain. Characters seem trapped inside a subjectivity they cannot share with others. In Jean Cocteau's stunning films *The Blood of a Poet* (*Le sang de un poète*, 1930, France) and *Orpheus* (*Orphée*, 1950, France), social reality completely dissolves into a mysterious world of magic and wonder based on classic myths. In other words, subjectivity goes hand in hand with a profound sense of social alienation.

Michelangelo Antonioni's films render the subjective dimension to individual lives with a powerfully enigmatic quality. Communication and comprehension no longer seem possible. His early trilogy of *L'avventura* (1960, Italy/France), *La notte* (1961, Italy/France), and *L'eclisse* (*The Eclipse*, 1962, Italy/France) present striking representations of characters who drift through urban environments, share what should be intimate moments, and shuffle to the next encounter without ever establishing a clear sense of intimacy.

Antonioni uses existing social space (city streets, apartment rooms, urban architecture) brilliantly to suggest that this manmade world has turned against its creators, isolating individuals from one another and making genuine relationships impossible. Antonioni makes no attempt to assign causes to this condition. He explores effects, not causes, and makes no diagnosis of the sources of alienation and offers no proposals for its elimination. His social perspective dwells on what it feels like to be spiritually adrift but in the presence of others.

The European art cinema associated with great postwar auteurs like Antonioni, Ingmar Bergman, Federico Fellini, Jean-Luc Godard, and Alain Resnais often adopted a modernist tone in its examination of subjective states of mind and new ways of representing social reality. Resnais's *Last Year at Marienbad* (*L'année dernière à Marienbad*, 1961, France/Italy), for example, like his earlier film, *Hiroshima mon amour*, and his stunning documentary, *Night and Fog* (1955, France), explores questions of memory as a subjective experience. Social engagement, in fact, becomes an endless series of conversations that attempt to establish a common past for the central characters at the Marienbad spa, a traditional resort destination for the leisured classes of Europe. These efforts to affirm a common past and shared experience prove unsuccessful. The trademark modernist qualities of heightened subjectivity, ambiguity of motivation, and uncertainty of time and place abound. The hero's world possesses a past (encounters tied to monuments, architecture, landscape) but it lacks continuity, meaning, or connection. Characters drift through the gardens and baroque palace as if in a dream, talking and meeting. The seemingly aimless or random encounters draw attention to the capacity of film to arrange realistic images into patterns that become subjective and surreal.

BRECHTIAN ALIENATION

For the Dadaists, constructivists, and other socially engaged artists, modernism was a tool to equip an audience to engage with a new social reality. The playwright Bertolt Brecht (discussed further in Chapter 8) questioned the commodification of art and the limitations of realism as a style, but continued to value the pleasures of art as a means of expression. Brecht adopted techniques to distance the viewer from emotional involvement with individual characters but did so in order to intensify involvement with underlying social issues and conflicts. The strategy of distancing viewers from emotional identification and heightening engagement with a broader social perspective became known as the "**alienation effect**."

Brecht adopted many popular elements of theater and the circus to produce lively, engaging plays. He had little patience with high art limited to a select elite; accessibility was a key quality to all his work. Brecht called for the separation or fragmentation of formal elements (music, speech, acting, set design, projected titles or images, and so on) to generate a conscious awareness of how these different elements contribute to an overall effect. He wanted each scene to stand on its own, separated from what came before or after by various devices. An assembly of fragments exposed the work of constructing a story rather than reproducing a social reality; it also conveyed the idea that reality consisted of splintered pieces that modernist technique could reassemble into a fresh way of seeing the world.

Many directors have adapted Brecht's modernist ideas. Godard, for example, uses segments of black leader (film that has been completely exposed to light so that is entirely black), chapter numbers, and titles to break down his film *Vivre sa vie* (1962, France) into twelve discrete segments. It tells the story of Nana, a young prostitute trying to free herself from others so she can live her own life. The film has strongly Brechtian overtones in its high degree of fragmentation and in the collage-like mixture of different source materials, from *The Passion of Jeanne d'Arc* (Carl Dreyer, 1928, France) to an interview between Nana and an actual philosopher (Brice Parain) who offers apparently off-the-cuff insights into the relationship between contemplation and action. Similarly, director Luis Valdez brings a Brechtian aesthetic to *Zoot Suit* (1981). He casts Edward James Olmos as a flamboyant, critically astute commentator on the actions of the characters, together with fragmentation, vivid stylization, and thematically pertinent songs. The film, adapted from Valdez's play, retells the history of racial and class conflict that led to the Zoot Suit Riots of 1943 in Los Angeles. The film is highly theatrical and engaging; it addresses an important historical event but does so in a thoroughly modernist, and decidedly Brechtian, manner.

Postmodernism

The most recent of the three major stylistic schools, **postmodernism** presents two alternative characteristics to those of realism and modernism:

1) Formally, the storytelling process draws attention to itself through a high degree of quotation, homage, borrowing, copying, and otherwise recycling previous work. Postmodernism lacks the anti-commercial, elite quality of much modernism; it readily mixes popular and high art references, traditions, and conventions to stress the artifice of any imagined world.

2) Socially, postmodernism emphasizes how any one imagined world is more like other imagined worlds than like reality itself. This autonomy, and isolation, of art from life licenses rampant borrowing from previous works in any medium. Consequently, the sense of an external social referent (a shared social reality) decreases as the story world positions itself in relation to other imagined worlds governed by the same formal conventions.

HISTORICAL BACKGROUND

Postmodernism represents a radical transformation of realism and a rejection of modernist elitism. In contrast to most modernist work, postmodernism embraces the marketplace, although it often takes an ironic or cynical attitude toward the process that converts art into a commodity to be traded for a profit. In terms of social context, postmodernism responds to issues of transnational globalization since World War II in which the nation-state and its distinctive culture fade from a position of centrality. Issues like exile, diaspora, ethnic cleansing, immigration, the global economy, and terrorism all take place across national borders. Individual nations no longer act in isolation from other nations to any significant degree. Under these conditions, the traditional association of art with national identity (French films, British comedy, the Russian novel, and so on) through a distinct cultural tradition breaks down. Postmodernists detach fragments of existing works from their local context and throw them into a global stew. The phenomenon of world music is one example of postmodern art. Its borrowings of rhythms and instruments from an eclectic array of sources create a new form that has no base in any one national or local context and does not represent any one national culture. (Paul Simon's *Graceland* epitomizes this process.)

The individual, firmly rooted in realist time and space, and whose subjective experience of a fragmented world occupies a key position in modernism, becomes just one more ingredient in the postmodern aesthetic stew. That is to say, if the hero of realist films embodied qualities of agency and self-determination that were characteristic of early capitalism, and if the hero of modernist films embodied qualities of uncertainty and doubt that were characteristic of late capitalism, the hero of postmodern films embodies qualities of interchangeability and adaptability characteristic of transnational capitalism. Like the migrant worker, he functions as a small cog in a global economy.

CHARACTERISTICS OF POSTMODERN STYLE

MIXING AND MATCHING SOURCE MATERIAL As a subversion of realism and a rejection of modernism, postmodernism makes use of similar techniques and emphases but to different ends. To a large extent the difference is one of perspective or attitude. Postmodern work often adopts a seemingly devil-may-care attitude toward recycling such as we find in films like *Brazil* (1985, UK) or *Fear and Loathing in Las Vegas* (1998) by Terry Gilliam or Quentin Tarantino's *Pulp Fiction* (1994). Films like *Pulp Fiction* and *Run, Lola, Run* (Tom Tykwer, 1998, Germany) shuffle the temporal sequence of events in ways that violate realist conventions.

Postmodernist mixing and matching spans high and low culture. References to *I Love Lucy* may be as common as references to Shakespeare. Familiarity with the great tradition of high culture is no longer an implicit prerequisite for appreciating the work. Francis Ford Coppola's *Apocalypse Now* (1979), for example, which constructs an image of the Vietnam War that rejects both jingoistic patriotism and radical protest, mixes references to Playboy bunnies and water skiing with allusions to Joseph Conrad's *Heart of Darkness* and T. S. Eliot's *The Wasteland*. Awareness of these references may enrich the experience of the film, but they are far from essential to enjoying it.

QUESTIONING INDIVIDUALISM Like modernism, postmodernism questions the power, autonomy, and self-control of the individual, but places less stress on interiority and subjectivity. The prevalence of **irony**—where what is said is not necessarily what is meant, or where what is said is said as if in quotes, as if it didn't quite mean what it appears to mean—undercuts the sense of a character's autonomy. Characters turn into pawns in the author's own game, a condition stressed in films like Quentin Tarantino's *Kill Bill, Volume 1* and *2* (2003–04), where Uma Thurman plays "The Bride," a figure who embodies the principle of revenge more than the traits of a well-developed character in the realist or modernist traditions.

Draining characters of their apparent autonomy is also at work in *Performance* (Donald Cammell and Nicolas Roeg, 1970, UK), where a gangster (James Fox) and a rock musician (Mick Jagger) coyly interact with each other until their identities merge into a single entity, and in *The Rocky Horror Picture Show* (Jim Sharman, 1975, UK), where the characters seem to be little more than a witty, irreverent amalgam of stock characters from earlier, realist genre films, now uprooted to the blatantly stylized world of an imaginary Transylvania where the usually displaced sexual motifs of horror films blossom into full view. In such cases, characters are less realistically portrayed individuals than citations from or allusions to a treasure chest of previous film characters, and none more so in *Rocky Horror* than Dr. Frankenfurter himself. The desire to bring a new life into being, which the original *Frankenstein* portrays as a flagrant case of male hubris, becomes in *The Rocky Horror Picture Show*'s postmodern view of things, an explicitly homoerotic desire to "make me a man," as Frankenfurter says—and by a man he clearly means more a hunk than a monster.

Characters can also seem like pawns in the larger, extra-cinematic game of the global economy, as in Gianni Amelio's *Lamerica* (1994, Italy/France/Germany), where a somewhat naïve Italian con artist goes to Albania in the hopes of pulling off a financial scam and making a fortune, only to find himself abused and exploited by those whom he assumed would be no more than pawns in his game. A similar theme runs through Franco Brusati's *Bread and Chocolate* (*Pane e cioccolata*,1973, Italy), a comic tale of an Italian worker who goes to Switzerland to better himself, only to discover that betterment is far less common than exploitation no matter in what nation he finds himself. Identity, nationality, and professional standing all dissolve in these films to suggest how a global economy makes such qualities, which were once sufficient to define someone, anachronistic figments of a bygone world.

POSTMODERNIST ALLUSION AND CITATION Postmodernism uses quotation or allusion as a more casual form of borrowing or "sampling" that is not tied to invoking a hallowed tradition. This allows the filmmaker to build his own work from the fragments of previous work without claiming the originality of form characteristic of most realist and modernist work. Quentin Tarantino, for example, playfully adapts and quotes from several Hong Kong films in *Reservoir Dogs* (1992) and in *Kill Bill*, but these allusions do not identify him as part of that tradition or in serious dialogue with its themes and style so much as a **bricoleur** (someone who "makes do" with what's available) who uses these "ready-mades," or found objects, for his own ends.

Quentin Tarantino has readily professed his admiration for Ringo Lam's *City on Fire* (1987, Hong Kong). Tarantino's famous scene of the climactic four-way shoot-out, clearly borrowed, has itself been imitated by others and is sometimes credited to Tarantino as purely his own invention. But as he has said in an interview, "I steal from every movie... Great artists *steal*, they don't do *homages*" (in Jeffrey Dawson, *Quentin Tarantino: The Cinema of Cool*, p. 91). This use of the word "theft" marks a sharp division from the references and allusions of the modernists who wanted their work to be in serious ongoing dialogue with previous work. Tarantino measures originality by how well he can produce novelty more than engage in artistic dialogue.

Postmodern works can offer a serious meditation or commentary on popular forms as well as elite forms. Jim Jarmusch's *Dead Man* (1995, U.S./Germany), for example, does so by presenting a self-conscious, stylized version of the western. *Dead Man* features a hero, William Blake (Johnny Depp), who lacks the charismatic powers of the traditional hero, who fails in his effort to find a place for himself in the West, whose only friend is an Indian named Nobody (Gary Farmer), and whose journey through the wilderness includes a series of surreal encounters that involve perversion, destruction, and loss. Not unlike Antonioni's *The Passenger* (*Professione: Reporter*, 1975, Italy/Spain/France), Jarmusch's film unfolds as if it were reenacting the subjective experience of a man who is emotionally and spiritually lost. Jarmusch uses that experience as a critical commentary on the larger culture from which Blake comes and on the traditional celebration of rugged individualism in westerns.

FORMALISM IN A NEW KEY: THE COLLAPSE OF SUBJECTIVITY For the most part, postmodernism rejects the complex explorations of subjectivity that make modernist works difficult to comprehend. If modernism sought to give aesthetic form to reality as a fragmented, subjective terrain, postmodernism treats reality as a grab bag of cultural debris from movies to websites, comics to paintings, whose highest purpose is to be recycled. Postmodernism possesses a political dimension, discussed below, but the assumption that history is no

longer accessible or meaningful except through the recycling of previous styles can diminish its political bite significantly. Sometimes the
result is cynical detachment or nostalgia for something lost, but as
Dead Man or *How Tasty Was My Little Frenchman* (Nelson Pereira dos
Santos, 1971, Brazil), a critique of colonial exploitation, demonstrate,
critical engagement with previous forms of historical understanding
remains possible. These alternative perspectives of detachment or
engagement relate to the two political emphases within postmodernism discussed below, resistance and reaction.

THE SURFACE OF THINGS AND THE LOSS OF HISTORY   Postmodernism
stresses the surface of things. Best epitomized by the work of Andy
Warhol with his reproductions of soup cans and newspaper photographs, it is also a basic feature of Peter Greenaway's stunning films
such as *The Cook, the Thief, His Wife and Her Lover* (1989, France/UK)
and *The Pillow Book* (1996, France/UK/Netherlands). The refusal to
hint at a hidden depth can signify a capitulation to superficiality, or it
can mean an insistence that it is only through our various signifying
systems such as language, painting, or film that we can allude to a
depth that cannot be represented any more directly. Depth becomes
a dubious category for postmodernism. Signifiers now seem to refer
mainly to other signifiers, one work to other works, one moment to
other equally fleeting moments.

   One consequence of the loss of depth is the simultaneous loss of a
sense of depth in time, or history. References to the past function like
quotations or cutouts, elements of earlier moments and discourses that
recirculate as reminders, mementos, or as an overall nostalgia for histories that are no longer directly accessible or meaningful. The dense
invocation of the world of Louis XIV in Roberto Rossellini's realist
study, *The Rise to Power of Louis XIV* (*La prise de pouvoir par Louis XIV*,
1966, France), turns into the disjointed bits and pieces of American history that Forrest Gump wanders through as if they were little more

than stage props for his own life in *Forrest Gump* (Robert Zemeckis, 1994). History becomes a scrapbook, a playing field for nostalgic recall, rather than a vital force that gives shape to the present and future.

Robert Zemeckis's *Back to the Future* (1985) takes nostalgia for the past to an extreme. The past is no longer over and done with, exerting the pressure of its enduring presence on the current moment. It has become, instead, a gigantic sketchbook that a character, Marty McFly, can enter, erase, and transform in order to produce the future he desires. Technology and resourcefulness (part of the great myth of American know-how) have found a way to banish fate and, along with it, history as a repository of what has happened with a finality that can be understood but never altered.

Without the orientation historical awareness provides, characters lack a social compass. This can encourage paranoia. Characters can readily fall victim to a belief that a giant conspiracy controls their destiny and that what has gone before offers no principles or ideals with which to confront an unseen, immoral foe. *JFK* (Oliver Stone, 1991), for example, is a postmodern film that tries to provide a clear interpretation to an historical event, the assassination of President Kennedy, but does so by presenting evidence of a conspiracy of vast proportions. Facts, propelled by leaps of imagination, drawn from numerous sources both real and imagined, and mixed together into a complex brew, yield a paranoid tale of industrial-military intrigue that propels historical narrative into the realm of speculation. This conspiracy functions as a metaphor for global capital and the postmodern condition: large, impersonal forces drive the system forward but remain unseen and therefore beyond the reach of direct confrontation. Political criticism joins forces with a psychotic state of mind (paranoia) as the very system it scrutinizes becomes nebulous, far-reaching, and beyond control.

Postmodernisms of Reaction and Resistance

Postmodern work, like realist and modernist work, need not be aloof, neutral, or apolitical. Conservative and reactionary postmodernism tends to look backward with nostalgic eyes, whereas liberal and radical postmodernism takes up a position of resistance to the dominant social forms and practices. Nostalgia and resistance are terms that themselves suggest a weak form of political engagement, distinct from the strongly political *Battleship Potemkin*, which sets out to remake reality, or *They Live*, which sharply criticizes the status quo.

Films such as *Fear and Loathing in Las Vegas*, *Apocalypse Now*, *House of Games* (David Mamet, 1987), *Pulp Fiction*, *The Rocky Horror Picture Show*, and *Forrest Gump* belong more fully to a postmodernism of reaction than resistance. Films of reaction abandon history as a decisive concept in favor of nostalgia, reinventing the history one wishes to have (as in *Back to the Future*), or simple forgetting, a tendency epitomized by *Forrest Gump*. Such films typically adopt a conservative perspective that sanctions the status quo through their inability to imagine an alternative. *Apocalypse Now* follows the journey of a confused assassin as he seeks out the infamous Kurtz, a renegade soldier who has "gone native." This displacement of the socio-political context for the Vietnam War into a vague allegory about evil eliminates the need for protest or understanding: war is hell; bad apples corrupt others, men journey to the heart of darkness to find individual redemption.

The development of a postmodernism of resistance is most strongly evident in work by members of ethnic minorities and in **Third Cinema**. Third Cinema, from developing countries in the 1960s and '70s, rejected both the Hollywood model and the state-controlled cinemas of Communist states. Third Cinema typically adopted a liberal or radical perspective on social issues, and it often used fragmentation and irony to examine the effects of colonialism and globalization. The Brazilian film

Macunaíma (Joaquim Pedro de Andrade, 1969) and the Philippine film *Perfumed Nightmare* (Kidlat Tahimik, 1977), for example, mix and match lively visual styles and popular narrative techniques to tell stories that undercut the naturalness of a postcolonial world order.

In a similar spirit, Nelson Pereira dos Santos's *How Tasty Was My Little Frenchman* interjects close-ups of authentic engravings from the sixteenth century along with quotes from the journals and diaries of the first colonialists to arrive in Brazil to fragment the tale of a Frenchman who, mistaken for Portuguese, is captured by an indigenous tribe loyal to the French and assigned by the chief to various members of the tribe—after he is slain, barbecued, and "absorbed" on both a literal and metaphorical level. The main character, who has no name, is a prime example of the individual as an interchangeable, disposable cog in a much larger system, colonialism in this case. The film adopts techniques of modernist fragmentation but couples them to an ironic, postmodern treatment of history and memory. Rather than turn such a treatment into a nostalgic longing for a primitive, pre-contact past, the film celebrates the subversion of colonial power by indigenous people who learn how to assimilate a foreign culture before it can overwhelm their way of life.

How Tasty Was My Little Frenchman also draws on a bold, surrealist-influenced movement in Brazil in the 1920s known as the "anthropophagist movement." Artists in this movement defiantly assimilated and transformed elements of European art to make something distinctly Brazilian and wholly their own. They spoke of it as a form of creative cannibalism. As a postmodern recycling of this earlier movement, *How Tasty Was My Little Frenchman* demonstrates how postmodernism can function to tell a story of history from below, from the perspective of ordinary participants and everyday events, that subverts the official version of an epic clash between cultures at the time of colonialism.

6

THE INSTITUTIONAL AND NATIONAL CONTEXTS: HOLLYWOOD AND BEYOND

Four Social Contexts: Constraints and Opportunities

The study of the social context for film involves understanding how social forces and historical conflicts find representation in films, in the specific style and structure of individual films, and in the ways in which films function in society at large. Larger social issues manifest themselves in both the specific issues taken up by films (issues of ethnicity and identity, or the consequences of committing a crime, for example) and in the operating assumptions that govern each part of the infrastructure for the production, distribution, and exhibition of films. This **infrastructure,** or basic system of organization that exists to achieve particular goals such as the transportation of goods or the production of films, includes:

1) Film-oriented institutions and organizations like the Library of Congress (which stores and preserves films), the Academy of Motion Picture Arts and Sciences (which maintains an extensive film archive and library, and sponsors the Academy Awards, or

Oscars) and IDA, the International Documentary Association (which serves the needs of documentary filmmakers)

2) The film industry, consisting of studios (Paramount, MGM, and Universal); management companies that provide agents and managers for stars, directors, and other creative personnel (e.g., ICM [International Creative Management]); and exhibitors like United Artist Theaters and Carmike Cinemas. In other film-producing countries like Germany, France, Japan, India, and China, similar commercial organizations exist.

3) Technology (color or black and white film, specific lenses, digital editing systems like Avid and Final Cut Pro, Dolby and THX sound systems, HDTV, online delivery systems such as YouTube and Netflix)

4) The nation-state (laws regarding censorship or standards of decency, quotas for imported films, subsidies and grants, tax regulations, and other forms of support or constraint pertaining to film)

This vast infrastructure creates both opportunities and constraints for filmmaking. The fact that Paramount Studios, Home Box Office (HBO), the Public Broadcasting System (PBS), the National Endowment for the Arts (NEA), the Ford Foundation, Sundance Institute, British Broadcasting Corporation (BBC) in Great Britain, Canada Council, and Canal Plus in France all support the development or production of films makes opportunities available that might not otherwise be so. All these organizations also have a specific goal or mission, which limits what they support. Experimental films like *Wavelength* (Michael Snow, 1967, Canada/U.S.) or *Variations on a Cellophane Wrapper* (David Rimmer, 1970, Canada), with their absence of character, dialogue, and noticeable drama, are unlikely choices for Paramount Studios, whereas dramatic action films like *Saving Private Ryan* (Steven Spielberg, 1998) or *Iron Man* (Jon Favreau, 2008) are unlikely to get support from the NEA, since this congressionally funded institution primarily sponsors individual, artisanal work.

Opportunities and constraints always coexist. Every opportunity that nonprofit organizations, granting agencies, or the film industry make available is both supportive and restrictive, and every constraint invites creative solutions that bypass it. Creative solutions were common during the heyday of the Hollywood Production Code Association (PCA) from the 1930s to the '50s (the PCA enforced a set of restrictions about what could be shown on screen, discussed further below). Since the Code prohibited direct reference to homosexuality, for example, some writers and directors coded male characters as homosexual by effeminate gestures, overly meticulous dress, a gaze that seemed to linger on other men slightly too long, and so on, without ever identifying the character as homosexual. Many audience members recognized the allusion, but it was done in such a way that the filmmakers could deny they made it. That such characters were almost always associated with evil deeds or sinister deceptions may have helped persuade the Production Code enforcers to look the other way as well.

Technology also creates opportunities and imposes constraints. The state of the art of the cinema constantly evolves. At any given moment, more than one form of technological solution to specific needs will exist, be it the choice between black and white or color film or between distributing a film theatrically or on the Internet. Technology presents, in effect, choices for the selection and arrangement of shots and scenes from which filmmakers choose. Sounds and images can only be shaped by the instruments available to do so. The Internet and handheld digital devices, for example, impose severe restraints on the quality of the image compared to 35mm film, at present, but they simultaneously drop the cost of distribution from the multimillion-dollar level customary for theatrical release to almost nothing. The phenomenal success of YouTube is a prime example of how technology creates fresh possibilities even if it also has limitations. Digital technology in general allows filmmakers to make feature-length films for minuscule budgets. A highly personal documentary about growing up with a schizophrenic mother and coming out gay, *Tarnation* (Jonathan Caouette, 2003), had a reported budget of $218, not counting the price of the Macintosh computer Jonathan Caouette made it on. As a result many individuals who could not possibly manage to distribute a film in movie theaters—not only due to cost factors but also due to an unconventional form or controversial subject matter—now have an outlet for their work.

TWO FORMS OF FILMMAKING SUPPORT

The Motion Picture Association of America (MPAA) vividly demonstrates how competing corporations can also share common interests. The Ratings System, used by all the studios and discussed below, falls under the jurisdiction of the MPAA. The MPAA also oversees the film industry's lobbying efforts in Washington, where it has won strict revisions of copyright law, especially in relation to digital copying and distribution. The MPAA is quite aggressive about this, since large sums of money are at stake. Its policy statement reads, in part:

> People often steal movies on the Internet because they believe they are anonymous and will not be held responsible for their actions. They are wrong. Illegal distribution of digital movie files on the Internet is a serious crime, and individuals who engage in piracy via the Internet can easily be tracked. The movie industry has and is taking a firm stance against Internet thieves who steal millions of dollars in copyrighted material with complete disregard for the law.

The International Motion Picture Association, a subsidiary of the MPAA, addresses foreign trade. The IMPA tends to favor free trade, meaning that American films should be able to enter other countries to compete on a level playing field with domestically produced films, even if reciprocation, foreign films entering the American market on a level playing field, is not very plausible for small nations that lack the resources to enter the American market. Many other countries have resited this position ever since the rise of Hollywood in the 1920s, arguing that their own national cinema is part of their cultural heritage and deserves protection. Quotas that limit the number of foreign films that can be imported, or the number of theaters in which they can play; tariffs, which raise a financial barrier to importation, and taxes, which turn money from film exhibition back to the local film industry, are measures adopted by different nations and opposed by the IMPA.

The San Francisco Film Society (SFFS) and the Film Arts Society (FAF) have provided an entirely different kind of support for filmmaking. FAF had operated on a shoestring for several decades, providing support no other organization could provide such as equipment rental, viewing facilities, fundraising advice and accounting assistance. In 2008 the SFFS, sponsor of the city's international film festival, assumed the responsibilities of FAF. The Filmmaker Services division of the SFFS has taken up FAF's role for independent filmmakers and given it a more financially stable foundation. It does not take an official position on issues like copyright protection, fair use, or foreign trade, and it conducts no lobbying. It offers informal courses on everything from how to edit digitally to how to fund a documentary. The SFFS's Filmmaker Services serves a community of individuals whose mode of production is artisanal rather than industrial.

ARTISANAL FILMMAKING

Sharply distinct from the Hollywood studio system is **artisanal production.** Artisanal filmmaking revolves around one individual's distinctive way of seeing the world and making films to express that vision. Some individuals, like the documentary filmmakers Ken Burns and Errol Morris and the feature filmmakers Atom Egoyan and Woody Allen, may have long-term collaborators, just as some artists have studio assistants, in a tradition that goes back to the Renaissance, but the individual artist retains decisive control over what gets made. This is the mode commonly adopted by experimental and documentary filmmakers, by many independent feature filmmakers, and by most filmmakers who belong to the modernist tradition. Such filmmakers are often dependent on granting agencies for support, a potential constraint, but they also enjoy freedom from the assumptions and conventions governing big-budget feature productions.

The remarkable flowering of art films from Europe in the 1950s and '60s was almost entirely artisanal in nature. Individual filmmakers distinguished themselves and received financial backing for new films based on their distinctive styles more than their ability to make films that fit a predetermined mold. Jean-Luc Godard (*Breathless* [1960, France],

SAMPLE BUDGETS FOR TWO LOW-BUDGET FILMS

Independent, artisanal films have low budgets compared to studio films with major stars. A major star commands a salary of $5,000,000 to 25,000,000, enough to fund an entire low-budget film. Low-budgets impose limitations but also allow more risk-taking since it takes less revenue to recoup costs.

Budgets at all levels of funding break down into several major categories. One key division is between **above-the-line** and **below-the-line** expenses. **Above-the-line** personnel exercise a significant degree of creative control over the entire project. **Below-the-line** personnel perform tasks at the behest of the above-the-line personnel, but nonetheless possess distinct talents and skills of considerable value. Budgets also break down into **pre-production** (costs to prepare to shoot the film, such as screenplay development), **production** (the actual shooting of the film), and **post-production** (the editing of sound and image, special effects). On a blockbuster film, the budget for marketing, not included here, can equal the cost of production, which can easily land in the neighborhood of $100,000,000 or more.

Category	Low Budget	Ultra-Low Budget
ABOVE THE LINE		
Producer and pre-production	$500,000	$15,000
Director	100,000	15,000
Screenplay	150,000	5,000
Principal actors	500,000	20,000
Director of photography (DP)	70,000	8,000
SUBTOTAL	$1,320,000	$63,000
BELOW THE LINE		
Assistant cameraman	30,000	3,000
Art director	40,000	5,000
Production manager	70,000	7,000
Assistant director (AD)	50,000	5,000
Sound recording	40,000	4,000
Costume designer	30,000	5,000
Wardrobe	40,000	3,000
Makeup	25,000	2,000
Production assistants (PAs)	30,000	4,000
Other crew members	70,000	12,000
Sets and props	160,000	5,000
Equipment rental	130,000	45,000
Travel and lodging, meals	500,000	80,000
Lab costs	120,000	35,000
Editing, sound, and image	300,000	35,000
Music, original or rights	125,000	5,000
Insurance, taxes, misc.	350,000	18,000
SUBTOTAL	$2,110,000	$273,000
TOTAL COSTS	$3,430,000	$336,000

Vivre sa vie [1962, France], *Contempt* [1963, France/Italy]), François Truffaut (*The 400 Blows* [*Les quatre cents coups*, 1959, France], *Jules and Jim*
[1962, France], *Day for Night* [*La nuit américaine*, 1973, France/Italy]),
Ingmar Bergman (*The Seventh Seal* [1957, Sweden], *The Virgin Spring*
[1960, Sweden], *Persona* [1966, Sweden]), Federico Fellini (*La strada*
[1954, Italy], *8½* [1963, Italy/France], *Amarcord* [1973, Italy/France]),
Michelangelo Antonioni (*L'avventura* [1960, Italy/France], *La notte*
[1961, Italy/France], *L'eclisse* [1962, Italy/France]), and Agnes Varda (*Cleo
from 5 to 7* [1962, France/Italy], *Le bonheur* [1965, France], *Lion's Love*
[1969, U.S./France]) were among the dozens of directors who came to
prominence. Their distinctive approaches gave added impetus to the
auteur theory, with its emphasis on the combination of a consistent style
and thematic preoccupations across a body of work.

Artisanal filmmakers remain dependent on entities like the traditional studio distributors or smaller boutique distributors to get their
films seen, if not made. Some boutique distributors specialize in niche
markets for experimental, documentary, independent, or foreign feature films, sometimes relying on video, DVD, or the Web to reach
their audience. The Hollywood studios entered into the arena of
niche marketing in the 1990s by creating subsidiary units that focused
on independent films, domestic or foreign. From *Repo Man* (Alex
Cox, 1984) to *Little Miss Sunshine* (Jonathan Dayton and Valerie Faris,
2006), these units have brought to the public films that might not have
otherwise been seen.

THE INDUSTRIAL CONTEXT

Hollywood is the industrial context for film that first comes to mind
for many individuals, but there are actually a number of equivalents to
Hollywood around the world. Japan has long had a number of major
film studios, such as Toho, Daiei, and Shochuki, whose structure and
function closely resembles that of the classic Hollywood studio. Hong

Kong cinema has enormous international popularity along with the highest per capita film attendance in the world, and Bollywood, like Hollywood a term part mythical and part reality, serves as a worldwide emblem for the phenomenal size and popularity of feature films from India. The constraints and opportunities sketched out here apply to all these national industries. The Hollywood system itself receives further consideration later in this chapter.

OPPORTUNITIES CREATED BY AN INDUSTRIAL CONTEXT

The opportunities offered by the studio or industrial context are legion. Individuals can rise to the heights of fame and fortune. The popular press thrives on Horatio Alger tales of how people with little expertise or experience make their way to the top of the motion picture industry. Such tales go back to the very beginning of cinema with the first stars, people like Charlie Chaplin and Mary Pickford, working their way from relative poverty and obscurity to worldwide fame. Stars often proved to be ordinary people who possess palpable charisma and a magnetic attraction for the camera. The discovery, cultivation, success, and decline of a star has become such a mythic cliché that several films have retold this tale in different ways, from *A Star Is Born* (William A. Wellman, 1934, and George Cukor, 1954) with Janet Gaynor in 1934 and Judy Garland in 1954 to *Inside Daisy Clover* (Robert Mulligan, 1965) with Natalie Wood. *Singin' in the Rain* (Stanley Donen and Gene Kelly, 1952) also incorporates this tale, in the form of Kathy Selden's ascendancy from serving as the unseen, off-screen voice for the reigning star of the moment, Lina Lamont, to genuine stardom as the true partner to Don Lockwood (Gene Kelly). Histories of Hollywood never fail to recount how a set of poor Jewish immigrants rose to the heights of power as the founders of the major film studios in the 1920s and '30s, a story not unlike that of Harvey and Bob Weinstein, who rose from being small-time music

promoters in Buffalo, New York, to running the most financially successful company dedicated to promoting offbeat, independent, and
quality films. Miramax was eventually purchased by Disney and then,
following a series of disagreements, sold back to the brothers as Weinstein Films.

Within an industrial or studio context, financial interests and the
executives who represent those interests have significant control over
what gets made. They fund, own, and therefore control the final product, just as the artisan owns and controls her own work. Work done on
a studio film, whether by a hairdresser or a director, is done under contract or "for hire." The individual sells his labor to the studio and
receives payment in exchange. At the same time, he forfeits ultimate
control over what happens to his labor, over what the end result will be.
That remains up to studio executives. Much of the creativity of the Hollywood system involves finding ways to honor artistic goals while also
satisfying the financial needs of the studios that fund the films, but this
arrangement is also the source of considerable conflict.

Hollywood, of course, also offers the opportunity to make the type
of films for which it is best known: popular films that entertain sizable
audiences. Genre films are the bread and butter of such a system and
many of the best-known directors began by making them. Martin
Scorsese's first Hollywood-based film was *Boxcar Bertha* (1972), a tale
of a union organizer who meets up with a female drifter. They become
a pair of politically motivated criminals who seek revenge on an avari-
cious railroad company in this low-budget imitation of *Bonnie and Clyde*
(Arthur Penn, 1967). Similarly, Steven Spielberg's first major film
was *Duel* (1971), a television movie about a man on a trip who unwittingly gets drawn into a deadly battle with the (never seen) driver of
a menacing big rig. It was produced at Universal TV, the movie studio's television production arm, as a suspenseful road movie, and it was
first aired on the ABC television network. Many of the best respected
directors from the period of Hollywood's greatest fame—John Ford,

Charlie Chaplin, Frank Capra, Howard Hawks, Vincente Minnelli, and others—made genre films almost exclusively, but of considerable distinction.

Some studios or other producing entities become known for their willingness to support risk-taking, while others are best known for avoiding risks by repeating what proves commercially successful. An example of the latter is the producing team, Don Simpson and Jerry Bruckheimer and, after Simpson's death in 1996, Bruckheimer on his own. They have specialized in male actions movies with spectacular chases, shoot-outs, and attacks, such as *Enemy of the State* (Tony Scott, 1998), *The Rock* (Michael Bay, 1996), *Black Hawk Down* (Ridley Scott, 2001), and *Gone in Sixty Seconds* (Dominic Sena, 2000), and they also produced the *Pirates of the Caribbean* series (Gore Verbinski, 2003-2007). The producer Ed Pressman exemplifies a more risk-taking approach. Over his career he has produced almost 100 films, including *Das Boot* (*The Boat*, Wolfgang Petersen, 1981, West Germany), *The Cooler* (Wayne Kramer, 2003), *Thank You for Smoking* (Jason Reitman, 2005), *Amazing Grace* (Michael Apted, 2006, U.S./UK), and *Fur: An Imaginary Portrait of Diane Arbus* (Steven Shainberg, 2006), all offbeat, quality productions.

In recent decades the studios have shifted to banking their hopes on a few "tent pole" or blockbuster "event" movies. These are heavily publicized, franchise-like films that not only include major stars but often include marketing tie-ins such as toys, videogames, and sequels. The success or failure of such films becomes extremely important and the studios make great efforts to attract as much attention, and paying customers, as possible, especially in the opening week. This "bet the house" approach that has replaced the concept of a steady stream of **A-** and **B-budget films** has also brought what may appear an unexpected opportunity for newer filmmakers. (**A-budget films**, while not necessarily blockbusters, have enough funding to utilize a studio's best talent; **B-budget films** have more limited budgets and were, historically, the standard genre films that filled double bills as the second feature.) Slowly releasing a film over a period of months, allowing reviews and word of mouth to build an audience while advertising modestly, put a premium on experienced directors who knew how to meet basic expectations dependably. The blockbuster movie, by contrast, depends on the modern practices of **packaging**, assembling most of the above-the-line personnel as a single package to market to a studio for funding, and **saturation booking**—filling as many theaters with as many people as quickly as possible. It has, perhaps surprisingly, given some relative newcomers an opportunity to direct. Such projects depend on the market research, script development, star power, producing talent, and marketing skills of the team that brings the film to the theater more than on an individual director's distinct style. A less established director may prove easier to control by the producers, stars, and others who have already invested considerable time and money in the project by the time they need to hire a director to shoot it.

For example, Roland Emmerich, director of *Independence Day* (1996), enjoyed prior commercial success in Germany and had a few credits as a Hollywood producer before taking on this blockbuster, budgeted at $75 million, which grossed over $300 million by the end of its first year of release. Shawn Levy graduated from Yale and had worked mainly on television shows like *Beverly Hills 90210* before assuming responsibility for the $110 million budget on *Night at the Museum* (2006, U.S./UK). The film grossed $235 million within the first two months of its release. Zack Synder had directed a couple of music videos and just one feature film, *Dawn of the Dead* (2004, U.S./Japan/France), before getting a chance to direct the R-rated *300* (2006), a graphic comic book–style but live-action tale of the battle of Thermopylae. The film grossed $70 million on its first weekend alone, approximately double what Warner Brothers had predicted it would earn and already well in excess of its estimated budget of $60 million. A relatively inexperienced director can shave some money off the costs while more readily ensuring that the production team gets to make the movie it wants, for better or worse.

CONSTRAINTS ASSOCIATED WITH AN INDUSTRIAL CONTEXT

To an appreciable extent, the film industry is a meritocracy: it rewards those with talent and weeds out those without it. Money and power alone cannot create the type of film chemistry that occurs when a Scarlett Johansson, Kate Winslet, Brad Pitt, or Leonardo DiCaprio steps before the camera, nor can it produce the kind of powerful flights of imagination and originality that mark the films of a Martin Scorsese (*Taxi Driver* [1976] and *Goodfellas* [1990]), or Tim Burton (*Edward Scissorhands* [1990] and *Sweeney Todd* [2007, U.S./UK]). By the same token, many are attracted but few chosen. The odds of rising to a position of major prominence as an actor, writer, producer, or director are slim, given the enormous amount of competition. The suggestion that "Someone else will do the job the way we want if you don't" can promote considerable conformity. A very sizable number of individuals nonetheless do find niches in which their talent and the industry's needs match to such a degree that an extended career of gratifying accomplishments proves entirely possible.

Originality must accommodate itself to the basic conventions that lie at the heart of commercial success: a realist style, strong characters whose psychological makeup is relatively easy to understand, a plausible story world, goal-driven plot, suspense, and a satisfying resolution. Such constraints leave enormous room for individual variation and exceptional achievement, to be sure, but they also rule out projects that stray too far toward an episodic, modernist style, enigmatic or unintelligible characters, a stress on situations more than plot development, lack of suspense, an emphasis on ambiguity, and a lack of resolution. Such films do get made, but they seldom come from the Hollywood studios.

PRODUCT PLACEMENT

Product placement, the practice of using specific products in a film in exchange for financial consideration, exemplifies one way in which an industrial context creates both opportunities and constraints. The manufacturer enjoys a form of embedded advertising and the filmmaker adds revenue to her budget. Product placement depends on the audience's recognition of a given signifier's referent (the product) in the external world. That item—be it a brand of cigarettes, a line of clothing, or a soft drink—will now be associated with the myth and magic of Hollywood, giving a boost to the product's appeal.

Is this a financial compromise or can it be turned to advantage? Some directors find ways to exploit the concept to enrich their story. The Giorgio Armani clothing that is worn by Richard Gere's character, a male escort, in *American Gigolo* (Paul Schrader, 1980), is meant to suggest his refined taste. The appearance of specific beverages, cars, or computers in other films, by comparison, makes no real difference to our understanding of the characters or the story: they may, in fact, distract from the story if they suggest to the viewer that the characters are there to promote products rather than tell a story.

The Production Code of old and the current ratings system also establish limits as to what can be shown on the screen. Ratings are issued after the completion of a film. A filmmaker can show just about anything, if willing to accept the most restrictive rating, NC-17 (no one less than 17 years of age admitted). There is, however, considerable risk of diminished box office return if a large segment of the younger audience that accounts for a disproportionate share of box office revenue cannot see the film at all. Producers and the studios usually do all they can to ensure that a film receives no worse than an R rating (anyone under 17 must be accompanied by a parent or guardian).

TECHNOLOGY

Technology defines the range and limits of the possible. It generates an ever-changing sense of the possible. Before Technicolor perfected its three-strip color film process, the great majority of films were shot in black and white because the existing technology made shooting in color complicated, expensive, and aesthetically unsatisfying. Similar opportunities and limitations apply to:

- Cameras—relative silence, medium (film, tape, digital storage), and portability;
- Lenses—sharpness, speed, and depth of field;
- Sound recording—range, directionality, ability to separate signal from noise, and wireless capability;
- Post-production sound—ability to add sound effects, improve the quality of dialogue through **ADR** (additional dialogue recording: the replacement of sync sound recorded on the set or location with more carefully controlled recording done on a sound stage as the original scene is projected on a screen in front of the actors), and **sound mixing** (the careful blending of as many as 48 different soundtracks into one master soundtrack);
- **Special effects**—such as blowing up a building, or having a character fly through the air as several characters did in *Crouching Tiger, Hidden Dragon* (Ang Lee, 2003, Taiwan/Hong Kong/China/U.S.) These effects expand the director's dramatic options considerably, and **CGI (computer-generated images)** can create entirely imaginary worlds, as it does in *The Incredibles* (Brad Bird, 2004) and *Wall-E* (Andrew Stanton, 2008), or add imaginary elements to otherwise real ones such as the Gollum character in *The Lord of the Rings* trilogy (Peter Jackson, 2001–03, New Zealand/U.S.).

All these options involve trade-offs, from the shallow depth of field of telephoto lenses to the fuzzy, poor contrast ratio of low-cost digital recording. But each brings advantages as well. The filmmaker's challenge is to make optimal use of available technology to achieve the greatest gains with the fewest losses. The potential of digital images to match celluloid film in color fidelity, sensitivity to contrast, and the capture of detail, along with the emerging capacity to project films digitally in movie theaters, augurs the all-digital cinema of the future. This, too, will open up new opportunities and limitations.

Special effects as a way to do things that cannot be done in reality is as old as the cinema. Early filmmakers such the Lumière brothers or Georges Méliès quickly discovered that action could be speeded up or slowed down, and that startling jumps from one time or one place to another would fascinate viewers. By the 1910s individuals began to specialize in devising special effects, distinct ways to produce the image seen by the viewer that supplement what a camera can record on its own. These involved such techniques as **superimposing** one shot on top of another so that the two images are seen at the same time. Superimpositions can show a character and her dream, for example, at the same time. The **Schüfftan process** allowed filmmakers to shoot a miniature model of a set through a mirror and superimpose this shot onto the same strip of film that recorded the principal actors. The actors would now appear to stand before a vast, possibly fantastical set, such those in Fritz Lang's *Metropolis* (1927, Germany). Much the same thing is now done using computer-generated images (CGI) alone. Backgrounds and actions can be blended into the same shot as the one that contains the actors, making it seem as if they possess magical powers or occupy fantastic spaces, as when Eddie Valiant (Bob Hoskins) stands opposite and talks to cartoon characters in *Who Framed Roger Rabbit* (Robert Zemeckis, 1988), or when Neo dodges bullets torpedoing toward him in *The Matrix* (Andy and Larry Wachowski, 1999, U.S./Australia). Digital effects can create an array of remarkable worlds, such as the ones in *Sky Captain and the World of Tomorrow* (Kerry Conran, 2004, U.S./UK/Italy), *Sin City* (Frank Miller and Robert Rodriguez, 2005), and *300*.

THE NATION-STATE

CREATING A CLIMATE FOR FILM PRODUCTION Finally, the institutional, industrial, and technological contexts all function within a national framework. The national context includes the general cultural attitude adopted toward the arts or toward the cinema in particular in comparison with other areas. Self-promotion by the relevant institutions, organizations, and industry, the nature and quality of commentary about film in the mass media, the types of awards and prizes offered for work in film as well as the general disposition of the public to value the cinema relative to other forms of art and entertainment, all play an important role in creating a national context that situates the cinema relative to other forms of art and leisure activity. These factors join with the role assumed by the state directly to create a climate for the arts in general and cinema in particular as part of a broader national identity.

The French, for example, are avid moviegoers, embracing a wide variety of films from around the world as well as locally produced ones. They are enthusiastic followers of American cinema in all its manifestations, from major, big-budget, big-star studio films to small, quirky independent movies and avant-garde films. This enthusiasm, supported by a lively book and magazine culture, television talk shows with movie personalities, and an abundance of theaters that range from movie palaces to tiny shoebox operations, fits a broader national pattern in which matters of culture occupy a prominent position in day-to-day French life. The national Ministry of Culture works closely with the commercial film industry and supports the arts and film in a wide variety of ways.

In almost all countries, official agencies carry out governmental policies toward the arts, applying specific measures that may range from foreign trade to censorship. In many countries, for example, television is under state control and many feature and documentary films get funded by the television networks. This is commonly true throughout Europe. Many important films have received backing from Canal Plus in France, Channel Four in Britain, and RAI in Italy. In Germany, the television networks provided significant support for the films of the New German Cinema. New German cinema was a loose movement of filmmakers with core members such as Rainer Werner Fassbinder, Werner Herzog, Margarethe von Trotta, and Wim Wenders. They all took a fresh, detached, often critical look at German history and the postwar legacy of a divided country (into East [Communist-controlled] and West [democratic] Germany). Their films often drew funding from the state television system but quickly found an international audience thanks to their offbeat and probing qualities. Television funding, in turn, often derives from fees or taxes attached to the purchase or use of televisions by citizens. Such fees often replace or reduce the amount of advertising, and place creative control more squarely in the hands of the networks rather than corporate sponsors.

In the United States, the state's promotion of the cinema is primarily done at arm's length through a tacit endorsement of Hollywood film as an ambassador for American culture internationally and as a successful industry domestically. There is a comparative lack of government support for artisanal filmmaking, and the modest efforts of the NEA pale in contrast to the degree of support found in Canada, Great Britain, or France. The arts—theater, ballet, opera, jazz, painting, sculpture, literature, poetry, and avant-garde, documentary, and independent feature films—play a significant role in American society as a whole but do so without anywhere near the degree of support that some other governments provide.

Some countries regard film primarily as another industry that can generate employment, provide tax revenue, and improve the balance of trade. Such a view was, ironically, quite strong in the early days of the Soviet silent cinema, when, despite the Soviet Revolution, many government officials considered the Soviet film industry, like the vodka business, as a way to fund the revolution by generating foreign exchange. The artistic success of the great silent Soviet films of Sergei Eisenstein, Vsevolod Pudovkin, Aleksandr Dovzhenko, and others encouraged the Soviet government to allow the concept of film as cultural capital to coexist alongside the idea of film as a source of foreign exchange revenue for some time.

Other countries promote film primarily as a form of **cultural capital**, which is to say as an art form from which the country as a whole profits in terms of prestige, status, and international reputation as much as or more than in financial terms. When seen as cultural capital, film production may receive government support even if, and sometimes specifically because, it is not commercially viable in the marketplace. For example, Iran has used the international success of key directors such as Jafar Panahi, Abbas Kiarostami, Mohsen Makhmalbaf, and Rakhshan Bani-Etemad as a way to enhance its reputation as a modern, culturally diverse, and artistically rich country, an image that contrasts sharply with the one advanced by the American government of a dangerous, even terrorist regime. Strong support—with equally strong constraints—comes from the government's Ministry of Culture and Islamic Guidance and from organizations like the International Festival of Films for Children and Young Adults.

IRANIAN CINEMA AND THE STATE Over the course of time, many nations have had film industries that earned international recognition. The French and Italian cinemas were among the very first to produce a range of highly engaging work in the early part of the twentieth century. At different moments Denmark, Sweden, Germany, the Soviet Union, Japan, India, Brazil, Cuba, and Senegal, among others, have produced films that have circulated widely and earned both popular and critical respect.

Iran is a relatively recent addition to this list. Iran has a long history of over 2,500 years of social development and cultural achievement. It is a nation that has never experienced colonial rule, and lacks a legacy of colonial influence. After the revolution of 1979, in which a fundamentalist theocracy replaced the repressive monarchy of the shah, the cinema gradually began to grow in importance. This was only partially a matter of government subsidy, since such aid went primarily to films that promoted the revolution. The birth of a new Iranian cinema depended more on small pockets of opportunity that happened to allow some exceptionally talented individuals to demonstrate what might be possible within the strict constraints demanded by the new government. For example, the ayatollah and his clerical followers prohibited films from showing any physical contact between men and women, let alone intimacy. Women in public, in film as in ordinary life, had to wear a veil, and no direct criticism of the government could be made.

Perhaps it is not surprising, then, that much of the impetus for a new Iranian cinema came from Kanun: the Institute for the Intellectual Development of Children and Young Adults. Focusing on children made it relatively easy for filmmakers to sidestep the constraints that strict religious rules imposed. Films like Amir Naderi's 1985 film *The Runner* (Iran), about a young orphaned boy who ekes out a scant living on the waterfront of Abadan while consumed by a passion to run, evokes the simplicity and down-to-earth quality of Italian neorealism.

Iranian cinema has tackled a wide range of subjects, including a wide array of adult themes, since its birth in the mid-1980s. It has run afoul of censorship from time to time, but it has also proven an invaluable form of cultural capital in the arena of international opinion. The government has supported the films that wind up in film festivals and art houses as well as encouraged a more strictly domestic film industry that produces imitation Hollywood films and films that promote government policies. Promoting a positive, culturally sophisticated image abroad clearly plays a role in this support. That a sizeable group of distinguished directors can make films that compete successfully at festivals like the Venice, Cannes, New York, and Toronto film festivals stands as a clear indication that the state, despite explicit and detailed constraints, can nonetheless foster a cinema of considerable quality.

The Dynamic Tension between Art and Business in Cinema

Just as the cinema incorporates both intense realism and vivid fantasy, it has also functioned both as an art form and a business. The business side of things is never very far from sight even in independent and avant-garde filmmaking, since making a film is but the first step on its journey to the public via organizations and businesses devoted to film distribution and exhibition. Whereas the bulk of television shows are **green lit** or approved and funded by the very outlet that will eventually broadcast the work to the public, guaranteeing the maker an audience, films are made in one context, whether artisanal or industrial, but seen in others—movie theaters, museums, media centers, schools, at home, and on the Web—which means that every single film must be promoted as a distinct entity competing in a common marketplace.

Historically, U.S. federal and state law treated film as a commodity like any other. In legal terms films were a commodity pure and simple, far removed from the realm of art. Movies fell into the same category as pork bellies, dairy products, and quack remedies. Their regulation involved issues of safety (early nitrate-based film stock was highly flammable) and morality (most courts and legislatures felt an obligation to protect the public from the corrupting influence of movies). Because movies were a product marketed for the purpose of making a profit, **prior censorship** seemed entirely appropriate, even if this practice ran counter to the principle of free speech: filmmakers could not say what they wished to say, but had to follow the state's restrictions regarding what was and was not permissible. (**Prior censorship**, also known as **prior restraint**, determines what can and cannot be said or done prior to the saying or doing of it. It approximates the regulation of standards and practices in the food, travel, and health industries, where government acts to protect the public from unscrupulous entrepreneurs and unsafe practices. Prior censorship often involves lists of prohibitions, along with penalties for violations.

Prior censorship contrasts with the principle of **free speech** in which individuals, or filmmakers, can say and do what they choose. It is then only after they have done so that courts may become involved in cases that question whether the utterance or film violated certain standards, such as those of obscenity, slander, or libel.)

It was not until a Supreme Court ruling in 1952, involving a forty-minute fiction film by Roberto Rossellini, *The Miracle* (1948, Italy), which had been banned as "sacrilegious," that the cinema gained the protective status of free speech. (The film tells the story of how a stranger seduces a naïve peasant woman by convincing her she is the Virgin Mary and he is Joseph. The Catholic Church regarded her delusion and subsequent pregnancy as an attack on church dogma and condemned the film.) Following this Supreme Court decision, film received the same protection from prior censorship as journalism or literature. (With few exceptions, courts have interpreted the First Amendment guaranteeing freedom of speech to mean that speech cannot be restricted, or censored, prior to its utterance or dissemination.) After the *Miracle* ruling the Hollywood Production Code, the multiple forms of prior censorship at the state level, and the formidable power of organizations like the Catholic Church to determine the acceptable content of films before they arrived in the marketplace began to erode.

With the court ruling, which arrived just in time to welcome the wave of exceptional postwar European films by directors like Rossellini, Vittorio De Sica, Luchino Visconti, Ingmar Bergman, and the French New Wave, the art of cinema gained new opportunities for expression. Without prior restraints, films could be judged by viewers in a marketplace of ideas, giving those with merit the opportunity to succeed, even if their content proved offensive or distasteful to some. Dissent, debate, and even protests and boycotts remained possible. The regulation of content would have to take other forms now that prior censorship was no longer valid.

MUTUAL FILM CORPORATION V. INDUSTRIAL COMMISSION OF OHIO (1915): *The Birth of a Nation* AND FILM AS ART OR COMMODITY

The Mutual Film Corporation, a distributor, challenged the state of Ohio's right to censor portions of films prior to their exhibition, in this case D. W. Griffith's *The Birth of a Nation* (1915). Ohio argued that it had the same right to reject work that did not meet its standard for film as for any other consumer product. Mutual's core argument was that films were a form of speech and should receive the protection guaranteed to a free press in the First Amendment. The Ohio court rejected this argument. The unanimous, nine-judge opinion prevailed until 1952. In his majority opinion, Justice McKenna wrote:

> The exhibition of motion pictures is a business pure and simple, originated and conducted for profit. . . . [Movies] are mere representations of events, of ideas and sentiments published or known; vivid, useful, and entertaining, no doubt, but . . . capable of evil.

Given the low quality and lack of serious intent in the majority of early films, such a view of the cinema was not at all unusual in the early part of the twentieth century. Many middle-class citizens held similar views, regarding movies as a titillating entertainment aimed primarily at immigrant and working-class urban populations. This social context made it quite reasonable to think of films as similar to other novelty items hawked on street corners, like home remedies, rather than as comparable to journalism or serious literature. The result was that prior restraint became a common practice, both within the film industry and in society as a whole, until the 1950s, a span of time that more or less coincides, ironically, with the golden age of Hollywood.

Hollywood Production and the Studio System

PRODUCTS, FILMS, AND THE DUAL PRACTICE OF STANDARDIZATION AND DIFFERENTIATION

The entertainment industry, like other industries devoted to the production of a commodity or provision of a service, must subordinate aesthetics and art to commerce and profit. As already discussed, however, the commodity produced by Hollywood—movies—is an unusual one. Films bear emotional impact and convey a range of meanings. Unlike a hammer, bedsheet, or vegetable, a film is valued for its expressive capacity as a language more than for its usefulness as a physical entity. As such, film's have the characteristics of a commodity that can be bought and sold, a language that makes communication and expression possible, and an art form that yields aesthetic pleasure.

Not only its commodity status, but the process of making a film is unusual. Hollywood can produce a large number of films and do so by cost-effective means, but, unlike most manufacturers, it cannot, indeed it dare not, mass-produce exactly the same thing over and over. Consumers expect all cars of a specific version of a model to be essentially the same, but audiences expect *Scream 2* (Wes Craven, 1997) to be different from *Scream* (Wes Craven, 1996) no matter how similar they might also be (hence the long tradition of genre films and sequels).

The Hollywood infrastructure produces a continual flow of distinct **prototypes**, that is, films that are similar to but distinct from previous films and that are also possible models for future films. Creative personnel who can tell new stories that will attract a sizable audience while not straying too far from the tried and true are highly prized. The practice of conceiving of every film as a prototype, based on successful previous films, increases the odds that a given film will capitalize on the achievement of earlier films but without any guarantee that it will actually do so. *Elektra* (Rob Bowman, 2005), starring Jennifer Garner, adapted the comic book hero prototype that had been applied successfully to the Batman, Superman, and Ironman films, not to mention *Lara Croft: Tomb Raider* (Simon West, 2005, U.S./Germany/UK/Japan), with its female heroine played by Angelina Jolie. *Elektra* also threw in scenes with Japanese dialogue to enhance its international box office potential. It was, nonetheless, a flop. With a budget of $40,000,000, it only grossed $24,000,000 theatrically, whereas *Lara Croft: Tomb Raider*, with a budget of approximately $80,000,000, was still profitable, grossing over $131,000,000 theatrically. Additional income would accrue to both films from **ancillary markets.** These comprise all the ways a film can be distributed outside of U.S. movie theaters: foreign theater distribution, foreign and domestic television, cable, satellite, as well as videotape and DVD rental and sales. **Tie-ins** such as **novelizations** (novels based on the film that closely follow the same plot), and clothing, toys, or video games associated with the original film, also provide additional income for certain films.

Contemporary Hollywood leans heavily toward the blockbuster megahit, released in one to two thousand theaters nationwide behind a massive wave of publicity. Films like *Independence Day*, *The Terminator* (James Cameron, 1984), *Titanic* (James Cameron, 1997), the *Pirates of the Caribbean* series, *The Lord of the Rings* trilogy, *The Bourne Identity* (Doug Liman, 2002, U.S./Germany), and the *Harry Potter* series (Chris Columbus, Alfonso Cuarón, Mike Newell, and David Yates, 2001–07, UK/U.S.) follow in the footsteps of *Jaws* (Steven Spielberg, 1975) and *Star Wars* (George Lucas, 1977) as media events. Their goal: maximize box office returns as quickly as possible. This newer type of marketing requires massive expenditures for radio, television, newspaper, and online advertising. Enormous effort focuses on the opening weekend before reviews, word of mouth, and more extensive commentary accumulate. Films without **"legs,"** the ability to continue to bring in appreciable revenue over time, quietly sink from sight after their splashy opening.

The concept of each film as a prototype serves both to standardize film production and to differentiate between specific films. **Standardization** involves all those narrative conventions, filmmaking techniques, skills, and facilities that can be carried over from one film to another. An entire layer of personnel—typically executive producers, producers, studio heads, marketing personnel, boards of directors, and so on—see to it that new films conform to the assumptions and expectations that characterize previous films and distinguish them from, say, documentaries or European art cinema films. **Differentiation** involves all those innovations to narrative convention, variations on familiar plots, stylistic idiosyncrasies, distinctive forms of character development, and specific choices of selection and arrangement that mark any given film as unique. This effort requires blending the talents of two relatively separate groups: above- and below-the-line personnel. Their collective goal is to make the particular film they are working on distinct from every other film.

All personnel, above and below the line, must agree on answers to the three key questions: Exactly what story shall we tell? Exactly how will we tell it? And how much can we spend to tell it? Individuals committed to standardization and those devoted to differentiation often clash in defining what is and is not acceptable in terms of form and content. How different can a film be without losing broad audience appeal? Different members of a production team (an actor and writer, or a director and producer) can also clash in terms of the structure of a scene, development of a character, or shape of the final film. The collaborative but tension-laden nature of the filmmaking process magnifies the possibility, inherent in all art, of ambiguous or even conflicting values and meanings residing in a single work. This is another dimension of film that formal-social analysis, sensitive to contradictions, ambiguities, and mixed messages, can help interpret.

During its classic period from the 1920s to the 1960s, each major studio retained a set of key personnel on long-term contracts. The studio heads then mixed and matched actors and directors, writers and producers to ensure a steady stream of films. This system leaned toward the steady production of dependable and modestly remunerative genre films. Publicity during this earlier period promoted the overall system (up-and-coming actors and actresses, the careers of stars, the studio system, genres, etc.) more than individual films. This practice made for a level of studio consistency, or style, as well as an overall Hollywood style: Warner Brothers featured hard-hitting action films, whereas MGM maintained prominence in more lavish productions such as musicals.

But despite its efficiencies, this system inevitably left many of the studio's assets—sets, sound stages, equipment, and back lots, along with individuals—underutilized. Equipment, space and personnel, often very costly personnel such as directors, writers, and stars, were often **between pictures**—a term used to indicate that they were not productively employed in making a film at that particular moment. Cost-conscious managers questioned the wisdom of retaining expensive personnel on long-term contracts, and many prominent actors, producers, and directors sought the greater independence that came with single picture deals. In the 1950s, well ahead of other industries, Hollywood broke away from upholding long-term commitments and standing obligations.

Since the 1960s studios most commonly have played the role of chief financial agent and green-light, or approve, individual projects based on the personnel and screenplay. A team assembles for the purpose of making one particular film; then, at the conclusion of their contribution to the film, individuals move on to other projects, usually with entirely different sets of collaborators.

Constraints and Censorship in Hollywood

Internally, the studio system has established constraints, and made opportunities possible, in three ways:

1) *Internalized conventions.* The first implicit method of constraint has an "It goes without saying" quality, since it is simply the accepted norms that govern standard business practice, the "rules of the game," as it were.

2) *Prior restraint and censorship.* The second involves external pressure groups and the restrictions created in 1934 by the Production Code to limit what could be said and done in movies. This was a form of **prior restraint**—the Code banned certain forms of expression before they reached the public, usually by reviewing screenplay proposals or by examining a finished film and demanding the elimination of objectionable material. Prior restraint became unacceptable after the 1952 court decision involving *The Miracle* gave the cinema the same rights to free expression as other media.

3) Ratings system. The third set of constraints is the current ratings system, which classifies films into broad categories according to what is deemed appropriate for minors. This system acknowledges the extension of the freedom of speech guarantee to the cinema by not attempting to block objectionable films from theatrical release in the first place. Instead it labels all films submitted to it as suitable for all audiences (G), for those under 13 with parental guidance (PG-13), for those under 17 if accompanied by an adult (R), and for those over 17 only (NC-17). Producers are understandably eager to avoid the more restrictive R and NC-17 labels, which remove a large part of the most active portion of the moviegoing public, those 25 and under, from seeing their film.

Each of these forms of constraint will be examined in turn.

INTERNALIZED CONVENTIONS An emphasis on the conflicts faced by a central character, often played by a star, reliance on continuity editing, a linear narrative structure, and a happy ending would be formal aspects of a "This is how we do things here" understanding inside the Hollywood system. It corresponds not only to the norms of the business but to broader social values: (1) the centrality of the individual to any problem-solving activity, (2) a belief in the basic coherence and continuity of the social fabric, (3) an understanding of time and history as progressive, forward-moving forces, and (4) the successful resolution of conflict as a highly desired social goal. All of these qualities are often said to be particularly characteristic of American society.

Despite these common assumptions, individuals retain the opportunity to subvert, challenge, or subtly modify what is expected of them. This allows for innovation. When this happens repeatedly in a given direction, the system itself changes. Graphic violence is far more routine now than in the past, for example. Disturbing to some and offensive to others, it is also an area in which filmmakers can display their creative skills in a compelling way. Questions of taste and convention, though, establish boundaries for creativity. The 1943 movie, *The Leopard Man* (Jacques Tourneur), for example, depicted the death of one character at the hands of a leopard obliquely: his cries cease and a pool of blood slowly seeps under the threshold of the door. His fate is clear, although we see nothing more. The 1995 film *Se7en* (David Fincher) left little to the imagination; and by 2004, *Saw* (James Wan) had upped the ante considerably in terms of how much the audience could be drawn into the perpetration of ghastly acts, with its vividly depicted, prolonged tortures and murders that the victims (and viewers) seem completely unable to avoid.

PRIOR RESTRAINT AND CENSORSHIP Another source of limits or constraint follows from the efforts of the entertainment industry to forestall outside interference. The regulatory agencies of state and federal governments, and pressure groups such as the Catholic Church, whose Legion of Decency actively sought to block the screening of morally unacceptable films, posed a financial as well as free speech threat to Hollywood. Like the automobile industry or medical profession, Hollywood preferred to set its own standards and police them internally rather than allow this task to fall to others. It has done so, over time, in three basic ways. These were the Production Code, the Hollywood blacklist, and the current ratings system.

THE LEGION OF DECENCY

Prior to the 1952 *Miracle* decision that granted motion pictures the protection of the First Amendment, the Legion of Decency functioned as a powerful force to prevent the production and exhibition of films that violated basic tenets of the Catholic Church. The Legion, which took form in 1934, ranked films into three broad categories: "A: Morally unobjectionable, B: Morally objectionable in part, C: Condemned." The Legion continues to function as the Office for Film and Broadcasting under the United States Council of Catholic Bishops, but its influence has diminished considerably. In 1938, however, the Legion promoted a pledge that it expected faithful churchgoers to take once every year:

> I condemn all indecent and immoral motion pictures, and those which glorify crime or criminals. I promise to do all that I can to strengthen public opinion against the production of indecent and immoral films, and to unite with all who protest against them. I acknowledge my obligation to form a right conscience about pictures that are dangerous to my moral life. I pledge myself to remain away from them. I promise, further, to stay away altogether from places of amusement which show them as a matter of policy.

Such tactics encouraged studios to modify their films to earn an A or B rating from the Legion. Nonetheless, numerous films received the Condemned rating, including *The Outlaw* (Howard Hughes, 1943), a mediocre western that gave excessive attention to Jane Russell's bust;

The Miracle, labeled "sacrilegious for its treatment of the Virgin Mary"; and, in more recent times, *Dawn of the Dead* (George A. Romero, 1978), about zombies who lay siege to a shopping mall.

In 1978 *Grease* (Randal Kleiser) earned a PG (parental guidance advised) rating from the MPAA's ratings system, but an "O," for "Morally Offensive," a newer rating category that replaced "Condemned," from the Legion. The objection stated: "Though director Randal Kleiser plays it for simple-minded fun, the teen fantasy glamorizes negative role models and is preoccupied with sex in its dialogue and lyrics (O)."

Hollywood's answer to outside efforts to censor films was the Production Code. The Production Code, also known as the Hays Code after Will Hays, who oversaw its implementation, began in 1930 but became an active force in 1934. It arose as a response to state and federal pressures to safeguard public morality as well as to the threat of sanctions and boycotts by the Legion of Decency and other pressure groups. The Code imposed strict standards that slowly eroded during the 1950s and '60s. Here are some excerpts from the Code:

General Principles
- No picture shall be produced that will lower the moral standards of those who see it. Hence the sympathy of the audience should never be thrown to the side of crime, wrongdoing, evil or sin.

Particular Applications
II. Sex
- The sanctity of the institution of marriage and the home shall be upheld. Pictures shall not infer that low forms of sex relationship are the accepted or common thing.
- Adultery, sometimes necessary plot material, must not be explicitly treated, or justified, or presented attractively.

- Scenes of passion should not be introduced when not essential to the plot.
- Excessive and lustful kissing, lustful embraces, suggestive postures and gestures, are not to be shown.
- In general passion should so be treated that these scenes do not stimulate the lower and baser element.
- Sex perversion or any inference to it is forbidden.
- White slavery shall not be treated.
- Miscegenation (sex relationships between the white and black races) is forbidden.
- Scenes of actual child birth, in fact or in silhouette, are never to be presented.
- Children's sex organs are never to be exposed.

The Code was aimed at filmmakers rather than consumers. Enforcement was essentially a voluntary agreement among the major studios to abide by the Code's decisions in determining if a film violated any of the sanctions. Restrictions on "perversion," which was the common term for homosexuality but would have included sadism, fetishism, voyeurism, and other perversions as well, "white slavery," the forced prostitution of white women, and "**miscegenation**," or mixed-race sexual relationships, especially between blacks and whites, although seemingly pious and straitlaced to many today, paralleled existing laws in the 1930s. In most states, homosexual acts were a punishable crime. The marriage of people of different races, particularly blacks and whites, were expressly banned in most states until after the civil rights movement in the 1960s, just as marriages between members of the same sex are often banned today. Many aspects of the Code thus were in keeping with mainstream American values at the time. What they revealed about American culture is another question. The Code sought to steer Hollywood through the rocky shoals of contemporary moral controversy with minimal damage. (The complete Production Code text can be found at *www.artsreformation.com/a001/hays-code.html*.)

WOMEN AND THE PRODUCTION CODE

Prior to 1934 strong women characters often broke the law openly and rejected sexual conventions defiantly. The Code, though, had a chilling effect on female characterizations. Josef von Sternberg's *Blonde Venus*, in 1932, made none-too-subtle hints that Helen Faraday's (Marlene Dietrich) efforts to raise money to help her ill husband as the spectacular entertainer, the Blonde Venus, involved extramarital affairs, if not prostitution. By 1934 such innuendo was a red flag for the Hays Office. A number of 1920s films, following the flapper craze and the emergence of the "New Woman" who had joined the workforce and refused to be little more than a housewife and mother, presented female characters who were brazen, calculating, ambitious, and sometimes criminal. After the strict application of the Production Code in 1934, such characters all but disappeared from the screen, not to be seen again until the postwar emergence of film noir. Similarly, depictions of heterosexuality conformed to the image of a hierarchical relationship between a male breadwinner and a female homemaker, a figure whose primary role often became urging her husband not to undertake a dangerous task and worrying about his well-being once he did.

Given the enormous success of Hollywood films during the 1930s, '40s, and '50s, the Code must be considered something of a success in steering feature films toward a large, receptive, but perhaps middle-of-the-road audience of young and old alike. This ability to appeal to the great majority of potential viewers clearly made the film industry a powerful social and economic force even if it did come at the expense of more daring, probing works that explored the underbelly of social customs and common practices. Movies were no longer seen as a salacious, immoral force or merely the entertainment of crowds that didn't know any better.

Most of the daring films of the 1950s and '60s, such as *Baby Doll* (Elia Kazan, 1956) and *Lolita* (Stanley Kubrick, 1962, UK), about older men and the teenage girls they love, *The Man with the Golden Arm*

(Otto Preminger, 1955), about drug addiction, and *Detective Story* (William Wyler, 1951), about abortion when it was illegal, attracted comparatively small audiences. Some decried the loss of moral standards that seemed to follow in the wake of this transformation, but others heralded the Code's demise as paving the way for the rise of a more mature and complex view of life in the American cinema, especially in the 1970s.

PRIOR RESTRAINT, CENSORSHIP, AND THE HOLLYWOOD BLACK-LIST The most vivid example of prior restraint, or internal censorship of work before its completion, was the Hollywood blacklist that began in 1947 in the wake of congressional hearings to determine the extent of alleged Communist influence in Hollywood. In this case, the goal was not to formulate rules about what could or could not be seen in films but to eliminate subversive elements (Communists and **fellow travelers**, individuals who were not party members but supported many of the same causes as those who were) from the film industry altogether. The blacklist aimed at individuals more than at film content. (Considerable inventiveness was required to find any Communist content in Hollywood films at all.)

A major congressional hearing took place in 1947. A group of screenwriters and directors were subpoenaed to testify before the House Un-American Activities Committee (HUAC), whose mission was determining the extent of Communist activity in the United States. This House committee, like Senator Joseph McCarthy's later investigations into alleged Communist activity, found Hollywood, along with the entertainment industry generally, an attractive target not because so many films had appeared with clear Communist themes (virtually none were identified), but because investigating Hollywood brought widespread notice to the activities of the committee. The studio heads were not eager to have the federal government probe their industry or interfere with their power to run it as they saw fit. They wound up opting for a blacklist as the best way to stave off the threat of interference.

Many of the events leading up to the blacklist had the quality of a staged ritual. HUAC invited studio bosses and conservative, anti-communist directors and stars to point fingers. Names began to appear identifying left-wing activists. Many of these individuals were screenwriters. Almost all were well known to HUAC from their private investigations before the public hearings began. Some writers and other industry personnel belonged to the Communist Party, but whether they belonged or not, almost all their political activism addressed broad issues such as racism, trade union organizing, or the rise of fascism rather than the development of a left-wing movement in film.

HUAC also subpoenaed "unfriendly" witnesses: those who had alleged Communist affiliations. These individuals believed that a government committee posing questions about political affiliation infringed on their freedoms of speech and association. Furthermore, membership in the Communist Party was entirely legal, as was participation in political organizations that might include Communist Party members. If a witness admitted he was a Communist or knew Communists, however, HUAC then required him to "name names": he would have to identify everyone else he knew to be a Communist or fellow traveler. For the nineteen unfriendly witnesses, this was tantamount to being stool pigeons. They refused, and drew citations for contempt of Congress.

The raucous tenor of the exchanges, the loss of decorum, and apparent disrespect for a congressional committee hurt the Hollywood Ten, as the first ten unfriendly witnesses to testify became known. Other Hollywood guilds, and even the Ten's own Screen Writers Guild, refused to back them. The studio bosses quickly realized that unified protest against attacks on alleged Communists within the unions and guilds would not take place. Later, the U.S. Supreme

Court denied the Hollywood Ten's appeal of their contempt citation. They were then sentenced to one-year jail terms; the industry did not defend them, and the blacklist spread to hundreds of others.

In November 1947 the studio bosses issued what became known as the Waldorf Statement, saying that they would fire the Hollywood Ten and ban Communists from the industry. Because the Ten could not be fired simply for being Communists, since that was legal, the studios invoked a "morals clause" in their standard contracts and argued that the Ten had brought "disrepute" to the industry. This provided grounds for dismissal. The Waldorf Statement launched the formal system of the blacklist. Studios and guilds initiated loyalty oaths in which employees or guild members had to assert, under oath, that they were not and had never been members of the Communist Party. At subsequent hearings of HUAC the two key questions required witnesses to say if they had belonged to the Communist Party and to name the names of anyone they suspected of belonging to the Communist Party. Failure to answer these questions meant the loss of employment. Many named names, while others refused and left the industry.

Between the late 1940s and early 1960s a shadow industry had grown up of blacklisted writers who sold screenplays through intermediaries known as **fronts**. The front, usually a writer and guild member, would represent the work as his own and pass along payment to the blacklisted writer. The film *The Front* (Martin Ritt, 1976) gives a fairly accurate picture of how this system worked. Some blacklisted writers like Albert Maltz, Ring Lardner, Jr., and Abraham Polonsky published novels under their own names, or wrote for television shows such as CBS's *You Are There*, again using fronts. A heavy toll had been exacted, but the industry heads succeeded in remaining masters of their own house. When Dalton Trumbo received official screen credit as writer of *Spartacus* (Stanley Kubrick, 1960), cracks in the blacklist began to appear. But the blacklist remains a contentious, lively subject for many in the Hollywood industry to this day.

THE END OF PRIOR RESTRAINT AND RISE OF THE RATINGS SYSTEM

The acknowledgment that films are a form of speech and deserve the protection of the First Amendment, along with the gradual erosion of moral prohibitions through the 1950s and early 1960s, made the Production Code less and less viable. A new approach was needed, and it took the form of a ratings system. The MPAA ratings system applies to finished films and does not block their release as the Code had done; instead it identifies the intended audience by age. Ratings function as a form of consumer report, self-administered by the Hollywood studios, and designed to warn viewers of the potentially offensive aspects of any given film. It offers no critical assessment of a film's aesthetic or social merits, but it does gauge each film's potential to offend or disturb younger viewers, thereby assisting parents in their choice of what to allow their children to see, or to see themselves, primarily in terms of sexual or violent content, including profanity. Like the Code, it has functioned more strictly in terms of sexuality than violence, and it has also succeeded in fending off pressure from outside groups or government agencies.

The ratings system itself has gone through permutations, dropping the original X rating for adult-only content and substituting the R and NC-17 ratings. G and PG-13 ratings ensure the largest possible potential audience and promise the least controversial subject matter. The stricter the rating the more difficult it is to reach a younger audience, and younger audiences have made up a disproportionately large percentage of the overall movie audience since the 1970s. The adult movie industry, a very big business in its own right, has adopted the old X rating, usually multiplied into an XXX, as a virtual logo. In this way they parody the ratings system by trumpeting the forbidden nature of their non-Hollywood product.

To get a sense of how the ratings system handles sexual and violent content, consider this verbatim excerpt from an MPAA statement on the topic:

If nudity is sexually oriented, the film will generally not be found in the PG-13 category. If violence is too rough or persistent, the film goes into the R (restricted) rating. A film's single use of one of the harsher sexually-derived words, though only as an expletive, shall initially require the Rating Board to issue that film at least a PG-13 rating. More than one such expletive must lead the Rating Board to issue a film an R rating, as must even one of these words used in a sexual context. These films can be rated less severely, however, if by a special vote, the Rating Board feels that a lesser rating would more responsibly reflect the opinion of American parents.

The seemingly scientific terminology that reduces complex social behavior to a word count and adopts terms with enormous range for interpretation such as "too rough or persistent" points to the difficult task a ratings system sets itself: to assuage responsible, generally middle-class parental viewers that the movies are a safe, respectable form of entertainment. What one of the "harsher sexually-derived words" might actually be remains undefined, as if the mere mention of such a word would be a lapse of taste. This is indicative of the "you know what we mean" tone adopted by the MPAA as if there were one, tacit standard that would suit all viewers. That said, the ratings do serve effectively the dual purpose described earlier: to ward off outside interference and to give customers some sense of what they are getting at each ratings level.

The documentary *This Film Is Not Yet Rated* (Kirby Dick, 2006) views the workings of the MPAA from an irreverent, satirical perspective. In it, director Kirby Dick submits his film about the ratings system for rating, only to receive, perhaps not surprisingly, an NC-17 rating (based on some of the clips that Dick includes from other films already rated NC-17). He then appeals. The film has a comic tone to it but also raises significant questions about the multiple motives that fuel the ratings system.

The Social Context and the Vitality of the Cinema

Every mode of production, be it intensely artisanal or entirely industrial, on the cutting edge of technological innovation or a function of the tried and true, only persists over time if filmmaking remains possible within it. If the opportunities do not outweigh the constraints, the viability of a given mode comes into question. Clearly, the Hollywood system and its counterparts around the world have had tremendous viability. They offer a remarkable range of opportunities to filmmakers as well as audiences.

Artisanal modes have also continued to flourish, but the constraints that weigh against commercial success and a successful career are great. Those who pursue independent feature filmmaking, art cinema, experimental and documentary filmmaking often do so despite an institutional and organizational context that offers support but lacks the financial means to establish a solid commercial base. This relates back to the dynamic tension between film as an art and as a business. Some will make films for the sheer love of doing so, despite the economic hardships their mode of production entails; some will make films more as a job that provides the considerable rewards of a remunerative career; and some will combine both a love of cinema and an ability to establish a stable economic niche for themselves. From this diversity of modes, motives, and accomplishments, the cinema continues to renew itself.

7

GENRE FILMS

The Appeal of Genre Films

G enre films exert an inexhaustible fascination, not least because of their power to draw us into worlds well beyond the bounds of everyday reality. They also dramatize, explore, and, often, imaginatively resolve an enormous range of personal and social conflicts. Almost everyone has favorite genres. These choices may reveal something about the individual, but the genre system as a whole also reveals something about the kinds of worlds and forms of conflict that preoccupy society as a whole. Not only do genres divide into two large groups; taken collectively, they address many of the most significant, underlying issues in society. Table 7.1 provides a brief sketch of some genres, the type of world we experience in them, the emotions these films activate, and the forms of conflict they address. It gives a sense of how fully genre films, despite the exaggeration inherent in their different worlds, which can range from the highly realistic to the breathtakingly fantastic, nonetheless tap into widely shared feelings and desires, values and beliefs.

Table 7.1 The Specific Appeal of Representative Genres

Genre	We enter a world...	Emotions activated	Conflicts addressed
Science fiction	altered by time, technology, or aliens	Awe, wonder, fascination, fear, dread	Human values vs. technology, civilization vs. aliens
Western	where law and community must be created by rugged, individual men; the land is both precious and dangerous	Respect or admiration for tough men and expansive landscape, awe at natural beauty	Civilization vs. wilderness, frontier rules vs. rule of law (e.g., vigilantism vs. due process); community vs. individual
Gangster	revolving around men whose ambition spills beyond the law, for which they often pay the price	Respect or admiration for self-willed individuals, identification with greed, egotism, ruthless tactics	The rule of law vs. survival of the fittest, due process vs. taking law into one's own hands, loyalty vs. betrayal
Mystery	full of intrigue, false clues, and a mystery to be solved	Anticipation, second-guessing, problem-solving skills, suspicion, suspense	Identification and isolation of perpetrators who threaten the social order
Thriller	where individuals must strive to achieve goals against severe, life-threatening odds and, often, a time limit	Tension, anxiety, anticipation, suspense, thrills, shock, relief	Threats and challenges to the individual vs. individual skill and determination; threats to the social order vs. heroes who can overcome them

Genre	We enter a world...	Emotions activated	Conflicts addressed
Horror	in which dangerous figures or spirits, sociopaths, or evil threaten individuals who have little external help	Fear, suspense, horror, shock, surprise, disgust, repulsion, relief	Anxiety and doubt about self-worth; irrational or intangible threats vs. our ability to overcome them
Musical	that revolves around song and dance, exuberance, spontaneity, togetherness and love	Joy, happiness, delight, pleasure, escape, affection, light-heartedness, release	Everyday, numbing routine, kill-joys and sour-pusses vs. zest, joy, carefree spirit, and community
Film noir	where trust and honesty prove rare, seduction and betrayal abound; no one can be trusted; darkness engulfs people	Suspicion, worry, anxiety, distrust, fascination, admiration, attraction, wariness, caution	Distrust and instability vs. trust and a stable social order; a secure masculinity vs. threats to male identity
Melodrama	where the emotional intensities of family dynamics receive close attention	Worry, concern, distress, empathy, moral judgment, sadness, sorrow, distrust, hope	Family as a haven vs. family as hell; benevolent vs. malevolent figures

Genre	We enter a world...	Emotions activated	Conflicts addressed
Comedy	in which situations and events lead to comic, humorous results	Light-heartedness, amusement, laughter, frivolity, delight, release of aggressivity	Decorum vs. indignity; predictability vs. unpredictability
Adult	in which situations and events lead to prolonged sexual interaction	Sexual arousal	Sexual propriety vs. sexual license

Additional genres can be added, from romantic comedies like *When Harry Met Sally* (Rob Reiner, 1989) to epics like *Lawrence of Arabia* (David Lean, 1962, UK), and from courtroom dramas like *To Kill a Mockingbird* (Robert Mulligan, 1962) to slasher movies like *Friday the 13th* (Sean Cunningham, 1980). Adult movies will not be discussed further here, but several authors have examined them as a genre related to horror and thrillers, on the one hand, in their express intent to arouse certain feelings or desires, and like musicals, on the other, in their use of a relatively flimsy plot to focus on extended sex acts, which, like musical numbers, do not advance the story significantly but are the main reason for the genre's existence.

Glancing at the table, similarities and differences are apparent among the genres. The gangster, western, and sci-fi genres all address basic questions about the core values supporting social order, whereas horror, melodrama, and film noir focus on hardships, threats, and dangers individuals must encounter and vanquish essentially on their own. These differences and similarities are pursued in greater detail later in the chapter.

Genre Films as a Distinct Way of Viewing the World

Genre films pursue social conflicts in an imaginative manner. Viewers experience what it feels like to live in a certain type of world and to see this world from a particular perspective. The behavior and actions of characters build on patterns or conventions peculiar to the type of imaginary world they inhabit. These are familiar to the viewer not only as conventions but also as behavior derived from real life as well as previous films. It may be exaggerated or set in an unfamiliar world, but the behavior itself—acts of jealousy, courage, curiosity, seduction, loyalty, and so on—has a familiar ring to it. Genre films explore aspects of the actual world in imaginative ways, magnifying certain conflicts and intensifying various emotions.

With every new story, even in a familiar genre, viewers see the world as they have never quite seen it before. They experience what life in an alternative world feels like through the actions of characters, the qualities of settings, the shape of the story, and the film's own perspective on the world it represents. Broadly speaking, these stories provide viewers with a perspective similar to the one Paul Feyerabend claimed scientific researchers need in order to understand the physical world:

> Now—how can we possibly examine something we are using all the time? How can we analyze the terms in which we habitually express our most simple and straightforward observations, and reveal their presuppositions? How can we discover the kind of world we presuppose when proceeding as we do?
>
> The answer is clear: we cannot discover it from the *inside*. We need an *external* standard of criticism, we need a set of alternative assumptions or, as these assumptions will be quite general, constituting, as it were, an entire alternative world, *we need a*

*dream-world in order to discover the features of the real world we think
we inhabit* (and which may actually be just another dream-world).
[Paul Feyerabend, *Against Method*, pp. 31–32; italics his]

For Feyerabend, the goal of scientific discovery is to see things
anew. Genres constitute an aesthetic rather than scientific dream
world from which we can explore and discover qualities of the real
world we think we inhabit. Does the imagined world of a genre film
affirm the existing social order, or does it question its legitimacy? Does
it explore social limitations or pose alternatives? What kind of work
does a film perform to resolve problems peculiar to its own world and
familiar to our own, and how does it do it?

Genre Films and Conflict

Genre films allow Hollywood realism to depart from a matter-of-fact
portrayal of everyday life. This is true for modernist and postmodernist
genre films as well as the more prevalent realist ones. The important
point in this context is that characters in genre films encounter the
same types of problems repeatedly. Characters in musicals need to find
a way to express their enthusiasm, joy, and love, often in relation to a
show they must put on; characters in horror films constantly find
themselves caught up in ominous, threatening situations with which
they seem unable to cope, at least initially, and characters in melodramas are plagued by heart-wrenching issues of rejection, betrayal,
and self-sacrifice over and over. None of these problems occur in
everyday life with anything like the same frequency and hence they
cannot be said to be realistic representations of life. Genre films offer
allegorical suggestions about how similar problems might be tackled
in reality; but within the story world, the resolution primarily functions

to bring the story itself to a close. The goal is to produce not so much a realistic blueprint for solving social problems as an imaginary world in which pleasure and insight weave together in a complex way.

Standardization and Differentiation in the Genre System

Genre films conjure up fabulous imaginary worlds of lone cowboys, mad scientists, dancing couples, rampaging monsters, *femmes fatales*, anguished mothers, and more. Some of these thematic patterns took root in cinema in the first few decades of the twentieth century: a series of challenges or dangers confront the hero, the hero resolves conflict by battling a villain, the imperiled woman awaits rescue, and so on. When these conflicts received a particularly engaging form of representation, as did the derring-do of the outlaw bandits in *The Great Train Robbery* (Edwin S. Porter, 1903), that film functioned as a prototype for other films. Soon, recurring thematic and stylistic elements gelled into conventions and different clusters of conventions gradually took on the familiar genre titles of science fiction, melodrama, comedy, the western, horror film, and so on.

The mix of a familiar form with variable content has proven tremendously popular in film as in other media. The balance between the standardization of form in terms of generic conventions and the differentiation of content in terms of specific plots, performances, and styles lies at the heart of the main film genres. Early feature-length westerns like *The Covered Wagon* (James Cruze, 1923) and *The Iron Horse* (John Ford, 1924) portray the efforts of pioneers to settle the West as heroic. A repertoire of challenges that recur in later films are already in place in these early films: greed and ambition versus the harm caused the little guy; the heroism, and toll, involved in projects like building a transcontinental railway; wagon trains that must battle nature (storms, rivers, etc.), competitors, dangerous versus honorable leaders, and Indians, and love interests that struggle to flourish amidst all the hardships. Sergio Leone's spaghetti westerns of the 1960s, like *The Good, the Bad and the Ugly* (1966, Italy), focus almost exclusively on the shifting alliances among solitary men out for personal gain, and sometimes revenge. He takes a theme established in westerns by the 1920s but amplifies it to an exceptional degree.

A similar process is evident in the rise of the melodrama. Early works like Frank Powell's *A Fool There Was* (1915), the story of a seductive vamp who lures a foolish young man away from his wife, and D. W. Griffith's *Broken Blossoms* (1919), about the fragile, long-suffering daughter of an abusive boxer-father, helped standardize melodramatic conventions: a stress on emotions (compared to the western's stress on action and landscape), domestic turmoil, individual isolation, and emotional suffering. Griffith made a notable contribution to the genre through his use of Lillian Gish, who became a perfect embodiment of the noble but suffering female. Her remarkable performances helped differentiate his melodramas from those of others.

The economic value of standardization and differentiation was quite apparent from early on. There is a common struggle among personnel not only to make each film different from every other film but also to make each film familiar in its basic use of genre conventions. As discussed in Chapter 6, standardization and differentiation also contribute to the efficiency of the filmmaking process. The principle applies to all filmmaking but has particular value for genre films, since so many of the same elements recur in different films. An example of this economical efficiency is *Rescued by Rover* (Lewin Fitzhamon and Cecil Hepworth, 1905, UK), a film that clearly pioneers many of the techniques that yield a distinct story in a familiar form that can be economically achieved. Although it predates the full-blown development of the genre system, it is an important precursor to the film melodrama.

NARRATIVE ECONOMY AND GENRE CONVENTIONS:
Rescued by Rover

Rescued By Rover tells the story of a happy, middle-class family at a moment of crisis: a bitter and vindictive beggarwoman abducts the family's baby. The disruption of the happy family unit by an external, malevolent force clearly returns in *A Fool Like This*, as well as in F. W. Murnau's stunning silent film *Sunrise* (1927), about a young married man who succumbs to the allure of "the other woman" and the bright lights of the city. In this sense the film strikes a familiar thematic chord. It addresses a perceived social problem, for the middle class, and does so with considerable aplomb. In *Rescued by Rover* the kidnapping fills the father and mother with paralyzing grief, but Rover, the family's dog, jumps out a window, dashes down different streets, crosses a stream, and discovers the kidnapper and baby in a garret. Rover retraces his steps and convinces the father to follow him to the woman's lair. The father does so, taking a route that is now familiar to the viewer, rescues the child, and berates the woman. The film ends with the entire family happily reassembled in their parlor.

What is striking about this approximately five-minute-long film is its prototypical plot line: it raises and answers the two most classic melodramatic questions of "Does this man have the right to rule this family?" and "What suffering or sacrifice must this woman [most often the mother] endure?" In *Rescued by Rover* the pathos of female suffering is relatively slight, with only one shot of the mother crying over the news of the baby's abduction. Later films that pursue the basic melodramatic elements of the imperiled family and suffering mother will give fuller attention to the family dynamic itself and the agonies of the mother who loses her child. Here, action, which will validate the father's paternal role, prevails. Hepworth and Fitzhamon encapsulate these basic questions into a five-minute film that restores a sense of order in just twenty-one shots and even fewer camera setups.

Rescued by Rover uses the classic melodramatic structure of noble hero, loyal sidekick, helpless victim, and evil villain. The film affirms cultural ideals of love, wisdom, sacrifice, and community, that is, the status quo. It answers the question of "Does this man have the right to rule this family?" affirmatively. It adopts the conventions of what will soon become the standardized melodrama, but it also differentiates itself from other proto-melodramas by means of the specific shots selected and how they are arranged. Performance, camera angle and position, editing, and *mise-en-scène* join together to produce a film like but not identical to other melodramatic tales.

Standardization, based on conventions like the chase or pursuit, allows Hepworth and Fitzhamon, the directors, to tell their tale economically. They film the story with great simplicity, based on the already standardized process of filming out of chronological order according to physical convenience. Only nine camera setups create the film's twenty-one shots. For example, shots of Rover fording a stream, recrossing the stream to bring home news of his discovery of the baby, and of both Rover and the father going back across the stream a third time to retrieve the baby, were filmed one after the other from the same camera setup. Hepworth then distributes the shots according to their narrative logic—where they need to go to tell the story clearly. The film flows in an efficient manner from shots obtained out of sequence, but joined by continuity editing to create a smoothly told, engaging story. With the passage of time, these production techniques have become increasingly standardized, but the specific choices of actors, gestures and expressions, composition, lighting, and editing, for example, continue to give individual films their distinctiveness. These distinctive stylistic qualities guarantee the constant differentiation of one film from another despite generic and thematic similarity.

Film Genres as a Total System

Each genre has its own characteristic conventions in terms of character types and typical narrative conflicts. Genre films, more than any other form of cinema, thrive on conflict. Every genre presents dramatic confrontations, crises, issues, and dilemmas. The western (*The Searchers* [John Ford, 1956], *Johnny Guitar* [Nicholas Ray, 1954]), for example, typically presents stoic male heroes who confront conflicts between settlers and Indians, community and loners, the law and the renegade. The melodrama (*All That Heaven Allows* [Douglas Sirk, 1955], *The Ice Storm* [Ang Lee, 1997]) has complex family units with conflicts between loyalty and desire, parents and children, trust and betrayal. The comedy film (*Modern Times* [Charlie Chaplin, 1936], *Borat: Cultural Learnings of America for Make Benefit Glorious Nation of Kazakhstan* [Larry Charles, 2006]) has conflicts between propriety and impropriety, the expected and unexpected, mischievous pranksters and those who become the butt of jokes. The war film (*The Bridge on the River Kwai* [David Lean, 1957, UK], *Flags of Our Fathers* [Clint Eastwood, 2006]) has a tough leader and conflicts between the warring sides, among members of the same side (who often represent different ethnic groups), and between those in command and those who must fight in the field. Each genre possesses a rich array of stories that develop these conflicts in specific ways.

When we examine any one genre of Hollywood film in isolation, however, we miss the way it the genre system as a whole generates a meta-world. If we look at genres collectively, we can see that the spheres they address are overlapping and complementary. From this standpoint, we can categorize them as:

1) Genres that address the social order and public sphere: the world of politics and social policy.
2) Genres that address the domestic order and private sphere: the world of interpersonal relationships and family ties.

CULTURAL IDEALS

Cultural ideals give utopian, or ideal, embodiment to the values and beliefs that lie behind day-to-day activities, social policies, and institutional functions. Values and beliefs are typically intangible concepts like wisdom or love, status or power. Cultural ideals—like the image of the Pietà, representing the unconditional love of Mary for her son, Jesus, or the American flag, representing the United States and feelings of patriotism—set standards and establish goals. In this sense, cultural ideals are the visible face of ideologies: they are the concepts and images people have that link to a particular way of imagining one's relationships, rights, and responsibilities in the world. In a pluralistic or multicultural society, different cultural ideals, such as entrepreneurial freedom versus market regulations for the common good, obtaining justice by means of revenge or due process, maintaining a subcultural identity or assimilating to a dominant national identity, may compete with each other and become manifest in different social practices.

Cultural ideals take more tangible, down-to-earth form in **social practices**—the speech, behavior, and actions that individuals exhibit and institutions adopt in day-to-day activity. Struggles over the organization and control of institutions such as the film industry, television, education, the judicial system, health care, corporations, and so on are commonly waged in the name of various cultural ideals and the values and beliefs that comprise them. Once internalized, a cultural ideal fuels effort to make an imperfect social reality conform to a more ideal version of itself. Chapter 8, "Ideology and the Cinema," discusses this concept further.

Between them they span the breadth of social reality as we normally understand it. This division also runs along the historical fault line of masculine and feminine roles. Relying to a noticeable degree on stereotypes, and subject to subversion, active masculine characters commonly occupy the public sphere. They engage in social practices fueled by cultural ideals of creativity, sacrifice, wisdom, and community.

Correspondingly, feminine characters populate the private sphere. They engage in the management of sexual relations and social organization at the level of the family, fueled by the cultural ideals of love and kinship.

In westerns and gangster films, the cultural ideal of sacrifice and self-restraint—allowing the law to take its course, respecting due process—often conflicts with an ideal that defends revenge or vigilantism as a necessary way to right wrongs. These two ideals clash in *The Naked Spur* (Anthony Mann, 1953), for example, a western in which Howard Kemp (Jimmy Stewart) must wrestle with the degree to which he can justify taking the law into his own hands as he brings a killer to justice. Melodramas often juxtapose self-sacrifice with self-fulfillment. Some melodramas seem to say that it is only through sacrifice and a vicarious relation to another person, most often one's own child, that individuals find fulfillment. Such a view converts any desire to change the existing social order into a desire to help prepare others to enter into it, often by means of personal sacrifice.

In the classic 1930s melodrama *Stella Dallas* (King Vidor, 1937), Stella (Barbara Stanwyck) eventually realizes that her own limited resources and unsophisticated background will not help her daughter, Laurel, advance into the upper social strata where Stella believes Laurel belongs. Stella makes a dramatic sacrifice for her daughter: she excludes herself from the high society world Laurel fits in but she doesn't. This may make greater social mobility possible for her daughter, but it guarantees profound loss and suffering for Stella. In this case, the cultural ideal of self-sacrifice provides fulfillment, but the sacrifice and fulfillment are split between different characters. It is the opposite lesson from that of the Horatio Alger myth in which hard work and sacrifice bring eventual reward to the actual individual who practices these virtues rather than to someone else.

Westerns and melodramas confront large-scale social issues but from different directions: the western reflects on the price of westward expansion as a key ingredient in American national identity; the melodrama reflects on the quality of family life and the issues that tear parents and children, husbands and wives apart. Some other genres are more fundamentally affective, aimed at giving viewers a kick in the solar plexus or a chill down the spine. The genres of horror, melodrama, some performative documentaries, and, in a different sphere, adult movies, are sometimes called body genres due to their emphasis on visceral or bodily response.

In any case, the sum total of all genre films is greater than the parts. The overall system addresses many of the basic issues that can be found in contemporary society, sometimes in the displaced form of past or futuristic spaces, sometimes in the condensed and overheated confines of the present. We can summarize this genre system as in Table 7.2.

Some types of film, such as film noir, avant-garde films, and many documentaries, do not fit neatly into this table. Film noir, for example, takes place mostly in public spaces such as urban streets, cafes, bars, and offices. It treats such spaces as laden with danger, but film noir also uses the private space of apartments and bedrooms to generate a subjective sense of danger not apparent to all. Similarly, these films explore cultural ideals of law and justice but do so by placing their characters in situations where trust, suspicion, and anxiety run high. Frequently, neither the public nor the private sphere is fully secured by the hero's actions. In fact, there is often the strong sense that fundamental cultural ideals are deeply imperiled and that powerful but corrupt men and attractive but dangerous women deserve the blame. From *Double Indemnity* (Billy Wilder, 1944) and its tale of murderous greed to *Kiss Me Deadly* (Robert Aldrich, 1955), with its story of a mysterious box and a rogue detective who gets in way over his head, film noir blurs the distinction between the social and domestic orders to suggest how both may be out of kilter.

Even though different genres typically emphasize the public or the private sphere, the goal of achieving their harmonious merger, or of witnessing the failure of this merger, is pursued across the entire spectrum of genres. It usually takes the form of the parallel plot. One plot involves the male character's quest for something within the social order. The other involves courtship or his family life within the domestic

Table 7.2 The Two Basic Types of Genre Film

BASIC TYPE	SPACE	HERO
Social Order and the Law of the State		
Science fiction Western Gangster Detective Adventure War	Public: Unstable, dangerous; highly charged (objective danger, seen by all)	Male loner or buddies on a quest; enters and exits the social space of others
Domestic Order and the Law of Patriarchy		

Musical
Comedy
  of manners
  romantic
  silent
  screwball
Melodrama
Horror
Gothic
Slasher
	Private/Domestic:
	May be imperiled
	or neutral
	(subjective
	danger, seen by
	some, not all)
		The couple,
		individual, or
		nuclear family
		Suitability of
		male or female
		figure for their
		roles, tests, and
		trials; hero faces
		obstacles or threats
		to domestic order

CONFLICT	RESOLUTION	THEMES
Among social values or cultural ideals: Law, order, justice, authority, power, hierarchy; what counts as fruitful labor, controlled violence or sacrifice, knowledge, and good governance	Reestablish social order; eliminate evil, chaos, villains, creatures, aliens, etc.; affirm ideals of creativity, sacrifice, wisdom and community or dramatize failures to achieve such ideals	Charismatic heroes redeem or secure the public sphere; male independence and pursuit of self-interest secure cultural ideals; dystopias undermine these values
Within inter-subjective values: Trust, love, suspicion, fear, anxiety, paranoia, and commitment; social practices involved in sexuality and labor	Establish social harmony with absorption of the individual into a couple or family unit; secure the safety of the couple or family; overcome threats or obstacles; affirm love and creativity	Romantic love secures the domestic sphere; traditional family values secure cultural ideals; dystopias undermine these values

order. Success in one—defeating the villain, restoring a loss, achieving a goal—is frequently matched by success in the other—marriage. In the 1940 screwball comedy *His Girl Friday* (Howard Hawks), Hildy (Rosalind Russell) and Walter (Cary Grant) successfully get the exclusive news story that is central to the question of the social order and they also plan to marry, bringing harmony to the domestic order.

In Alfred Hitchcock's suspenseful *Strangers on a Train* (1951), Guy (Farley Granger) both defeats Bruno's (Robert Walker) efforts to frame him for a murder and reaffirms his engagement to Ann (Ruth Roman) when he frees himself from a cloud of doubt. In James Cameron's sci-fi *The Terminator* (1984), the efforts of the cyborg from the future to assassinate the mother of the world's future champion suffers defeat, and the mother finds romantic fulfillment with the man from the future sent to help protect her so that her child will be born. And, in Steven Spielberg's sci-fi *Minority Report* (2002), John Anderton's (Tom Cruise) foiling of a diabolical murder plot reunites him with his estranged wife. Domestic order and social harmony typically hinge, in genre films, on the ability of the male character to overcome obstacles and achieve goals in both public and domestic spheres. This makes film noir exceptional in the sense that these films present a strongly negative view of the possibility for individual success in the social order and for love and marriage in the domestic sphere.

The Individual and Society

Viewing any genre film invites awareness of both its formal and social context. This social context invariably includes reference to the tensions that are most volatile in a given culture. In relation to both the public and private spheres, almost every film has the potential to activate various forms of binary conflict that lend themselves to the largely black-and-white, good-and-evil vocabulary of genre films. (Chapter 8 compares the model of binary conflict with a model of webs of social conflict.) Among the most basic conflicts are:

1) Urban development vs. rural escape
2) Class struggle vs. social mobility
3) Individualism vs. community
4) National autonomy vs. the fear of external threats

These socially based forms of conflict embody typical patterns of tension such as:

- Urban vs. rural: anonymity/community; sophisticated/primitive; manipulative/sincere; unnatural/natural
- Lower vs. upper class: subordination/independence; lack of control/control; hierarchy/equality; conformity/rebellion
- Individual vs. community: autonomy/interdependence; go-it-alone/collaborative effort; individual identity/group belonging; charismatic leaders/prudent spokespeople
- National autonomy vs. external domination: liberation/colonization; attack/defense; independence/dependence; self-determination/exploitation

Similar tensions come into play in relations between the sexes and between different ethnicities or races. (Chapters 9 to 11 pursue these issues.) All of these conflicts raise questions of power, hierarchy, authority, and justice. Who has power and who doesn't? Who has the right to decide, rule, or act? How do they gain that right? Who must have decisions made for them, be ruled, or acted upon? What justifications are offered and how well do they hold up? Such questions apply to the world constructed by each genre film, but they quite often have metaphorical resonance: the issues and tensions, presented from the distinct perspective of the filmmaker, commonly hint at how similar issues in the actual world might be understood and addressed.

Answers to these questions emerge not only from what characters say and do but also from how the film represents the imaginary world it has constructed. Whose side is the filmmaker on? What moral weight does she lend to a position taken by a character, or how does she undercut it? Solitary individualism, for example—commonly represented by men who go their own way and make their own rules—is a typical trademark of more conservative perspectives, cooperative dependence of more liberal ones. John Wayne's character in *The Searchers*, Ethan Edwards, follows no man's rules but his own. He rescues the child abducted by a renegade band of Indians and restores her to the community, doing what the military, the sheriff, and the community cannot do for itself. Edwards is, and John Wayne himself embodied, the tough-guy loner, beholden to no one. His perspective fits comfortably within a conservative framework. The director, John Ford, does, however, suggest limitations to Edwards's character: he ends the film by literally shutting the door on him, excluding him from the greater community. In other films like *The Wild Bunch* (Sam Peckinpah, 1969) and *Ocean's 11* (Lewis Milestone, 1960), individuals who operate outside the confines of the law nonetheless find fulfillment in a group to which they contribute and from which they draw a sense of belonging.

In general, genre films that justify hierarchical relationships tend to fall within a conservative or reactionary spectrum, since these political positions respect authority and the necessity if not the right of some to manage the affairs of others. Films that stress the problems and limitations of hierarchy tend to fall within the liberal to radical part of the political spectrum, since these positions value equality and find fault with the abuse of power and authority. Westerns, detective films, and thrillers often celebrate the charismatic hero who takes matters into his own hands to save the day or solve the problem. If the film presents the hero's actions as fully justifiable and appropriate, it lends credibility to the idea of a natural hierarchy that deserves to be upheld against the leveling tendencies of bureaucracies and legal safeguards.

By contrast, other films explore the consequences of a concentration of power and what it does to those who both abuse it and suffer from it. In the 1950s a number of epics used the Roman Empire to give embodiment to what a world ruled by tyrants would feel like. On the one hand, such films are historical fiction, based on actual events; a large-scale uprising of slaves against their Roman masters became the basis for Stanley Kubrick's *Spartacus* (1960). On the other hand, the films were allegorical commentaries on the horrors of Communism. Corrupt emperors conveniently stood in for tyrannical dictators like Joseph Stalin or Mao Tse-tung.

Larger social structures, of which the government is a prime example, often mediate the relation between individuals. To regard social structure (especially government regulation) as a limitation on self-fulfillment goes with a conservative stress on individualism, whereas viewing government as a way to meet the collective needs of the people and safeguard civil liberties goes with a liberal stress on community. King Vidor's remarkable social drama, *Our Daily Bread*, made in 1934 during the thick of the Great Depression, celebrates the resourcefulness of a diverse group of unemployed individuals who band together to create a garden of Eden, a farm community, without any government assistance whatsoever. The film represents a utopian vision that harkens back to the days of tribal society and leaves behind the dilemmas of modern, urban complexity, but does so with a compelling style and exceptional verve. The film stresses both community over individualism and personal liberty over government intervention.

Condensation and Displacement in Genre Films

As visual languages, dreams, daydreams, fantasies, and films possess unusual properties: time and space prove highly malleable (great leaps in time or space are readily possible); characters may have remarkable powers; problems and conflicts from waking life may appear in distorted forms, and what may be unrealistic resolutions become entirely plausible. Of the distinct qualities of thinking in images that stem from the creative resources of the mind, it is the procedures of condensation and displacement that will primarily concern us in relation to genre films.

CONDENSATION

Condensation is the process of loading something up with more meaning or importance than it would normally receive. Condensation usually packs a variety of values and meanings into a single signifier or image. Traditional symbols such as national flags, the Christian cross, or the Nazi swastika are vivid examples of condensation. Each of these symbols can evoke strong if not necessarily identical feelings among a broad spectrum of individuals. Condensation functions equally for symbols that are particular to one character or film: "Rosebud" was a symbol in *Citizen Kane* (Orson Welles, 1941) that carried a heavy load of condensed meaning for Charles Foster Kane, but for the other characters it was essentially an enigma.

In films, like dreams, almost any object or person can be the target of condensation. In *Flags of our Fathers*, the historically loaded meaning of the American flag becomes yet more symbolically burdened through a carefully orchestrated public relations campaign to turn a photograph of raising the flag on the island of Iwo Jima during World War II into a profound, and soon famous, symbol of American resilience and determination. The photograph of the flag becomes a condensation of patriotic feelings and nationalistic loyalties even as the work of constructing this symbol takes a heavy toll on the young soldiers who actually raised the flag. They must now tour the country to raise money for the war effort, exaggerating and distorting what actually happened in the process, unable to rejoin their comrades in battle or to get treatment for the traumatic stress they suffered.

Condensation makes the hero into a lightning rod. Great actors and almost all movie stars attract the conflictual "electricity" in a situation and intensify its charge. Expressivity or, more precisely, the sense that gestures and facial expressions open a window onto inner emotional states plays a crucial role in our engagement with characters or stars who effortlessly captivate our attention. As a result, the close-up occupies a

prominent position in star-centered films. The face itself is a condensation of the star, actor, and character: it is where we feel we can fathom
depths of feeling that would otherwise be inaccessible. Some films,
such as *The Way We Were* (Sydney Pollack, 1973), featuring Robert Redford and Barbra Streisand, or *Troy* (Wolfgang Petersen, 2004,
U.S./Malta/UK), featuring Brad Pitt, consist of long stretches of nothing but close-ups of the "talking heads" or pensive faces of their stars.
The star system itself relies massively on condensation as a way to load
individuals who become stars with a rich array of qualities and traits
through publicity, gossip, and typecasting.

The star system owes its existence to the tendency of early audiences to identify with some actors more than others. Whereas many
early films were sold to exhibitors for so many cents per foot, distributors soon began to charge higher fees for films with popular performers such as Lillian Gish and, of course, the comedians: Fatty
Arbuckle, Harold Lloyd, Buster Keaton, and Charlie Chaplin. As the
1927 film *It* (Clarence Badger), starring Clara Bow, proposed, some
people simply possessed "it." Clara Bow's success in portraying a
young woman with "it" made her a star. The Hollywood publicity
machine quickly turned an actress of considerable gifts into the "It
Girl" for the rest of her career.

The star system has grown not only as a result of audience fascination with certain charismatic performers but also as the result of the
concerted effort of exhibitors, distributors, studio producers, directors,
screenwriters, publicists, agents, fan club organizations, gossip colum-
nists, and, later, TV talk show hosts, all of whom devote considerable
energy to the promotion of stars. By the 1920s the studios developed
an elaborate system to cultivate new stars. It involved training newcomers in how to dress, talk, and behave as well as how to act. Successful actors were usually signed to seven-year contracts with a specific studio and assigned to films that fit the image that studio had
created for them.

Stars like Brad Pitt, Uma Thurman, Tom Hanks, and Kate Winslet have emerged after the heyday of the studio star-making machine. Some, like Johnny Depp and John Travolta, began their careers with parts on television shows (*21 Jump Street* and *Welcome Back, Kotter*, respectively). Others, like Brad Pitt and Jack Nicholson, gained attention for outstanding performances in minor, supporting roles. Nicholson's portrayal of an alcoholic small-town lawyer who decides to go along for the ride in *Easy Rider* (Dennis Hopper, 1969), and Brad Pitt's turn as an easy-going, apparently naïve but scheming young outlaw in *Thelma and Louise* (Ridley Scott, 1991) propelled them to new heights.

Charismatic characters resemble stars: they exude a magnetism and power over other characters by dint of their commanding personalities. **Charisma** is a form of personal magnetism that draws people to those who possess it. Charisma was a term originally used to describe the power of early Christians to persuade converts: the Holy Spirit seemed to speak through them. The word retains this sense of an extraordinary power or mysterious gift. It is most often associated with the ability of leaders, be they spiritual or secular, to induce others to follow them on the basis of their magnetic personality rather than the clarity or wisdom of their ideas. For this reason charismatic heroes can be wise or dangerous, benevolent or tyrannical.

Charismatic heroes, commonly played by stars, are a staple of Hollywood cinema. Charismatic figures give dramatic expression to collective longings. They condense within themselves a wide range of desires, from the desire for national unity and pride that Frank Capra's ordinary citizens turned civic leaders exemplify in films like *Mr. Smith Goes to Washington* (1939) or *Mr. Deeds Goes to Town* (1936), with James Stewart and Gary Cooper respectively, to the longing for direct, decisive action against criminals who manage to elude the slower paced workings of the law that Clint Eastwood's Harry Callahan character represented so vividly in *Dirty Harry* (Don Siegel, 1971) and that Jodie Foster updates in *The Brave One* (Neil Jordan, 2007, U.S./Australia). The hero's triumph gives visible expression to the ways in which the charismatic individual reinforces, protects, or even creates the social bonds that let society flourish.

The reliance on a charismatic hero is especially frequent in cartoon-based tales. The star power of Arnold Schwarzenegger in *Conan the Barbarian* (John Milius, 1982), Angelina Jolie in *Lara Croft: Tomb Raider* (Simon West, 2001, U.S./Germany/UK/Japan), and Tobey Maguire in *Spider-Man* (Sam Raimi, 2002) multiplies the charismatic effect of their preexisting cartoon characters. The hero of these genre films, like the mythic figures of Hercules, Prometheus, and Robin Hood, typically performs valiant deeds and saves society from a villainous threat. These heroes epitomize the degree to which charisma serves as a problem-solving mechanism in genre films.

Finally, condensation can create evil as well as good characters. Just as the charismatic hero condenses the forces that might result in positive change into the figure of a single, powerful leader, the bad apple condenses the forces that might lead to negative change into the figure of the rotten-to-the-core villain. Both tendencies discount social and environmental factors, instead placing the burden of social responsibility on the individual and then praising or blaming him for his conduct. Films such as *Natural Born Killers* (Oliver Stone, 1994), *Star Wars* (George Lucas, 1977), *First Blood* (Ted Kotcheff, 1982), and the *Batman* series all present clear-cut villains who serve as lightning rods for what might otherwise be treated as a more socially dispersed set of factors such as sociopathy, despotism, and egomania. Dispose of the villain to dispose of the problem. This is what charismatic heroes can do, in a genre film, even if actual governments and social systems cannot.

DISPLACEMENT

Not only do social conflicts undergo condensation, they also go through a process of **displacement**. **Displacement** means that in their treatment of volatile social issues, genre films frequently shift attention from their most troubling to less troubling manifestations.

Condensation forcefully concentrates tension, conflict, and emotional energy into a single figure. Displacement shifts tension, conflict, and emotional energy from its primary source to a secondary, less inflammatory focus.

For example, effects may receive greater attention than causes. These effects may be emotionally charged, even highly disturbing, but, by de-emphasizing their cause, a film may fail to identify the actual source of a real problem. John Ford's great western *Cheyenne Autumn* (1964), for example, shows the tragic consequences of forcing the Cheyenne Indians to undergo a relocation across desolate terrain to a new reservation. It makes the destructive impact of western expansionism on the culture of Native American people patently clear, but it refrains from identifying any causes for the specific ways in which expansion affected Native peoples.

This is not an unusual tactic for narrative storytelling in general: stories allow us to understand what a given situation, action, or experience feels like, but the attempt to identify causes for personal and emotional effects may seem reductive. This may be one reason why a number of films choose to weave several parallel plot lines together. Films such as *Nashville* (Robert Altman, 1975), about how multiple lives eventually intersect in powerful ways, *Traffic* (Steven Soderbergh, 2000), about the international traffic in drugs and its consequences, *Syriana* (Stephen Gaghan, 2005), about behind-the-scenes U.S. manipulations in a fictitious Middle Eastern country, *Crash* (Paul Haggis, 2004, U.S./Germany), about how vested interests and personal values produce divided loyalties and conflicted actions, and *Babel* (Alejandro González Iñárritu, 2006, France/U.S./Mexico), about the consequences of imperfect communication and bad judgment across cultural divides, all explore the complex causes for specific actions. They adopt a multi-character perspective to do so. This strategy indicates how exploring the causes of social conflict can be as complex and multifaceted as examining their effects.

In addition to this common displacement from the causes of a social issue or conflict to its effects or consequences, displacement takes a number of forms of which three hold particular significance.

THE COLLECTIVE BECOMES PERSONAL In this form of displacement, class or group conflict is shifted to the level of interpersonal conflict. *Gentleman's Agreement* (Elia Kazan, 1947), for example, shifts the widespread social issue of anti-Semitism to one specific case: a journalist (Gregory Peck) who poses as a Jew. *Mortal Thoughts* (Alan Rudolph, 1991) displaces the general issue of wife-battering and spousal abuse to a question of how Demi Moore and Glenne Headly cope with Headly's lout of a husband (Bruce Willis). Domestic violence clearly has more widespread relevance, but the displacement of a large social issue to an individual case has taken on the status of a genre convention.

Similarly, the large-scale economic, political, and racial implications of the Civil War are shifted to the trials and triumphs of one Southern belle in the classic epic film, *Gone with the Wind* (Victor Fleming, 1939). And, in a similar manner, *Schindler's List* (Steven Spielberg, 1993) displaces the question of how Germans with a moral conscience could respond to the genocidal policies of the Nazi regime to exterminate all Jews from the German population as a whole to the actions of one man in particular, Oskar Schindler.

Resorting to displacement often occurs in relation to the question of responsibility for crime or social disorder. Social problems are condensed and displaced from the social to the personal. This process allows films to heap all the blame onto bad apples, the villains and secondary characters like henchmen, underlings, gang members, and so forth. The James Bond films are a stunning litany of the evil perpetrated by villainous masterminds and their sadistic underlings. Eliminate the evil character and the world becomes once again essentially good. In this case displacement joins with a conservative perspective that rejects bad environments and poor social conditions to focus on evil as a more eternal or mythic threat.

The postwar phenomenon of film noir frequently combined the "bad apple" of seductive women who led decent but fallible men astray and the "bad environment" of a postwar world in which corporate and financial forces appeared to eliminate many of the traditional avenues for upward mobility. Behind many of the plot lines that featured ways to get rich by a little murder, such as "kill the husband and collect the insurance" (*Angel Face* [Otto Preminger, 1952]), "turn circus skills in handling a gun into armed robbery" (*Gun Crazy* [Joseph H. Lewis, 1950]), or "kill the husband and get the wife" (*The Postman Always Rings Twice* [Tay Garnett, 1946]), the audience discovers frustrated, smart, but vulnerable working- or middle-class male characters who are led down the wrong path by the combination of unsettled times and unsettling women. None of these films acknowledged the social upheavals of the 1940s directly, but all made their effects plain to see.

POLITICAL ISSUES BECOME MORAL ISSUES The displacement of the political to the moral allows a large social issue to express itself through the troubled conscience of an individual character. This usually involves issues of motivation in which a potentially good character (the hero) hesitates to get involved or take sides. He has, it seems, no political ax to grind and no social wrong to right. When he does finally act, this action appears free of any specific political perspective. It becomes a matter of individual conscience and doing the "right thing" in a given situation.

This is another version of the naturalizing impulse utilized by ideology to make some behavior seem natural and self-evident. Ultimately, the hero acts, but in order to do so the looming social issue must first be condensed and displaced into a personal form, typically a "bad apple." In *Casablanca* (Michael Curtiz, 1942), Rick (Humphrey Bogart) acts to save Ilsa (Ingrid Bergman) and Victor Laszlo (Paul Henreid) from the Nazis and the local police, not because he staunchly opposes fascism (he seems quite unaware of it) but because Ilsa is his old flame whose act of desertion some time before is now understandable to him as devotion to Victor. Rick becomes a reluctant warrior, just as the United States became a reluctant participant in World War II over two years after it began. He only responds when Nazi aggression threatens his own vital interest—the woman he loves. He does so in a noble, sacrificial way—he doesn't get the girl but he knows that his action will help Ilsa and Victor carry on the good fight that is Victor's passion. Displacement allows the film to address a highly topical issue at the time of its release—America's recent declaration of war following the Japanese attack on Pearl Harbor at the end of 1941—but to do so in a displaced form that camouflages any sense of partisan politics beneath the guise of a bittersweet love story.

In *On the Waterfront* (Elia Kazan, 1954), Terry Malloy (Marlon Brando) knows full well that the union is corrupt and thousands of workers exploited by the crooked, authoritarian union boss, Johnny Friendly (Lee J. Cobb). He only confronts Friendly, though, after union goons kill his brother. His ethic of silence, in which informing to the authorities about illegal activity is dishonorable, finally yields to a personal need for vengeance. Personal vindication vanquishes social injustice. Government investigators turn up to promise that they will take care of corruption. It is as if a broader form of social justice would not be possible without the catalyst provided by the individual act of moral conscience carried out by Terry Malloy.

POLITICAL POWER BECOMES PERSONAL AUTHORITY The displacement of issues of political power to issues of personal authority facilitates a focus on individual character rather than social justice. Instead of a critique of the social system as such, this form of displacement shifts the issue to the quality of one individual's actions. Questions such as the abuse of power, insensitivity to those less powerful, cruelty, blind ambition, deception, or the manipulation of others, which operate in tension with the yearning for a responsible, democratic system, becomes displaced from the political arena as a whole to the idiosyncratic behavior of a particular leader.

A vivid example is the war movie *Patton* (Franklin J. Schaffner, 1970), which explores the personality of this famous World War II general. His abrasive, "can do" style is shown to cause serious harm to others and to cost Patton himself some of the respect he might otherwise earn, but it is also celebrated as a necessary form of decisiveness in tactical battles against the German army. The television show *24* elevates the portrait of the by-any-means-necessary hero to new heights by devising ticking time bomb scenarios almost every week in which counterterrorism agent Jack Bauer (Kiefer Sutherland) must resort to torture to extract information that will help prevent an imminent attack. Such scenarios are rare in real life, but they bring into extremely sharp focus what it feels like to know that desperate measures are the only hope of saving others. Similarly, three films, the original 1949 *All the King's Men* (Robert Rossen), its 2006 remake (Steven Zaillian, Germany/U.S.), and the documentary *Kingfish: A Story of Huey P. Long* (Thomas Schlamme, 1995), examine the career of Huey Long, a populist reformer and cruel demagogue in Louisiana politics. The question of how a democratic system can remain democratic while tolerating the misuse of power to get things done is displaced onto the question of whether Huey Long did more harm than good during his reign as governor.

Another way in which political power becomes a question of personal authority is by displacing conflict from the public sphere to the private. The broad question posed in different ways by *On the Waterfront, Patton,* or *All the King's Men,* "Does this man have the right to rule this land?" shifts to the more restricted question, "Does this man have the right to rule this family?" The family as microcosm condenses questions of power into the agonizing issues faced by individuals, while the displacement from the public to private sphere allows large issues to gain visible representation in a less controversial form.

In the classic melodrama *Written on the Wind* (Douglas Sirk, 1956), for example, the family business—Texas oil—becomes secondary to the **family romance**—a term of Sigmund Freud's representing the various emotional currents that play out within family relationships. In this case these currents circle around whether the wealthy but deeply troubled Kyle Hadley (Robert Stack) can make a good father and decent husband. Does he have the right, and the ability, to marry the attractive Northerner (played by Lauren Bacall), handle his out-of-control sister, and run the family business successfully?

Director Douglas Sirk makes his critique of power not by exposing exploitation in the oil industry but, on the one hand, by making Kyle paranoid and impotent and, on the other, presenting his solidly middle-class, hard-working right-hand man, Mitch Wayne (Rock Hudson), as a paragon of virtue. Mitch has worked his way up. He wasn't born with the proverbial silver spoon in his mouth, and his self-reliance and level-headedness make him admirable. Power, Sirk seems to suggest, should fall on the shoulders of those who rise by merit, not those who inherit and abuse it. The film in this sense metaphorically defends democracy over aristocracy.

Kyle's sister Marylee (Dorothy Malone) plays an important part as a supporting character. Kyle's impotence contrasts with Marylee's lust. She is in love with Mitch, but he treats her like a sister. She attempts to seduce Mitch and throws herself at men who resemble him, but to no avail. Between them, she and Kyle suggest that the Hadley family has reached the end of the line, morally, if not economically. In one scene, Marylee, dressed in a striking red chiffon gown, dances with sensual pleasure and wild abandon in her bedroom as, elsewhere in the house, her father dies. The editing makes it appear as if her dancing has the power to kill: we see her twirl and kick and thrust and then, in an abrupt cut, her father staggering and collapsing.

The shift from public to private is equally vivid in *The Godfather* (Francis Ford Coppola, 1971), where the process of centralizing economic control by means of ruthless business practices becomes displaced from the domain of corporate America to the world of a Mafia don. This displacement brings large issues into sharp focus but at a remove from the terrain of most corporate culture. *The Godfather* displaces the pursuit of profit onto the question of loyalty to those with power, but with equally negative consequences, a point underscored by the great emphasis on murder as the way to resolve conflict. *The Godfather* questions the wisdom of Michael Corleone's business methods by chronicling his gradual slide into total isolation even as he remains ostensibly dedicated to creating an image of respectability for his alienated and fractured family.

Coppola uses rooms, doors, and distance to convey the psychic experience of isolation effectively. These physical elements take on added meaning as signifiers of the high price the once idealistic and innocent Michael has paid for his power as the family's don. He achieves power but loses any sense of deep connection with those around him, especially with his own family members.

THE VALUE OF CONDENSATION AND DISPLACEMENT IN NARRATIVE STORYTELLING

In sum, condensation provides symbols, icons, archetypes, stereotypes, and heroes who often stand in for larger collectivities and issues. Displacement shifts the emphasis from conflicts at the heart of the body politic to issues that seem more localized and particular, if not domestic. These processes alter the original conflict and introduce a metaphorical or allegorical dimension to the story. The narrative no longer says what it means directly. Audiences experience a successful story as one that achieves closure, resolving underlying conflicts. Real issues receive an imaginative resolution with the pleasure of a wish fulfilled. The realization of a basic desire for imaginative solutions to vexing problems provides an emotional reward for the audience's involvement.

Genre films routinely address social issues but customarily displace them to a safer, more limited context. The film narrative then speaks metaphorically to the underlying but now disguised issues, with specific situations and conflicts in the film standing as allegorical references to real-world problems. This convention has become an assumption in the mainstream film industry that large issues must be reduced to the story of individuals, but the examples of the silent Soviet cinema (*The Battleship Potemkin* [Sergei Eisenstein, 1925, Soviet Union], *Man with a Movie Camera* [Dziga Vertov, 1929, Soviet Union]), many Third World films (*Emitai* [Ousmane Sembene, 1971, Senegal], *The Battle of Algiers* [Gillo Pontecorvo, 1966, Italy/Algeria]), and multiple plot line films like *Crash* and *Babel* indicate that narrative conflict need not be represented solely through clashes among one set of individual characters.

The oblique, allegorical, or metaphorical means of expression makes stories appealing to a wider audience than those who favor one or another political perspective on social issues. Condensation and displacement recast issues in forms that allow for imaginative resolution— the elimination of a bad apple, fixing a bad environment, assessing a man's right to rule his family, and so on.

In interpreting genre films, viewers cannot treat the worlds produced by unconscious thought process like condensation, displacement, or storytelling itself as objective fact. These worlds may contain facts as well as fabrications, but they are always seen from a distinct perspective and communicated with expressive techniques that work affectively. That is why we speak of representations of the world and perspectives on social issues rather than primarily of records, documents, and facts. Stories are allegories, not literal transcriptions of actual events, and are valued precisely for the license this approach gives to the imagination. Our means of entry into such worlds reveal the filmmaker's social attitude or political perspective indirectly. Films represent wishes and desires, meanings and values, cultural ideals, and competing ideologies: a reactionary regression to earlier social forms of organization, conservative defense of the status quo, liberal modifications to the way things are, dystopian cautions, and radical urgings. Individuals have no more direct way of showing what it feels like to enter into a particular state, wrestle with a particular issue, or discover a particular form of resolution than storytelling. The oblique but vivid forms of social commentary in most genre films allow audiences to take aesthetic pleasure in the imaginative resolution of dramatic conflicts that retain the allure of metaphorical references to real social issues.

Interpreting the Genre Film

APPLYING A DUAL FORMAL-SOCIAL ANALYSIS TO GENRE FILMS

As we have seen in previous discussions, this interpretive model attends to both the formal and social contexts for a particular film or set of films. It is quite applicable to the genre film. Socially, the approach asks how a film disguises certain aspects of social life, usually by means of techniques such as condensation and displacement, on the one hand, and how it helps viewers see aspects of social reality in a fresh light, on the other. Formally, it asks how a given film revitalizes a particular genre versus how much it simply repeats established conventions. *Blade Runner* (Ridley Scott, 1982), for example, offers, in a formal context, striking innovations in the look and feel of a dystopic, future society, and, in its social context, a fresh way of seeing where dangerous tendencies in artificial intelligence, ecological imbalance, and human vulnerability might lead.

HISTORY, FORM, AND SOCIAL ISSUES IN *Blade Runner* **AND** *Forbidden Planet* Genres adapt to changing times. On a formal level the conventions and techniques common to the genre will alter, and on a social level the actual conflicts they address will shift. This sometimes means that, at a formal level, a genre will go through something like an organic cycle of birth, growth, maturation, and decay. In science fiction, for example, silent films like Yakov Protazanov's *Aelita: Queen of Mars* (1924, Soviet Union) or Fritz Lang's *Metropolis* (1927, Germany) became prototypical models for later work in as much as these two films explored where society might be headed. *Forbidden Planet* (Fred M. Wilcox, 1956), *The Day the Earth Stood Still* (Robert Wise, 1951), and *The War of the Worlds* (Byron Haskin, 1953) rank among the classic sci-fi films of the 1950s in their mature exploration of technology, alien worlds, and questions of human survival. In the 1970s *Soylent Green* (Richard Fleischer, 1973) and *A Boy and His Dog* (L. Q. Jones, 1975) represent a significant darkening of the genre toward black humor and a post-apocalyptic future, which *Blade Runner* carries to a logical conclusion. Yet later works, like *Spaceballs* (Mel Brooks, 1987) and *Mars Attacks!* (Tim Burton, 1996), turn to postmodernist parody as if the genre were exhausted. Useful as broad generalizations, schemes like this cyclical one need to be balanced by scrutiny of the range of work produced in a given period and by comparison between works from different periods. No group of films will conform entirely to any one scheme of genre growth and decay.

That said, *Blade Runner* is a remarkable manifestation of how the sci-fi genre not only demonstrates a formal, semi-autonomous cycle of development but also responds to a changing social context. The film tells a **dystopic** story of the collapse of community and social order. (**Dystopias** are imagined worlds gone awry. Instead of a Shangri-La of dreamed perfection, a dystopia presents a world where balance is lost, a tyrannical bureaucracy prevails, technology runs amok, aliens scourge the land, and so on. Many sci-fi films have strongly dystopian elements.) In *Blade Runner*, Deckard (Harrison Ford), a man trained to terminate rogue cyborgs, agrees to track down four cyborgs for their maker, the Tyrell Corporation. The cyborgs have returned to earth, determined to modify their operating programs so that they will never self-destruct. Deckard meets Rachael (Sean Young), an administrative assistant at the Tyrell Corporation, only to discover that (1) she is a cyborg, (2) he is in love with her, and (3) (in the director's cut) he is also a cyborg. Deckard also discovers that the Tyrell Corporation is corrupt and exploitative. The film demonizes the corporation and humanizes the cyborgs in a spirit common to the cynical, detached tone of much sci-fi in the 1970s and '80s and to post-modernism in general. This outlook is considerably at odds with the classic sci-fi films of the 1950s such as *The Forbidden Planet* (1956).

As an expression of utopian longing, *Blade Runner* condemns the existing social order—but offers no alternative. True utopias were long ago and far away. Here, as in *Brazil* (Terry Gilliam, 1985, UK), *Dark City* (Alex Proyas, 1998, U.S./Australia), *Johnny Mnemonic* (Robert Longo, 1995), *Strange Days* (Kathryn Bigelow, 1995), *28 Days Later* (Danny Boyle, 2002, UK), and *The City of Lost Children* (*La cité des enfants perdus*, Jean-Pierre Jeunet and Marc Caro, 1995, France), a feeling of apocalypse-from-now-on prevails. And yet the characters retain a vision and a desire for something better, be it the fantasy of union with a cyborg entertained by Deckard or the mysterious splendors of inter-galactic travel which the cyborg Roy Batty (Rutger Hauer) remembers just before he perishes. Roy's last words are a poetic reminder of the desire for something beautiful and enduring to hold onto, spoken, iron-ically, at the moment of his death: "I've seen things you people would-n't believe. Attack ships on fire off the shoulder of Orion. I watched C-beams glitter in the dark near the Tannhauser Gate. All those moments will be lost in time like tears in rain. Time to die."

In *Blade Runner* the nation-state as the focal point for society yields to the corporation as the dominant force; rugged individualism succumbs to cyborg collectivism, and the dream of community transforms into an urban nightmare. These shifts in the social structure appear in other genres as well, from comedy (*Get Shorty* [Barry Sonnenfeld, 1995], which demonstrates, with an abundance of black humor, how a Mafia hit man makes a perfect film producer), to westerns (*The Quick and the Dead* [Sam Raimi, 1995], in which the classic gunfight degenerates into a sadistic contest and honor becomes a fleeting afterthought), to animation (*Waking Life* [Richard Linklater, 2001], in which the characters drift through a drug-induced haze of paranoia and confusion, something virtually unimaginable in the heyday of Disney's greatest work). The shifts respond to an altered social context, but how these responses gain representation is a matter of concrete questions of selection and arrangement for any given film: of, in other words, style and the modifications of convention.

Forbidden Planet, from 1956, contrasts sharply with *Blade Runner*. It tells the story of a spaceship crew that visits a lone scientist, Dr. Morbius (Walter Pidgeon), and his beautiful daughter, Alta (Ann Francis). They were part of a group stranded on a "forbidden" planet. (The film has numerous parallels to the plot of Shakespeare's *The Tempest*.) Dr. Morbius, a widower, has accepted his isolation and has no desire for rescue. A bizarre, murderous force terrorizes the planet, but Morbius has devised defenses to keep it at bay. This force, the visitors discover, is a "monster from the id," namely Dr. Morbius's own unconscious desires which he tries to suppress and deny. They return as a destructive force that threatens the stability of the social order. The monster's violent aggression toward the visiting crew, it turns out, has a strong connection to Morbius's possessive relationship toward Alta. Her innocence and physical beauty attract several of the spaceship's crew members.

What the film makes visible is the doctor's unconscious, violent jealousy toward anyone who threatens to take his daughter from him. The "monster" is a projection from his psyche: perhaps of his fear of abandonment, or of his emotional incest with his daughter. His unhealthy attachment takes an oblique form that allows it to escape censorship, both by Dr. Morbius, who thinks the monster is purely external, and the motion picture industry's Production Code, since there is no hint at all of actual incest, just intense emotional dependence.

Forbidden Planet has a liberal perspective on the doctor's unconscious desire. It stresses, as horror and science fiction films with a liberal perspective generally do, that what at first seems an entirely alien monster bears a vivid affinity with, and, in fact, stems from, the hero, not nature gone amuck. In a liberal perspective, threats, aliens, and monsters may be real, but they take on exaggerated and distorted proportions to the extent that needs, anxieties, and desires get projected onto them or create them in the first place. The implication is that a fuller understanding of the self will lead to more balanced and receptive relationships with others who are different from us.

Forbidden Planet by no stretch of the imagination condones Dr. Morbius's excessive attachment to his daughter. (By contrast, *Blade Runner* has considerable sympathy for Deckard's attraction to a cyborg, an attraction that the dominant social code of his time also judges wrong.) What *Forbidden Planet* suggests is that Morbius's own blindness to his actual desires, somewhat akin to Oedipus's ignorance of his own lineage, has catastrophic consequences. He entertains needs or desires that he cannot openly admit or accept. This failure on his part, rather than the threat posed by an entirely external force, is what causes his downfall.

Forbidden Planet adopts a visual style characteristic of the 1950s that supports its fundamentally optimistic view of the future: outer space exhibits qualities of depth that recede toward a vanishing point. Significant objects that stand out sharply from their surroundings populate it, thanks to backlighting and composition. Space represents a frontier to colonize, civilize, and defend. Designed objects are clean, sleek, and uncluttered. An elegant, powerful servant, ready to aid in civilizing space, taming nature, and defending culture, embodies the dream of a technological utopia. Robby the Robot, a benevolent android, shuffles about in service to Dr. Morbius, clearly the prototype for R2-D2 in *Star Wars*. The film celebrates rationality, science, and technology and its capacity to overcome the threat of "monsters from the id."

THE POLITICAL SPECTRUM COVERED BY GENRE FILMS At any given historical moment, a range of political perspectives receive representation within each genre. For example, classic science fiction films from the 1950s often celebrate the hierarchical command and control structure of the military and its ability to annihilate destructive threats from outer space. Such films adopt a them-against-us perspective and a conservative point of view. The threat is always external, with no apparent connection to the lives or values of those who find themselves threatened.

The opposite, less frequently presented view in the 1950s tends to see the threat of aliens as a projection: individuals project their anxieties and fears outward onto others, most notably onto aliens and monsters. This is the case in *Forbidden Planet*. Some '50s sci-fi classics even extol the virtues of the curious, well-intentioned scientist or ordinary citizen who finds a way to communicate with alien beings and profit from their wisdom, a liberal-minded perspective that is well represented by films like *The Day the Earth Stood Still* and *It Came from Outer Space* (Jack Arnold, 1953). Later sci-fi films like *Close Encounters of the Third Kind* (Steven Spielberg, 1977) and *E.T.: The Extra-Terrestrial* (Steven Spielberg, 1982) continue this tradition.

The Power and Fascination of the Genre Film

Style is a vital source of a filmmaker's power. The common stylistic qualities, or conventions, of a given genre emphasize, but do not necessarily explain, the conflicts and desires that propel characters forward. Their application and innovation gives every filmmaker an opportunity to convey her own distinct perspective on the world she places before us. Music is used lavishly in melodrama and horror films, often to signal the enormous emotional stakes of particular scenes (something of which the characters, of course, remain totally unaware). Similarly, the expressive use of composition, camera angle, or color may serve as an outward manifestation of a character's inner emotional state. Characters are only aware, however, of how they present themselves to others within the story. Film style, like the acting skills of actors—which the director must also harness as an effective element in the overall design—is what generates fascination with and attraction to the world conjured up by the film and populated by characters. It is what shifts a film into an expressive and allegorical form of communication.

A film rarely shows awareness of its own style, just as actors seldom show awareness of their acting skill. The represented story world and what happens within it simply is like this or like that. And yet, style allows the director to adopt an attitude and present a perspective on this imagined world that usually reverberates with implications for the larger historical world to which it belongs. Style, a crucial component of the formal context, fosters the viewer's emotional participation, intellectual engagement, and ideological involvement. It does so, as dreams, metaphors, and allegories generally do, without saying exactly what it means. Interpretation is the task of the viewer. The film's goal is to achieve an effect, to move, please, or persuade, to convey what life in a certain world feels like rather than to analyze and resolve social issues and conflicts directly. Narrative storytelling and the genre system of filmmaking remain among the most powerful ways to achieve these goals.

8

IDEOLOGY AND THE CINEMA

Ideology Demonstrates Both Repressive and Productive Qualities

IDEOLOGY AS PRODUCTIVE AND INEVITABLE

As discussed in the Introduction, ideology is an internalized image of one's place within all of the social dynamics related to power and hierarchy. Put differently, ideology describes the lens through which individuals see and understand how they fit into the social world around them. The internalized image of one's place in the world bestows on each individual an idea of what goals to strive for, which values and beliefs count most, what groups inhabit society, how to use and adapt common social practices, and what cultural ideals deserve emulation. Ideology allows individuals to frame specific actions within a more comprehensive framework. No one has to decide what to think or do from scratch in each new situation.

In this sense ideology is tremendously valuable. It is a productive force, allowing people to go about their business in relation to an already established sense of purpose and direction. It is as if ideology says, "This is how we do things here, and this is how you fit in." In this sense, each person knows his or her place in advance, even if this place

remains subject to modification in many ways. Individuals can operate on the basis of ingrained habits or attitudes, and express themselves
via conduct that's commensurate. Individuals routinely do what seems
natural and obvious based on the image they have of themselves and
the world. Reliance on ingrained, customary ways of seeing and acting allows individuals to reserve their conscious attention for problems
that resist routine treatment.

Ideology, as an internalized, imaginary, or image-based relation to
an actual situation, presents a picture of how one ought to conduct
oneself. It guides behavior. What actions or statements will do justice
to a given view of the world? Ideology lays the groundwork for
answers to such a question. In some cases it is likely that individuals
will tender agreement with the established, prevailing, or dominant
way of doing things, without full knowledge of doing so. It is as if a
map or blueprint had already been internally installed.

When ideology is understood this way it is as if an image of the
world presents itself, full-blown, of how to act. This image may, in fact,
have been gradually constructed over considerable time via the family, media, church, schools and universities, the legal system and other
institutions, as well as by friends and peers, but now it is in place. Such
an image becomes part of how individuals see themselves. When they
have need of a guide to conduct, this already existing image provides
it. A villain doesn't need to think twice about shooting someone in a
gangster film, for example: he sees the world in them-against-me
terms and has already internalized an image of how to act that puts self-
preservation first, even if it requires criminal violence.

Similarly, Jefferson Smith (Jimmy Stewart) arrives in Washington
as a hopelessly naïve senator in Frank Capra's *Mr. Smith Goes to Washington* (1939), but is not at a loss in terms of how to act: he has an
ingrained sense of honor, decency, and fair play that guides his conduct. His slow discovery that others are more scheming and callous
than he is presents a series of problems that he must then consciously

address. Dissonance between his ideological map and the actual political terrain generates the conflict at the heart of the film.

In any given time and place, one view of the world will tend to prevail. This is known as the **dominant ideology**: it upholds the existing relations of power and hierarchy. Agreement with the dominant ideology consists of accepting and upholding this particular belief system rather than seeking an alternative. The dominant ideology maintains the status quo, but whether the status quo serves an individual's needs and interests adequately can only be determined in a specific context.

In a complex society there are almost always **alternative ideologies** that resist, challenge, or subvert the dominant ideology. These are the belief systems of individuals who feel that the dominant ideology does not meet their needs. Adherents of dominant and alternative ideologies will inevitably present contrasting propositions about the nature of social reality and one's place within it. For example, the liberal belief in social change and the role of government to ensure equal opportunity for all contrasts with the conservative belief in social stability and individual autonomy from government supervision or interference. These two views often struggle for dominance. Each carries a different image of the individual's place in relation to the distribution of political power and the effects of social hierarchy. Subcultures and subordinate ethnicities, classes, or genders typically develop alternative ideologies of their own.

An ideology also entails an emotional investment in a particular way of seeing things. It is what makes both a conservative patriot and a radical activist fervent: they see the world in a particular way, with particular values and beliefs, and have a distinct emotional investment in their view of things. They regard the world as heading in a given direction, for better or worse, and find their own conduct and behavior propelled by specific ideals that will reinforce or alter that direction. For adherents of a given worldview, such ideals are worth fighting for. That these ideals differ leads to patterns of conflict. Almost all of the stories a culture tells itself refer back to these conflicts, be they tales of family discord or romantic harmony, social prejudice or social justice, the abuse of power or personal responsibility, greed or generosity. How these conflicts get resolved and a dominant ideology established, and what alternative ideologies contend for followers, defines the characteristic values and beliefs of a society at a given point in time.

IDEOLOGY AS A REPRESSIVE FORCE

Any specific way of seeing the world will inevitably discount or disparage alternative ways of seeing. A dominant ideology, for example, operates to normalize or naturalize social practices that preserve the status quo. It must constantly discredit, misrepresent, censor, or otherwise fend off alternative ideologies that threaten its dominance. The commonsensical voice of the dominant ideology says something like, "The way things are is perfectly natural, isn't it?" and "This is how we do things here, isn't it?" Typically, this voice treats the existing social arrangement as mythic, natural, or eternal, outside of time.

Whether individuals heed this voice or set out to contest it will be part of the ongoing struggle for hegemony, or control. There is not only an invitation to consent, but also the suppression of dissent. Mockery or ostracism may be directed at those who depart from the dominant way of seeing and doing things. Shaming or ignoring, rejecting or punishing the views of those who see things differently may occur. Providing rewards for those who see things the right way also wins compliance without resorting to brute force. Recognition, respect, status accrue to those who go along.

In this sense, a dominant ideology creates a set of constraints on what counts as acceptable conduct. Like constraints within an institutional context such as the Hollywood studio system, this allows for opportunities at the same time as it sets limits. This process has definite value: it gets things done; it makes routine behavior more or less automatic. Whether it proves to be a problem or not depends on the specific values and beliefs promoted, the power relations supported, the social hierarchy established, and where this leaves specific individuals or groups.

It is almost inevitably the case that any dominant ideology will dissatisfy some. Racism, sexism, and class bias are but a few of the social practices that have, in certain times and places, belonged to a dominant way of seeing things. As we saw in Chapter 6, numerous state laws prohibited interracial marriage, or miscegenation, in the 1930s. Such statutes clearly suppressed alternative values and beliefs just as prohibitions on gay marriage do in the 2000s. Whether individuals perceive these laws as a problem or not will hinge on how they picture themselves fitting within the social system that results. When a repressed alternative begins to feel more desirable, when it appears that it might be more productive for a given group, **consciousness-raising** (discussed below)—bringing alternative values and beliefs to a heightened level of awareness—proves a valuable tool for achieving social change.

Ideology as Blind Adherence to a Specific Point of View

The concept of ideology has a lengthy history, and its meaning has evolved over time. Earlier understandings of the term linked it to a specific cause or set of values that adherents follow blindly. This view overlooks ideology's productive value and treats the term as a derogatory one. It suggests that someone has both a fixed agenda and a blind belief that elude rational control. This makes ideology a characteristic of zealots of all stripes and, as a corollary, makes the non-zealot free from any ideological straightjacket. **Ideologues** are then an extreme case of those who proselytize for a given way of seeing things. Labeling these individuals or their ideologies pejoratively, though, doesn't mean that others lack internalized values and beliefs to guide their conduct, even if they apply them more judiciously.

Ideology is not the exclusive preserve of zealots. Zealots may support the dominant or alternative ideologies, but non-zealots will also act in relation to one or another ideology. Rather than treating ideology as blind belief and an absence of ideology as common sense, this chapter proposes a range of ideologies, with one typically dominant (its dominance makes adherence appear commonsensical) and a set of alternatives to it.

The film *American History X* (Tony Kaye, 1998), for example, tells the story of a skinhead, Derrick Vinyard (Ed Norton), who goes to jail for committing a monstrous hate crime only to "see the light" and discard an all-consuming, racist ideology. The latter part of the story involves Derrick's efforts to steer his younger brother, who has consistently idolized him, away from the obsessive racism he has abandoned. Derrick's transformation represents a classic form of heightened consciousness (discussed below) in which he gains an ability to see the big picture and to realize how wrong his former beliefs were.

The film adopts the idea of ideology as a pejorative term by making his conversion from racist zealotry an escape from ideology entirely. His respect for others appears to be a commonsensical, entirely natural state of affairs. Non-racist behavior is not seen as an alternative ideology that must also be "bred in the bone," that is, slowly internalized as a way of seeing the world through repetition and social reinforcement so that it becomes a habitual way of acting. Because Derrick's change is made to appear effortless, his brother's persistence as a skinhead seems like a stubborn, misguided belief that he should readily correct. This approach associates ideology with moral blindness, creates a realm of nonideological behavior, and links this realm with natural goodness. But if ideology is an omnipresent, productive as well as repressive force, the conflict between racism and anti-racism becomes a genuine struggle between alternative ideologies.

Ideology and Consciousness-Raising

Consciousness-raising describes the process of arriving at a new state of awareness. Through this process individuals or groups see things in a fresh way. Often, there is a moment of sudden revelation, although the process can also be gradual and painstaking. Saint Paul's conversion on the road to Damascus is a classic example of an "aha!" experience that suddenly leads to an altered state of consciousness. From that point on, Paul understood his mission in life in a new light. In political terms consciousness-raising means seeing the existing structure of society in a new way. Typically, it also entails working to bring a different social structure, whether reactionary, a reversion to the past, or radical, a brand-new alternative, into being.

In terms of narrative storytelling, consciousness-raising involves a character's sudden shift of awareness and perception: things aren't what the character thought they were. A new form of awareness clicks into place. This type of "aha!" experience provides a crucial pivot for the story. Typically it is the hero or central character who undergoes the most profound change. The main character can now chart a new path forward based on an altered consciousness as Derrick Vinyard does in *American History X*.

From a progressive perspective, consciousness-raising involves seeing conflicts or injustice not as individual problems but as common problems affecting an entire group or class of people. Correspondingly, a conservative moment of consciousness-raising comes with a realization that government intervention makes problems worse or that it denies people their personal autonomy. From a feminist perspective consciousness-raising has typically meant seeing oppressive conditions as a result of systemic bias that targets all women rather than just individuals. From a religious perspective, consciousness-raising often means seeing the structure and meaning of the world as a result of divine intervention rather than the product of nature or human endeavor alone.

Films from the Soviet Union in the 1920s and '30s, and proletarian literature from various countries during this period, frequently told the story of a worker who, realizing his exploitation, decided to act to confront this situation. He threw off misguided ideas, adopted new ones, and served as a model for others. This model drew on Marx's view of ideology as a misguided, upside-down conception of how the world really is rather than a more contemporary view of ideology as a necessary, productive as well as repressive force that, when deficient, must be confronted by an alternative ideology. In most of these films and novels, the big picture pops into view via an "aha!" experience in which a final straw or inciting incident prompts a dramatic change of perception. In *Battleship Potemkin* (Sergei Eisenstein, 1925, Soviet Union), the realization that the ship's doctor is quite willing to deny that the crew's meat is crawling with maggots is one such moment: a sailor lifts a plate and smashes it to the deck in an act of outrage that spurs the rest of crew toward mutiny against the ship's cruel, oppressive officers. The crew no longer see themselves as loyal sailors but as mutineers against unjust tyranny.

The idea of consciousness-raising goes in the opposite direction from narrative displacement. Displacement means shifting political issues to less volatile terrain, for example, dealing with the morality of seeking personal revenge rather than testing the adequacy of the legal system. Instead of converting social issues into personal conflicts, consciousness-raising prompts characters to identify personal conflicts with larger social issues directly, usually in the form of acting in concert with others for a common goal.

Ideology, Hegemony, and Hierarchy

HEGEMONY AND CULTURAL IDEALS

Cultural ideals, described in Chapter 7, preside over social practices as a motivating force. They say something like, "And here's the payoff. Here's why you should agree with the way we do things here."

Cultural ideals from creativity to love, and from success to freedom, are the embodiment of the values and beliefs that fuel a given ideology. Once internalized, these ideals guide behavior and motivate action. They fill routine conduct with meaning. They imbue ambitions with purpose. They provide a measure of what ought to be when what is does not quite measure up, when conflicts and compromises generate confusion. Their replacement is usually piecemeal rather than wholesale; and, as values and beliefs, shared cultural ideals, like ideologies, cannot be jettisoned entirely in any case. They must be replaced by viable alternatives.

It is not uncommon to contest the existing social hierarchy in one area but remain under its sway in others. Workers in one country may unite under a cultural ideal of class solidarity, but also remain hostile to foreign workers who want to immigrate to earn better pay if this need seems threatening to their own job security. In this case, patriotic or nationalist ideals may take priority over class solidarity. Similarly, a male liberal may display a patronizing attitude toward women at the same time as he champions the cause of an oppressed ethnic minority. Such contradictions can be identified and addressed in concrete situations. Film is one way to give concrete expression to such contradictions. Different genres, for example, explore typical conflicts inherent in different cultural ideals. Film noirs, like gangster films, explore contradictions between individual ambition and the law, westerns explore tensions between personal autonomy and the need for community, and science-fiction films examine conflicts that arise around the use and abuse of technology.

THE MEANING AND FUNCTION OF HEGEMONY

Hegemony refers to the process by which a given social system wins the voluntary consent of its members to accept their place within a hierarchical structure. This process if often referred to as socialization, but the concept of hegemony puts a sharper focus on the political stakes involved: how to get individuals to freely accept the constraints of a given ideology in exchange for the benefits of:

1) social belonging,
2) a ready-made template for handling routine situations, i.e., not needing to rethink how to deal with every situation, and
3) acquiring a concept or picture of what the world is like and what one's place within it is.

Hegemony is the mechanism by which ideologies take hold within individuals, and groups and establish consent for the existing distribution of power and hierarchy. It operates across a spectrum of institutions and social practices.

Hegemonic processes lead to social hierarchy or the uneven distribution of power. The **hegemonic order** refers to the social distribution of power and hierarchy that results from the work of this mechanism in practice. Hegemony strives to make any uneven distribution of power seem natural. The owner of a business has considerable power over his employees, for example. This seems only right, since he has the largest stake in the success of the business, but it is also clear that this power can lead to abuse and exploitation. Rather than level the playing field to prevent abuse, hegemony works to justify the uneven distribution of power and to have those affected by it internalize the justifications as part of how they see the world. In this case, it might mean that workers come to see their fate tied to their boss's and hence be willing to accept his autonomous decisions and actions as necessary for the good of all, rather than militate for a substantial say in such decisions to guarantee that their perspective and needs get fully represented.

Hegemony works in the opposite direction from consciousness-raising: instead of seeing things anew, the individual becomes accustomed to the ways things are as the natural order of things. The media, along with education, the workplace, family, church, and legal system, assign positive values to behavior that supports the customary way of doing things. These values establish dominant, hegemonic relationships. They are, at root, hierarchical. It is from this imbalance that most narrative conflict arises. Narratives commonly revolve around what it feels like to experience particular forms of hierarchy at a day-to-day level: for example, the abusive family patriarch (*This Boy's Life* [Michael Caton-Jones, 1993], *The Edge of Heaven* [Fatih Akin, 2007, Germany/Turkey/Italy]), the boss who is overbearing (*Wall Street* [Oliver Stone, 1987], *The Devil Wears Prada* [David Frankel, 2006]), the political leader who becomes a demagogue (*All the King's Men* [Robert Rossen, 1949], *The Last King of Scotland* [Kevin Macdonald, 2006, UK]), or the military commander who fails to lead wisely (*Paths of Glory* [Stanley Kubrick, 1957], *The Caine Mutiny* [Edward Dmytryk, 1954]).

How the Behavior of Individuals and Characters Relates to Ideology

Ideology is thus not a pejorative reference to zealots or other people's (distorted) views, not simply explicit statements of doctrine and belief we can take or leave, and not false consciousness waiting to be converted to full awareness. Instead, a hegemonic tug-of-war between contending values and beliefs, principles and practices occurs in relation to what individuals identify with and how they act. As an internalized guidance system, ideology frees individuals to focus on specific problems rather than constantly reinvent the social order and their place within it. For this reason, ideology manifests itself in many forms of behavior. Behavior and action, whether by an actual individual or by a fictional character, is ideology's most natural form of expression.

Richard Leacock, a distinguished documentary filmmaker, once said that he refused to do interviews and preferred instead to film people going about their business while he unobtrusively observed them. He justified this choice by saying he was uninterested in hearing what people said they did. He wanted to observe what they actually did. The difference can be considerable. A fundamental premise of almost all narrative storytelling is that people reveal who they are through what they do. Dividing behavior into four, somewhat overlapping categories will help us understand how ideology functions in the ordinary, day-to-day activity of individuals conducting their lives and pursuing their interests. These categories differentiate between ideological (or normal), idiosyncratic, symptomatic, and resistant forms of behavior.

Ideological or Normal Action and Behavior

Ideological behavior involves conduct that models, exemplifies, demonstrates, reinforces, or supports the dominant ideology, whatever that ideology might be. Such behavior says, in effect, "I am acting in a way that leaves unquestioned how we do things here." Anti-Semitism was normal action and behavior in Nazi Germany, whereas tolerance and multicultural acceptance are models of normal, ideological action and behavior in present-day Germany. Within a given subculture, normal action and behavior will conform to what is deemed normal within the specific context of that subculture, be it an immigrant, gay or lesbian, or religious community.

The man who whistles at a woman passing on the street is acting ideologically. Such behavior, to the whistler, seems perfectly normal. His action draws from and reinforces an ideology of **male chauvinism** or **machismo**. It reinforces and endorses the presumption that men have the right to objectify women in public. **Male chauvinism, masculinism**, and **machismo** are terms adopted by the women's movement to describe male behavior that derives from an assumption of male superiority, such as deciding whether a wife should work and under what conditions, or having the right to make crude passes at women. These acts deny the woman a sense of dignity and a right to her full individuality. (Masculinism is discussed further in Chapter 10.) In a different context, the military officer who issues orders to men under his command also acts ideologically. And the soldiers who obey his order act ideologically. Together they affirm the hegemonic order and the distribution of power across different military ranks. Whether this distribution is just, or a given order wise, is a separate question. Given ideology's productive value, behavior that adheres to a given ideology is not necessarily misguided or wrong.

In *The Conformist* (Bernardo Bertolucci, 1970, Italy/France/West Germany), Marcello Clerici's obsessive urge to be taken as normal in fascist Italy drives him to commit murder to prove his loyalty to the cause. The murder is an ideological act in a context where normal behavior includes such extreme acts. In *Wall Street*, the tremendously successful Wall Street broker Gordon Gecko (Michael Douglas) proclaims as his motto "Greed Is Good" and proves it through dishonest and illegal dealings with one and all. He regards his actions as entirely normal and perfectly in accord with the underlying ethic of the marketplace. The film, by focusing on a young, impressionable newcomer to Wall Street, Bud Fox (Charlie Sheen), explores the darker consequences of this concept of normalcy. In each case, normalcy is judged against a norm or standard that may not be explicit. It is more a tacit understanding of "how we do things here" and it may be represented sympathetically or critically by the film. In these two cases, the films display a critical distance from the behavior of their main characters.

In *The Lives of Others* (*Das leben der anderen*, Florian Henckel von Donnersmarck, 2006, Germany), Hauptmann Wiesler's (Ulrich Mühe) boss orders him to spy on a successful playwright. Wiesler is a surveillance specialist working for the Stasi, the East German police unit that rooted out dissidents and subversives when East Germany was a Communist state. His behavior is, at this point, professional and entirely ideological, in support of the existing status quo and the relations of power and hierarchy it entails. Unquestioning obedience is fully expected, and Wiesler obeys. Gradually, though, Wiesler learns that the surveillance operation is not in the name of national security but an attempt by the minister of culture to frame the playwright so that the minister can more freely pursue his affair with the playwright's girlfriend. Wiesler realizes that his normal, ideological behavior, in service to the state and to political ideals he cherishes, has led him astray. His behavior begins to shift from support for the dominant ideology to active resistance. He secretly lends assistance to the playwright, whom he now sees as an innocent victim. His actions and behavior no longer reinforce the status quo, or, more precisely, assist in the abuse of power by his superior, even if his resistance requires him to disobey orders and risk his own life. He adopts an alternative ideology that places exposing the abuse of power above obedience to orders.

Normal behavior includes behavior that may not consciously endorse or reaffirm the dominant ideology but nonetheless conforms to it. Such behavior sometimes goes by the name of **coping behavior**. Coping behavior plays a vital part in negotiating hierarchy. Instead of rebellion, the individual learns how to go along whether his heart is in it or not. He copes or makes do rather than making waves. To the proposition, "This is how we do things here and this is how you fit in," coping responds by saying something like, "So I'd better play along, not rock the boat, and hope for the best even if I don't fully believe in the way it all works." Coping often encourages the individual to overestimate the odds of success and to minimize the obstacles that may prevent it.

Arthur and William, the two young men who are the focal point of the stirring documentary *Hoop Dreams* (Steve James, 1994), cope with their family problems and economic hardships by buying into a long-shot dream: life as a professional basketball player. Such a dream comes with a high price attached, even at the high school level. William switches to a predominately white, suburban school to benefit from a superior sports program, but he is treated as an outsider. Arthur becomes a leader on an inner-city team that does quite well. The filmmaker follows the two men over a three-year period. At film's end both are headed to college but their ultimate success is not yet clear. The emphasis is on what it takes to cope with adversity and hold onto a dream. Neither man wants to change the system so much as become a full-fledged part of it. Neither buys into everything he is told, but they go along in the hopes that there will be a significant pay-off. The filmmaker makes clear how low the odds of success are, how ruthless the system can be, and how much race and class enter into the equation in complex ways. The film implies that those who dream of professional sports as the path to a better future have the odds heavily stacked against them. This does not deter William and Arthur from making the effort.

In *Mystic River* (Clint Eastwood, 2003) Jimmy Markum (Sean Penn) and his friend, Sean Devine (Kevin Bacon), witness the same childhood tragedy in which two men abduct and rape Dave (Tim Robbins). They struggle to cope with this experience the rest of their lives. Sean winds up a police officer, whereas Jimmy becomes the owner of a corner business and a small-time crook. Jimmy has adopted a cynical view of the law and playing by the rules, but family life and normal parental behavior are also a crucial component of his identity. When his daughter is murdered, Jimmy cannot passively wait for Sean and the other cops to bring the killer to justice. He becomes a vigilante. Unfortunately, he misinterprets Dave's idiosyncratic behavior after the murder as symptomatic evidence of guilt, erroneously concluding that Dave is the killer. Dave's actions could be those of a guilty man but, in fact, they are not. Jimmy also believes that "a man must do what a man must do." His belief derives from the dominant ideology of masculinism and of frontier justice. Dave serves as the sacrificial figure for ideologies that demand men demonstrate their manliness in acts of vengeance that place them above the law.

Director Clint Eastwood's early career celebrated just these ideologies in films like *Dirty Harry* (Don Siegel, 1971) and *Pale Rider*
(Clint Eastwood, 1985), but his later films have called vengeance and
masculinism into question. *Mystic River* stresses the tragic dimension
of masculinist assumptions. The restrained, solemn music, the frequent
flashbacks to Dave's childhood trauma, and the method acting styles
of the male leads, which hint at inner turbulence beyond the reach of
language, all emphasize how the childhood attack on Dave lingers as
an emotional trauma that shapes the men's behavior. Dave finds himself shattered as a man, unable to express his feelings or affirm his own
dignity. His two friends, forced to be bystanders, bear lingering guilt
for what happened. Sean wants to prove the system can work; Jimmy
is convinced it never will. Eastwood leads the audience to experience
what it feels like for emotionally damaged men to try to cope with
trauma in ways that only intensify and perpetuate the damage.

Idiosyncratic Action and Behavior

Idiosyncratic behavior involves those forms of conduct peculiar to an
individual. Like style, idiosyncrasies (mannerisms, favorite expressions,
and an unusual way of moving or gesturing) help distinguish an individual from others in the same social category (doctors, gamblers, busi-
nessmen, or parents, for example). Idiosyncrasies often involve minor
deviations from normal behavior. They seldom represent a challenge to
or subversion of the norm from which they in some way depart, but they
do distinguish the individual as a unique person. Marcello Clerici's tendency to hold his straight fingers in a rigid block in *The Conformist* may
be a way to display an idiosyncrasy that he thinks will make him look like
a good fascist—rigid, in control, free of hesitation. It suggests how eager
he is to appear to be one of the group even through idiosyncrasies. As
in this case, idiosyncrasies quite often serve to signal something of a character's identity. At other times, idiosyncrasies are carried by actors from

film to film. Stars are often targets of parody based on their distinctive mannerisms: John Wayne's swagger and his verbal pauses, for example, were frequently imitated by comedians, and Tallulah Bankhead likened Katherine Hepburn's patented form of rapid-fire, staccato speech to "nickels tumbling in a slot machine." These quirks can make the difference between a charismatic star and a competent supporting actor, although everyone possesses idiosyncrasies to one degree or another.

NEUROTIC OR PSYCHOTIC ACTION AND BEHAVIOR

Neurotic or psychotic behavior involves those forms of conduct indicative of mental pathology. Action and behavior now serve as symptoms of a disorder. In the cinema, a film's tone or perspective often indicates whether the filmmaker considers the pathology to be of unknown origin and strictly an individual disorder or something that stands for larger scale social disorders.

If the dominant ideology says, "This is how we do things here and this is how you fit in," neuroses and psychoses respond, through behavior far more than words, to say something like, "I can't fit in; I've lost control of what I do despite the consequences." *Psycho's* (Alfred Hitchcock, 1960) Norman Bates (Anthony Perkins), for example, is clearly psychotic; he lacks the ability to sustain social relationships, although he is also able to talk about what is normal and abnormal in a way that appears, at least to Marion Crane (Janet Leigh), to have a helpful perspective on situations similar to her own. His actions, though, tell a very different story. *Psycho* explains Norman in terms of individual mental pathology, whereas *American Psycho* (Mary Harron, 2000, U.S./Canada), the story of a well-to-do Wall Street investment banker whose life becomes subsumed by terrible, psychopathic acts of violence and murder, offers no individual explanation. It suggests, through a narrative structure that makes his psychotic self the nighttime Mr. Hyde to his seemingly normal daytime Dr. Jekyll, that his behavior is a lurid symptom of a divided self, torn by unchecked greed and narcissism. This, in turn, can be interpreted as a metaphorical critique of a socio-economic system whose fundamental values and beliefs fuel such a division, a critique that goes back at least as far as *The Cabinet of Dr. Caligari* (Robert Wiene, 1920, Germany).

Mental disorders like these often demonstrate the individual's inability to cope with or adapt to the expectations of the dominant ideology. Voyeurism, for example, replaces normal expectations regarding mature sexual expression in terms of physical intimacy with experiences based solely on looking while remaining unseen and unengaged directly. Michael Powell's powerful and disturbing exploration of voyeurism in *Peeping Tom* (1960, UK) suggests that the main character's urge to photograph women as a prelude to killing them with the camera tripod he uses to film them derives from traumatic childhood experience.

Whether such experience serves as a metaphor for larger social ills remains ambiguous in *Peeping Tom*, as it does in *The Blue Angel* (Josef von Sternberg, 1930, Germany). In Josef von Sternberg's memorable film, Professor Rath's slavish infatuation with Lola (Marlene Dietrich) can be interpreted as individual illness or as a symptom of some men's longing to escape from the demands of a masculinist ideology. Rath finds power a burden and surrender a relief. From this perspective the film serves as a critique of an ideology of male superiority.

Professor Rath's neurotic obsession pales alongside the apparently paranoid delusions of Ben Marco (Frank Sinatra and Denzel Washington in the 1962 and 2004 versions respectively) in *The Manchurian Candidate* (John Frankenheimer, 1962; Jonathan Demme, 2004). Ben tries to figure out why he has nightmares and whether a fellow soldier actually deserved a Medal of Honor. By film's end we learn that Ben is not paranoid, but both the original and the remake give a vivid sense of what it feels like to experience the world from an apparently paranoid perspective. They make such a perspective feel justified. Ben's paranoia, it turns out, corresponds to a world in which clandestine machinations by sinister forces (Communists in the original and, as a revealing comment on changing times, corporate powers in the remake) exploit democratic principles (elections and free speech) for their own, very undemocratic ends. A psychotic state of apparently paranoid behavior becomes symptomatic of a world ruled by forces that disregard the codes of democratic conduct.

RESISTANT ACTION AND BEHAVIOR

MOCKING OR REJECTING THE EXISTING SOCIAL ORDER WITHOUT CHANGING IT Resistant, subversive, deviant, or confrontational action and behavior are at odds with the dominant ideology. Subversive behavior usually does not set out to change the dominant system but to undermine, mock, or exploit it. Irony and satire are aesthetic forms that commonly perform these actions. Satire, cynicism, ironic detachment, and the pose of the beatnik, hippie, or slacker all let the existing system persist but undercut or reject its values and beliefs. Such perspectives respond to the voice of dominant ideology when it says, "This is how we do things here and this is how you fit in," with a "That's what you think; here's another way to fit in," or "No thanks; I won't bother you if you don't bother me." These responses don't confront the dominant way of doing things directly in order to found a new social order, as the rebel, discussed next, often does. The result, though, provides insulation from the indignities of a system that remains unaltered.

The numerous characters who pass through *Slacker* (Richard Linklater, 1991), for example, exhibit a singular lack of ambition in terms of finding a place in the existing social system. Instead of coping with adversity by holding to a dream and a plan, they slide through the present absorbed in their particular obsessions and interests. They build a subcultural community in the course of doing so. It is a classic case of "dropping out" not to militate for change but to find a viable place at the margins of mainstream society. The dominant ideology presents an image of adulthood as a time when individuals become successful, productive members of society. The slackers here have little sympathy with this view. They adopt values and beliefs that run quite deep, but productivity and success as measured by careers, income, social status, and material comforts are not among them. Like the Beats and hippies before them, they respond to a society whose dominant values they do not respect by opting out rather than coping or rebelling. *Animal House* (aka *National Lampoon's Animal House*; John Landis, 1978) offers a raucous, insolent form of rebellion meant to defy convention but not to overthrow the social order. The gross, deliberately offensive nature of the students' actions becomes a vital aspect of their rejection of the dominant ideology. They will have nothing to do with discipline and preparation for the respectable life as responsible citizens. At least not yet. First there comes the moment of wild oats, sown with flamboyant irreverence, then, perhaps later, these rebels will settle down and take their place in society. The tradition of giving offense that the surrealists and Dadaists reveled in during the 1920s lives on. It bears similarity to the **carnivalesque**, in which for a limited time and in a specified place, the normal order of things is suspended and a festive, defiant, subversive spirit breaks loose. Such defiance may not shake society to its foundations, but it does frequently present a mocking display of the values and beliefs that support the status quo.

REBELS AND THE SOCIAL ORDER Alternatively, individuals can adopt the role of the outsider, outcast, loner, misfit, martyr, or rebel as a way of breaking with the dominant ideology. Such individuals often exude great appeal. As condensed images of broader currents of discontent, they often possess charismatic personalities that attract others magnetically. Outsiders and rebels often embark on journeys or quests, challenge wrongs, serve as exemplary models or as cautionary warnings. Without a movement or following, however, their efforts may not spark social transformation. Rebels, in this sense, prove to be leaders or loners. Just as neuroses and pathologies may suggest deeper social ills or merely individual disorders, so rebels may represent splendid loners who march to the beat of a different drum or social leaders who challenge the hegemonic order of a given social structure.

From the perspective of the dominant ideology, misfits and rebels help define the boundaries of what counts as normal versus deviant behavior. Society often needs such figures to point to the limits beyond which behavior is no longer acceptable. The risk is that rebellious behavior will act as an incitement rather than a warning. The Hollywood Production Code guarded against this risk by stipulating that films could not present criminals in a positive light and that crimes could not go unpunished.

In the 1960s, however, *Bonnie and Clyde* (Arthur Penn, 1967) capitalized on earlier couple-on-the-run films such as *They Live by Night* (Nicholas Ray, 1948) and *Gun Crazy* (Joseph H. Lewis, 1950) but imbued the couple with a vividly romantic aura, thanks to the inherent glamour of Warren Beatty and Faye Dunaway plus cinematography that cast them in golden light and soft focus. Viewers root for them to beat the system and spark a popular uprising against the callous, moneyed interests. But the couple steps beyond the pale, inadvertently killing innocent people and setting off a chain reaction of violent revenge by the police. They develop a following that admires and idealizes them from a distance through newspapers and newsreels, radio and wanted posters rather than as dedicated rebels against the social order. The sense of vicarious excitement, a displacement of social discontent into identification with defiant but loner rebels, replaces any more direct form of social action.

RESISTANCE BECOMES REBELLION: SOCIAL ACTIVISM AND POLITICAL MOVEMENTS For most political theorists, lasting change primarily arises from concerted forms of social action. This, however, requires a shift from the personal to the political, from individual rebellion against discrimination, oppression, hardship, and injustice to group revolt against such practices. Films such as *Zero for Conduct* (Jean Vigo, 1933, France), *Battleship Potemkin, Storm over Asia* (Vsevolod Pudovkin, 1928, Soviet Union), and *The Battle of Algiers* (Gillo Pontecorvo, 1965, Italy/Algeria) exemplify a more radical perspective in which rebels embody shared values and common goals that galvanize others to join together to overthrow tyranny and create a more egalitarian community.

The French director Jean Vigo had an anarchist's view of society, not unlike that of Luis Buñuel but with a more acerbic tone. His feature film *Zero for Conduct*, like the earlier German film *Mädchen in Uniform* (Leontine Sagan, 1931), tells a story of repression and frustration, discipline and rebellion in a boarding school. Unlike *Animal House*, there is a deeply felt sense of injustice at work. The students dream of a more utopian world, free from tyranny and oppression. The dream belongs to all the students; the rebellion is collective rather than solitary. Their defiance, in Vigo's hands, becomes cinematic reality as he gives visual embodiment to their dream. The result is a symbolic defiance of authority that comes closer to an ecstatic riot, beautifully and poetically presented, than a revolution. Clearly, though, for Vigo, it is prelude to more substantial forms of rebellion rather than a passing moment of sowing wild oats as it appears to be in *Animal House*.

What *Zero for Conduct, Battleship Potemkin*, and *Mädchen in Uniform* have in common is that if there is a rebel or leader, usually someone who achieves a heightened form of consciousness, her actions galvanize others to action. Rather than settling for vicarious excitement, other characters actively work toward a common goal. For example, Ali la Point, the central character in *The Battle of Algiers*, is an angry, unemployed young man who winds up in jail for a petty crime. He witnesses an execution of a fellow Algerian radical and hears the man's final words urging others to fight back. Instead of reverting to his life of crime, Ali joins the FLN, the group working for Algerian independence from France.

Having done so, he eventually becomes a leader of the entire movement. Likewise, in *Norma Rae* (Martin Ritt, 1979) Sally Field plays an ordinary textile worker trapped by an oppressive situation in a Southern mill town that offers no obvious escape. Thanks to a union organizer from the North, she undergoes a consciousness-raising experience. Norma Rae's change becomes an inspiration to others and their collective efforts bear fruit, winning important concessions and improved work conditions.

In a classic example from one of Sergei Eisenstein's best films, *Battleship Potemkin*, the extraordinary shots of people streaming through Odessa, on streets, bridges, and piers, on foot and by boat, to mourn the death of Vakulinchuk, a leader of the rebellious crew aboard the *Potemkin*, give vivid embodiment to the idea of a mass movement. In this case, there is no hero or romantic rebel at the head of the crowd. Instead, Eisenstein imbues the crowd itself with a sense of spontaneous and dynamic determination. The mutiny against injustice spreads through the population as if it were itself a charismatic actor. The city's population becomes a multiheaded character, moved by the funeral for Vakulinchuk, and prepared to declare itself for the revolution against the czar which this incident represents in embryo.

In this funeral sequence, Eisenstein locates power and decision-making squarely in the hands of the people. The dead leader, Vakulinchuk, can only provide a symbolic center, not actual leadership. Lenin himself had died just two years before this film was made, and the allusion to him was no doubt vivid when the film was first released. Responsibility passes from the vanguard leader to the massed citizenry.

As different speakers exhort the crowd, Eisenstein assembles a montage of attractions, among which are fleeting shots of fists being clenched. Every character we see bobs and sways within the frame. Like the waves that beat upon the shore at the film's beginning, the crowd exhibits a force and vitality of its own. The motif reaches its climax as the mass of citizens finally thrust their fists in the air and declare their solidarity with the *Potemkin*'s crew.

Eisenstein provides a compelling demonstration of how an alternative ideology spreads across a wide spectrum of people. He makes this process of rebellion the center of the film, rather than the individual characters who embody it. In this way, *Battleship Potemkin* remains a memorable example of what it feels like to experience collective, revolutionary action itself rather than to find it condensed and displaced into the actions of a heroic rebel.

The Uses of Film Form to Challenge the Dominant Ideology

Because realism creates the impression that aspects of the world are transported directly, faithfully, and authentically to the screen, free from formal distortions, some film theorists conclude that if form is crucial to a film's impact, realism cannot be a useful style. This conclusion, however, runs contrary to the evidence of a wide range of realist fiction and documentary film that convey a distinct perspective and simultaneously allow viewers to see aspects of the world in a fresh, revealing way. Many filmmakers who have adopted modernist and postmodernist styles have also retained elements of realism. They have sought to combine the pleasure and power of popular cinema with the more expressly stylistic qualities of these other styles. The modernist work of Bertolt Brecht in the theater is a prime example of this tendency.

Brecht wrote extensively about his ideas for the theater and made clear that he sought to create a popular theater that had a politicizing effect. A popular play cannot be so formally sophisticated that most of the general public find it off-putting. It has to provide what Eisenstein called "attractions" or a "montage of attractions," terms that referred to the three-ring circus, with its exciting, simultaneous acts.

But, like many other artists who sought a transformative effect on their audience, Brecht felt that attractions could quickly become distractions. He wanted the sense of seeing things anew to touch on the social and political organization of society. The uses and abuses of power, the struggle for hegemony, the effects of hierarchy, the conflicts between dominant and alternative ideologies—to see such issues in a new, revealing light need not lead to specific political action, need not connect to the platform of any one party or group. It could be politicizing in the more general sense of urging the viewer to understand the world in terms of discipline, power, hierarchy, subversion, and consciousness. An aware audience member was a potential activist, eager for change. Like many artists, Brecht, who had clear leftist leanings, refrained from spelling out any concrete political program. It was enough to create a catalyst for change, and it was crucial that this catalyst be the form and structure of the work of art, be it play, novel, painting, or film.

BERTOLT BRECHT'S CONCEPT OF THE EPIC THEATER

Much great art can challenge and disturb. Greek tragedy held to just such a notion: the fall of the hero produces an emotional catharsis for the audience. But for Brecht this was not enough. Catharsis remains contained within the dramatic experience, and it remains centered on a single character. Rather than identify with characters, he wanted the audience to examine the characters' behavior to see its ideological dimensions. Brecht wanted to incite the audience to see their place in the world afresh. Let the audience enjoy the show but have the show unveil relations of power and hierarchy in a way the audience had never seen before.

Brecht sought to find ways to make the work of art less easily consumable as a distraction. Brecht felt that he had to take specific artistic measures to achieve this result. Table 8.1 summarizes some differences between Brecht's view of theater and more traditional views (adapted from Brecht's original formulations; see Further Reading).

Table 8.1 A Comparison of Traditional and Brechtian (or Epic) Theater

Traditional Theater	Brechtian (or Epic) Theater
Continuity and an overall harmony of elements prevail. Each element (lighting, music, action, dialogue, and so on) blends with the others so that they achieve one, harmonious whole.	Collage and fragmentation remind us that wholeness and harmony are aesthetic constructions. Uses a "separation of elements" to make music, dialogue, and action semi-independent of each other.
Wears down the spectator's capacity for action.	Arouses the spectator's capacity for action.
Gives the spectator sensations that provide distraction	Forces the spectator to make decisions that pertain to the real world
Ideological perspectives are implied and often remain subordinate to the dominant ideology.	Ideological perspectives are put baldly, in projected titles, signs, songs, or dialogue.
Instinctive feelings are preserved (as if they were natural and obvious).	Instinctive (ideological) feelings are brought to the point of recognition.
The human being is taken for granted: individualism is a core premise that allows action to revolve around a hero.	The human being is the object of inquiry: individualism itself and the function of the hero becomes subject to scrutiny.
Humans possess a timeless essence.	Humans are alterable and able to alter.
Thought determines being: putting on a happy face abolishes unhappiness, for example.	Social being determines thought: we adopt the perspective promoted by the ideology that prevails unless we achieve critical distance from it.
Feeling: a theater of sensations, spectacle, and distraction.	Reason: a theater of thought, reflection, and perspective.

Brecht's view that the spectator needs to gain a certain distance from a performance that is nonetheless engaging, led him to oppose many acting conventions for stage and screen. His approach is antithetical to **method acting**, for example. It refuses to heighten emotional investment through identification with the character's state of mind. It stresses an intellectual engagement with the social or ideological aspect of individual behavior. Brecht was after what he termed **social gests**. These **social gests** correspond to ideological action and behavior such as treating a subordinate discourteously and a superior obsequiously.

Brecht argued that actors should remain external to the actions and emotions they display. The actor, like the filmmaker, can adopt an attitude toward his character and convey a perspective on that character's conduct. Brecht puts it this way: "The attitude which [the actor] adopts is a socially critical one. ... In this way his performance becomes a discussion (about social conditions) with the audience he is addressing. He prompts the spectator to justify or abolish these conditions according to what class he belongs to." (See Willett's edition of Brecht's writings in *Brecht on Theatre*, listed in Further Reading.)

The techniques that have become most vividly associated with Brecht's name involve an **alienation effect** or **distanciation**. These techniques counter the tendency of much realism to make things seem natural and familiar. Graphic titles might be projected above the characters, identifying some of the issues they confront or presenting slogans whose validity the audience must assess. The music, catchy and familiar as it is, may seem out of place or excessive for a given moment in the play: again, the audience is given something to ponder. Scene changes may be done with no effort to disguise them by drawing a curtain. And the actors, by adopting personas that resemble those of familiar social types and delivering dialogue as if they were reporting what was said rather than fully embodying it, prompt the audience to reflect on what group or class a character represents and to what extent her attitudes correspond to members of such a group.

Like surrealism, expressionism, and formalism, Brecht's epic theater strives to make the familiar strange. This idea stems from the work of the Russian formalists in the 1920s, who argued that *ostranenie* or "making strange" was the technique that best distinguished literature from ordinary prose. To treat something artistically was to impede the habitual way of seeing it and to move an audience to see it in a new way. One of the formalist leaders, Victor Shklovsky, describes how Tolstoy defamiliarizes the ordinary act of a peasant whipping a horse to get it to pull a cart by recounting such an event from the point of view of the horse. Readers see the event with fresh eyes. The actions that are entirely habitual, and ideological to the peasant, become a form of social gest: they expose the hierarchical relationship of man and beast but also demonstrate the physical vulnerability of the horse to his owner. Tolstoy lifts the cloak of normalcy. A fundamental act of cruelty stands exposed in all its stark brutality. As Brecht would no doubt want to add, the reader is also put in a position to read the event metaphorically, where a horse stands for the peasantry or working class and the physical violence represents the habitual or ideological exploitation of these groups by the ruling class.

Brecht knew that a character saying that workers need to revolt or to trust the owners meant very little without the affective impact that came from style, structure, and, in his case, the specific work of alienating devices. These qualities work to convey something of what it feels like to live a certain way or see the world from a certain perspective. The Roman poet Horace once said the art should both please and instruct. This was Brecht's view as well.

Taking Brecht's views as a starting point, we will survey some of the ways in which filmmakers have explored the relationship between form and content. This survey will not yield formulas, but it does sketch out some of the general tendencies and possibilities that filmmakers have considered. The survey examines each of the four possible relationships between radical or conventional form and politicizing or non-politicizing effect.

Possible Relationships between Aesthetic Form and Social Impact

Radical Form with Politicizing Effect Bertolt Brecht's own plays fall into this category, as does Luis Valdez's *Zoot Suit* (1981), discussed in Chapter 5. In addition, many of the great works of the early Soviet cinema exhibit qualities that resemble those championed by Brecht. Dziga Vertov's *The Man with a Movie Camera* (1929, Soviet Union), which may have influenced Brecht's own theories, uses techniques such as stopping the action of filming passengers in a horse-drawn carriage with a freeze-frame, cutting to a shot of a strip of film that now contains the freeze-frame we just saw, and then observing the film's editor as she assembles different shots into the final film. The effect distances viewers from a purely realist style and engages them in the process of understanding how productive, material forces actually construct a social reality.

Vivre sa vie (1962, France) is one of Jean-Luc Godard's most overtly Brechtian films. Susan Sontag called it "a perfect film." It is the story of Nana (Anna Karina), a young Parisian woman whose relationships flounder as she drifts into prostitution and comes to a bad end. This tale is not told in a realist or melodramatic style, although it retains the ability to engage an audience emotionally. Michel Legrand's music for the film is moving, even haunting, but in keeping with the principle of separating the elements, Godard cuts the music off abruptly at times. He also breaks the film into twelve separate episodes. The first episode, for example, has the simple title, "Nana and Paul. Nana feels like giving up."

In episode 8, Godard adopts the techniques of participatory documentary to describe what a typical day in the life of a prostitute is like. We see Anna with clients and hear a voice-over commentary, speaking in a monotone, chronicling the details of her work. What we see of Nana begins to function simultaneously as the story of any woman, as a study of the negative impact of women's oppression (her pimp winds up selling her off to another man when she wants to quit, but the deal goes bad). This descriptive portrait can also be read as a metaphorical commentary on the fate of most individuals at the hands of capitalism. As in a number of his other films such as *Contempt* (1963, France/Italy), *Weekend* (1967, Italy/France), *2 or 3 Things I Know About Her* (1967, France), and *Tout va bien* (Jean-Luc Godard and Jean-Pierre Gorin, 1972, Italy/France), Godard couples elements of a popular, engaging style with a more modernist, defamiliarizing one to promote thought as well as feeling.

RADICAL FORM WITHOUT POLITICIZING EFFECT   Another term for this combination is formalism. This is work that is innovative on a formal or stylistic level and therefore capable of guiding the viewer to see formal conventions and the world they reveal in a new light. In cinema, it is the avant-garde that has taken up the call for radical innovations in form most ardently. The tendency of much avant-garde film to prompt viewers to rethink their relation to cinema and only secondarily to rethink their relation to society gave rise to the idea of a political avant-garde and a formalist avant-garde, as discussed in Chapter 2.

In *Window Water Baby Moving* (1962), for example, Stan Brakhage films his wife giving birth to their own child in a highly impressionistic, compelling way. Little of the actual birth is discernible, but the camera's movements and framings are highly engaging. The formal lyricism of the film uses its radicalism for aesthetic rather than social ends. Like much modernist art, such work certainly throws down a gauntlet at the feet of realist representation. It helps redefine the possibilities of the film medium, and can achieve a defamiliarizing effect, but it does so indirectly, in a much more oblique manner than that proposed by Brecht.

The highly innovative feature film *Time Code* (Mike Figgis, 2000) pursues the cubist concept of a fracturing of space and time in a highly formalist manner. In this case director Mike Figgis recorded a set of real-time events with four different digital cameras and then placed the footage in the four quadrants of the film screen. Viewers watch all four long takes of identical length (approximately ninety minutes) as they offer four different views of events that occurred simultaneously. By raising and lowering the sound levels for each quadrant, Figgis is able to guide the viewer's attention to the most salient quadrant at any given moment. The characters and events, however, fall into the familiar mold of the anti-Hollywood story. The head of a faltering, offbeat film studio debates whether to fund various film projects, including one identical to the film we are watching! *Time Code* could be said to convey ironic criticism of an entertainment industry too conservative to support the very work we are, in fact, viewing. The irony, although an effective element of the overall film, remains at some distance from the politicizing effect sought by Brecht.

CONVENTIONAL FORM WITH POLITICIZING EFFECT For Brecht such a category is inconceivable: the commodity status of conventional work overwhelms its politicizing potential. Many critics and filmmakers have disagreed with Brecht on this point. To alter conventional forms may make audiences unwilling to engage with the work at all rather than be disposed to see things anew. Political efficacy, in this view, depends on using a conventional form like realism, familiar to general audiences, but then adapting or subverting it for more pointedly political goals. As the principle of a dual formal-social analysis suggests, any film can be examined in terms of what is conventional and what innovative, what in line with and what contrary to a dominant ideology. As other chapters have demonstrated, popular films are not of one political stripe. In fact, conventional but politicizing films operate across the political spectrum from reactionary to radical.

Conservative and Reactionary Films Both the left and right sides of the political spectrum can make use of conventional form. Conservative and reactionary work is often quite content to use familiar forms, since its goal is to present the status quo as the obvious, unquestionable way things are. Defamiliarizing a realist representation of the world might encourage the idea that things could be otherwise. Films from the right tend to favor a straightforward, no-nonsense approach that has popular appeal. Vigilante characters who take the law into their own hands to right egregious wrongs, for example, often articulate precisely this type of shoot-from-the-hip, get-the-job-done mentality. *Dirty Harry*, with Clint Eastwood as the no-nonsense cop who gets his man, a serial killer, set the mold for such characters. The *Batman* films have a similar theme in which a personal trauma—witnessing the murder of his parents—serves to bring out Bruce Wayne's latent vigilantism.

War often provides a clear testing ground for political perspectives, with conservative films taking up themes of loyalty, patriotism, and self-sacrifice against an enemy who typically embodies repugnant qualities exclusively. *300* (Zack Snyder, 2006) does so in relation to ancient history and the battle of Thermopylae, in which the valiant three hundred soldiers of the Spartan king Leonidas fend off tens of thousands of invading Persian hordes. That the king's plan calls for taking a stand in a remote mountain pass to spare Sparta from the worst of a direct assault and that the assailants are Persian has led some to read an even more explicit conservative theme into the film than its celebration of a tough-minded masculinism. The strategy has clear similarities to the war in Iraq, promoted as a way to spare the United States from terrorist attack. In this regard, the film functions, as conservative films about the Vietnam War did, to support specific policies of the U.S. government as well as a generally conservative perspective on the world.

The Green Berets (John Wayne and Ray Kellogg, 1968) and *We Were Soldiers* (Randall Wallace, 2002, U.S./Germany), although made thirty-four years apart, both provide explicit endorsements of the U.S. government's rationale for the war in Vietnam. They celebrate the heroism of American military leaders, symbolized by John Wayne and Mel Gibson, respectively, and the men who follow them into combat. They deploy a realist style, with continuity editing and a full measure of condensation that reduces broader social issues to the hazards faced and responses made by their gallant heroes. Their politicizing effect lies in their presentation of an image of the world that makes government policies seem like a natural and necessary response to a black-and-white threat. They assert, like the vigilante films, "This is the way it is, isn't it?" or "This is how we should do things here, isn't it?" From a conservative perspective, such films represent individualism in its finest hour.

Progressive (Liberal and Radical) Films The combination of a conventional form and a politicizing effect exists in a wide variety of progressive films as well. *My Beautiful Laundrette* (Stephen Frears, 1985, UK), *Norma Rae, Three Kings* (David O. Russell, 1999, U.S./Australia), *Z* (Costa-Gavras, 1969, Algeria/France), *Malcolm X* (Spike Lee, 1992), *Judgment at Nuremberg* (Stanley Kramer, 1961), *Erin Brockovich* (Steven Soderbergh, 2000), and *The Insider* (Michael Mann, 1999) all present appealing central characters, familiar, resolvable problems, and conventionally constructed worlds. They do so, however, in relation to a pointed social agenda:

1) The acceptance of gay love and ethnic identity in *My Beautiful Laundrette*,
2) Working-class solidarity and a female leader's raised consciousness in *Norma Rae*,
3) The elements of hypocrisy and greed within a war waged in the name of democracy in *Three Kings* (the film is set during the first Gulf War),
4) Political assassination and the quest for social justice in *Z*,
5) A militant insistence on black power rather than civil disobedience as a political strategy in *Malcolm X*,

6) The issues of responsibility and guilt for war crimes in *Judgment at Nuremberg*,

7) A heroic crusade against corporate abuse of the environment and the endangerment of human lives in *Erin Brockovich*,

8) The abuse of power by tobacco companies versus the intrepid heroism of a whistle-blower in *The Insider*.

Such films hope to achieve a politicizing effect through character identification with the intrepid Norma Rae (Sally Field) or the feisty Erin Brockovich (Julia Roberts), for example. As in the conservative films, condensation remains heavily in use through the stress on a crusading hero who can do what others cannot. Displacement, though, is relatively slight, as social issues are openly acknowledged and addressed. Both conservative and progressive films count on emotional identification and intellectual engagement with the central characters to align the viewer with heroes whose actions exemplify a particular political perspective.

This combination of realist conventions and politicizing goals has underpinned films with an even more radical perspective, such as Ousmane Sembene's *Camp at Thiaroye* (Ousmane Sembene and Thierno Faty Sow, 1987, Senegal/Tunisia/Algeria), on the rise of a nationalist consciousness among Senegalese men recruited to serve as soldiers by the French during World War I but treated as inferiors at war's end, and *Salt of the Earth* (Herbert J. Biberman, 1954), a film made by blacklisted personnel from Hollywood that traces the course of a miners' strike and gives pointed emphasis to the role played by the miner's wives.

The genre of the social problem film also depends on coupling conventional form to politicizing effect. Often successful with audiences—as *Kansas City Confidential* (Phil Karlson, 1952), *Underworld U.S.A.* (Samuel Fuller, 1961), *The China Syndrome* (James Bridges, 1979), *Silkwood* (Mike Nichols, 1983), *City of Hope* (John Sayles, 1991), and

Traffic (Steven Soderbergh, 2000) were in the 1950s, '60s, '70s, '80s, '90s, and 2000s respectively—these films strike a popular chord by combining stylistic accessibility with a political message about cover-ups and corruption. They have their counterpart in socially conscious documentaries, from Barbara Kopple's *Harlan County, U.S.A.* (1976), on an intensely fought coal mine strike in Appalachia, to Michael Moore's *Sicko* (2007), on the inadequacies of the American health care system. Television movies that have addressed issues from AIDS to domestic abuse have also adopted this combination of conventional form and politicizing effect, often with surprisingly successful results in terms of attracting large audiences.

CONVENTIONAL FORM WITHOUT POLITICIZING EFFECT The majority of works fall into this category, from run-of-the-mill TV movies to blockbuster films. These works affirm our customary way of viewing the world, and film. They provoke viewers neither to reaffirm the rightness of the existing social order nor to activate disbelief in its values and ideals. They avoid the potentially politicizing messages of conservative films like *The Green Berets* or liberal ones like *Erin Brockovich*. They take few formal chances and provoke mild political controversy, at best. They put the individual hero at the center of things and rely heavily on condensation and displacement to shift any political or social overtones toward more exclusively personal issues. The stories take a familiar form: a central character attempts to resolve a problem within a plausible world governed, for the most part, by realist conventions.

Ben-Hur (William Wyler, 1959), for example, gives us Charlton Heston as the hero. He addresses the problem of his social status as a Jew under Roman rule and of his childhood friendship to Messala, who, as an adult, becomes a Roman ruler. He does so in a world where family values and social conflicts that would be familiar to 1950s Americans are common, and where the film's continuity editing and smooth linear development follow Hollywood's realist conventions to a T. Various interpretations of the film are possible, including symptomatic or politically motivated readings, but the film itself refrains from taking a political stand or striving for a politicizing effect. *Spartacus* (Stanley Kubrick, 1960), *Braveheart* (Mel Gibson, 1995), *The Gladiator* (Ridley Scott, 2000), and *The Patriot* (Roland Emmerich, 2000, U.S./Germany) also use a historical setting in which we find charismatic heroes solving the social issues of the day. These films often provide echoes of conservative or liberal sentiments but without any attempt to alter preexisting assumptions or provoke fresh ways of seeing things. Like films from *Gone with the Wind* (Victor Fleming, 1939) to *Gone in Sixty Seconds* (Dominic Sena, 2000), the emphasis is on the effortless telling of an engaging tale whose focus seldom strays from the plight of the central characters, not matter how symbolic or symptomatic their predicament may be.

Form, Content, and the Ever-Changing Social Context

This survey of film form and political effect runs the same risk as Brecht's advocacy of specific methods to achieve political effect. There is, in fact, no guarantee that a given work will have a specific effect or generate a given response. There is no guarantee it will continue to have the same effect over time or in different places with different audiences. These points have been stressed in earlier chapters and they remain valid here.

As an example of how meaning changes in different contexts, Eisenstein's montage theory, along with the body of work produced by constructivist artists and other Soviet filmmakers in the 1920s, originally served to support a political revolution; it sought to find radical forms to convey radically new ideas. In more recent times, what were once radical forms have found far less radical use in the striking montage work of many television advertisements and in the rapid-fire cutting techniques of MTV-style music videos. Music videos and television advertising generally have been particularly eclectic in borrowing stylistic influences from just about anywhere, regardless of their original intent.

The reception of *Triumph of the Will* (Leni Riefenstahl, Germany), in 1935 and ever since, demonstrates the variability of audience response to a given combination of form and content. Some critics continue to hail the film as a cinematic milestone, preferring to focus on its formal accomplishments such as the innovative and compelling use of editing. Others decry the film and its form as a repellant justification for the rise of Nazism. Agreement has never been unanimous because different critics and viewers give different emphasis to the balance between formal innovation and political advocacy (for the Nazi ideology that was then dominant in Germany).

In another case, some regard *The Battle of Algiers* as a suspenseful, politically progressive drama, but others take offense at the recourse to violent, terrorist acts, which it depicts without judgment. For example, the film follows three Algerian women who disguise themselves as French women to slip into the French quarter of Algiers to plant deadly explosives. Cutting back and forth between the women, the strategists who conceived the plan, the French soon to become victims, and a clock builds great dramatic intensity. Some viewers regard this as a measured demonstration of the lengths a population that lacks the means to wage a conventional war must resort to, whereas others consider the attacks as unconscionable acts of barbarism. The film's form remains immutable; it possesses the same selection and arrangement of shots regardless of the interpretation, but the interpretations vary considerably, depending on the emotional investment, intellectual engagement, and ideological involvement of the viewer.

In all fairness to Brecht, he never claimed that a radical form amounted to any one set of techniques or guaranteed any one result, even if some took this message away from his work. It all depends on execution, the audience, the particulars of form or style, and the specific context. A work bristling with radical form and radical impact might find itself severely limited due to clumsy execution or cliché set pieces. Conversely, conventional form in the hands of an inventive filmmaker might achieve unexpected results, as many progressive and conservative films that adopt conventional forms indicate.

It is on this point that Brecht's indebtedness to the rhetorical tradition as well as the poetic and narrative traditions reveals itself. A classic perspective for assessing rhetorical discourse is a contextual one—did it move the audience for which it was produced?—whereas aesthetic discourse often invites a decontextualized assessment of seemingly eternal qualities—does this work stand the test of time? Brecht understood that his plays, like an orator's speech, were aimed at specific audiences at a specific historical moment and that their effect would vary markedly according to who attended them and the predispositions with which they came.

Different times call for different measures. A once radical element of form can quickly become another convention, available for commercialization. Form, ideology, and politicizing effects enjoy a shifting, unstable relationship that is best understood when located in relation to a given historical moment and a particular audience, the task for which a dual formal-social analysis—asking what is disguised and what seen afresh— proves a particularly useful tool.

9

RACE AND ETHNICITY IN FILM

Hierarchy, Prejudice, and the Social Imaginary

Individuals see themselves not simply as individuals but also as members of different groups. A sense of belonging solidifies a sense of identity. Individuals want to identify with representations of the groups they belong to. As a result of this desire for collective as well as individual representation, the arts and the cinema in particular portray a rich array of nationalities, ethnicities, subcultures, and communities. These representations can be highly affirmative, offering images of a relation to the rest of the world that validates and solidifies group membership.

At the same time, the representations of groups can function divisively if they demean one group or subordinate it to another. In these cases, a more powerful group characterizes a subordinate group in discriminatory ways. Prejudice asserts privilege for some and subordination for others. It justifies and supports the existence of a power gradient or hegemonic order. Prejudice or bias denies individual difference in order to assert group homogeneity. Individuals are lumped together and judged according to the group they belong to. Individuality, a cornerstone of democracy, succumbs to generalizations that diminish and objectify individuals. The person is no longer judged as an individual but labeled with characteristics attributed to an entire group.

A term used to describe the how this type of collective bias creates a prejudicial worldview is the **social imaginary**. The **social imaginary** contains all the prejudicial images assigned to different groups within the social dynamics related to power and hierarchy. It is the arena within which members of one group picture members of another group in terms of stereotypes and clichés. The word "imaginary" is not used in the sense of fictitious or made up but in the sense that real but stereotypical images overwhelm individual distinctions. The social imaginary licenses both

- **Institutional racism,** or prejudice in which the social practices of an institution embody discriminatory patterns, and
- **Individual racism,** or prejudice in which individuals regard others as inferior to themselves.

Institutional racism involves forms of discrimination built into the legalized, everyday activities of institutions. Prior to the civil rights movement of the early 1960s, redlining, in which banks would not lend money to residents of areas with high percentages of minorities, was a common practice, as was the practice, institutionalized by state law in much of the American South, of requiring African Americans but not whites to pass literacy tests before they could register to vote. These practices discriminated against one group and denied them privileges readily available to members of another group. School segregation, prior to *Brown v. the Board of Education* in 1954, which declared the doctrine of "separate but equal" school systems for blacks and whites unconstitutional, is another example of institutional racism.

In **individual racism**, prejudiced individuals internalize an image of themselves as superior to a stereotypical image of members of another group. These images become habitual and lead to prejudicial and ideological behavior of which the individual may not be fully conscious. The more a person longs for a sense of fixed, permanent identity, impervious to the flux of time and the fluidity of encounter, immune to the rewards of empathy and the hazards of love, the more powerful the allure of the social imaginary becomes.

In John Cassavetes' brilliant and pioneering independent film *Shadows* (1959), he explores the unraveling of a budding romance between Lelia (Lelia Goldoni) and Tony (Anthony Ray), a man she meets at a party. Lovemaking isn't what she hopes it will be, but an even worse disillusionment lies ahead. Tony comes to pick up Lelia at her apartment. Lelia introduces Tony to her two brothers, and as she does, Tony's face silently reveals the shock coursing through his body: her brothers are black. Tony has always seen the very light-skinned Lelia at predominantly white gatherings and made the assumption that she, too, was white. Now he discovers that he is dating a woman of another race, and the shock runs across his face as if he had been slapped.

His reaction is obvious to her oldest brother, Hugh (Hugh Hurd), who escorts Tony out of the apartment, his own rage barely constrained. The word "racism" is never spoken, but its presence is deeply felt. Behavior—in this case, facial expression and body language—speak volumes, and are unmistakable in their meaning to Hugh and Lelia, the two siblings. They have seen it before. They know all too well what a certain look means, a certain bodily tenseness, a subtle edging away. Tony is less aware. He does not know how obvious his recoil is, since he tries to maintain a polite front verbally. Generously, in his own mind, he invites Hugh to join Lelia and him for dinner, another time, but the damage has long since been done. In this case it is in what is unspoken that prejudice makes itself most glaringly visible, as normal and habitual but highly ideological behavior.

Racism, anti-Semitism, sexism, homophobia, jingoism, classism, and even biases against certain lifestyles (of dress, mannerisms, values, and behavior) are other cases that lump individuals into categories and assign demeaning qualities. The subordinate group often bears the burden of a stigma: dark skin in contrast to presumably pure white skin in American society, for example; or allegedly Semitic features compared to a presumably "Aryan" standard; the vulnerable, weak female body in contrast to the hard, tough male body; "effeminate" versus "manly" traits for males; foreign accents and strange customs in contrast to the ("This is how we do things here") "normal" behavior of a dominant national group, and regional or working-class accents and behavior compared to a tacit middle-class standard for speech and conduct.

In any discussion of racism, it is important to begin with an acknowledgment that humans constitute a single species. The very idea of multiple "races" of humans based on physical differences is itself a discredited, nineteenth-century concept whose correlation with any other set of human characteristics, from athleticism to intelligence, has been strongly rejected by science. The cultural ideals of racial separation under apartheid rule in South Africa and of Aryan supremacy under Nazi rule in Germany represent extremely powerful values and beliefs precisely because defenders claimed their beliefs derived from nature, and, in the nineteenth and early twentieth century a great deal of pseudo-science proposed direct correlations between intelligence and so-called racial characteristics such as skull size, facial appearance, or skin color. It is now widely agreed that there is no such thing as a racial hierarchy. The word race remains in use, however, partly by force of habit, partly by those who still adhere to racist doctrines, and partly as a way to refer to the historical legacy of racism. A more apt word that does away with the implication of any genetic hierarchy among peoples is "ethnicity."

Institutional and individual prejudice function ideologically to internalize an image of one's relation to the world. They also function hegemonically to gain consent for discrimination based on group identity.

Prejudicial behavior may be treated as normal in terms of a dominant group's image of itself, but such behavior will be seen as discriminatory and hurtful from the perspective of a subordinate group. The dominant group or prejudicial institution always has reasons to justify its behavior. These reasons invariably depend on stereotypes for their power.

Institutional racism leads to experiences of privilege or bias, depending on one's group identity. A white male may take it for granted that he will not be pulled over for driving through an affluent neighborhood, whereas an African American or Mexican American may not. Individual racism leads to experiences of the power of hierarchy to affirm or hurt. A white male worker may say of a worker from another ethnic group, "He's a lazy _____; what do you expect?" If others agree, the speaker will gain a sense of belonging but a member of the other ethnic group who hears the comment will feel that a piece of his humanity has just been taken away.

Behavior—action, gesture, dress, tone of voice, gaze—serves as an indicator of someone's sense of identity, her values and beliefs. Behavior also functions to indicate prejudice, sometimes without an individual's awareness. To put a little more distance between yourself and another person at a party *after* learning that he is gay (or to move a little closer, for that matter) serves to signify, through physical action, how you conceive of your sexual identity and of how you sustain that identity at the expense of, or in alliance with, others. Such behavior in a film becomes a potent way for a filmmaker to develop characters and for the audience to see what it feels like to experience prejudice firsthand. Just such a reaction occurs in an extreme form, for example, in *Boys Don't Cry* (Kimberly Peirce, 1999). After a group of male friends discover that Brandon is female and not male, despite the fact that Brandon acts masculine and dates a female friend, they not only recoil but violently attack Brandon for the deception, as if her choice of gender role had put their own masculinity in jeopardy.

WHITE SKIN PRIVILEGE AND PREJUDICE

What characters say and do, behavior—ideological or normal, subversive, idiosyncratic, neurotic or psychotic—lies at the heart of visual media like film, television, and theater. Films represent behavior extremely effectively, highlighting and dramatizing it with different camera angles and distances, compositional choices, lighting, music, editing, and the other expressive techniques. Behavior is habitual. Sometimes this involves discriminating against others and other times it involves assuming rights or privileges for oneself. In terms of race in the United States and other predominantly white countries, the latter is sometimes referred to as **white skin privilege**. Elsewhere, other skin colors may be privileged.

Under the banner of an automatic white skin privilege, white people, for example, can enter almost any situation and know that they will not be expected to act as a representative of their race. If they handle themselves well, they will almost certainly not be called a credit to their race, and if they act badly, it will not be blamed on their racial background. They can assume that they will see other whites in leading roles in most of the media they watch. They can seek financial, legal, or medical assistance without fear that their race may prove an obstacle.

Films may reinforce prejudice if they, too, take prejudicial behavior for granted; or they can draw attention to how what seems natural or taken for granted rests on stereotypical assumptions. In *Willie Wonka and the Chocolate Factory* (Mel Stuart, 1971), despite the fact that the candy bar contest is open to kids around the world, the winners all turn out to be white. Each kid is a little strange, or obnoxious, perhaps, but white nevertheless, as if this result were entirely natural.

In *Guess Who's Coming to Dinner* (Stanley Kramer, 1967), by contrast, Matt Drayton (Spencer Tracy) and his wife Christina (Katherine Hepburn) assume that their daughter will find a suitable marriage partner. She does. He is a successful, highly respected doctor, polite, charming, poised, and well-dressed. He is the ideal of the tall, dark, and handsome suitor, except that he is also African American. To the parents this quality initially nullifies all the others. That Dr. John Prentice is played by Sydney Poitier doesn't change the fact that, for them, the doctor is no longer a suitable marriage partner. The film, a romantic comedy, treats the underlying theme of racism lightheartedly, poking fun at the crusty, old-fashioned ways of the parents. It also demonstrates how simple assumptions, such as ideas about the type of person someone will choose to marry, can contain unexamined ideological dimensions. The awkward conversations that constantly hint at the racial problem that Matt and Christina are too polite to name directly is a prime example of how ideology functions at the level of ingrained, habitual ways of seeing the world and one's relation to it.

WHITENESS AS THE UNIVERSAL ETHNICITY OF CLASSIC HOLLYWOOD FILM

Feature films that tackle institutional racism usually belong to the **social problem genre** of film that draws public attention to a serious public issue. A spate of films after World War II, including *Gentlemen's Agreement* (Elia Kazan, 1947), *Pinky* (Elia Kazan, 1949), and *Lost Boundaries* (Alfred L. Werker, 1949), drew attention to racism in American society. Historically, however, films have usually not regarded race as a divisive issue (the Production Code discouraged it), and if they presented minority characters they did so in stereotypical roles that went unquestioned. More recently, many Hollywood films have given supporting roles to minority group members, but their racial identity plays no part in the drama. A police supervisor, judge, waiter, or doctor may belong to an ethnic minority, but their behavior exemplifies their social role, not their racial identity. In this way many recent films accommodate social pressure to include minorities while still avoiding race as a primary issue.

Whether race or ethnicity contributes to the dramatic conflict or not, racism may be at work in another way: in the convention that white actors represent universal human values whereas ethnic minority actors, if their race comes into play, represent stereotypes. This convention has led to the celebration in the great films made by the Hollywood studio system, from *Scarface* (Howard Hawks, 1932) to *The Godfather* (Francis Ford Coppola, 1972), from *Sergeant York* (Howard Hawks, 1941) to *Saving Private Ryan* (Steven Spielberg, 1998), and from *Sunset Boulevard* (Billy Wilder, 1950) to *The Player* (Robert Altman, 1992), of a world in which white actors and actresses represent Everyman and Everywoman. Whiteness, specifically a non-denominational but generally Protestant version of whiteness, comes to represent a universal reference point against which other ethnicities are made to appear amusing, sinister, untrustworthy, or otherwise lacking.

The doctrine of America as a great melting pot buttressed this system of representation. A basic American identity came into being as those from other lands, with other customs, abandoned their old ways to adopt new ways in a new land. The idea of the melting pot applied primarily to European immigrants who were themselves white. It made less accommodation for the sizable populations of Chinese and Japanese Americans who had immigrated to the United States in the 1800s and early 1900s, and it excluded the long-term presence of African Americans, who remained heavily segregated from white culture until the 1960s. The melting pot ideology encouraged the ideal of whiteness as a universal norm. It did not treat whites as another ethnicity with their own strengths and limitations, including a presumptive privilege based on skin color.

STEREOTYPES AND THE BURDEN
OF REPRESENTATION

The assumption that individual white characters will be judged on their merits, and that their successes or failures will not be chalked up as a credit or embarrassment to their race, has led to an undue burden of representation on nonwhite actors. Their challenge is to find roles that allow a sense of individual complexity and dignity comparable to that of white characters, to emerge. Historically, this has proven extremely difficult. The great African American actor, writer, singer, and political activist Paul Robeson never found the roles or studio support that would allow his career to flourish. Other actors like Sidney Poitier turned down villain roles almost entirely in favor of dignified heroes such as Doctor Prentice in *Guess Who's Coming to Dinner* or Homer Smith, an ex-GI, who, after World War II, becomes savior to a group of nuns in the American West. He builds a church for them, treats them with respect, and abstains from all romantic involvement. Homer Smith is a virtual saint. (The film, *Lilies of the Field* [Ralph Nelson, 1963], received five major Oscar nominations, including Best Picture; Poitier won the Oscar for Best Actor.)

The history of popular cinema is, in part, a history of the evolution of stereotypical representations of different races and ethnicities, along with nationalities, gender orientations, and subcultures. In John Huston's classic tale of greed and betrayal from 1949, *The Treasure of the Sierra Madre* (1948), for example, the bandits who ominously turn up as the men prospect for a treasure in gold, evoke the image of scheming, deceptive, murderous Mexicans. This is the typical **Greaser** stereotype. It goes back to the early days of cinema when films like *Tony the Greaser* (William F. Haddock) in 1911 and *The Greaser's Revenge* in 1914 first portrayed Mexican characters as thieves, drunks, or killers. Over time a complimentary but still reductive stereotype arose of the Latin Lover, initially epitomized by Rudolph Valentino.

For African Americans, a range of stereotypes date back to the days of slavery and continue to crop up in television and film to this day. The **Mammy** and the **Coon** represent comic stereotypes of female and male blacks. The large, cantankerous Mammy speaks her mind but is basically ineffectual. She is like the Greek chorus of old, speaking truths, but with a comic manner that makes her more laughable than forbidding. The Coon condenses all of the assumptions of intellectual inferiority assigned to blacks. Fumbling, full of comic malapropisms and antic gestures, he is invariably the butt of the joke, if he is not, in fact, the joke itself. In 1905, *The Wooing and Wedding of a Coon*, about the antics of a Coon character on his honeymoon, made clear that the stereotype already had a firm purchase in popular culture. Spike Lee's trenchant examination of this stereotype, *Bamboozled* (2000), demonstrates that, despite its offensive nature, it can continue to be enjoyed by many viewers. In this case, these are viewers of a television show that a black TV writer concocts thinking that neither the network nor the public could possible tolerate such a spectacle. Director Lee proves him wrong, leaving the film's viewer to ask himself if he, too, enjoys the blackface TV show as harmless entertainment or takes it as an offensive affront.

Closely related to the Coon but without the buffoon-like element is the **Uncle Tom**. Harriet Beecher Stowe's 1852 novel *Uncle Tom's Cabin*, about a good-hearted slave who suffers his master's tyranny in heroic silence, gave rise to this term. (Ironically, Stowe's novel was strongly anti-slavery, and Uncle Tom's suffering was meant as an indictment of an inhumane system. Over time, the character's subservience overshadowed the author's critical perspective.) The Tom stereotype is benign, innocent, trusting, compliant, obedient and faithful. Nothing can rouse him to regard his master in a bad light; he remains loyal to the end even when subjected to physical threat or violence. He is the Good Negro who never presents a threat of any kind, an idealized projection of the type of person the bigot wishes to see: someone who will tolerate discrimination without complaint. In the 1911 short, *For Massa's Sake* (Joseph A. Golden), for example, a freed ex-slave willingly returns to his former life when his old master's plantation is in danger of failure. The Camerons' house servants in *The Birth of a Nation* (D. W. Griffith, 1915) also fulfill the stereotypes of the Mammy and Uncle Tom.

The **Tragic Mulatto** stereotype has historically functioned as a dramatic warning of the perils of miscegenation. The Mulatto is the light-skinned black who often tries to pass for white. Doom awaits. Once the secret of mixed blood gets out, no matter how white the character may not only look but behave, the Tragic Mulatto plummets from the white world back into the African American culture he or she sought to escape. Douglas Sirk's 1959 remake of the 1934 film *Imitation of Life* explores the fate of such a character, a light-skinned daughter of an African American maid who tries to pass as white, only to break her mother's heart and suffer a vicious physical attack from her white boyfriend when he discovers the truth of her racial identity. It is a richly melodramatic exploration of the racial issues that are handled in a more low-key style in *Shadows*, made in the same year.

Finally, the **Buck** represents a black variation on the Greaser. Sometimes brutal, often ruthless, and almost always oversexed, the Buck stereotype represents a hyper-masculine image of the African American as a powerful, magnetic physical force. Whereas the Coon forfeits intelligence for buffoonery, the Buck subordinates intelligence to physical and, often, sexual prowess. At worst, the Buck is a lustful, rapacious figure such as Gus (Walter Long, a white actor playing an African American role), who stalks Flora Cameron (Mae Marsh) in *The Birth of a Nation*. In other cases, the Buck can be an avenging force for good, a turn of the stereotype toward a somewhat more positive figure that was common in blaxploitation films of the 1970s such as *Shaft* (Gordon Parks, 1971).

Almost every minority suffers from stereotyping. Chinese American characters, for example, may be typed as mysterious, clannish, unwilling to assimilate, passive, and extremely tight-lipped. In the 1920s and '30s, they were also frequently associated with opium dens and crime. Ang Lee's *The Wedding Banquet* (1993, Taiwan/U.S.) and Wayne Wang's *The Joy Luck Club* (1993) dismantle some of these stereotypes and explore the dense layers of complexity that lie beneath first impressions.

In an earlier historical moment, the Rogers and Hammerstein musical *South Pacific*, first a Broadway play, then a 1958 film (Joshua Logan), examined the prejudices regarding interracial love: the white nurse in love with a widowed French plantation owner is disturbed to discover that the half-Polynesian children in his house are his; and a young white sailor and a Polynesian woman fall in love—all at a time when miscegenation was anathema to many whites and illegal in many states. The film stresses the pain and agony of having to forfeit a socially taboo love, sometimes lightheartedly ("I'm gonna' wash that man right outta my hair . . .") and sometimes poignantly as the ill-fated lovers realize that social pressure and the white characters' ingrained prejudices make union impossible. The exploration of how characters find themselves balking and struggling with mixed emotions can seem surprisingly frank for a film from the 1950s; in its Broadway revival in 2008 after some fifty years, its treatment again provoked considerable discussion.

Creating Boundaries between Groups and the Rise of Otherness

BOUNDARIES AND TABOOS

The **Other**, with a capital O, is often used to signify an abstract other that is the product of hegemonic processes. It is what becomes of others when they are subordinated, demeaned, and reduced to a stereotype.

A hierarchy comes into existence. One group dominates by making another group subordinate. The idea that "Colonial people need our (the colonizing power's) guiding hand in order to earn a place in the league of civilized, industrial nations," for example, assumes that the "white man's burden" is to bring education as well as discipline, culture as well as order, to an Other who presumably lacks such qualities. The same idea justifies colonial exploitation of an Other who does not know how to take advantage of precious metals and natural resources that the colonizing power knows full well how to use to maximum advantage.

Establishing a division between a dominant group and its Other, or Others, requires boundaries and **taboos**. (**Taboos** are prohibitions that carry a strong emotional charge. Violating them may jeopardize one's social status. Incest is often cited as the most fundamental social taboo, since the taboo guarantees that individuals will seek sexual partners outside the family unit and thereby create a network of kinship relations that can broaden into an entire social order.) The border zone between one group and its Others is where taboos operate to ensure that the two groups remain separate and unequal. Taboos and the boundaries they create reinforce the sense that individuals of the dominant group have a solid, impermeable identity: it is bound and delimited by the ability to contrast Us with Them, those beyond the boundary line. Boundaries, sometimes invisible, as in the psychic barrier that prohibits incest, and sometimes entirely visible, as in the strictly segregated school systems that sent African American children to one set of schools and whites to another until 1954, maintain hierarchy and order. Some sense of boundaries is necessary and inevitable, but some boundaries come at the expense of Others; these latter boundaries inevitably distribute power and maintain hierarchies that favor one class, gender, or ethnicity over another.

The psychic and sometimes physically real border zones that function to maintain a separation between one group and its Others often provide the emotionally charged setting for narratives that address the issues of ideology and the social imaginary. John Sayles's complex and engaging film *Lone Star* (1996), for example, explores issues of family, ethnic, and national identity that are made all the more acute by the film's setting on the Texas-Mexico border. Most of the characters do not belong to singular categories purely and simply. Mixture and hybridity create a far more complex social reality that the central characters struggle to comprehend and accept.

Lone Star reaches its emotional peak as the hero, Sheriff Sam Deeds (Chris Cooper), comes to realize that his racist, violent father was profoundly implicated in a series of events that now deeply affect his attraction for Pilar Cruz (Elizabeth Peña), his childhood sweetheart and a Mexican American. They were driven apart by racial prejudice and now, years later, they gradually learn that Pilar is herself the result of an interracial intimacy that moves their own relationship into the territory of the taboo.

Sayles does a brilliant job of examining the price stereotypes exact from everyone involved and of exploring the hypocrisy, or contradictions, that allow individuals such as Sam's father to uphold stereotypes on the one hand and to pursue sexual attractions their own prejudice would seem to forbid them on the other. He multiplies the central story with other subplots that serve to compound and complicate the issues even further. The simple either/or dichotomy that make clean and simple divisions between a dominant group and subordinate Others fractures as characters gain a heightened awareness of their interdependencies and mutual needs.

IDENTITY, PROJECTION, AND THE OTHER

One basic dynamic that governs hegemonic relations in the social imaginary involves **binary oppositions** (either/or categories such as us/them, black/white, good/evil, and so on) that are, in turn, based on fixed images of others. Although prejudice would make it seem that the

Other would always be regarded negatively, this is not entirely correct. The Other often provokes an ambivalent response of attraction and repulsion. The Other not only possesses an external reality of its own but also becomes a source of internal anxiety for the bigot: an individual's sense of identity may revolve around his relation to an Other that can confirm or deny his identity. Without others to provide acknowledgment of a hierarchy, as stereotypes like the Coon, Uncle Tom, and Mammy have done, identity may lose its solidity.

Prejudice is an ideologically loaded remedy for the instability and insecurity that is part and parcel of identity. If the Other can be fixed into a constant image governed by a stereotype, then the self or a group can be similarly fixed as permanently "not like that." "That's how they are," takes on a refrain: "And I'm not like that." Members of a dominant group can project onto the stereotyped Other a negative image of themselves, the self they do not wish to be or to accept. A negative self-image is projected outward onto the Other so that its actual presence within a member of the dominant group can then be denied ("They're like that; I'm not"). Institutional racism reinforces this process by granting it legal embodiment, as in the anti-Semitic laws passed in Nazi Germany, the apartheid laws that segregated whites from blacks in South Africa before the democratic elections of 1994, and the laws against miscegenation in the United States that have since been revoked.

Some films explore what it feels like to occupy the position of a person discriminated against because of his group identity. For example, Phil Green (Gregory Peck), a journalist, experiences both institutional and individual prejudice when he agrees to pretend to be Jewish to see if anti-Semitism really exists in Elia Kazan's 1947 film *Gentleman's Agreement*. In one phase of his experiment, his attempt to check into a hotel fails not because of a personal dislike of Jews on the part of the hotel clerk but because the clerk must adhere to the hotel's unspoken policy and deny accommodations to any and all Jews, even when they look just like Gregory Peck! As soon as Peck indicates, in a casual remark, that he is Jewish, his fate is sealed by the invisible hand of a "gentleman's agreement"—a tacit form of institutional racism—that still functioned, in the 1940s, to maintain a social barrier between gentiles and Jews in public establishments, private clubs, and residential neighborhoods.

In the case of his fiancée, the issue is not institutional but individual prejudice. Kathy Lacy (Dorothy McGuire), who is white, Anglo-Saxon, and Protestant, encourages Phil Green to become Phil Greenberg so that he can write an exposé about anti-Semitism, but she begins to worry when Phil wants to remain in character when he visits her well-to-do family in Connecticut. Kathy doesn't want to embarrass herself by bringing home a Jew, someone her parents might consider an inappropriate suitor. She doesn't reject Phil violently the way the white boyfriend of Sarah Jane does in *Imitation of Life* when he discovers she is black passing for white. Kathy's bias takes the more muted form of not very subtle hints that Phil would make things much easier if he would just be himself rather than play his Jewish character in her parents' home. Her clear discomfort, conveyed by body language and tone of voice rather than by espousing any explicit doctrine, makes it painfully clear that he has proven his point in more ways than Kathy realizes.

Gentleman's Agreement, although somewhat didactic and mechanical in execution, gives a vivid sense of what prejudice feels like as experienced by its victim. It is a prototypical social problem film. The audience readily identifies with Gregory Peck, a star whose whiteness usually functioned within the terms of studios' star system to represent universal human qualities. By adopting a Jewish identity, Peck brings the audience along with him so that it can see what it feels to be the object of hurtful, demeaning experiences. Given the degree of institutional bigotry still at work in the 1940s, the same audience might not have identified quite so readily with discriminatory practices against a Jewish character played by a Jewish actor like John

Garfield. Much of the audience might consider it natural for discrimination to occur in such a case. By using Gregory Peck as the victim, the film made it possible for an audience still heavily accustomed to racial and ethnic prejudice to experience discrimination from the point of view of the victim.

In Ousmane Sembene's *Black Girl* (*La noire de . . .* , 1966, France/ Senegal), Diouana (Mbissine Thérèse Diop), an African woman, agrees to go back to France with the couple whose child she tends. Her identity now depends almost exclusively on her recognition by the French couple for whom she works. They, however, cannot see her as a fully human person like themselves. The couple thinks they are doing her a favor. They assume that life in France is far superior to life in Senegal.

Having hired her as a governess, the couple assumes Diouana should also be their maid and servant. Small acts of insensitivity accumulate, such as insisting that she wear a maid's apron and remove her high heel shoes when she cleans, even though it lowers her self-esteem. At another point, the couple discusses her culture's traits in her presence at a luncheon with friends as if she were not there or could not contribute anything to the discussion herself. These hurtful acts grow into a pattern of systematic abuse that ends tragically.

Throughout *Black Girl*, Sembene puts the audience in the position of Diouana. We see events from her point of view and experience the affronts to her dignity and self-respect directly. In a reversal of the usual pattern of stereotyping, it is the French couple who hire her that appear to lose individuality as they begin to stand for general characteristics of a colonial attitude. Sembene makes it clear that Diouana must maintain a **double consciousness** when she deals with her white employers. **Double consciousness** was African American scholar W. E. B. Du Bois's term for the acute awareness a victim of discrimination must have of the intentions and dispositions of those who wield social power over her. The victim must be highly vigilant: misjudging the meaning or intention of someone who has the power to cause harm, emotionally or physically, can have dire, even deadly consequences.

Recognition, so vital to a healthy sense of identity, can be offered or withheld, seemingly on a whim. As Du Bois put it in his famous book, *The Souls of Black Folk*, "It is a peculiar sensation, this double-consciousness, this sense of always looking at one's self through the eyes of others, of measuring one's soul by the tape of a world that looks on in amused contempt and pity" (p. 3). In a similar spirit, another great writer on the experience of racism, Franz Fanon, wrote in *Black Skin, White Mask* about going to a movie theater, "And already I am being dissected under white eyes, the only real eyes. I am *fixed*. . . . I am laid bare. I feel, I see in those white faces that it is not a new man who has come in, but a new kind of man, a new genus. Why, it's a Negro!" *Black Girl* emotionally involves and intellectually engages the audience in understanding what it feels like for an African woman to see herself through the eyes of a white couple. It is one of Sembene's most powerful films.

Stereotypic images of the Other often represent a projection of anxieties about an individual's sexual as well as ethnic identity. A particularly vivid example occurred in the case of the murder of Vincent Chin, a Chinese American beaten to death in 1982 by an unemployed Detroit auto worker, Ronald Ebens, who mistook Chin for Japanese and blamed him for taking his job away. (Many American automobile factories were closing down at the time partly due to strong economic competition from the Japanese auto industry.) Mr. Ebens also regarded Chin as a sexual rival when they encountered each other in a bar and took opposing views of a strip dancer. An argument that began around a woman's sexual appeal turned to resentments about foreign workers before it escalated into deadly violence. Mr. Ebens's identity as a worker was so tied up with his identity as a male that a threat to one was a threat to the other, as the tragic death of Mr. Chin was to demonstrate. The documentary *Who Killed Vincent Chin?*

(Christine Choy and Renee Tajima-Peña, 1988) explores these dynamics in great detail. (The film received an Oscar nomination for Best Documentary in 1989.)

In Arthur Dong's powerful documentary *Licensed to Kill* (1997), Dong, a gay Chinese American man, bravely sets out to interview men convicted of murdering gay men. Every one of the men he interviews admits that he was drawn toward the very people he professed to hate, as if his own identity depended on proving he was not like them by being near them. One example is particularly extraordinary: a black, formerly closeted gay man with AIDS, Jay Johnson, internalizes both the longing for and loathing of other men in an exceptionally acute way. He prowls a park where gay men cruise for partners and, on two different occasions, kills men he encounters there. Afterwards he openly admits his own sexual orientation and the conflicting feelings of desire and loathing that he feels. He realizes that these killings stand in stark contradiction with his own homosexuality. Johnson's murders land him in jail, where Dong's remarkably calm interview style allows Johnson to reveal the almost unfathomable mixture of hatred, self-hatred, and ambivalence that make his sense of personal identity profoundly troubled. When he confides, "Mentally, I'm just a lot healthier now, because everybody knows," it remains completely unclear whether he fully understands just how lethal this mixture of attraction and repulsion was to his victims.

Liberalism, Tolerance, and the Family of Man

Many people assume that prejudice is a sign of a conservative or reactionary political perspective, since it tends to reinforce the status quo, but some types of prejudice are more often linked to liberalism than conservatism. The liberal is willing to acknowledge the otherness of others, to accept them as different in degree, with customs and practices of their own. Tolerance prevails. But the liberal's acceptance typically reduces to what a famous 1950s exhibit of photography called "The Family of Man." Underneath the surface differences of clothing and custom, a human essence prevails. Wherever we are born, whatever our color, whatever language we speak or role we play, we find ourselves united by common concerns and mutual needs: work and play, love and marriage, birth and death.

At heart this liberal perspective accepts Otherness but only on the liberal's own terms. The dominant group reserves the right to accept or tolerate others for who they are but also to set a boundary when others become too assertive, too argumentative, or too insistent on differences that make a difference. This liberal approach to others, as Roland Barthes recognized in a trenchant critique of the photographic exhibit "The Family of Man," overlooks the hierarchy tolerance often assumes. It also ignores the social and historical specificities that make different ethnicities and cultures truly distinct. In his short essay collection *Mythologies*, Barthes wrote,

> That work is an age-old fact does not in the least prevent it from remaining a perfectly historical fact. Firstly, and evidently, because of its modes, its motivations, its ends and its benefits, which matter to such an extent that it will never be fair to confuse in a pure gestural identity the colonial and the Western worker. . . . Secondly, because of the very differences in its inevitability: we know very well that work is "natural" just as long as it is "profitable," and that in modifying the inevitability of the profit, we shall perhaps one day modify the inevitability of labor.

Locating the formation of group identities in specific forms of historical experience as Roland Barthes suggests we should—whether the slave trade, the Chinese diaspora, the Holocaust, or the oppression of women—threatens the liberal-democratic desire to pretend that differences of race, class, sex, nationality, and so on do not make a real difference to people's fundamental identity. A liberal view is often a sentimental view. It prefers to wish away real tensions and conflicts and paint a rosy picture of conflict-free harmony.

In *Mississippi Burning* (Alan Parker, 1988) two FBI agents, Rupert Anderson (Gene Hackman) and Alan Ward (Willem Dafoe), come to a Southern town to determine who murdered three civil rights activists, flush out the racists, and guarantee equal opportunity and civil rights for all. Not only does this reverse the historical record, which indicates that the FBI spent more effort spying on and subverting the work of civil rights groups and their leaders, from Martin Luther King to Malcolm X, than investigating the conduct of the Ku Klux Klan and other racist organizations; it also minimizes the efforts of the local African American population to change their own situation. The townspeople depend on the two agents to solve the murders and arrest the killers. In a formal context *Mississippi Burning* is a powerful drama, but in a social context it is problematic history. It condenses and restricts human agency to two FBI agents, displaces systematic, institutional discrimination onto the bad apples responsible for one murder, and paints a picture of African American impotence in the face of injustice. Because its liberal perspective celebrates a moral and judicial victory, however, the film can leave its audience feeling that good has triumphed over evil, even if it entails historical misrepresentation.

Two Models of Social Conflict

BINARY OPPOSITIONS

Many films address issues that arise around the basic social practices that surround the management of labor, power, sexual desire, aggression, and the use of knowledge. Conflicts between the overall good of the society or the state and the needs and desires of individuals arise in areas like economics, governance, kinship, discipline, and know-how. It is here in the heart of actual social practices, concrete behavior, and specific situations that hegemonic struggles take place. Different cultural ideals of worker control versus corporate control, social integration in one big melting pot versus subcultural autonomy, protecting hierarchy from erosion versus distributing power equitably, heterosexual monogamy versus alternative forms of relationship, self-promotion versus self-sacrifice, reward for individual success versus insistence on equal opportunity for all, the use of know-how to serve the common good or to get ahead, are fought out in the nitty-gritty particulars of how existing social institutions and practices operate. As this list suggests, the conflicts often appear to boil down to a binary opposition between two distinct positions: good/evil, black/white, right/wrong. Such oppositions have considerable value when polarization and clarity are needed, but they can also obscure much of the complexity of difficult issues.

The "social problem" films *Gentleman's Agreement, Pinky, The China Syndrome* (James Bridges, 1979), *The Insider* (Michael Mann, 1999), and *The Constant Gardener* (Fernando Meirelles, 2005, UK/Germany) build up a single, primary polarity to stress how important it is to address anti-Semitism, racism, nuclear safety, the health risks of tobacco, or the unscrupulous ethics of the pharmaceutical industry, respectively. In many films, particularly genre films, the conflict jells into a binary opposition, represented most persistently, thanks to the work of condensation, by a hero and a villain. A western, for example, is likely to focus on a single social conflict. Any one western might have as its specific conflict:

1) The homesteader versus the cattle baron (*Shane* [George Stevens, 1953])
2) The honest prospector versus the greedy merchant (*The Far Country* [Anthony Mann, 1954])
3) The "show girl" versus the "respectable" woman from back east (*Stagecoach* [John Ford, 1939])

4) The younger son or cowhand versus the grizzled boss or patriarch (*Red River* [Howard Hawks, 1948])

5) The sheriff versus the outlaw (*High Noon* [Fred Zinnemann, 1952])

6) The Army versus the Indians (*Fort Apache* [John Ford, 1948])

7) The scout versus the Army commander (*Ulzana's Raid* [Robert Aldrich, 1972])

8) The vengeful westerner who tracks down a pathological enemy (*The Searchers* [John Ford, 1956])

9) The Indian woman married to a white man versus prejudiced whites (*Broken Arrow* [Delmer Daves, 1950])

10) The belligerent Indian tribe versus a peaceful Indian tribe (*Dances with Wolves* [Kevin Costner, 1990])

This type of conflict structure suggests that society divides into opposing camps over one particular issue. As examples cited earlier in the chapter suggest, this issue may involve group identity and institutional or individual prejudice. Films based on binary conflicts try to find an imaginative resolution to this particular conflict. Chapter 7 examined in further detail how such films operate. The model of binary conflict is less common in non-genre films such as independent American films, European art cinema, films from developing nations, or documentaries. In these cases, we often encounter a different model of social conflict.

THE WEB OF SOCIAL CONFLICT

In this model, a vast number of conflicts of different magnitudes and origins characterize society. The idea of a complex array of conflicts and alliances that are not reducible to a single either/or polarity has great resonance in a society where there are numerous forms of social division based on categories that can be used to discriminate among individuals according to group membership or affinity. A multicultural society is often rife with such conflicts. A vivid tension exists in many modern nation-states between national unity and ethnic or other divisions. Among the most prominent divisions are class or economic status, race, ethnicity, language, nationality of origin, family, education, lifestyle or value system, religion, and gender. Groups that represent one or more of these divisions experience inclusion and exclusion, identity and prejudice, affirmation and discrimination, individuality and stereotyping, depending on the context.

Each category provides for relations of hierarchy (owner/worker, parent/child, male/female) and for relations of equality (worker/worker, cousin/cousin, woman/woman) so that bonds of affiliation coexist with potentially conflictual relations within as well as between groupings. In this model, association and dissociation, cooperation and competition, equality and hierarchy, inclusion and exclusion align individuals with and against others in a fluid and variable way. A child may attack his mother at one point and defend her against outsiders at another; a union member may support a decision made by his company on one occasion but reject another decision fiercely; an immigrant may compete against other immigrants at one point and join forces with them at another. This web of conflict and affiliation runs through all the groups and social practices in a society. They add up to an overall social structure that is dynamic, provisional, and at least potentially explosive. Hegemony must struggle to maintain the status quo.

This idea of a web of social conflict comes from the German sociologist Georg Simmel. Simmel was born in 1858, in Berlin, and became one of the leading sociologists of his day. Simmel saw social conflict as a productive engine that drives society forward rather than as the unfortunate result of exploitation and power, as Karl Marx did. Simmel did not intend to condone injustice but, instead, to stress that any belief in the fundamentally harmonious nature of social organization, even in a future, utopian form, may be little more than wishful thinking or a myth. If this is the case eliminating conflict entirely is less the goal than confronting and minimizing injurious conflicts such as those based on prejudice whenever possible.

Simmel's model is a particularly suggestive one for those categories where prejudice is often deeply entrenched as part of an ideological image of a group's place within the social dynamics of power and hierarchy, such as race, class, and gender. In these categories people relate to each other in relations of dominance and dependence, equality and hierarchy, association and separation, inclusion and exclusion. Hegemony, then, maintains a provisional balance of power among these competing social groups. Ideology functions to make this balance appear natural and encourages individuals to internalize their relation to the world in accord with the provisional balance ("This is how we do things here and this is where you fit in"). The balance will, however, place some groups in one-down positions and others in one-up positions. From this disparity, prejudice is apt to flower as those one-up begin to stereotype or stigmatize those one-down to reinforce the sense of a taboo or boundary separating Them from Us.

Individuals may change status or social position, and social groups may redefine themselves relative to other groups, forming new alliances and breaking old ones, confronting stereotypes and overthrowing them, but, for Simmel, these dynamics become a permanent characteristic of modern society rather than a process that will eventually eliminate hierarchy and prejudice. Movement toward affiliation in one direction is matched by heightened resistance from another direction. A son drawn to a gay community may be pulled back toward a straight one by family, (old) friends, or personal experience with stereotyping. An immigrant who seeks to assimilate and adopt behavior deemed normal by the dominant group may be pulled back by other immigrants who hold to the old ways.

Racism and the Social Imaginary in
Do the Right Thing

AMBIVALENCE, RESENTMENT, AND
LIFE ON THE STREET

The clash between the dream of equality and a politics of resentment provides the motor force behind Spike Lee's *Do the Right Thing*, released in 1989. This is not posed as a binary opposition, however, but as a complex web of conflict involving all the principal characters found on a single urban street. Sal (Danny Aiello), the proud owner of a pizzeria in a predominantly black Brooklyn neighborhood, acts like a benevolent plantation owner looking after his children, which include his actual sons, the angry, openly racist Pino (John Turturro) and the generally passive Vito (Richard Edson), as well as the African American "children" who come to Sal's for a slice of pizza. Near the end of the business day, Sal proclaims his vision of peace and harmony:

> We did good business today. We got a good thing going. Nothing like a family in business working together. One day the both of you [Pino and Vito] will take over ... and Mookie [Spike Lee's character], there will always be a place for you at Sal's Famous Pizzeria. Y'know, it should be Sal's and Son's Famous Pizzeria.

For Sal the pizzeria is a "place of business," an image that receives the reverence normally accorded a "place of worship." Sal, in fact, hangs what amounts to a family album of photographs signed by famous Italian Americans (Joe DiMaggio, Frank Sinatra, Al Pacino, Luciano Pavarotti, etc.) on the restaurant's "Wall of Fame."

It is just after Sal defends the family business to the disgruntled Pino, who feels degraded by the daily journey to a different, (for him) inferior 'hood and the ribbing his friends give him for spending his time "feeding the Moulies," that the hotheaded Buggin' Out (Giancarlo Esposito) mounts his campaign for a boycott. He wants to force Sal to add African American photos to his Wall of Fame. Such a demand runs directly counter to Sal's liberal sense of tolerance—he is happy to accept the fact of racial difference but only on his own terms—coupled with patriarchal authority. He sees himself as the provider of a valuable service, and no one can tell him how to run his business, or, what amounts to the same thing, family. African Americans are customers to Sal, not icons and heroes.

Sal and his sons become caught up in a love/hate dialectic that two black characters, Radio Raheem (Bill Nunn) and Stevie (Luis Ramos), articulate: Radio Raheem does so with his knuckles labeled "LOVE" and "HATE," a clear homage to Robert Mitchum's tattooed knuckles with the same words in *The Night of the Hunter* (Charles Laughton, 1955), and Stevie, with his photographs (nominees for the Wall of Fame) of the pacifistic Dr. Martin Luther King and the confrontational Malcolm X. Although these characters appear to set up binary oppositions between love and hate and between militancy and civil disobedience, Lee does not organize the film to match these terms. Characters find their loyalties pulled in more complex, conflicting directions. Pino, for example, squirms to explain to Mookie his attraction to black athletes and performers: "It's different. Magic [Johnson], Eddie [Murphy], [The Artist formerly known as] Prince are not niggers, I mean, are not Black. I mean, they're Black but not really Black. They're more than Black. It's different."

To this frank confession of ambivalence, Mookie replies, "Pino, I think secretly that you wish you were Black. That's what I think." In the social problem film *Gentleman's Agreement*, Gregory Peck can expose prejudice by revealing—to the audience from the very start and to different characters at the right dramatic moment—that he isn't Jewish after all. Their anti-Semitism toward him is therefore utterly unfounded. Spike Lee offers no such convenient out. The black characters are not really white actors done up in blackface, and Pino's bigotry is fully his, even if he cannot own up to it. Antagonisms, conflicts, and biases are real, with deep psychological roots accompanied by ambivalent feelings of envy, attraction, and barely suppressed desire.

VISUAL STYLE AND THE WEB OF SOCIAL CONFLICT

Do the Right Thing examines the issue of race in America with a style that marks a sharp departure from the genre of the social problem film. The social problem film revolves around a binary conflict and a hero. The seriousness of the issue and the determination of the hero prove a formidable match, but the hero prevails and the problem finds a solution, as we see when Erin Brockovich (Julia Roberts) holds a major public utility accountable for the damage it caused by releasing toxic chemicals into the environment in *Erin Brockovich* (Steven Soderbergh, 2000). Most social problem films combine conventional form with a politicizing effect, and sometimes they do so quite successfully.

Do the Right Thing does something different. Lee adopts a radical form with a politicizing effect. His style is more akin to Bertolt Brecht's ideas for an epic theater than to social problem films or to documentary realism. (See Table 8.1 for a summary of Brecht's views on epic theater in comparison with traditional theater.) The color scheme, for example, is chosen to accentuate the heated passions of the various characters. It is bright and defiant with abundant hot reds—from brick walls to shirts—that mirror the summer heat and the racial tensions. The theme song under the opening credits and stylized, energetic images of Mookie's girlfriend Tina (Rosie Perez) shadowboxing in the street is Public Enemy's "Fight the Power," with its angry refrain of "Fight the power that be." Graceful tracking shots capture the weave of several dozen characters as they move to and fro on the film's block-long set. Unlike the tracking shots in *Slacker* (Richard Linklater, 1991), Lee's tracking shots follow characters as they leave and enter the space claimed by other characters, heightening or alleviating tensions as they do so. Static, carefully composed shots of specific characters and groups who look off-screen at other characters and actions also convey dynamic tension: the characters may occupy a fixed position, but it is always relative to the larger web of conflict that surrounds them.

At the heart of Lee's effort to convey what it feels like to live within a racially divided society is his effort to give visual embodiment to a web of conflict that puts every character into complex, often ambivalent relationships with other characters. Lee avoids the tendency to rely on stereotypes to represent good intentions and bad attitudes among characters. Each character displays a mixed set of emotions and needs that makes it impossible to view the film as a simple conflict between whites and blacks, Koreans and African Americans, young and old, male and female, and so on. Each of these zones of potential conflict flares up at different times, but no one conflict polarizes the characters into a clear-cut binary opposition like the oppositions that structure most genre films, until the film's climax, and that is clearly coded as a catastrophe from which everyone must recover.

A vivid example of how Lee gives visible form to invisible hierarchies and patterns of dominance, as well as to how these patterns are constantly renegotiated, is the way in which Sal's request that Pino sweep the sidewalk at the start of their workday gets passed along by Pino to Vito, word for word. The mimicry and Pino's shirking of responsibility immediately signal his ambivalent relationship to his father, whom he does not want to cross but also does not want to blindly obey. Vito, in turn, complains. Vito is the put-upon younger brother who finds it difficult to stand up to those who give him orders but is even more reluctant to express his true feelings. At this point, Da Mayor (Ossie Davis) enters, asking if there's any work to do.

Da Mayor is the last resort, the bottom rung on the chain of command, and the only one who will be paid for doing the sweeping, which keeps him in liquor for the morning. Sal gives him a dollar, a gesture of largesse that is typical of his paternal attitude, but one that annoys Pino, who thinks of it as money wasted even though he refuses to do the menial work himself. These interactions, revolving around a minor task, are a brilliant example of how Lee visualizes a web of conflict that is unstable and liable to explode at any moment.

The fragmentation of the film into a rich array of scenes following well over a dozen significant characters not only functions to limit the audience's identification with a singular hero, of which there is, in fact, none, but to draw attention to the interdependencies of individuals who must constantly establish and maintain their position. The most dramatic example of this Brechtian principle of fragmentation is the series of racial diatribes launched by five of the film's characters as they stare directly into the camera (and at the audience). The venomous string of invectives is shockingly blunt, but yet it is not embedded in the dialogue between characters as it is in, say, Quentin Tarantino's *Jackie Brown* (1997), where the "n" word is hurled about with extraordinary frequency and naturalized as something acceptable in the context as just the way some people talk. Here, language retains its capacity to shock and offend. Like Tina at the start of the film, the characters stare out at the audience with defiance and anger. Spike Lee has noted that audiences often find the diatribes humorous and laugh, perhaps a bit nervously, unless they happen to be members of the group attacked.

Lee's presentation of these outbursts of racist hatred to the audience breaks the illusion of the narrative's independent status as a world apart. The audience no longer has to interpret the behavior of characters inside a fictional world, but to assess the effect of words within a social context (the larger context of racism in America today). Lee boldly refuses to displace racism into self-deceptive forms of liberal tolerance such as Sal's paternalism, which amounts to a variation on white skin privilege, as if it were all a matter of individual psychology, or to limit it to specific characters who then can be labeled "bad apples." The invective hurled at the viewer in these diatribes becomes a Brechtian demonstration of the hateful, stereotyping thoughts that exceed the story world. Lee sets out to have the audience experience the shock of hearing these slurs addressed at them directly so that they may recognize them as elements in a pervasive reservoir of hatred from which individuals draw.

Many of the usual forms of condensation and displacement found in fiction films are also set aside in Lee's film. No hero emerges as the lightning rod for larger social conflicts, and no displacement of racial issues into questions of moral conscience or personal authority obscures the underlying conflicts. Lee adopts a combative, confrontational style that is similar to the street talk and social manner of many of the characters. They live side by side but they also fight, sometimes fiercely, for what they need to maintain their dignity. The web of conflict leaves room for levity and humor, but it also puts characters on guard and sets situations on edge. Characters contest hegemony—the effort to maintain a hierarchical status quo—over and over, in every interaction. From these interactions the final, catastrophic conflict erupts. But Lee also makes clear that it is only from frank interracial and cross-cultural interactions that meaningful social transformation can take place.

Do the Right Thing brings great energy to the conflicts and contradictions surrounding racial and ethnic identity. It constructs a rich tapestry of characters and their complex positions within a web of social conflicts that include, in addition to Sal and his sons: the ambivalent position of the Korean fruit and vegetable stand family owners; the precariousness of the single white homeowner; the solitary but unifying black radio DJ, Mr. Señor Love Daddy; Mookie's independent, level-headed sister and his straight-talking Puerto Rican girlfriend, Tina; and the young and restless teenagers, the slightly older and more assertive Buggin' Out and Radio Raheem, and the considerably older generation of street corner philosophers, dreamers. and alcoholics. *Do the Right Thing* explores what it feels like to experience, with visceral force, a complex web of tensions and contradictions from multiple perspectives.

An Alternative to Conflict: The Social Symbolic

Many feature films evoke fragments of a utopian moment within the realm of a social reality that remains fundamentally besieged by ideologies of either/or, them/us oppositions or dense webs of social conflict. Symbolic acts of understanding and empathy shine a light on cultural ideals that otherwise often disappear within the darkness of prejudicial social practices. These acts comprise a distinct realm that we can call the **social symbolic.** Such acts often arise in relation to events that have a ritual quality to them such as weddings or carnivals like Mardi Gras where social hierarchy dissolves, at least momentarily. They occur even in westerns and other genre films that otherwise play out a drama based on either/or polarities. The barn-raising sequence in *My Darling Clementine* (John Ford, 1946), for example, gives visible expression to the type of ideal society that remains in scant supply in a world marred by bad apples and wanton violence. The entire community gathers as one to celebrate the completion of the barn-raising by joining in a ritual celebration of song and dance; hierarchy dissolves as each person becomes the equal of every other.

Children of Men (Alfonso Cuarón, 2006, U.S./UK/Japan) also conveys a sense of optimistic fellowship in its concluding scenes. Theo (Clive Owen) succeeds in delivering Kee (Claire-Hope Ashitey) and her baby, the first child born in the last eighteen years as the world descends into cataclysmic doom, to a utopian community that can protect and raise the child safe from the urban violence of the previous society's final days. Similarly, despite the either/or polarity that pits the citizens of Pepperville against the Blue Meanies, the animated feature *Yellow Submarine* (George Dunning, 1968, UK), through its exuberant style and winsome music, conveys a feeling for what relationships lived largely within the terms of mutual respect might feel like. This animated feature brilliantly captures the sense of innocence and fun that characterizes the Beatles' songs. Their music infuses the film with a sense of community beyond the social and racial divides that linger. *Wall-E* (Andrew Stanton, 2008), with its triumphant victory over loneliness and isolation, its celebratory resettlement of a nearly ruined earth, and its romantic union of Wall-E and Eve, his perfect mate, sings a similar song that pays tribute to qualities of perseverance, optimism, and love.

Music and dance are often expressive of the utopian, communitarian qualities of the social symbolic, where the oppositions and conflicts that populate the social imaginary yield to a sense of cooperation and mutuality. They represent moments when worries and cares can be put aside, when rivalries and schemes can be suspended, when the sheer joy of the present moment can shine in all its radiance on characters and audience alike. In this form, exuberant musical expressiveness is a vivid reminder of what many people long for in their everyday lives and only find on special occasions. In *My Darling Clementine*, Wyatt Earp becomes thoroughly absorbed into the community from which he must more often set himself apart in order to defend it, when he joins in the barn-raising celebration. In *Singin' in the Rain* (Stanley Donen and Gene Kelly, 1952), the three characters express their creative, harmonious joy through dance. In *Yellow Submarine* the characters exude a grace and innocence that captures a sense of genuine community, and in *Wall-E* the cartoon characters possess innocence and charm, coupled to resolve and resourcefulness, so that a despoiled earth can once again become a Garden of Eden.

Music and dance, like the happy endings of many films, sometimes displace the cultural ideal of community to distinct, ritualized activities or moments that give little sense of how the more routine social practices of day-to-day life, from family interaction to workplace dynamics, can be infused with the open-ended give-and-take of the social symbolic. These almost ecstatic moments of spontaneous pleasure nonetheless provide a cornerstone for cinematic representations of a symbolic harmony.

Social practices predicated on acceptance and mutual respect, trust and honesty, rather than on prejudice and racial bias, are difficult to achieve. Hierarchy and power constantly intrude; they take root in the social and psychic dynamics that drive the dominant social practices forward. The power of cinema very often correlates precisely with film's ability to perform certain actions difficult to perform by any other means. Among these actions is the ability to give viewers a sense not only of what bias or discrimination feels like but also of what communitarian ideals feel like in the concrete, embodied form of a cinematic world not entirely unlike our own.

10

GENDER AND MASCULINITY

The Fluidity of Sex: Biological Sex, Sexual Identity, and Gender Identity

THE SHAPING OF SEX

The social imaginary, discussed in Chapter 9, operates with exceptional force in relation to categories that appear to be grounded in nature or biology such as sexual or ethnic identity. Why, we may ask, do we need to erect and maintain powerful, fixed images of ethnic, gender, or sexual identity if nature had already provided forms of indisputable difference? The very fact that these identities are enormously loaded concepts suggests that any apparently obvious difference between ethnicities or between men and women is not quite so obvious after all. Summarizing uses of the terms **biological sex**, **sexual identity**, and **gender identity** will help highlight areas of continuing debate.

The **biological sex** of an individual refers to his or her anatomical sex characteristics. The great majority of people clearly exhibit either a male or female biological sex identity, although some people possess the genitalia of both sexes. Possessing either male or female genitalia, however, does not guarantee any one sexual or gender identity. **Sexual**

identity or **orientation** is sometimes used interchangeably with biological sex, but sexual identity also refers to whether a person is attracted to the same sex or the opposite sex. Same-sex attraction goes by terms such as homosexual, gay, or lesbian, while opposite-sex attraction is commonly known as a heterosexual and straight orientation. The word "orientation" is often used to indicate that sexual attraction is not primarily a matter of conscious choice. Feelings of attraction to others typically emerge as a felt preference in childhood and early adolescence. Individuals can later consciously choose to affirm their sexual identity openly or mask it. For individuals who are not heterosexual, a masked sexual identity is often called **closeted,** and making an open acknowledgment of a non-heterosexual identity is known as **coming out.**

Gender identity refers to how individuals act in relation to norms of masculinity and femininity in a given culture. A male can adopt feminine behavior and be sexually attracted to men or to women. A woman can adopt masculine behavior and also be attracted to men or to women. Similarly, a man can adopt a very masculine gender identity and yet be attracted to other men, just as some women may adopt a very feminine gender identity and be attracted to other women. These options begin to suggest how diverse and fluid sexuality among humans is. The fact of real anatomical differences between the sexes is one thing, but the way individuals display mixtures of masculine or feminine traits, seek same- or opposite-sex partners, attach meanings and values to different orientations (sometimes with strong negative or positive charges), and assign considerable responsibility for the management of sexual identity, gender identity, and the corresponding forms of acceptable behavior to social institutions, from the family and schools to medicine and the courts, is quite another.

To summarize the three key terms:

Biological sex: possession of male or female genitalia

Sexual identity or **orientation**: erotic attraction to members of the same or opposite sex. (Someone attracted to both sexes has a bisexual identity.)

Gender identity: display of traits, mannerisms, and general behavior that falls somewhere along a spectrum from very masculine (rational, independent, self-sufficient, stoic, "tough") to very feminine (emotional, relational, dependent, vulnerable, "soft") (the specific traits assigned to each biological sex may vary somewhat in different cultures). All individuals possess masculine and feminine characteristics. A given society may value one part of this spectrum more than another.

ATTRACTION VERSUS IDENTIFICATION

When individuals find themselves attracted to other people, those other people become objects of erotic desire. When individuals find themselves identifying with other people, those other people become models for an internal sense of identity. In the dominant ideology of heterosexual relationships, men typically identify with men and desire women, while women identify with other women and desire men. The initial identification, in both cases, is often with the parent of the same sex, but this identificatory process continues throughout life and includes, among many other possibilities, the images of others found in the cinema. Identification is crucial for the construction of identity: internalizing qualities of others is how a stable ego and sense of self come into being. Gender identity depends in considerable measure on what qualities in others become emulated and made into qualities of one's own. A male who identifies with James Dean may envision his masculinity in softer, more vulnerable terms than someone who identifies strongly with Sylvester Stallone, for example.

Attraction is equally crucial, since it is through feelings of desire for others that each individual establishes his sexual identity. The male who finds himself sexually attracted to James Dean, as does Pluto (Sal

Mineo), the main supporting actor in *Rebel without a Cause* (Nicholas Ray, 1955), may have a gay sexual identity, whereas a male attracted to Natalie Wood, Dean's girlfriend in *Rebel*, exhibits a heterosexual or straight sexual identity. The cinema offers models for both identification and attraction. It typically does so in accordance with the dominant ideology of heterosexuality.

Identification with those one wants to emulate and desire for those to whom one experiences attraction are subjective matters. Such relations are difficult to measure and even more difficult to explain. They fall outside the province of most social science research although they are the virtual bread and butter of the arts. The analysis of viewers' identificatory and erotic attachments to actors, stars, and characters is a staple of film criticism. Some time ago, Sigmund Freud proposed that the processes of identification and attraction operate primarily at an unconscious level. Whether this idea proves entirely valid or not, and whether empirical research provides useful insights into how and why we identify with some and desire others, film study has relied heavily on the idea of the unconscious to explore the function of these processes of identification and attraction in the cinema.

Referring to processes of identification and attraction as unconscious has the value of acknowledging the seemingly automatic way in which these feelings arise. Gender and sexual identity are not decided by rational thought; they well up as forms of behavior whose exact origin remains unclear. Their power, like the power of ideology as an internalized (unconscious) picture of one's place in the world, can be all the greater as a result, since neither whom we identify with nor whom we desire is fully under conscious control. It is no accident that the magical spark that sometimes occurs between certain actors like Katherine Hepburn and Spencer Tracy is called chemistry: just as some chemicals automatically react to form new compounds in each other's presence, some actors interact in ways that ignite the identificatory and erotic impulses of their audiences.

The Power of Others: The Vulnerability of Identity

Like social identity more broadly, sexual and gender identity lack absolute solidity. If a person's identity more or less conforms to that expected by the dominant ideology, it will match a preexisting image of ideological or normal behavior and seem quite natural for that reason too. The result can be a very strong feeling that identity is an inborn trait that resists change and persists through time. Images of others, embedded, for example, in photographs or films, exhibit a similar quality: they persist as timeless icons available for others to identify with or desire. The fixed image—be it a mental picture or a photograph—arrests time; it eludes decay or change. The power of ideology, stereotypes, and identity all draw heavily on this distinctive quality of the image.

But conflicts and crises, the bread and butter of cinema, make clear that social identity, including sexual or gender identity, displays a high degree of vulnerability. In *The Blue Angel* (Josef von Sternberg, 1930, Germany), a strict teacher, Professor Rath (Emil Jannings), winds up as a pathetic sideshow clown as a result of his infatuation with Lola (Marlene Dietrich), a nightclub performer. Rath's masculinity depends on an authoritarian streak he can uphold with students, but his power evaporates in the presence of the seductive Lola. His entire demeanor changes; his behavior suddenly becomes servile. In many ways Lola emasculates him, but the professor not only allows this to happen, he earnestly wants it to happen. His formerly solid identity crumbles; he becomes a laughingstock to Lola's friends, but he also feels a bliss he had never known before.

In *Performance* (Nicolas Roeg and Donald Cammell, 1970, UK) a gangster on the run, Chas (James Fox), hides out with a fallen rock star, Turner (Mick Jagger), only to find his identity dissolve into that of a man who appears to be his total opposite. In *The Night Porter*

(Liliana Cavani, 1974, Italy) a staid hotel clerk (Dirk Bogarde) encounters a former inmate (Charlotte Rampling) of the Nazi concentration camp where he was an officer. The encounter spirals into a destructive cycle of sadomasochistic interactions that completely unhinge the formal, proper, and humorless clerk. His life, like that of Professor Rath's, suddenly spins out of control and he, like Rath, is heedless of the consequences.

In such films, identity as the rock-solid core from which an individual's personality emerges with its normal, idiosyncratic, neurotic, or resistant behavior patterns, proves quite fragile. Identity has a vulnerable side, and this vulnerability is a crucial consequence of our dependence on others to form and maintain all aspects of our identity. This is particularly true when we examine male identity, which has a strong investment in appearing autonomous, independent, self-sufficient, achievement-oriented, and, as represented by action heroes, invulnerable. It is, instead, as numerous films demonstrate, far more fragile than it might at first appear.

Action heroes fulfill teenage fantasies of male power and autonomy. That these heroes also benefit society further valorizes them, imbuing them with worth. The action hero's Achilles' heel—his vulnerability—counterbalances his power. For Achilles, it was literally his heel, the one part of his body not dipped in the magically protective waters of the river Styx, that left him vulnerable to his foes. For a typical action hero it might be the woman he loves, who, if she falls under the control of his enemy, can be used against him. A wife held captive may compel the hero to deeds he would not otherwise commit. Typically, his resourcefulness enables him to rescue his wife and restore social and moral order, as we find in the first season of the television series *24*, when terrorists capture hero Jack Bauer's wife and compel Bauer to attempt to assassinate a presidential candidate. The theme recurs in the sixth season, when the Chinese kidnap Audrey, the woman he loves. His determination to rescue her imperils U.S.-Russian relations and jeopardizes his own life. A comic reversal of this plot occurs in *The Incredibles* (Brad Bird, 2004), where it is Mr. Incredible himself who is kidnapped. His overeagerness to escape his humdrum, post–action hero life as a normal, retired dad is the Achilles' heel that leads him to fall into the hands of his nemesis. His wife and children are the ones who must rescue him.

Perhaps most literally of all, Superman, who can leap tall buildings in a single bound, nonetheless falls helpless in the presence of kryptonite. The Achilles' heel of the superhero is a reminder of the vulnerability of masculine identity in all its forms. It is this quality of vulnerability, however, that adds conflict and drama to tales of derring-do. If the hero had no weaknesses whatsoever, far less would be at stake in terms of the challenges that confront him.

Masculinism, Patriarchy, and the Question of Male Privilege

Privilege as the Apparently Natural Order of Things

An image of the autonomous, independent male promotes self-reliance and initiative; it motivates action, it get things done. The spirit of independence and the longing for freedom plays a vital role in both the history and mythology of western culture, from the myth of Prometheus to the birth of the Renaissance to the exploration of space. However much such a spirit may need tempering with respect, humility, prudence, or wisdom, its fundamental value lies beyond question. What feminists have asked is not so much how the drive for independence can be quashed as why such a drive must be limited to men and whether it must be at the expense of intimate relationships. Should such a spirit and desire not be understood as common to all? Is its parceling out between the sexes something other than the natural order of things, something that might be considered ideological?

Such questions may seem impertinent. They threaten to disrupt what some consider the natural order of things. In fact, the linkage of certain rights and privileges to men, most of which involve autonomy and initiative, bears resemblance to the linkage of certain rights and privileges with white skin discussed in Chapter 9. Some men accept as natural that women will make marriage and family life their priority, that their wives will play a supporting role, that men will make basic family decisions, that when things need doing it will be they who do them, and that women who do not go along with these assumptions are more a threat or hindrance than a help. Films have traditionally supported many of these assumptions with the parallel plot structure in which men act and women wait, or men rescue and women await rescue. From *The Birth of a Nation* (D.W. Griffith, 1915) to *No Country for Old Men* (Ethan and Joel Coen, 2007), men venture forth into public space while women await the outcome in the private space of hearth and home.

The assumptions at the root of male privilege can, indeed, be seen as natural and fair, based on claims of innate differences between the sexes or through appeals to tradition that "This is how we've always done things here," or to religious doctrines that justify this arrangement. Assumptions, basic starting points, are usually ingrained or habitual and therefore difficult to change. And yet they are seldom universal. Just as gender hierarchy may seem natural to some, it will seem unnatural to others, based, for example, on (1) direct experience, as a woman, of this hierarchy as oppressive or exploitative, (2) alternative views of biological difference that disputes its basis for social hierarchy, or (3) feminist theory that dissects the relations between the sexes as a social construction and calls for equal opportunity and an end to stereotyping. Films from pioneering fiction films *Alice Doesn't Live Here Anymore* (Martin Scorsese, 1974) and *Girlfriends* (Claudia Weill, 1978) to more recent feminist films such as *Divine Secrets of the Ya-Ya Sister-hood* (Callie Khouri, 2002) and *North Country* (Niki Caro, 2005) take up various aspects of male privilege by exploring its consequences for women.

Performing like a Man

Another way to understand the attempt to stabilize and secure an autonomous male identity from vulnerability relates to what Herbert Marcuse, a sociologist, termed the **performance principle**. In *Eros and Civilization* Herbert Marcuse distinguished between the performance principle, which revolved around work, toil, sacrifice, discipline and obedience, and the **pleasure principle**, which centered on play, pleasure, spontaneity, creativity, and joy. (Marcuse reverses Sigmund Freud's more pessimistic view that civilization must repress the individual's urge to seek and obtain pleasure so that it does not become socially disruptive. For Marcuse the possibility of social disruption was an inviting prospect.) The pleasure and performance principles can also be considered as different points on the spectrum of gender identity, from the highly masculine to the strongly feminine. The performance principle is represented by Prometheus and his daring theft of fire from the gods. Prometheus is a solitary, defiant hero who risks his life for the greater good. He epitomizes the autonomous male hero for Marcuse.

The alternative hero, Orpheus, was, according to legend, the greatest musician to ever live. He could charm and soothe any and all with his magical play. Orpheus, like Narcissus and Dionysus, boldly bears the trace of a feminine sensibility. He opposes the logic of domination and control, defiance and mastery. His is an image of joy and fulfillment, the voice that does not command but sings, the deed that gives rather than conquers and controls. This is the image of what Marcuse called the Great Refusal, a rejection of the dominant ideology and dominant social practices in favor of a social order revolving around utopian values, beliefs, and ideals. Using the two categories discussed in Chapter 9, Orpheus aligns with the social symbolic, Prometheus with the social imaginary. For Marcuse, Orpheus is the "poet of redemption," a male figure who invites others toward a world with far fewer barriers between desire and its fulfillment.

Marcuse claimed that although societies could be organized around either principle, western culture keeps the pleasure principle strictly subordinated as a distraction and compensation. The entertainment industry carried out, for Marcuse as for Brecht, hegemonic strategies of subordination by offering empty distractions. Marcuse did not try to distinguish, as a dual formal-social analysis might, between the ideological and utopian aspects of a popular work, what that work saw afresh versus what it took for granted. His judgment of what he and others called the "culture industry" may therefore be overly harsh, but his distinction between two opposing principles, one centered on autonomy and getting the job done, the other focused on relationships and being true to oneself, retains considerable value.

Under the dominant performance principle, men, threatened by the risk that power will be denied them, must measure up. Measure up to what? In practice, they must measure up to impossible cultural ideals of autonomy, mastery, and self-control, even though these ideals may be sugarcoated with notions of love, creativity, wisdom, and community. Striving to achieve the impossible takes its toll, not only on men but also on all those around them, as in the films *Walking Tall* (Phil Karlson, 1973), where a rough-and-tumble battle against crime leaves the town sheriff more and more incapacitated, and *There Will Be Blood* (Paul Thomas Anderson, 2007), where the humanity drains from Daniel Plainview (Daniel Day-Lewis, who won an Oscar for his performance) as he gains more and more power and wealth.

Men test how they measure up by means of comparison and competition. Deriving a sense of identity from what one does rather than from who one is feeds into the sense that the only thing that matters is performing successfully. In terms of successful performance, a common but deadly form of comparison is with the machine. In this competition men can become like machines, agents bereft of feelings and dedicated to a single purpose, regardless of the risk or harm to self. As an imaginary machine, a man demonstrates how tough he really is, how good he is, what he can overcome or endure and still get the job done despite all the obstacles and sacrifices.

In Martin Scorsese's searing indictment of the performance principle, *Raging Bull* (1980), this is the goal Jake LaMotta (Robert De Niro) sets for himself. The film recounts the up-and-down boxing career and failed personal life of Jake LaMotta, who defined his manhood in terms of a performance principle organized around his ability to shut out his pain and feelings while physically dominating others. We constantly see the toll LaMotta's obsession with the performance principle takes on his humanity, from having his brother punch him in the face simply to show that he can take it, to shouting at Sugar Ray Robinson, after Sugar Ray has reduced him to a bloody pulp, "I never went down, Ray; I never went down."

The image of the battered Jake is an ironic commentary on male prowess. As in his other films, Scorsese explores a male fascination with maintaining an impregnable façade behind which lurk enormous self-doubts and insecurities. From Jake LaMotta, Henry Hill (Ray Liotta) in *Goodfellas* (1990), and San Rothstein (Robert De Niro) in *Casino* (1995) to his remarkable portrait of a fallible, self-doubting Jesus in *The Last Temptation of Christ* (1988), Scorsese presents a portrait gallery of troubled males who strive to prove themselves. This impulse leads them into situations where they risk, and sometimes find, death itself.

Like the boxing film, action, adventure, and war films betray underlying insecurities and instabilities. *The Terminator* (James Cameron, 1984), for example, makes the hero into a nearly indestructible machine, albeit a machine with a heart of gold. Certainly *First Blood* (Ted Kotcheff, 1982), *The Road Warrior* (aka *Mad Max II*, George Miller, 1981, Australia), and *The Chronicles of Riddick* (David Twohy, 2004) enact fantasies of power and invulnerability that stand at palpable odds with what these films also hold out as the possibility of love, comfort, and trust. If such films enact male, adolescent fantasies of power, they also betray an underlying sense of insecurity and doubt.

Other genres like the western also include films that undercut or question the conventional celebration of a robust masculinity. In *Dead Man* (Jim Jarmusch, 1995, U.S./Germany), for example, William Blake (Johnny Depp) goes west but finds a promised job nonexistent. Within a day he's unwittingly committed a murder. Panicked, he then flees the frontier world of exploitation and savagery represented by the company town of Mechanic. He gradually rediscovers suppressed aspects of his humanity in an alternative world opened to him by his Native American companion and guide, Nobody (Gary Farmer). What Nobody teaches best, in the spirit of Orpheus far more than Prometheus, is the surrender of the ego rather than the celebration of individualism as the foundation of community. Blake's acceptance of his position outside patriarchy and rugged individualism renders him capable of openness and emotional surrender to another. As his slow journey through the wilderness proceeds, Blake learns to let go, to give himself over to another person, another culture, another world in his progress toward both understanding and death.

Johnny Depp, through his character portrayals in *Dead Man*, *Charlie and the Chocolate Factory* (Tim Burton, 2005, U.S./UK), *Edward*

Scissorhands (Tim Burton, 1990), and the *Pirates of the Caribbean* trilogy (Gore Verbinski, 2003-2007), has developed a special niche as an actor. His characters are close to adolescence in age or at least in spirit. The films may remain squarely anchored within a heterosexual world but they also grant his characters qualities of vulnerability and self-doubt that contrast sharply with more conventional representations of a performance-based masculinity.

For some men, **performance anxiety**—strong visceral feelings of self-doubt, feelings of inadequacy, and fear of rejection, humiliation, or failure—accompany the demands of the performance principle. A staple moment in war films is the lull-before-the-battle scene in which men get to confess their fear and anxiety prior to going out to face death. This tendency is often on vivid, humorous display in comedies that feature males who act hysterically, their bodies seemingly beyond the control of their conscious will, or who revert to childish antics. Jerry Lewis built his career on characters who display endless anxiety in films such as *The Ladies Man* (Jerry Lewis, 1961) and *The Nutty Professor* (Jerry Lewis, 1963).

In particularly vivid variations on this theme, Anthony Perkins in *Psycho* (Alfred Hitchcock, 1960) and Dennis Weaver in *Touch of Evil* (Orson Welles, 1958) represent the male as little boy who cannot respond as an equal to a mature, sexually alluring female. Their behavior borders on hysteria as they lose self-control and are reduced to the symptomatic behavior of fidgeting and stammering. Weaver is left speechless, and what speech Perkins possesses is a convoluted mix of curiosity, circumlocutions, and anxiety. Janet Leigh's character in each film triggers a crisis that goes to the core of their identity as males, which is found lacking. They revert, in the tradition of numerous American comedians such as Harpo Marx, Jerry Lewis, and, later, Pee-wee Herman, to the behavior of boys.

Normal and Alternative Sexualities as Signs of Trouble within Masculinity

REPRESSED DESIRE, SUBLIMATION, AND ALTERNATIVE COMMUNITIES

Another sign that the natural order of things in terms of normative sexual and gender identities may involve socially imposed constraints is the **repression** of alternative orientations. **Repression** can be external, in the form of social pressures that encourage individuals to conform to the status quo, or internal, in the form of a psychic process that removes some thoughts and desires from consciousness by pushing them into the unconscious. If repression is successful and the dominant forms of sexual and gender identity emerge in the adolescent, repressed desires can only escape from the unconscious in disguised or sublimated forms. These often take the form of neuroses or psychoses, but they may also join with the normal channeling of sexual energy into socially productive forms. In other words, there are cases where repressed desires contribute to socially acceptable but **sublimated** forms of expression such as creativity or sacrifice.

Sublimation involves the conversion of a basic drive, such as sexual desire, into a non-overtly sexual form. It is a form of displacement from a physical urge to a more creative or spiritual longing. Unlike the perversions, discussed below, sublimation is socially productive. Creative expression and sacrificial action afford personal fulfillment and social benefit. *Lawrence of Arabia* (David Lean, 1962, UK) is a case study in sublimation that turns one man's repressed sexual energies into the motor force for political transformations throughout the Middle East during World War I. The film leaves clear hints that sexual longings motivate Lawrence's heroic efforts.

In one scene, Lawrence rides into a group of Arab rebels he is assisting dressed for the first time in a burnoose. He acts utterly oblivious to the fact that he is the only man in white and that a white burnoose, like a white gown, is what a bride wears to her wedding. The image is a hint that Lawrence has repressed homosexual desires. The closeted quality of his desire can be attributed to the social codes of the 1910s when homosexuality in Europe and the Middle East would be highly closeted and to the formal film conventions of the early 1960s when the Production Code, with its strictures against the representation of homosexuality, still wielded real if diminished authority.

The image of Lawrence in white can be understood as a reference to his sublimated sexuality whether or not that sexuality is homosexual: his desire is to marry his own ambition to the Arab struggle against Ottoman rule and to marry the warring tribes into one great fighting force. Joining his Arab comrades, ready for battle, is a symbolic wedding of his organization skills and the Arab guerillas. The image, in other words, can be read on multiple levels, a common feature of fictional worlds that have metaphorical or allegorical overtones.

Seabiscuit (Gary Ross, 2003) is another case study in sublimation, this time through a story of how three men renew their self-esteem as men through the displacement of their sexual desires into the making of a champion racehorse. The film provides scant reference to any love life for the three main, male characters. The focus stays on their collective dedication to making Seabiscuit into a formidable racetrack champion. In these films where sublimated desires eliminate the parallel plot structure that balances action and adventure with courtship and romance, women play negligible roles or are nonexistent. The men's romantic or sexual energies find expression in sublimated, socially productive forms instead.

Sexual identities repressed by the dominant ideology of heterosexuality have also led to the formation of gay, lesbian, bisexual, and transsexual subcultures or communities. By redefining normal behavior within an alternative framework, individuals whose sexual or gender identity does not fit the prevailing mold find social belonging within a like-minded community. The proliferation of gay and lesbian characters in popular entertainment who are no longer represented as self-loathing or sadistic stereotypes, as they often were before the rise of a gay movement, is a sign of how this social movement has altered the larger society's perception of sexual difference. *Parting Glances* (Bill Sherwood, 1986), for example, was among the first to treat gay life as a subculture with its own internal norms and problems, from interpersonal conflict to the onset of the AIDS epidemic. None of the characters represents a stereotypical gay man. As with other films that adopt a gay or lesbian political perspective, the sense of what is and is not normal shifts to make the internal norms of a distinct subculture the primary point of reference.

Classic Heterosexual Desire and Alternatives to It

What serves as the normal expression of masculinity—heterosexuality, marriage, and family life—sits atop a vast array of alternative desires and practices. Some of these are modest variations, but others deviate quite substantially. In some cases, very different forms of erotic desire prevail. That diverse desires and social practices exist can be seen as a crack in the effort to make "normal" sexual identity natural and obvious. For some individuals it is not natural and far from obvious. Such desires and practices, sometimes referred to as **sexual perversions**, may be repressed, condemned, or made taboo, another indication of the threat they pose to the maintenance of a dominant norm. (**Sexual perversions** involve forms of sexual behavior that strikes many as strange, aberrant, unpleasant, or distasteful partly because they are typically uncoupled from any reproductive goal.)

Sigmund Freud considered alternative sexual identities and sexual perversions to be forms of psychic disorder rather than evil intent. Since his pioneering work many others have also tried to understand the so-called perversions in a morally neutral manner. Freud himself stressed four things:

1) The norm from which perversions were viewed as aberrations was itself a social invention rather than an inviolate moral standard;

2) Perversions were part of an unbroken spectrum of sexual and gender identities that did not divide into good versus bad. They might involve activities that others would find distasteful or not erotic, but they brought distinct gratification to the pervert;

3) Perversions were not necessarily a medical problem, although the dominant ideology might well consider them a moral problem; and

4) If a perversion appeared to handicap an individual's ability to function socially, it could be treated by psychoanalysis.

The perversions of greatest interest in the cinema include voyeurism, fetishism, sadism, and masochism (discussed below). These four perversions are not limited to men, but they do seem to occur more often in men than women.

Behavior, as noted in Chapter 8, often functions symptomatically. It points to patterns and possible disorders of which characters remain but dimly aware. A character may go to great lengths in the pursuit of a desire but, if asked, show very little ability to say why he does so. At times, perverse desires become crippling to the individual. Neurotic and especially psychotic behavior seems to run an uncontrollable course no matter how self-destructive they become. Not surprisingly, given that it is women who usually suffer the brunt of these perversions, as the targets of a voyeuristic gaze, for example, feminist film scholars have

done a great deal to explore how their manifestation in films both limits the possibilities for the representation of female characters and
reveals, symptomatically, fissures in a male or masculinist social order.
Each of the four main perversions deserves additional attention.

VOYEURISM Voyeurism represents an alternative form of sexual pleasure in which looking without being seen replaces direct physical contact as the source of erotic excitement. Looking can obviously
function as part of a normal process of sexual attraction, but it
becomes an alternative to it when it becomes an end in itself. A pattern of looking at someone who cannot look back with equal authority puts the typically male voyeur in control. Here the woman's
subordinate status is tacitly acknowledged in the inequality of gazes.
Typically, the male gaze surveys the scene, taking pleasure at will,
while the female remains unaware of the objectifying male gaze. In
both a literal and metaphorical sense, the female cannot see that her
own agency is denied her by the voyeuristic gaze of an other. She may
also be punished for her allure, for not grasping how her attractive-
ness incites men whether she is aware of it or not. The dynamics of
voyeurism and fetishism in film were first discussed in considerable
detail in Laura Mulvey's 1975 "Visual Pleasure and Narrative Cinema," which has since become the classic reference for study of these
perversions in film.

In films, voyeurism frequently correlates with violence. It is, for
example, only moments after Norman Bates peeps through the wall
at the semi-clad Marion Crane that she meets Norman's vengeful
mother in the bathroom shower and succumbs to a brutal knife attack.
The entire genre of slasher movies is predicated on a similar correlation between voyeuristic perversion and pathological violence. From
The Texas Chainsaw Massacre (Tobe Hooper, 1974) to the *Friday the
13th* series (1980–2009), slashers hand out violent punishment that is

closely, if not causally, linked to the sexuality of their female victims and the arrested, infantilized sexuality of male perpetrators.

The male voyeur can punish women or redeem them (for crimes often of his own imagining). He decides their fate. In *Murder, My Sweet* (Edward Dmytryk, 1944), the hard-boiled detective, Marlowe (Dick Powell), treats the young and innocent Ann (Anne Shirley) like a little girl, someone who is not a sexual threat. She stands in stark contrast to the highly sexual and dangerous Mrs. Grayle (Clair Trevor). The characters, in fact, amount to two sides of the same coin. Marlowe as a detective has a legal license to snoop, peep, and pry. He looks in on the lives of others and infers things about the nature and quality of their conduct. He can then orchestrate punishment—death for Mrs. Grayle, or redemption, that is, marriage, for Ann—in accord with the stories he has formulated about each of these women.

In *Gentlemen Prefer Blondes* (Howard Hawks, 1953), Marilyn Monroe and Jane Russell reduce a troop of male gymnasts to gyrating pawns entranced by their sheer physical presence. That the women are showgirls makes their alluring appearance natural, as if it is not in the least out of the ordinary. It is so arresting, though, and so inviting of a voyeuristic response that it completely discombobulates the male athletes, whose training session comes to a halt as they stare agog at the two women. The wink-like quality of the showgirl, in which films can say, "We are not encouraging voyeurism; these women actually want to be looked at," worked as an effective alibi to elude the Production Code when the film was made. Director Paul Verhoeven pushes this idea of the alibi to an extraordinary extreme in his more recent film, *Showgirls* (1995), set in Las Vegas amidst such abundant nudity that some critics have interpreted it as both a parody—mimicking stripper movies—and satire of the social values that support the whole business of stripteases, showgirls, and even the idea of an entire city devoted to gambling and spectacle.

FETISHISM Fetishism always represents a form of emotional overinvestment. The fetish object attracts excessive devotion. Its psychic value exceeds its intrinsic worth. Anthropologists noted that tribal people placed excess value on fetish objects that had only modest intrinsic worth (to someone outside the tribe). They overvalued these objects as signifiers of something else, perhaps a deity or spirit, which the object could symbolize but not become. For Karl Marx, fetishism in modern society took place in relation to commodities that received magical powers to please or gratify. The fetishization of commodities involved bestowing magical powers on objects instead of recognizing that their value derived solely from the human labor that went into producing them. According to Marx, the purpose of this fetishization, which ads for automobiles and alcoholic drinks trade on relentlessly, is to camouflage the value of the labor involved in their production.

A similar form of fetishization occurs with movie stars, whose aura propels them into celestial orbit. This process of star worship involves considerable overvaluation and overinvestment in the apparently magical powers of that particular actor. Mulvey's essay "Visual Pleasure and Narrative Cinema" extended this line of thinking in a more pointedly feminist direction.

Unconditional love is something men long for that is normally unattainable after childhood. The longing for a perfect, unconditional love, though, can lead men to create an idealized image of the woman who might provide it. This fantasy image, a "nurturing mother" stereotype, for example, promises to give men what they long for. The fetishist, in effect, invents an idealized image and then attaches it to actual people. He no longer sees the actual person, with all her strengths and weaknesses, but a fetish object or image that seems to possess exceptional powers. The **fetish** serves as a projection of the male's fantasy of female perfection; it overvalues a person or object because of the meanings or needs the fetishist projects onto it. When a real person, typically a woman, is converted into a fetish object for someone else, typically a man, this process denies her real limitations and needs in order to fabricate an image devoted entirely to the fulfillment of male needs.

The fetishist, like Professor Rath in *The Blue Angel*, may become the target of social derision for his excessive infatuation. Rath himself seems oblivious to what others think of him as he forfeits his social standing to dote on the elusive and taunting Lola. In her first encounter with Professor Rath, who comes to chastise her for distracting his students from their studies, she drops a pair of panties down a staircase. They land on the Professor's head as he ascends the stairs to see her. He pauses to examine them. From that moment on, his fetishization of her dominates his life. He lives to serve the one he venerates. He is never fully conscious of what drives him to risk all for an impossible object of desire. He loses his job and fails to live up to the dominant definition of adult manhood. He pays a painful price.

Dietrich's costume as Lola represents her as an erotic figure of desire; she is, as so many such figures are, a showgirl or, more precisely, a cabaret performer. Sternberg's camera converts her legs into fetish objects par excellence. They present an image of near impossible perfection, diverting attention from what others might recognize as her inevitable human limitations. In more recent times, cosmetics, airbrushing, and digital retouching to remove the usual blemishes and imperfections from the skin have proved a staple of *Playboy* magazine and of much fashion advertising. Such techniques create fetish objects that prove impossible for actual women to equal.

Female stars often embody an idealized image of feminine allure, sexuality, and power that converts them into fetish objects. They make men tremble at their feet. In the comedy *The Seven Year Itch* (Billy Wilder, 1955) the perfect body of Marilyn Monroe reduces the male protagonist, played by a nervous, fidgeting Tom Ewell, to a state of fumbling adolescent adoration. In *Basic Instinct* (Paul Verhoeven, 1992) Sharon Stone's fetishized body presents an image of perfection that the male hero (Michael Douglas) worships at his own peril. The fetish image, though capable of a powerful magnetism, is one that also masks the real person who remains, unseen and unacknowledged, beneath the mask. What lurks beneath may be a calculating opportunist, as in the **neo-noir** *Body Heat* (Lawrence Kasdan, 1981), where the alluring woman in white (Kathleen Turner) lures an unsuspecting private eye to his doom, or a woman with a heart of gold, as in the frightened and abused (Kim Basinger) in *L.A. Confidential* (Curtis Hanson, 1997), whom detective Bud White (Russell Crowe) vows to rescue from virtual captivity. (**Neo-noirs** are films made after the heyday of film noir in the late 1940s to late 1950s but in the same spirit and style.)

SADISM Men may also punish the woman trapped beneath an image that is not of her own making when she fails to delivers the goods this image promises. Men may assign blame to an image they themselves project onto women. Since women appear as irresistible sirens, it must be their own fault that they simultaneously pose a threat to male independence and autonomy. As Rita Hayworth knowingly sings during her defiant nightclub song in *Gilda* (Charles Vidor, 1946), "Put the blame on Mame, boys, put the blame on Mame."

The debasement of women who do not measure up to an idealized image and the punishment of women who undercut a man's sense of autonomy involve a sadistic relationship rather than a fetishistic one. Pleasure comes not from submitting to an ideal but from asserting power over an object of erotic attraction. Film noir's host of *femmes fatales* are a classic case of the woman punished for her fatal powers when these powers are, in fact, the product of male projection. Such a woman seduces and deceives and is ultimately punished for her deceptions, but not before she destroys the men who fall into the web they have unconsciously wanted her to construct. Some men go down for the count, like Fred MacMurray in *Double Indemnity* (Billy Wilder,

1944) and Bill Pullman in *The Last Seduction* (John Dahl, 1994), while others, from Humphrey Bogart in *The Maltese Falcon* (John Huston, 1941) to John Cusack in *The Grifters* (Stephen Frears, 1990), escape the clutches of scheming women by the skin of their teeth.

The Maltese Falcon finds a convenient metaphor for the punishment awaiting Brigid O'Shaughnessy (Mary Astor), the woman who has sweet-talked Sam Spade (Humphrey Bogart) into the treacherous labyrinth at the center of which lurks the fabulous jeweled treasure, the Maltese falcon. Brigid has used her female wiles in subtle but seductive ways. She has professed love and loyalty when her words were but a sham; she has misled Spade about her motives and intentions, and, at film's end, Sam Spade metes out the punishment that is her due with cool dispatch. He takes pleasure in sending her to prison for her calculating and dishonest ways.

In *Double Indemnity*, the seductive but two-timing Phyllis Dietrichson (Barbara Stanwyck) meets an even more gruesome end as she is shot down by her betrayed lover, Walter Neff (Fred MacMurray), but not before she fires the fatal shot that marks his ultimate demise as well. These films, with their heavy shadows, nocturnal figures, and dark urban settings, are vivid examples of the film noir style that arose in 1940s and 1950s postwar America. The hard-boiled heroes almost always have to prove their toughness by giving the long good-bye to women with the power to melt their impenetrable exteriors. It is but a short time later that Colonel Jack Ripper's fear that he is losing his "precious bodily fluids" during intercourse with women leads him to an even more extreme form of sadistic self-destruction: nuclear annihilation, in *Dr. Strangelove: Or, How I Learned to Stop Worrying and Love the Bomb* (Stanley Kubrick, 1964, UK).

A chilling variant on sadistic perversion is Michael Powell's film, *Peeping Tom* (1960, UK). The antihero, Mark Lewis (Carl Boehm), moonlights taking cheesecake photos of young women, although it is clear his interest is in photography and not the women. The most deviant part of his behavior involves a fascination with the effects of terror and fear on others, which drives him to film women that he brings to his studio as they realize that they face certain death. Their death comes in the form of a dagger concealed in the leg of his camera's tripod. Director Powell links Mark's pathology to his father's experiments on him as a child, filming the little boy's reactions to frightening, terrifying actions. Now, Mark's voyeuristic impulse becomes inseparable from a murderously sadistic one. Neurosis turns into criminal psychosis. *Peeping Tom* came out the same year as *Psycho*, 1960, but whereas *Psycho* gained praise as one of Hitchcock's greatest films, *Peeping Tom* earned condemnation as the depraved work of a once great director. Powell's career went into steep decline until the film's revival in the 1970s, thanks to the efforts of Martin Scorsese.

MASOCHISM If fetishism describes the overvaluation of an idealized image of women, masochism describes the compliant subordination of men who forgo male privilege for the pleasure of submission. Unlike the sadist, the masochist male does not set out to investigate, punish, save, or redeem the female. These narrative actions take place over time. Masochism, however, arrests time: it creates a state of surrender in which the male masochist hopes to remain indefinitely.

A willingness to be dominated rather than to dominate unsettles the idea that male privilege asserts itself in a relentlessly hegemonic manner, reducing women to a position of subordination. Women can attain considerable power in masochistic relationships, as we see in the case of Marlene Dietrich in *The Blue Angel*. Just as melodrama can provide a safety valve for the pent-up frustrations of women, masochistic fetishism can provide a safety valve for the pent-up anxieties of men. It provides an escape from the socially produced expectations, and anxieties, of the performance principle. At least since Leopold von Sacher-Masoch first described such a dynamic in his 1870 novel, *Venus in Furs*, masochism has had the peculiar quality of being a male-controlled perversion that compels men to render themselves defenseless and vulnerable to all-powerful women. It is another way in which repressed desires return to present a troubled picture of masculinity.

A prime example is *Blue Velvet* (David Lynch, 1986). It has the wide-eyed Jeffrey Beaumont (Kyle MacLachlan) fall under the spell of the mysterious Dorothy Vallens (Isabella Rossellini), a two-bit nightclub singer who croons "Blue Velvet" to an indifferent audience. Jeffrey embodies straightlaced innocence only to discover himself inexplicably drawn to Dorothy. The spell Dorothy casts over Jeffrey involves him in a process of maturation, as he becomes aware of the dark side of human nature, but even more potently, it draws him into a masochistic relationship, as he succumbs to Dorothy's perverse desires.

Jeffrey must also confront the utterly bizarre Frank Booth (Dennis Hopper), who combines masochistic regression before Dorothy with a violent, sadistic game of torment in which he holds her husband and son captive. Frank embodies an extreme version of male dependence on a nurturing figure, on the one hand, and a resentful sadism aimed at those who threaten his illusory sense of autonomy, on the other. Jeffrey triumphs in the end, or at least director David Lynch allows him to think he has, and, unlike Professor Rath, Jeffrey has a "good woman" (Sandy) to accompany him on his passage into adulthood.

Adolescence and the Longing for an Alternative Masculinity

The adolescent male is more than a child but less than a man. In the cinema, he often provides a malleable figure for the projection of unacknowledged, utopian longings for an alternative masculine identity. Adolescent male characters combine active qualities associated with masculinity with passive qualities associated with femininity. The result is a gender identity suspended in a moment of incomplete

development prior to its differentiation into clear-cut, either/or masculine and feminine alternatives. The adolescent upholds cultural
ideals of sensitivity, honesty, vulnerability, and principled conduct
that can seldom be consistently sustained by adult men. The male adolescent does not act out a perversion so much as serve a role similar
to that of the Greek chorus. He visibly and audibly reminds his adult
counterparts of what might have been. The world of the adolescent
invites a nostalgic return to or utopian longing for a moment in which
men can be men (as a biological sex) while being spared the negative
consequences of privilege and power (as a socially constructed gender).

The adolescent male can only maintain his innocence by remaining a son, but he can only remain a son at risk to his manhood.
Although this could be a paralyzing double bind, it is more often presented as a troubled, transitional moment, suspended in time. The
splendor of adolescent youth holds out an image of an idealized masculinity (sensitive, chivalrous, virtuous) before it must dissolve in the
harsher realities of a socially enforced manhood (tough, strong,
autonomous). Few films convey a fetishistic image of masculine innocence and perfection more poignantly than the scenes of the young
Brad Pitt trout fishing in the mountain streams of *A River Runs
Through It* (Robert Redford, 1992). These are the moments of harmony and communion that precede the fall, captured with Norman
Rockwell–like lighting and composition. Pitt must soon step into the
harsher currents of adult life, but for these brief idyllic moments he
presents a picture postcard of the male youth as a virtual knight, at
one with the wilderness. It is a figure revisited with doting reverence
in Sean Penn's *Into the Wild* (2007), the story of a young man (a virtual adolescent) who abandons society to rediscover himself through
communion with nature.

Not all adolescent figures are teenagers. The appeal of charismatic
heroes, particularly heroes of a populist stripe that stresses their rise
from the ranks of the common man, often lies in their innocence, their

immediate access to bedrock principles, their lack of guile, and their aversion to cynicism. Jimmy Stewart's Mr. Smith, in *Mr. Smith Goes to Washington* (1939), is one of Frank Capra's greatest creations. As a "dupe" picked to fill a vacant Senate seat so that the corrupt and wealthy can continue to plunder the public treasury, Jefferson Smith seems, at first, the perfect choice. Once he gets wind of what is at stake and how he is being used, however, he responds with a principled tenacity that shocks those who think they can manipulate him. Without growing up, without, that is, adopting the cynical or patriarchal posturing of his adult adversaries, Mr. Smith prevails.

Mr. Smith remains a gentle man, sensitive and vulnerable but also decent, honorable, and, to some, a bit too feminine. As Eric Smoodin reports in his book *Regarding Frank Capra*, the United States State Department considered blocking the distribution of *Mr. Smith Goes to Washington* to Latin America because it presented an insufficiently masculine image of the American political leader. The State Department appears to have noticed that Mr. Smith lacked the hard, tough, masculine political image it wanted the United States to project for the rest of the world.

The urge to fashion new possibilities for the adolescent male that escape the binary either/or logic of society's dominant adult gender roles takes exceptionally vivid form in *Rebel without a Cause*. Jim Stark (James Dean) winds up forming a new, alternative family with his girlfriend, Judy (Natalie Wood), and his adoring male friend, Plato (Sal Mineo). The mothers and fathers of all three adolescents present portraits of dysfunctional parents (weak, overbearing, incapable of love, or absent). The political conservatism of the film, however, underscores the impossibility of an alternative form of family unit. At the climactic ending Plato dies, shot by the police, while Jim and Judy return to the social fold and their presumably more understanding parents.

James Dean conveys with memorable power the yearning of the adolescent son for something different. He gives vivid expression to

an (impossible) ideal of a more Orpheus-like masculinity. He offers
audiences the opportunity to sense what it feels like to yearn to be a
man, but not the man who has a place reserved for him in the patriarchal order of 1950s America. (The recent cable TV program *Mad
Men* vividly explores what that place was like for a group of men at a
Madison Avenue advertising firm, and their female partners, at the
start of the 1960s.) Jim Stark's yearnings, however, dissolve into inner
emotional turmoil, well conveyed by Dean's method acting, rather
than gel into social activism. Dean agonizes between the conflicting
lures of discipline, strength, and self-control as masculine virtues and
intuition, empathy, and vulnerability as feminine ones with remarkable intensity.

The three main adolescent characters, Jim, Judy, and Plato, all arrive
at the police station near the start of the film, a clear sign that they are
troubled. Director Ray segregates them from each other using the
offices and glass partitions of the police station. This boxing off of each
character within one larger space signifies both their isolation and their
potential union. The *mise-en-scène* works to stress their inner, emotional state of distress, their inability to communicate or connect with
others in a satisfying way, and, through their presence in the frame
together and the occasional glances that pass among them, the strong
possibility that they will meet and get to know each other.

Later in the film Jim discovers his dad on his hands and knees
cleaning up a mess he made. Jim mistakes him for his mother because
of the apron he wears (it is the one we have already seen her wear at
breakfast). Jim has been challenged by Judy's boyfriend, Buzz, to a
"chicken run" (a dangerous car race) and needs advice about what to
do, but, at the very moment when Jim seeks to learn what a man
should do, his father appears to forfeit his masculinity. The film gives
evidence here of a common postwar theme of overbearing women
disrupting the healthy dynamics of a home by emasculating their husbands and sons. What the men's vulnerability to this process tells us

about the solidity of their masculine identity is typically left unexamined. Like the *femme fatale*, the domineering mother undermines a masculinity that cannot be very secure to begin with. The dad's advice boils down to evasive platitudes about not acting too hastily, getting advice, and so on. He does not try to find out exactly what the issue is that troubles Jim, and leaves him essentially to his own devices.

Although few reviews mentioned it at the time of the film's initial release in 1955, Plato is clearly coded as a closeted homosexual. The invitation that Plato makes to Dean's Jim Stark earlier in the film typifies the oblique way in which a subtext of unspoken desire hovers in the air, "Hey, you want to come home with me? I mean, there's nobody home at my house, and heck, I'm not tired, are you?"

Plato's ornate bedroom, with white lace curtains, rococo porcelain bedside lamps, glass chandelier and white walls, contrasts sharply with Jim's no-nonsense, sparsely decorated, wood-toned bedroom. It is unmistakably feminine in a way that reminds us of Jim's father wearing his wife's apron: men who do not live up to the socially defined norm for masculinity become coded as feminine. The feminine is the absence of a vigorous masculinity (in contrast to a positive set of alternative traits such as we will see in Chapter 11).

At the film's conclusion Plato lies dead at the planetarium, where the instructor had warned the class earlier that "Man, existing alone, seems an episode of little consequence." But now Jim does not exist alone. The two shot of him and Judy affirms his sense of belonging and his ability to overcome alienation. This shot is matched by a similar two shot of his parents. Jim wears his father's jacket, having left his red windbreaker on the fallen Plato. Jim and Judy are clearly represented as a newly formed couple, visually comparable to the adult couples they may replace. In this way, director Nicholas Ray suggests that Jim's quest for an alternative form of masculinity may not result in anything greater than eventually fitting into the social order epitomized by his parents. This less than utopian ambivalence is not stressed, however. The emotional weight of the film is clearly on the side of Jim Stark. He embodies an adolescent masculinity that offers hope of discovering a utopian ideal capable of reconfiguring the dominant sex-gender system.

The Gay Alternative

FORBIDDEN SUBJECTS, SUBVERSIVE MOMENTS, AND MAINSTREAM CINEMA

There is a mesmerizing moment in *Gilda* when Ballin, who has befriended Johnny and married Gilda, asks Gilda if she's decent before he and Johnny enter her bedroom. It is one of the great moments of fetishistic star worship in Hollywood cinema. As Gilda (Rita Hayworth) turns her head toward the camera, her long, radiant hair swirling about her beautiful face, she is the perfect image of the Hollywood star who embodies female beauty in her every gesture.

But why is Ballin bringing another man to his wife's bedroom in the first place? Why don't they wait in the drawing room for her to appear as men customarily do? Why does Ballin bring Johnny, a man he saved from serious danger with his "trusty little friend" (a very phallic walking stick whose tip conceals a stiletto), a man he has made into his right-hand man, to his bedroom door? There is here, as in many other film noir movies, more than a slight hint of homoerotic attraction, if not outright homosexuality. If this be love, however, it is truly a love that cannot speak its name. The mutual attraction Ballin and Johnny feel for each other emerges in lingering eye contact, glances at each other's bodies, and a common fascination with the same woman.

In mainstream cinema, homosexual love undergoes, for the most part, displacement. It is shifted into a more ambiguous homoeroticism where glances, gestures, mannerisms and inflections, an entire language of coded behavior, suggest unfulfilled desires. Its only fulfillment becomes what is known as **homosociality**, those sublimated forms of shared endeavor among men, from cattle drives and bank capers to putting on a show or fighting a war. These sublimated but emotionally charged forms of male bonding channel energies to nonsexual ends that might have otherwise taken a more overtly sexual turn. They provide some of the gratifications of sexual intimacy with none of the risks.

This is a formula at least as old as the silent Soviet films of Sergei Eisenstein, which consistently incorporated imagery that carried strongly homoerotic overtones, such as the sailors aboard the *Battleship Potemkin* (1925, Soviet Union) languorously draped among their hammocks, or the ecstatic spectacle of fireworks and erupting geysers that celebrate the success of the mechanical cream separator in *Old and New* (1929, Soviet Union). It can be found in Howard Hawks's 1928 film *A Girl in Every Port*, where two men vie for the same woman and which Hawks himself described as a male love story. Whatever stories such films told, however, they were never gay love stories. Love between men, or women, was displaced onto relationships of working together, in close physical proximity, with strong emotional bonds, to achieve an external task.

As Vito Russo's book *The Celluloid Closet* and the documentary film of the same name (Rob Epstein and Jeffrey Friedman, 1995) argue, decades of Hollywood film did not change much in their representation of gay and lesbian figures as stereotypes until the 1980s. Both Russo's book and the film suggest that a number of independently produced films have broken through the usual stereotypes and longstanding barriers to gay representation. *Parting Glances* (Bill Sherwood, 1986), *Go Fish* (Rose Troche, 1994), and *Swoon* (Tom Kalin, 1992) got their financing from outside the Hollywood studio system and opened the door for other, more mainstream films, and televisions shows such as "The L Word," to enter mainstream culture. A decade after the release of *The Celluloid Closet* in 1995, *Brokeback Mountain* (Ang Lee, 2005, U.S./Canada) cemented these gains by receiving numerous Oscar nominations and winning for Best Director and Best Adapted Screenplay.

Before that, in 2002, American independent director Todd Haynes took Douglas Sirk's classic 1950s melodrama, *All That Heaven Allows* (1955), and sharpened the original conflicts around age and class to address sexuality and race in his *Far from Heaven* (U.S./France). *Far from Heaven* converted Cary Scott's husband, who in the 1950s original has died before the film begins, into the heavy-drinking, closeted, and tormented homosexual Frank Whitaker. Still set in the '50s, *Far from Heaven* emphasizes how Frank struggles to accept his homosexuality at a time when coming out was almost impossible. *Far from Heaven* also sharpens what was meant to be a class and age divide in the original between Cary and the man she grows to love, her gardener, played by Rock Hudson. Cary, now named Cathy, still falls for her gardener, but he is now played by the African American actor Dennis Haysbert. Haynes gives poignant expression to what it feels like for Frank to hide his sexual identity and for Cathy to cope with overt racism. He flushes to the surface the tensions that swirl in more submerged forms in *All That Heaven Allows*.

Also in 2002, Pedro Almodóvar's beautiful film *Talk to Her* (*Habla con ella*, Spain) took gender stereotypes and turned them on their head. The film explores gender identity and sexual desire through its tale of a gentle, compassionate male nurse whose mannerisms evoke the closeted gay characters of the Production Code era. In Almodóvar's hands, however, Benigno (Javier Cámara) proves to be entirely heterosexual in his orientation. It never occurs to the other characters that the patient on whom he dotes ceaselessly, a comatose ballet student, might be the object of his affections in more than platonic ways.

The core of the film revolves around the relation Benigno has to Alicia and Marco to Lydia, a famous female bullfighter who also

happens to lie comatose in the same hospital. Instead of women bonding as they wait for their men to return, Almodóvar gives us two men
who learn to respect each other and share their intimate thoughts and
emotional insecurities. From Benigno, Marco learns how to talk to her,
to talk to Lydia as if she were fully conscious and aware of his tone and
feelings. The men learn to accept feminine qualities within themselves
without becoming gay characters. Instead, the film confounds the usual
combination of men and action, women and waiting, to demonstrate
some of the texture and complexity that relationships and gender identities actually possess. Almodóvar's films constantly invoke and then
subvert stereotypic images of both straight and gay characters.

MARLON RIGGS AND HIS TESTAMENT TO BLACK MEN
LOVING BLACK MEN: *TONGUES UNTIED*

Nothing epitomizes a cinema dedicated to the defiant desire for same
sex relationships better than Marlon Riggs's *Tongues Untied* (1989).
Riggs's previous work, including his highly successful account of black
stereotyping in the popular media, *Ethnic Notions* (1986, U.S./Canada),
and his later follow-up on the representation of black characters on television, *Color Adjustment* (1992), explored questions of race more than
sexuality. The overall structure of both films begins by establishing a
problem, goes on to explore its complexity, and concludes with a
guardedly optimistic expectation of better things to come. Like other
documentary filmmakers who made work for PBS, Riggs adopted the
network's standard documentary format to address an important issue
neglected by the mainstream media.

For *Tongues Untied*, Riggs chose a freer, more poetic form to stress
an evocative tone of exploration, eroticism, danger, and play. Rather
than introducing a problem and enumerating its complexities with
journalistic reporting, Riggs sought to engage the viewer directly and
viscerally in what it felt to be a black, gay male like himself in the late

1980s. Riggs puts his own body on the line as he begins the film in a darkened, empty studio space, dancing through the darkness in search of something he clearly desires, his naked body moving with guarded, protective steps. From here the film adopts multiple strategies as it sketches out the profiles of a vibrant but conflicted black, gay community. Sometimes there are interviews with other black gay men who discuss their experiences of racial discrimination at the hands of white gays. At other moments Riggs presents poems read and songs sung off-screen that stress the affective quality of gay life and its utopian longings for connection and community. Riggs's composite and complex structure makes *Tongues Untied* an extraordinarily vivid and compelling work.

Although roughly contemporaneous with other documentaries such as *Looking for Langston* (Isaac Julien, 1988, UK), a poetic, subjective reenactment and celebration of the life of black poet Langston Hughes, *Paris Is Burning* (Jennie Livingston, 1990), on the distinct subculture of vogueing and masquerade in the urban gay community, and *Silverlake Life* (Peter Friedman and Tom Joslin, 1993), a moving self-portrait of a gay couple as they struggle with AIDS, *Tongues Untied* remains at the symbolic center of the struggle to make visible the quality and tone, distinctiveness and complexity of a desire that defies dominant social practices and responds to a different cultural ideal.

Social Practices, Cultural Ideals, and Gay Cinema

By the 1990s, *Tongues Untied* had been joined by a considerable number of films that addressed questions of same-sex desire and the struggle to gain civil rights and a public identity in the face of social hostility and oppression. Riggs's film was itself preceded by other important documentaries such as *Before Stonewall* (John Scagliotti, Greta Schiller, 1984), on the early history of gay life in America, and

Word Is Out (Mariposa Collective, 1978), a series of profiles of gays and lesbians who describe what it felt like to live in a homophobic society before the rise of an openly gay community. A more poetic, experimental predecessor, Jean Genet's *Un chant d'amour* (1950, France) gave explicit, ritualized rendition to sexual longing among male prisoners. Not unlike *Zero for Conduct* (Jean Vigo, 1933, France), it reverted to silent cinema and a dreamlike form to represent a defiant desire, which the prison system, rather than suppressing, intensifies, as the guards' desires merge with those of the inmates.

John Greyson also adopted a prison setting in *Lilies* (1996, Canada), a complex, fascinating inquiry into the destructive power of repressed desire. The male inmates stage a play designed to explain how a bishop sealed one prisoner's fate by framing him for murder several years in the past. This same bishop comes to the prison, thinking he has come to hear a confession, but, in fact, lured there on a pretext so that he could be forced to see the play. The prisoners reenact moments from the earlier period when Simon was set up by Bishop Bilodeau in theatrical flashbacks. The film shifts from the harsh prison environment to the florid world of remembered passions with consummate grace. Seeing his past deed come back alive compels the bishop to face, once and for all, the enormous damage done by the homosexual longings and profound jealousies he denied within himself. Although not widely distributed, *Lilies* is a powerful example of how a gay cinema can use cinematic conventions innovatively to challenge social conventions provocatively.

Earlier works like *Chant d'amour* began the process of giving voice to desires that defy the dominant definitions of masculinity and femininity promoted by a sex-gender system that poet and feminist critic Adrienne Rich has termed "compulsory heterosexuality." More recent works often embed themselves within worlds in which gayness is taken for granted and issues take on new inflections. *Law of Desire* (*La ley del deseo*, Pedro Almodóvar, 1987, Spain), *Mysterious Skin* (Gregg Araki,

2004, U.S./Netherlands), *The Adventures of Priscilla, Queen of the Desert* (Stephan Elliott, 1994, Australia), and *Fox and His Friends* (*Faustrecht der Freiheit*, Rainer Werner Fassbinder, 1975, West Germany) explore, respectively, the comic implications of a gay love triangle, the subsequent impact on two men of childhood sexual abuse by a school coach, the strange adventures of three drag queens as they venture into the Australian outback to perform their campy cabaret act in a small town, and the tragic fate of a young man who is taken up and discarded by those wealthier and more powerful than himself. In all these cases, a matter-of-fact, celebratory, or defiant tone comes to replace the anguish and suppressed eroticism of an earlier era. The homosexual's right to exist is no longer in question even if the price exacted by sexual abuse, homophobia, and, in the case of *Fox and His Friends*, class bias, remain vivid.

In each case, these films lead the viewer to identify with openly gay characters and the narrative predicaments they face. Viewers see and experience the world as the gay characters see and experience it rather than from the perspective of straight characters who stereotype and marginalize others. Masculinity takes on a wider range of sexual and gender identities that allow men to choose other men as the objects of their desire without automatically becoming feminized, ostracized, or punished. Gay cinema proposes a distinct vision of what the widespread cultural ideal of love feels like in a realm in which men love men, facing familiar issues of trust, vulnerability, fidelity, and honesty. This vision is what makes a gay cinema a vital part of a broader gay subculture, and, simultaneously, a potential disturbance to social conventions that no longer seem quite as natural as they once did.

11

FEMINISM AND FILM

Feminist Film Criticism and the
Paradigm Shift to Formal-Social Analysis

QUESTIONS OF GENDER AND THE
SOCIAL-HISTORICAL SPECIFICITY OF FILMS

As noted in the preface, "To the Instructor (and the Curious Student)," a different set of assumptions has guided film studies over the last twenty years or so. Prior to this shift the prevailing assumptions gave primacy to the formal elements of film that yielded, at best, timeless works of art. These works, it was argued, engaged all viewers in a comparable way as a result of formal qualities embedded in the work itself. Newcomers had to learn to recognize these qualities so that they too could appreciate the greatness of distinctive works. As a corollary to this view, traditional film history told the story of the rise of the medium from its somewhat elemental and commercial beginnings to its status as an art form comparable to the novel, play, or symphony.

Feminist film theory and criticism challenged the notion of timeless works that had a uniform impact on all viewers, but it also remained highly attentive to the formal qualities of the cinema. Feminist scholars argued that the emotional impact and social significance of a given film, far from being timeless, will vary considerably in different times and places and in relation to the gender of the viewer. The standard genres of the western and melodrama gave evidence of this fact. Men and women typically do not respond to these genres in the same ways, even if the particular film considered is a great classic. Rather than discover aesthetic principles that elevate a film to the stature of the timeless, interpretation can focus on the specific techniques that give a film the particular impact it has for different segments of the audience, a point made especially vivid as women reexamined their response to films in relation to their position as women in society. Feminist criticism also asked if a male standard of aesthetics and taste has shaped a general understanding of art, cinema, greatness, formal sophistication, and timeless achievement, and how to modify it if it has. Other groups, from gays and lesbians to a wide variety of subcultures and minorities, have posed similar questions.

EARLY FEMINIST FILM CRITICISM OF THE 1970S

Women & Film magazine, begun in 1972, first posed the question of why women characters in feature films consistently occupied the recurrent, stereotypical roles of virgin, wife, mother, and seductress or whore. *Women & Film*, produced in Santa Monica, on the living room coffee table of its founders, Siew Hwa Beh and Saunie Salyer, opened the door to a rigorous reexamination of whether the glamour and pizzazz of beautiful stars giving powerful performances, predominantly in stereotypic roles, rightfully defined the limits of female representation.

Despite strong-willed women such as Scarlet O'Hara in *Gone with the Wind* (Victor Fleming, 1939) or numerous characters played by Bette Davis (*All about Eve* [Joseph L. Mankiewicz, 1950], *The Letter* [William Wyler, 1940]) and Joan Crawford (*Mildred Pierce* [Michael Curtiz, 1945], *Johnny Guitar* [Nicholas Ray, 1954]), in the majority of films, women characters remained caught up in a **sex-gender system** that trafficked in their desirability and availability for marriage. (A **sex-gender system** describes the ways in which the biological male and female sexes turn into a socially constructed and ideologically loaded range of sexual and gender identities, some of which may be treated as normal and others as deviant.) Acts of defiant independence were almost always measured in relation to the normal but ideological behavior that led female characters to the altar. As *Christopher Strong* (Dorothy Arzner, 1933), with its daring, defiant heroine indicates, women who step outside their assigned role as object of desire, however powerful or independent they might seem, had few alternatives: capitulation, defeat, or death were the most common choices, even as recently as the otherwise bold and provocative *Thelma and Louise* (Ridley Scott, 1991).

Strong women characters have not fared well in terms of happy endings. When women strike out on their own, using skills and resources normally associated with men, they tend to forfeit their eligibility for marriage and become expendable. In *Christopher Strong*, Katherine Hepburn plays Lady Cynthia Darrington, a daring and successful aviatrix perhaps partly modeled on the real-life Amelia Earhart. She commits the error, however, of falling in love with a married man, Sir Christopher Strong, who happens to be a member of Parliament, making her tacit threat to the established order all the more evident. This proves an impossible love, given the mores of 1930s upper-crust England, and the only honorable recourse she can find for herself is a final, doomed flight in her beloved plane.

Decades later, Thelma and Louise find themselves hunted down for killing in self-defense. Their only recourse: take a flyer over a canyon edge rather than submit to police pursuit. Like Lady Darrington, but as more down-to-earth, salty characters, Thelma and Louise present bold, adventurous figures. The narrative, though, cannot find a way to both preserve their independence and integrate them into society.

Women & Film called for more positive and less stereotypic representations of women. It galvanized readers to rethink the role of women as objects to be looked at and desired, as privately nurturing but publicly passive, as seductresses that men blamed for their own weaknesses. Eventually, these questions broadened into an examination of the formal means of representation as well as the social roles represented. **Looking relations**—the relationships between what the camera sees, what characters see, and what the audience sees—came to the fore as an issue. In film after film it seemed, the gaze of the camera aligned with male characters who beheld alluring women; the audience followed along. This led to asking whether the camera and male characters' gaze was simply a way to tell a story or an ideologically loaded way to reinforce gender hierarchy in terms of who gets to look at whom and under what conditions.

The sexual perversions discussed in Chapter 10, for example, are largely male perversions and involve the use of sight, most obviously voyeurism. This has clear implications for women. Voyeurism and fetishism require an object of desire, typically a woman. Sadism may be practiced on female characters who seduce and betray and must, therefore, be punished. Laura Mulvey's 1985 essay "Visual Pleasure and Narrative Style" dramatically shifted the focus from a call for positive images to the dynamics of the gaze. Mulvey astutely recognized that if the gaze is controlled by men—as it is in a great many film instances—it is women who are the object of this gaze, an objectification that worked to their disadvantage.

In the work of Hitchcock, she argued, women are the targets of sadistic urges, most vividly in the case of Marion Crane in *Psycho* (Alfred Hitchcock, 1960); whereas in the work of Josef von Sternberg, women are the objects of fetishistic veneration, most notably in the figure of Marlene Dietrich's Lola in *The Blue Angel* (1930, Germany). These patterns, she argued, pervade the cinema. Although Mulvey neglected to explore how the male gaze relates to male masochism or to a lesbian gaze attracted to the image of women characters, she convincingly argued that the formal system that linked the camera's gaze with male characters and identified the object of these gazes as women required transformation. For her this meant creating a feminist, avant-garde cinema, but for many feminist filmmakers and critics since it has also meant exploring the dominant system of looking relations with irony and innovation, subverting its usual intent.

Stereotypic Representations of Women

What does the camera see, and is it what men want? This question has a sociological component in the sense that what the camera sees often is women filling stereotypic roles. These roles—virgin, wife, mother, and vamp-seductress—are not invariably or automatically stereotypic. Like the representation of ethnic minorities, they become stereotypic when they serve oppressive ends, usually by categorizing people in objectifying ways that deny their individuality. The person becomes a one-dimensional generalization. Like ethnic stereotypes, the basic female stereotypes were already evident in the early days of cinema.

THE VIRGIN

As a stereotype, the **virgin** represents a male projection onto women of profound innocence and vulnerability. Men can then play the role of strong, resourceful protector. Some women are, of course, in fact virgins, but a stereotypic image of the virgin, as seen in D. W. Griffith's 1911 film *The Lonedale Operator*, or, more recently, in Terrence Malick's *The New World* (2005), about the love between the colonist and explorer John Smith and the virgin daughter (Pocahontas) of "the naturals," as the film calls the local Native Americans, reduces individuality to a single set of traits revolving around innocence and vulnerability.

The damsel in distress of *The Lonedale Operator* signifies helplessness, purity, and potential victimization. It draws on stereotypes of the virgin and the mother that preexisted the cinema. Although resourceful enough to barricade herself in a room and call for help after robbers attack, the operator's fate depends entirely on her rescue by the valiant men who ride to her rescue.

Innocence usually correlates with the virgin's vulnerability as potential victim, but it can also correspond to the image of the **dumb blonde**, a woman who may not actually be a virgin but whose innocence combines with obliviousness regarding her erotic effect on others. Marilyn Monroe—sweet, vulnerable and utterly alluring—often played this role to the hilt as she does in *Monkey Business* (Howard Hawks, 1952). Monroe is Miss Lois Laurel, dimwitted but sexy secretary to the absent-minded and very proper Dr. Barnaby Fulton (Cary Grant). One day Dr. Fulton accidentally ingests a chemical formula that has him romping around as if he were a hormone-crazed teenager again. Grant aims most of his amorous advances at the ever so accommodating and clueless Monroe, but the prospect of any actual sex between them remains as remote as if she were indeed a virgin.

Judy Holliday created a magnificent version of the dumb blonde who isn't so dumb after all in *Born Yesterday* (George Cukor), a role for which she won the 1950 Oscar for Best Actress. She plays Billie Dawn, an unpolished ex-showgirl who has become mistress to an uncouth junkyard millionaire. Her new boyfriend hires a reporter to smooth out some of her many rough edges, only to have her dumbfound everyone with plain-speaking truths that upset more than one applecart. Billie Dawn combines guileless innocence with naïve intelligence. Holliday converted the dumb blonde into a figure of admiration and respect, even if it remained a stereotype and even though the part led to her own typecasting as the perpetual dumb blonde.

The dumb blonde who is not so dumb after all is akin to the **good-bad girl**, the vamp who proves to have a heart of gold, a figure who appears in a number of film noirs. In *Thieves' Highway* (Jules Dassin, 1949), for example, Valentina Cortesa plays a hooker whom the underhanded, conniving dealer Mike Figlia (Lee J. Cobb), pays to seduce a gullible trucker, Nick Garcos (Richard Conte), only to realize how decent Nick really is. She befriends him and helps turn the tables on the corrupt Figlia.

Sometimes the virgin stereotype functions as a dangerous figure whose apparent innocence proves a seductive lure to unwitting men. This figure was immortalized in Vladimir Nabokov's novel *Lolita*, and Stanley Kubrick's film adaptation (1962, UK), in which the twelve-year-old Lolita (Sue Lyons) incites a much older, infatuated Humbert Humbert (James Mason) into the pursuit of a tragic, not to mention pedophilic, love affair.

When *Lolita* (Adrian Lyne, France/U.S.) was remade in 1997 no American studio would distribute it. The Child Pornography Protection Act of 1996 prohibited "any visual depiction that is or appears to be of a minor engaging in sexually explicit conduct." The "or appears to be" clause meant that even if these acts occurred off-screen or did not, in fact, involve a minor, they might still be judged a violation. The remake appeared on cable television and DVD but proved a financial failure, given its $62 million budget and lack of theatrical release.

THE WIFE

Wives, like husbands, are at the center of the enormously complex social dynamics that fuel family life. Melodramas plumb the emotional depths of this role. As a stereotype, the wife takes up a subordinate position as support, or impediment, to her husband. She remains strongly associated with domestic space and family life. She keeps the home fires burning as her husband does battle in the public sphere, or her complaints and worries weaken his resolve to act boldly as a public figure, something he must overcome by showing her how society requires his contribution to the greater good.

In the postwar period, wives and mothers who asserted themselves too forcefully, rather than serving as precursors of the feminist movement, emerged as dangerous, enervating figures who robbed men of their masculinity. The superb paranoid thriller *The Manchurian Candidate* (John Frankenheimer), first made in 1962, carried this motif to new heights. Eleanor Eislin's (Angela Lansbury) son is a war hero who's actually been made into the brainwashed agent of the North Koreans. Eleanor is wife to a spineless U.S. senator who does as she tells him. That is bad enough, but it also turns out that she is her son's Communist controller: on her command, he will assassinate the presidential candidate, making her stooge and husband the presidential front-runner. The film portrays her as a wife and mother, determined to let nothing stop her drive for power. As discussed in Chapter 10, *Rebel without a Cause* (Nicholas Ray, 1955) also presents a blatant portrait of the domineering wife who gets the final word in almost every scene. Her domineering ways, combined with her husband's weak-willed capitulation, cause the young Jim Stark profound anguish.

More recently, wives have continued the traditional stereotype of support or worrier, as in *JFK* (Oliver Stone, 1991) or *No Country for Old Men* (Ethan and Joel Coen, 2007), but they have also taken on more active roles that place them in the public sphere as well. In *A Simple Plan* (Sam Raimi, 1998, U.S./UK/Japan/Germany/France), the pregnant wife (Bridget Fonda) proves more cunning and cold-blooded than her husband. In a more comic vein, *Fargo* (Joel Coen, 1996) and *Mr. and Mrs. Smith* (Doug Liman, 2005) present wives who are every bit the equal of their husbands, and just about everybody else as well. *Fargo*'s Marge Gunderson (Frances McDormand) couples the apparent backwoods simplicity of a rural Minnesotan with astuteness and tenacity that stem from a clear sense of right and wrong. As the pregnant police chief she not only gets her man but completely outshines her husband.

The Mother

As a stereotype, the culturally vital role of mother turns into the be-all and end-all of a woman's life. Like other stereotypes its prejudicial force lies in its reductive power, its ability to obscure a wider range of possibilities and differences beneath a blanket generalization. In this case, qualities that threaten the autonomy of men—nurturing, caring, intimacy—get projected onto the mother who will do anything for the good of her children and nothing to compromise her single-minded devotion to family.

The mother stereotype exaggerates nurturing, sacrificial qualities above all. In this light, it is not uncommon for the mother to be represented as a compassionate figure, giving men the support they need. In *The Best Years of Our Lives* (William Wyler, 1946), an Oscar-winning film that tracks the fate of three ex-GIs after the end of World War II, Myrna Loy plays Milly Stephenson, the loving, understanding wife to her war-traumatized husband, Al (Fredric March). By contrast, Al's war buddy Fred (Dana Andrews) discovers he married a cheating, nightlife-loving woman (Virginia Mayo) who is no one's idea of a devoted mother. Luckily, Fred has Al's virginal daughter Peggy (Teresa Wright) to turn to as a more promising mate, while Homer (Harold Russell) learns that his fiancée Wilma (Cathy O'Donnell) does not pity him but truly loves him despite his loss of both his hands. Milly, Peggy, and Wilma are not all mothers yet, but all three demonstrate the qualities that coalesce into the stereotypic image of the perfect mother.

In *Mildred Pierce*, the title character (played by Joan Crawford), who had enjoyed a comfortable middle-class life, takes a waitress job in a desperate attempt to support her ungrateful and opportunistic daughter. Eventually Mildred realizes she can use her cooking skills to launch a restaurant of her own. Her skill and determination bring financial success, but not enough to put Veda (Ann Blyth) back on course. The film implies that Mildred's singleminded devotion to her entrepreneurial career makes Veda callous and greedy.

Tilda Swinton plays a different kind of mother in *The Deep End* (Scott McGehee and David Siegel, 2001). Money is not a problem, until two male strangers try to blackmail her. It seems that her son's lover, another man, lies dead in their Lake Tahoe boathouse. Margaret (Swinton) believes her son killed him. This drives her to do everything she can, despite complications that push her beyond the law, to protect her son and the family honor. Whatever dimensions her life had before the incriminating murder took place disappear from sight. With the determination of an avenging fury, she throws herself totally into the protection of her son.

SEDUCTRESS, VAMP, *FEMME FATALE*

When a woman's sexual energy condenses into this stereotype it is a projection of male anxieties about autonomy. The stereotype leaves the male blameless for his loss of independence, since he can no longer resist or help himself. Dedication or commitment proves deadly with women whose seductive charms overpower and exploit men.

The ultimate motive of the *femme fatale* proves to be economic gain, revenge, or power, but it is hidden beneath mystery and allure. In film noir, such women roam the urban landscape of nightclubs and bars. They wouldn't dream of staying at home. As women of the night, street, and bar, they become alluring but heartless seductresses who, in vivid contrast to loyal wives, draw unsuspecting men into their erotic spiderweb. Women like Rita Hayworth in *Lady from Shanghai* (Orson Welles, 1947) and *Gilda* (Charles Vidor, 1946), Jane Greer in *Out of the Past* (Jacques Tourneur, 1947), Mary Astor in *The Maltese Falcon* (John Huston, 1941), and Barbara Stanwyck in *Double Indemnity* (Billy Wilder, 1944) exude a power and fascination that had resonance with some feminist critics in the 1960s and '70s because of their ability to get their way, at least until the ending.

Such a character might die or go to jail in the end, but she also conveys a vivid sense of what it feels like to exert power, to fascinate and mesmerize, to control others, to outsmart those who think they can outsmart her, and to use seduction as a weapon of liberation. They are, in many ways, like the charismatic heroes of the populist tradition except that they convert their dedication from public causes to private schemes. The magnetic power of their personalities provides them with an opportunity to break into the all-male world of wealth and privilege.

As a **neo-noir**, a film that returns to the plot twists and visual style of film noir in its 1940s and '50s heyday, John Dahl's *The Last Seduction* (1994) retells a classic story, with a twist. A scheming woman lures men to their doom. But unlike the women in *Double Indemnity* or *The Maltese Falcon*, among others, Bridget Gregory (Linda Fiorentino) leads all the men she meets by the nose, steals a fortune, carries out heartless violence without missing a beat, and gets away with it. Originally released on cable when no theatrical distributor would handle it, *The Last Seduction* has gradually earned considerable acclaim.

Marriage, Family, and Women as the Foundation Stones of Culture

In her seminal 1975 essay, Gayle Rubin raised the idea of a "traffic in women" as the foundation of culture. For her, the trafficking in women occurs when a woman is given away in marriage to someone from another family. This forms the core of the sex-gender system, since it creates basic assumptions about sexual and gender identity within any given culture. Marriage serves as the cornerstone of culture because it is what creates the possibility of social affinity beyond family units. In the majority of cases, especially when marriages are social arrangements guaranteeing status and lineage, a woman's father gives her away and her fiancé takes her. Love, romance, and individual choice are late entrants into the marriage equation and are discussed further below.

Social organization, then, comes at the expense of women. Their circulation from one family or kinship unit to another is what secures their social standing as wives and mothers. They are subordinate, on the one hand, central, on the other, but always caught within a system under the primary control of men. This situation creates the paradox of a gender that is both defined by the physical body and denied full control over that body. This dilemma features prominently in the literature of nineteenth-century British authors like Jane Austen, and the films made from her work such as *Pride and Prejudice* (Robert Z. Leonard, 1940) and *Mansfield Park* (Patricia Rozema, 1999, UK). The law of primogeniture that prevailed in England at that time stipulated that an estate must pass to the eldest son. Daughters could only maintain their social standing by marrying well; without a "well-made marriage" to turn to, destitution, or worse, might befall them. Affairs of the heart could pose a great risk to one's prospects for security.

Ethnographic films have explored the traffic in women from a cross-cultural perspective. One such film is David and Judith MacDougall's *Wedding Camels* (1980, Kenya/Australia), which belongs to their trilogy of ethnographic films on the Turkana, a traditional tribe living in northern Kenya. It centers on the bride-price negotiations between Lorang, father of the potential bride, Akai, and the suitor, Kongu, one of Lorang's age-group associates. (Kongu is the same age as Akai's father.) Akai exists largely as an off-screen presence as the film follows the extended negotiations between the two men that finally establish her value in relation to cattle, camels, and goats. This exchange secures each man's social status and perpetuates the system of which it is an example. In her one interview on camera Akai wishes she could chose a younger man more to her own liking, but admits that such wishes are idle fantasies.

Romantic Love: Passion versus Marriage

Traditionally, marriage signifies a woman's transition from a position of anticipation and readiness as daughter and virgin to active participant in society as wife and mother. This path, or traffic pattern, makes the vamp, seductress, or whore, as well as the female homosexual, dangerous figures who threaten the system's stability by rejecting the belief that a heterosexual marriage is every woman's goal. Until recently, and even now in some cultures, the pursuit of sexual pleasure or use of sexual allure for purposes other than marriage may identify a woman as a tainted or "marked woman." The term is, in fact, the title of a 1930s American film about a group of women who engage in coded prostitution (as hostesses at a clip-joint nightclub) and only find redemption when a crusading district attorney rescues them. What women want has to be what society needs: wives and mothers above all, lest the social fabric disintegrate.

The first significant break with a literal traffic in women via arranged marriage arose during the Middle Ages. Around the twelfth century troubadours in Provence spread the spirit of romantic, often unrequited love for unavailable women that stirred the passions and inspired music and poetry as sublimated versions of sexual desire. This form of love gave passion a voice equal to or greater than socioeconomic calculation and the perpetuation of lineages in arranged marriages. The individual, whose full-blown individuality had become a central tenet of western civilization by the Renaissance, now had a form of love and courtship that did him or her justice.

The cinema consistently celebrates the power of romantic love, from *Titanic* (James Cameron, 1997), which revolves around an extramarital, high/low-class love affair as well as the sinking of the ship, to *Eternal Sunshine of the Spotless Mind* (Michel Gondry, 2004), which, with convoluted passages in time that alter memory and erase desire with each pass, leads to Joel's (Jim Carrey) discovery that his passion for Clementine (Kate Winslet) is far greater than his desire to forget her. These films do not denounce or subvert marriage so much as give far greater latitude to the blossoming of romantic passions, which become a near end in themselves. In them, women, like men, learn that they can desire more for themselves than what society is prepared to offer them.

A film that does subvert the basic tenet of marrying well is the memorable comedy and social satire, *The Graduate* (Mike Nichols, 1967). This film celebrates, until just before the end, romantic love at the expense of career, marriage, and social standing. It presents such love as part folly and part subversive threat. Ben Braddock (Dustin Hoffman), ultimately bored by a loveless liaison with Mrs. Robinson, a woman old enough to be his mother, develops a tremendous passion for her daughter, Elaine (Katherine Ross). After an endless, and what appears to be a fruitless pursuit, Ben defiantly rescues Elaine from a just-concluded wedding ceremony with the "make-out king," the man her parents have arranged for her to marry. In storming into the church and absconding with Elaine, Ben rejects parental authority and the sanctity of holy matrimony in favor of a fully individualized and democratic choice of love object, come what may.

But *The Graduate* also suggests that the desire *to be in love* is a narcissistic act of self-absorption in one's own feelings. It fuels both Ben's and Elaine's passion for each other. Rather than serving as an object of affection, the other serves as a goad. The lovers enjoy the delirious feeling of being in love more than they affirm a mutual commitment to a responsible, productive life together. Ben and Elaine wind up at the back of a bus going nowhere in particular, pushed to the edge of a social system that cannot easily accommodate individual desire at the expense of the social order.

Romantic love protests against arranged marriages that secure fortunes but deny happiness. Its emphasis on courtship and the emotional state of being in love also protests against the all too easy pleasures of the flesh that offer fleeting gratification. In this tradition passion stimulates being in love; this state thrives on being thwarted, blocked, suspended, delayed, and deferred. It is, therefore, perfectly suited for representation in narrative form, where the gap between the story's beginning and ending elaborates on all the obstacles and frustrations that keep the lovers apart.

Romantic comedies amplify the issues of romantic love, often from a strongly female perspective. Will she or won't she (marry)? Is he or isn't he (Mr. Right)? How can she decide and when will she know (if he's the man for her)? Films like *When Harry Met Sally* (Rob Reiner, 1989), *Four Weddings and a Funeral* (Mike Newell, 1994, UK), and *Bridget Jones's Diary* (Sharon Maguire, 2001, UK/France) revolve around the dilemma of finding the right match in a world where social standing and arranged marriages play next to no role at all. *My Big Fat Greek Wedding* (Joel Zwick, 2002, U.S./Canada) returns to the classic formula of the parents who try to nip an inappropriate marriage in the bud: their daughter Toula (Mia Vardalos) has fallen for a non-Greek! Toula has to come to terms with her Greek American identity, and with her parents, and the two families have to get to know each other, which they all do, humorously and successfully.

In *Down with Love* (Peyton Reed, 2003, U.S./Germany), many romantic comedy conventions, especially their 1950s foundation in the films of Doris Day, such as *Pillow Talk* (Michael Gordon, 1959), get gently parodied as Catcher Block (Ewan McGregor) sets out to win the heart of the one woman who doesn't fall at his feet. In fact, Barbara Novak (Renee Zellweger) proves as cunning and manipulative as Catcher himself, making the sparring between them a well-matched battle of wits.

In the Oscar-winning drama *American Beauty* (Sam Mendes, 1999), married, middle-aged Lester (Kevin Spacey) longs for an intimacy that his own sense of irony, and his misguided attraction to Angela (Mena

Suvari), one of his daughter's high school friends, undercuts. Lester's wife Carolyn (Annette Benning) also longs for love, but not with Lester. She seeks it in all the wrong places, principally with an egocentric, rival real estate agent. These misguided efforts combine with a case of mistaken sexual identity to lead to a tragic end for Lester. Director Sam Mendes uses set pieces and incendiary dialogue to intensify the tension between everyday reality and a seemingly impossible ideal. Imaginative and purely cinematic moments, such as the slow motion cascade of roses (American Beauties) that bathe Angela in Lester's fantasy of her, give added density to what it feels like to experience a gulf between actuality and a longed-for ideal that cannot be realized.

The Conflict between Mobility and Domesticity

The male child matures by giving up his emotional dependence on his parents, mainly his mother, to find someone else to meet his needs: a marriage partner. The search for such a partner, plus his social obligations as a man, sends him on an active quest into the world. By contrast, the female child's maturation has traditionally pivoted upon her passive but expectant anticipations of and preparations for the one who will rescue her from life at home. She is Penelope to his Ulysses, Juliet to his Romeo, Scarlet O'Hara to his Rhett Butler. Women now enter the workforce and have considerable freedom over their premarital choices of romance and sex, but these changes seem to multiply plot possibilities more than radically change the representation of the sexes. A woman may now appear as judge or private eye, soldier or executive, but if she faces personal and emotional dilemmas as well as professional ones, they tend to revolve around questions of trust and commitment, intimacy and love that call upon a man to show he is the one for her.

As films explore some of the career possibilities now available to women, the primary strength of melodramas—the rich, if not excessive exploration of emotional ties—has spilled over to other genres. *The Ballad of Little Jo* (Maggie Greenwald, 1993) and *A Thousand Pieces of Gold* (Nancy Kelly, 1991) as westerns, *Aliens* (James Cameron, 1986) and *The Terminator* series (James Cameron, Jonathan Mostow, McG, 1984-2009) as sci-fi, *Unfaithful* (Adrian Lyne, 2002) and *A Walk on the Moon* (Tony Goldwyn, 1999) as dramas of female infidelity, and *Thirteen* (Catherine Hardwicke, 2003) and *Kids* (Larry Clark, 1995) as adolescent coming-of-age stories, all present complex, often unexpected portraits of female characters. They flesh out some sense of what women want beyond the role of wife or mother. They also help define the feminine as more than what it is not, that is, not autonomous, tough-minded, adventurous, mobile, action-oriented, and achievement-driven. Some of these women embody precisely these masculine qualities, and couple them with dependence, trust, and openness.

Films that depict women gaining a profound sense of genuine gratification from activity in the public sphere, without regret or punishment, have special value for their validation of a feminine ethos. This is what makes *A League of Their Own* (Penny Marshall, 1992) such a memorable film. In a way it is a feature fiction version of *The Life and Times of Rosie the Riveter* (Connie Field, 1980): it tells the story of the creation of a women's baseball league during World War II, when the men were away at war. Framed by a reunion from which Dottie (Geena Davis) fondly remembers the past, the film also stresses the centrality of teamwork and how the women overcome their jealousies and doubts for common goals.

In the more offbeat spirit of independent film, this theme is also posed by Susan Streitfeld's *Female Perversions* (1996, U.S./Germany). As an ambitious attorney with a shot at a judgeship, Eve Stephens (Tilda Swinton) demonstrates from the outset that she knows just how to use her sexuality to gild, but not tarnish, her professional career.

Tilda Swinton's appearance and behavior are neither that of the overtly sexual *femme fatale* nor of the no-nonsense and asexual professional. Her legal savvy and fast-paced argumentation, delivered in a spirited style akin to Katherine Hepburn's, prevent her male peers from turning her into a fetish object. Tilda Swinton struggles to sustain a successful career, bail her resentful, self-destructive sister out of trouble, and pursue an amorous relationship on her own terms, terms which do not include marriage in the immediate future. The film suggests how perverse it is for women to find themselves limited to specific social roles that take on stereotypic qualities: the dutiful housewife, the loving mother, the supportive female companion, or, most ominously, the calculating seductress.

Women on the Move: Alternatives to Domesticity

FANTASY AS CREATIVE ESCAPE

The question Gayle Rubin's essay, "The Traffic in Women," ultimately poses is how to construct and represent a female gender identity as such. This challenge involves rethinking the power of an ideology that associates domesticity and passivity with the feminine and mobility and action with the masculine. What might a feminist film aesthetic and a feminine subjectivity look like when filmmakers set out to innovate and see afresh what is often taken for granted in terms of sexual and gender identity?

Women filmmakers have grappled with these issues since the early days of cinema. Many of these earliest efforts are remarkable achievements. Alice Guy-Blaché, for example, began work in film at the turn of the century. She made successful shorts in France and then set up a production company in New Jersey that flourished throughout the 1910s. Lois Weber and Germaine Dulac were among the women who followed in Guy-Blaché's footsteps. They opened the possibility of seeing the world as women see it, of addressing issues from a distinct perspective, and of giving hope for those who might come still later.

Lois Weber entered the fledgling feature film industry in the 1910s and built a solid reputation for work that consistently addressed social issues. In her feature-length narrative *The Blot* (1921, about the "blot" on society caused by the poverty-line wages paid college professors), Weber gives far less attention to the woes of the professor/husband than to those of his wife and daughter who must find ways to make do when the cupboard stands empty. Weber uses multiple point-of-view shots of the plump chicken and other food prominently placed on the kitchen windowsill of their neighbor's home, almost within reach of their own window, to show its tempting physical proximity. The shots give visual form to the idea of class division. Before a concluding plea for better salaries for college professors, Weber chronicles the woes visited upon the family of a man whose love of knowledge is not matched by an ability to provide for those who depend on him.

Germaine Dulac's short fiction film *The Smiling Madame Beudet* (1922, France) is a classic example of early feminist work. It tells a Madame Bovary–like story of a frustrated, unappreciated housewife who, rather than have an affair, takes revenge through fantasies of retribution against her obnoxious husband. Using a variety of innovative film techniques to give visible form to the wife's fantasies, Dulac draws us into the perspective of a woman who, without other women to turn to, discovers an alternative world of liberating daydreams. The film also demonstrates how humor can be a potent weapon in making visible attitudes and values that might otherwise continue to go unseen and unrecognized, when the wife's revenge fantasies function to make her straightlaced husband the butt of more than one joke.

Madame Beudet's fantasies grant her a sense of agency and imaginative potency. She acts in imagined rather than direct ways, but the viewer sees her fantasies of revenge carried out, even though they are framed as fantasies. These fantasies form the centerpiece of this trenchant satire of domestic life and the dull, habitual routines of her husband. Handsome men step out of magazine photographs to hold her in their arms, for example. Dulac demonstrates how a dream world can be a crucial form of resistance to oppressive features of the real world. It is a theme developed in a different direction in Maya Deren's *Meshes of the Afternoon* (Maya Deren and Alexander Hammid, 1943), discussed in Chapter 2.

EMBARKATIONS: WHEN WOMEN SET OUT FROM HOME

Women need not limit their escape from constraints and stereotypes to fantasy. They can also strike out on their own, embarking on alternative versions of the male quest narrative. Female protagonists of such adventures may act in distinctly different ways from their male counterparts, throwing some of the standard expectations and assumptions about narrative, social mobility, and gender into question. Dorothy Arzner, a well-known Hollywood director during the height of the classic Hollywood cinema, from the 1920s to the early 1940s, often gave her films a distinctly feminist slant, as is evident in *Christopher Strong*, discussed earlier, through Katherine Hepburn's free-spirited but doomed aviatrix.

In Arzner's 1940 film *Dance, Girl, Dance*, a group of young women have all left home to build show business careers rather than start a family. Arzner presents this troupe of female dancers who bond closely with one another as a levelheaded and serious group. Ambition and a willingness to sacrifice art (ballet) for economic success (burlesque) leads Bubbles (Lucille Ball) to steer aspiring ballerina-to-be Judy (Maureen O'Hara) toward the more lucrative, if lurid, world of dance-hall entertainment.

Judy, it turns out, proves fearless in confronting the leering gaze of a male audience-within-the-film. Rather than play to their desire to turn her into an erotic object to be ogled, she stops her performance. Standing defiantly on the stage, she looks the men straight in the eye. Remarkably, she also stares directly at the camera; the effect is that she is staring at the film's viewers as well. In a compelling speech, she confronts the reductive assumptions behind her audience's crass mentality. Her actions are entirely in character but still come as a shock. The world of song and dance, of women whose main goal is to entertain men, yields to a powerful feminist critique of the assumptions supporting that very world in terms surprisingly similar to those Laura Mulvey's essay later uses to spell out the formal foundations of a male-centered cinema. Judy's direct address comments to the audience within the film, like the diatribes delivered to the camera in *Do the Right Thing* (Spike Lee, 1989), break the illusion of a self-contained fictional world in which characters pretend to be unaware of the camera's gaze. Judy simultaneously challenges the actual movie audience to rethink its complicity with a seemingly natural system of looks, relayed between the camera and male characters by point-of-view shots that render women as objects of a gaze beyond their control.

In Maggie Greenwald's *The Ballad of Little Jo* genre expectations get disrupted by different means. In this case, a female character stands at the center of a western. After being duped into a deal that leaves her sold off to two men, she manages to escape, but she has nowhere to turn. Josephine Monaghan (Suzy Amis) must adapt to the rugged terrain and lawless ways of the West. The best way to do so? Act and dress like a man, adopt a masculine gender identity and appearance. The audience, however, is constantly aware that her masculinity is a masquerade, a performance, not unlike Rita Hayworth's deliberate performance as a *femme fatale* in *Gilda*, but here, the performance is more as average Joe than seductress. Her ability to pass as a man not only allows her to survive, it suggests that masculinity as performed by male characters may be no more or less a masquerade than it is for Jo. *The Ballad of Little Jo* functions both as a western and as a feminist commentary on the social construction of identity, the management of gender, the regulation of violence, and the qualities of community that the western normally addresses from a very different angle.

   Coming at these issues from a very different angle, Director Russ Meyer gained notoriety for his tales of buxom, aggressive women who broke conventions and defied the social order. Most of his films fit within the exploitation tradition (he began as a photographer for *Playboy* magazine in the 1950s). His soft-core fantasy film *The Immoral Mr. Teas* (1959) involves a salesman who fantasizes seeing all the extremely shapely women he meets nude. Meyer made enough money from this film to self-finance later ventures like *Faster, Pussycat! Kill! Kill!* (1965).

   Meyer typically used his female characters as spectacles in the mold of the seductress but with a heavy dose of dominatrix-like power. *Pussycat* chronicles the adventures of a rogue band of three buxom women led by Varla (Tura Santana), who breaks the back of a foolishly macho guy, drugs and kidnaps his girlfriend, and then arrives at the shack of a crusty old man and his two sons with a scheme to get the money he's hidden away. Varla is all menace and power. She brushes off sweet talk like dust from a table; she doesn't take no for an answer. Her martial arts skills reduce men to whimpering fools, if they survive. She and her band ramble freely across the American West, the idea of cultivating a domestic space utterly irrelevant to their marauding. Some critics have labeled Meyer's *Faster Pussycat*, like his *Wild Gals of the Naked West* (1962), as crude, sexist sensation mongering, but others have recognized a genuinely respectful, if fetishistic, attitude on Meyer's part toward his female characters. These characters, like many of the *femmes fatales* of film noir, present images of powerful, confident, self-assertive women.

   The double-edged quality of Meyer's work spills over to other sex-ploitation films such as *Women in Cages* (Gerardo de Leon, 1971, U.S./Philippines), where Pam Grier leads an escape through a tropical jungle, just one step ahead of her sadistic captors, and with just enough clothing to elude the censors. The female heroines demonstrate a level of skill and competence that stands comparison with that of most male action heroes.

The stilted acting and dialogue in these sexploitation films is not far removed from Madonna's banal lyrics and limited vocal range, coupled to deliberately tawdry and spectacular performances. She, too, projects the image of a powerful, confident, assertive woman. Some have argued that Madonna's stage persona is clearly indebted to Russ Meyer's films. Be that as it may, all these characters and performers cater to the very market in spectacle that someone like Bertolt Brecht abhorred, but they also celebrate powerful women who stand on their own.

A film that doesn't subvert or exploit the genre system as much as invent a distinctive aesthetic outside that system is Julie Dash's *Daughters of the Dust* (1991). The film examines an extended African American family during a moment of major transition. Shot in muted, elegant color, this film recounts the story of the Peazant family at the dawn of the twentieth century. On the single day observed by the film, members of the extended family gather at Ibo Landing, in the Gullah Islands off South Carolina, for one last reunion before several of them leave for the North and the promise of new opportunity.

The family members occupy a space that is neither fully integrated into the economic and racial relations of the mainland nor fully isolated either. This in-between, marginal or liminal zone allows them a degree of autonomy that becomes, in turn, the focus of the narrative. With intermittent commentary by "the unborn child" of Eula, one of Nana Peazant's (the family matriarch's) daughters, the film clearly brackets the present with a deep concern for the past and a voice from the future. What *Daughters of the Dust* discovers in the past is memory and tradition, pain and perseverance. What to cherish and what to abandon is a matter each of the characters must decide for herself as prelude to an epic journey.

The question of how to give voice to a female gender identity that also embraces a distinct ethnic identity preoccupies *Daughters of the Dust*. Nana Peazant (Cora Lee Day), the angular, determined grandmother, holds to fragments of her African culture. For Nana, shells, beads, rituals, and names serve as signifiers of struggles not yet concluded; they are far more than quaint references to bygone days. Nana counsels patience and resolve, acceptance and love. Easily said, these values are put to the test by the zealous Christianity of one daughter, Hagar, and the righteous anger of Nana's son-in-law, Eli. Eli, married to Eula, wants revenge on the white man who raped his wife, leaving her pregnant with "the unborn child."

Hagar wants to judge Yellow Mary, her sister, as a fallen woman. Like the unborn child, Yellow Mary (Barbara O) poses a moral test for her entire family. Yellow Mary returns with a companion, Trula (Trula Hoosier), who is clearly coded to represent an intimate, that is, lesbian, companion. Some of the family members, like some critics and audience members, fail to notice the sexual dimension to this relationship. Dash does not insist on it. Like the puppy love that was overlooked at the time of *Mädchen in Uniform*'s (Leontine Sagan, 1931, Germany) release, discussed below, this understated and partially acknowledged dimension of the two women's relationship underscores the invisible quality to a love that, at the start of the twentieth century, dared not speak its name. Any overt display of lesbianism was intensely taboo and often punishable by law or by the wrath of the mob. Yellow Mary and her companion enjoy a relationship that is not a closeted version of contemporary lesbianism but is instead a complex, distinct relationship, open to those who can see it for what it is and prudently hidden to those who cannot.

Nana Peazant appears to see and understand everything, recognizing that family ties and memory are a sustaining force no matter how complex the tie or painful the memory. Her spirit of fierce remembrance coupled with passionate acceptance persists most vividly in the spirit of "the unborn child" whose voice-over narration conveys a similar determination. The "unborn child" strives to preserve a living memory of the past as an integral part of her own yet to be completed story.

Daughters of the Dust is radical in both form and content. It favors wide shots that include family groups within the frame rather than close-ups of individuals. It also breaks with the usual conventions for continuity editing, especially regarding time. It uses match action editing between shots to join past and present events into one continuous flow of experience. In these ways, Julie Dash adopts qualities both of the griots, African storytellers who would orally recount tribal history in a spirit similar to Nana Peazant's tales, and of African filmmakers, who often favor wide shots that stress the group over the individual. *Daughters of the Dust* offers a vibrant return to the past not to pay a postmodern nostalgic homage to bittersweet memory but to discover the personal and political roots to present-day identity. It stands as a landmark work of independent American cinema and fits comfortably within a postmodernism of resistance.

Documenting Lives Previously Undocumented

The voice of a feminist perspective has transformed narrative expectations and existing film genres. It has also strikingly enriched the field of documentary filmmaking. Early documentaries, in the 1920s and '30s, typically addressed broad social concerns like labor and class division, war and poverty. They commonly adopted a perspective supportive of the policies of the presiding government, which, in turn, often funded the films. Women's issues and feminist perspectives were rare. Identity politics, with its stress on the values and beliefs, behavioral norms and social practices that define minority communities or subcultures, did not yet exist. The quest for a single national

identity, embracing everyone and epitomized by the ideology of the
melting pot, prevailed. Most documentary filmmakers, like their feature fiction counterparts, took masculinity, like whiteness, as a universal standard. An emphasis of broad social issues belonging to the
public sphere meshed readily with the assumption that such issues concerned and could be addressed by men.

The rise, beginning in the 1960s, of the civil rights movement, the
women's movement, the gay and lesbian movement, and struggles of
national liberation from colonized areas around the world promoted
a new form of political activism that moved away from the primarily
class and workplace politics of the past to embrace the rights of individuals to be free of exploitation and oppression on multiple fronts.
The development of lighter, more manageable 16mm equipment in
the 1950s and '60s, like the advent of digital video (DV) today, also
made documentary filmmaking more accessible to a broad spectrum
of political perspectives, of which the women's movement was, without doubt, the most important.

A great example of the rise of feminist documentary is Connie
Field's *The Life and Times of Rosie the Riveter*, released in 1980. This film
reverses the previous relationship of dependence on and subservience
to state programs and goals while recounting social history from
below, from the perspective of women who left their homes to go to
work during World War II. Field subverts key aspects of the conventional story of the war as told in magazine and news reports at the time.
Most significantly, she exposes government-sponsored documentaries
from the period for the propaganda they were.

Connie Field reverses the conventional genre story of men at war.
Five women, three white and two African American, recount their
experience as workers, not housewives, during World War II. The
women tell how they confronted discrimination and injustice in the
workplace and acted decisively to dispel it. Each woman is eager to
contribute to a war against fascism and brutality, but all five discover

that their presence in the workplace reminds their male co-workers of the men who have gone away to war and may not return. The African American Rosies also encounter racism that divides those the war effort would otherwise unite. The women's abilities are derided; their intelligence questioned; their equality denied. These five women do not take rebukes passively. Each woman insists on a chance to prove her mettle and get fair treatment. Each succeeds. Their individual triumphs, however, did not withstand the powerful ideological forces that arose after the war to return women to the home; they each lost the gains they had earned so valiantly.

Field would have told a compelling story of great historical value if she had simply told the stories of the five featured women, but she goes further. Just as the women combat the sexism and discrimination they encounter in the factories and shipyards of wartime America, Field combats the United States government's patronizing newsreels that idealized the war effort. Field repeatedly cuts between her interview subjects and scenes from state-sponsored documentaries. At first, these films urge women to help the cause: apply the skills they have as housewives to the needs of industry. But then, as the war concludes and GIs return, the films make an abrupt about-face and tell women their real place is at home, with their children, supporting their husband's adjustment back to civilian life and his role as family provider.

The disparity between the earnest, heart-felt testimony of the women interviewed and the patronizing tone of the propaganda films produces considerable humor. In one case a male voice-of-God commentary describes how women who work in an airplane assembly plant are "naturally" adept because cutting out plane parts with a blowtorch is like snipping out dress patterns with scissors. And in another breathtaking clip, a female doctor dictates a statement to her secretary: women are constitutionally unsuited for the workplace; their only source of true fulfillment comes as wives and mothers. Field's crosscutting between the five women's testimony, which has the ring of personal truth in every word, and the two-faced efforts to push women into and then back out of the workplace, makes for a powerful demonstration of how the government's focus on broad issues of national interest can be at the considerable expense of specific social groups, in this case, women.

Other documentaries carried forward the historical revisionism of *The Life and Times of Rosie the Riveter*. Rewriting the past and transforming the present were firmly established as principles of feminist filmmaking in work such as *Union Maids* (Jim Klein, Miles Mogulescu, and Julia Reichert, 1976), about women involved in union organizing in the 1930s, *Harlan County, U.S.A.* (Barbara Kopple, 1976), about a coal miners' strike and the impressive role women played in winning it, and *History and Memory* (Rea Tajiri, 1992), about the experience of Japanese Americans in the detention camps they were forced to enter during World War II. Each of these films couples archival footage of past events with first-person narratives captured in interviews. The combination gives a present-day context to past conflicts. Each film generates a tale of history from below, as experienced by ordinary people. All emphasize a feminist perspective on issues—strikes, national identity, immigrant experience—that had originally been told from a universalizing male perspective. Feminist documentaries bring a power and a passion to the interpretation of the past and an understanding of the present that stem from a desire to remember forgotten achievements, unsung heroes, and lost stories.

The Emergence and Significance of a Lesbian Cinema

LIMITATIONS AND CONSTRAINTS IN EARLY FEMINIST FILMS

Early feminist fiction films from the 1970s focused on the experience of women. They avoided the "L" word (lesbian) assiduously. For example, in *Girlfriends* (Claudia Weill, 1978) two women struggle to remain close despite numerous obstacles but remain focused on their heterosexual relationships as their primary source of love; *Clueless* (Amy Heckerling, 1995) offers a feminist satire of high school coming-of-age rituals that does not include same-sex relationships; and *Now and Then* (Lesli Linka Glatter, 1995) celebrates several decades of female friendship as four women remember their childhood friendship while one of them prepares to have a baby. The quality of relationships and their underlying significance receive considerable attention as the affective, emotional core of lived experience, but in a strongly heterosexual context.

These works contributed to a feminist aesthetic by prompting the viewer to understand what it feels like to enter into a world organized around women's subjectivity. Finding the right man vies for centrality with building a network of friendship and support with other women, with the latter effort receiving greater emphasis than the search for Mr. Right. What then looms as the next significant challenge is the possibility of finding a good woman. For women who value relationship and interdependence more than autonomy and single-mindedness, as well as for those who demand equality and recognition for their distinct perspective and values, this seems a logical conclusion. For some the logic goes one step further: women loving women becomes either the natural conclusion of the women's movement or a suppressed and tabooed orientation that must be acknowledged as a vital part of the greater feminist movement.

WOMEN LOVING WOMEN

Changing the dominant state of affairs involves changing the way stories are told in fundamental ways. For example, what if women are looked at as objects of desire not by men but by other women? This dynamic comes to the fore in lesbian-oriented films like *High Art* (Lisa Cholodenko, 1998), which is about the relationship between an ambitious young female editor at a photo magazine and a famous woman photographer who has given up her career to be with another woman. It also figures prominently in *Go Fish* (Rose Troche, 1994), a film about one young woman's courtship of and relationship with another woman, and in *She Must Be Seeing Things* (Sheila McLaughlin, 1987), in which two female lovers sort through layers of jealousy, fantasy, and commitment. In these cases it is women who look at other women, see them as objects of desire rather than role models, and romantically pursue them. The camera no longer relays what a male character sees but what a female character looks at and desires; this makes a new demand on spectators, as one would expect from a radical cinema.

These films also differ from "coming out" stories, in which the primary focus is on an individual's discovery of a homosexual orientation with which she must then come to terms. Films like *High Art* instead posit a subcultural world in which different forms of normal behavior prevail. This shift of social context for the narrative often goes along with a de-emphasis on the need for broad changes in dominant social values and beliefs: the films are not militant attacks on a heterosexual status quo and the institutions and practices that support it. Instead they embrace an alternative subculture and treat its internally dominant norms as natural.

Safely sequestered at home, women characters traditionally never had to give much thought to the idea that another woman might be a suitable lover. In traditional films, even those with strong women characters, other women served as friends and foils but only very rarely as potential objects of desire. One extraordinary exception is Leontine Sagan's 1931 German film, *Mädchen in Uniform*. The film tells the story of schoolgirls and teachers at an all-girls' boarding school. A newcomer to the school quickly develops a crush on one of her instructors, a caring, beautiful young teacher, Fräulein von Bernburg (Dorothy Wieck), who clearly possesses more tender feelings toward her young charges than the disciplinary regime of the school, embodied in a stern headmistress, considers desirable. Each night the girls eagerly look forward to the instructor's ritual act of kissing them good night.

Ostensibly an innocent form of normal behavior, the girls so eagerly await these goodnight kisses that some almost swoon with anticipation. The camera openly dwells on their eagerness in lingering close-ups, drawing the viewer into their state of reverie. For Manuela (Heretha Thiele), what begins as a schoolgirl crush becomes an all-consuming passion, one she cannot resist declaring publicly, despite the obvious risk involved. Nothing good can come from such a love at this point in time (as Hitler is beginning his rise to power) and the film makes very clear the personal and social price exacted from those whose actions and behavior appear to undermine the status quo. That things end badly is less significant than the prolonged, remarkably sympathetic attention given to the experience of unrequited love among women.

Mädchen in Uniform posits homosexual desire as a liberating force of comparable power to political activism. "What is the point of a repressive social order if it cannot repress errant sexual desires?" the school's supporters might ask. This film answers back with a vivid, moving expression of what it feels like to long for love more than discipline, intimacy more than distance, fulfillment more than sacrifice. At moments in the film the pleasure principle is in full bloom. *Mädchen in Uniform* was a truly remarkable, and unique, film. It had no immediate successors, and the rise of Nazism to power in 1933 guaranteed that it would remain a singular exception for some time.

Ironically, on its initial release German critics attacked *Mädchen in Uniform* not for its lesbian content but for its hostility to institutional discipline and social order. The girls' rebellious defiance of disciplinary action threatens the headmistress's control, just as the workers' rebellion in *Metropolis* (Fritz Lang, 1927, Germany) threatened the boss's control of the city. The erotic element is minor compared to this challenge to institutional authority. The homoerotic dimension remained literally unseen, written off by displacement into the trivial category of adolescent puppy love. This failure "to see" parallels the way in which some critics failed to see a sexual dimension to the relationship between Yellow Mary and her companion in *Daughters of the Dust*. In both case a sexual challenge to the heterosexual norm was clearly present, but in a form itself so barely visible and unexpected that it proved impossible to identify.

Some fifty years later women loving women could be openly presented as the primary theme of a film, as it is in *Desert Hearts* (Donna Deitch, 1985). Deitch's pioneering film borrows from the iconography of the western when a college English professor, Vivian Bell (Helen Shaver), leaves the city to visit a remote dude ranch. She soon finds herself drawn to the coltish charms of one of the ranch hands (Patricia Charboneau). The attraction causes much alarm as it moves toward physical consummation. *Desert Hearts* presents their moment of sexual intimacy as a warmly lit, carefully composed, discretely filmed interlude. Like *Word Is Out* (Mariposa Collective, 1978), the early gay and lesbian documentary about the experience of living both closeted and open lives as homosexuals, *Desert Hearts* aims at making the love that dare not speak its name as close to unthreatening normal behavior as possible. There can be no mistake that the primary focus of the film is on love between two women, however. The disconcerted, if not disapproving, looks given the two women by other characters makes the transgressive nature of their behavior fully evident, just as similar looks by observant characters do in *Brokeback Mountain* (Ang Lee, 2005, Canada/U.S.).

Stylistically tame, *Desert Hearts* exploits the conventions of the male journey of self-discovery to take an adventurous approach to the question of desire. It may offer a safe, tasteful representation of women loving women, but it also carries their simmering romance to its physical conclusion. The entire affair remains something of an adventure for Vivian, who has the option of returning to her life back east as an academic. In this it is unlike other films that have followed in its wake such as *Go Fish*. *Go Fish* takes same-sex relationships for granted so that coming out and dealing with the effects of doing so are no longer the main issue.

The central action in *Go Fish* involves the efforts of Max (Guinevere Turner) to establish a successful relationship with a woman she casually meets, Ely (V. S. Brodie). Shot in black and white, in a strongly realistic manner, and told with ironic wit and casual humor, the film introduces the viewer to a group of Max's friends whose individual qualities and social interactions provide the connective tissue for the film. These characters collude with Max as she attempts to develop her relationship with Ely. *Go Fish* conveys the feel and texture of day-to-day life in a world relatively isolated from larger social forces but brimming with a vitality and camaraderie entirely its own. By redefining normal behavior to revolve around the lives of a group of lesbian women and their romantic relationships, *Go Fish* validates the values and beliefs, social practices and cultural ideals of a distinct subculture.

In a highly satiric vein, this is also the goal of *But I'm a Cheerleader* (Jamie Babbit, 1999), in which a teenage cheerleader whose distaste for kissing her boyfriend and other odd behaviors convince her parents she's on the road to lesbianism. They send her to Camp True Directions to be straightened out. The entire film mocks stereotypic notions of gender identity; it casts RuPaul, famous for his extravagant costumes and drag queen performances, for example, as a straight camp counselor. Jamie Babbit's film uses satire and humor to undercut claims of a linkage between dominant forms of normal behavior and any natural order of things.

A Fusion of Sexual and Political Radicalism: *Born in Flames*

Born in Flames (Lizzie Borden, 1983) takes the challenge of constructing an alternative community one step further than the breezy neorealism of *Go Fish*. It adopts elements of the science fiction genre to represent a politically active women's movement, with lesbian and straight, liberal and radical subdivisions. It's set in New York City, some ten years after a democratic-socialist government comes to power. The women characters, and the audience, learn about the new government through fragments taken from newspapers and television, media that the social-democratic government controls. The media fully supports the government; it stresses gradualist rhetoric and co-optive strategies, branding dissidents as troublemakers and a threat to law and order. Like the government, the media casually accepts domestic surveillance, clandestine break-ins, police brutality, sexist conduct, and the promotion of disinformation—all to maintain itself as a purportedly progressive political force.

The issue of same-sex love exists as an easily accepted but underdeveloped and internally unproblematic dimension of the film's landscape. The film's casual acceptance of lesbian love contrasts sharply with the attitudes of the male characters, all affiliated with the state: they assume that lesbianism equates with subversion. Among the government's security forces, lesbianism is part and parcel of what defines these women as a danger to the social order.

The women's efforts, the film implies, require an alternative form of social organization so that a different set of shared values and beliefs can flourish. In one key discussion Zela Wylie (Florynce Kennedy), an old-time but wise radical, asks the younger Adelaide Norris (Jean Satterfield) which she would fear more: one big lion bounding through the door or five hundred mice. As Wylie puts it, "Five hundred mice can do a lot of damage."

The collage structure of the film, with its multiple characters, episodic structure, and parallel plots, is clearly on the side of "five hundred mice." The deliberate discontinuities in the flow of the film—it cuts from one feminist radio station to another, from Adelaide Norris to Zela Wylie, from surveillance footage to the government's media broadcasts, from the moderate editors of *Youth Review* to armed women guerillas in the Western Sahara—resists the construction of an autonomous hero, linear narrative, singular quest, and clear-cut outcome. The collage of scenes, like the activist coalitions themselves, comes together in the name of a common goal: completing the revolution begun but far from concluded by the existing government.

Born in Flames asks when revolutionary violence against the state is justified. Police operations have forced the women DJs and their underground radio stations to move their equipment to mobile units to continue their broadcasts. Their mobility and the grassroots, "five hundred mice" style of organization of the women activists contrast vividly with the ultra-stable phallic transmission tower atop the World Trade Center. The mass medium of television depends on this tower, which becomes a metaphor for the top-down, centralized organized power structure embodied by the government.

Born in Flames contextualizes the destruction of the communication tower as an act of nascent revolution. This destruction cripples the state's ability to propagate lies and distortions. The act contrasts vividly with the rebellious prank of Thelma and Louise when they blow up the big rig of a blatantly sexist trucker in the remote reaches of the American West, discussed in Chapter 4. Their act has all the markings of a wishful fantasy rather than an insurrection: the two women remain loners rather than leaders. Like *The Battle of Algiers* (Gillo Pontecorvo, 1966, Italy/Algeria), *Born in Flames* explores the role of violence in confronting an unresponsive, repressive government.

Feminist Aesthetics and the Power of the Image

The political challenge for a feminist cinema is to make visible subjectivities and perspectives, sensibilities and differences, values and beliefs that have gone unseen and undefined. This is a variant of the challenge for all art: to give tangible form to thoughts and feelings, dreams and longings that lack tangible form. It is a particularly acute challenge for marginalized communities. Both gay and lesbian cinema represent a dramatic coming out of an army of so-called perverts.

Sexual desire and gender identity are no longer organized around heterosexuality, romance, courtship, procreation, and the perpetuation of the nuclear family. Desires once labeled perverse are now adopted as new norms within a specific subculture. This may be regarded as an undesirable avenue that some will not wish to pursue. For others the advent of a lesbian cinema gives tangible form to a forbidden love that stood in need of representation.

The aesthetic breaking of habits, of reconfiguring the norms of action and behavior, of revising the cultural ideals that nourish values and beliefs, calls for a social constituency that can recognize and interpret what they see responsively, but critically. Works such as *Mädchen in Uniform*, *Daughters of the Dust*, *Go Fish*, and *Born in Flames* invite their audiences to rethink the customary and ponder alternatives. In that sense, gay and lesbian cinemas, along with a broader feminist cinema, fulfill a role similar to that of other social movements.

The films discussed in this chapter pointedly address the question of how women who leave home respond when they discover new possibilities and learn that other women may respond to their needs and desires as well as, or better than, men. To establish a space and voice of one's own makes possible a cinema of one's own. These works and numerous others mark out the contours of a feminist aesthetic—from the penetrating analysis of women in a socialist society by Marta Meszaros (*Adoption* [1975, Hungary] and *Free Breathing* [1973, Hungary]) to the defiantly lesbian, avant-garde films of Barbara Hammer (*Dyketactics* [1974] and *Nitrate Kisses* [1992]), and from the offbeat, perturbing films of Jane Campion (*Sweetie* [1989, Australia] and *The Piano* [1993, Australia]) and Catherine Breillat (*Romance* [1999, France] and *36 fillette* [1988, France]) to the ultra-low-budget, autobiographical love stories of Sadie Benning (*If Every Girl Had a Diary* [1990] and *Girl Power* [1993]).

These films clearly reject the marginalized position of women characters in mainstream cinema, no matter how beautiful, powerful, or intriguing such characters may appear. Feminist cinema agrees with Gayle Rubin's assessment of the problematic traffic in women and takes steps to redirect this traffic in new directions. It does so in terms of radical revisions to film form, narrative structure, and social representation. Feminist films, individually and together, make visible worlds we may think we have already seen but which have, in fact, never been seen in quite this way before.

Part III

12

WRITING AND SPEAKING
ABOUT FILM

Basic Types of Writing about Film

Everyone is familiar with writing about film. Every newspaper carries film reviews; every television viewing guide contains summaries and assessments, and numerous websites review films. Most of these commentaries are designed for the general public. They are not part of a course of study nor do they assume any special knowledge. Most are reviews, aimed at indicating whether a given film is worth seeing or not; some are essays, exploring a topic or idea at greater length with readers who are likely to be familiar with the film. Some reviews, especially on the Web, are written by amateurs, a word whose root meaning refers to those who do something for the sheer love of it rather than those who possess special qualifications. Many are written by professional critics, individuals who may or may not have formal training in film study but who are adept at responding to films and conveying their response effectively to readers. Some are the product of essayists and scholars who take particular interest in specific topics and try to explore them in greater detail. Susan Sontag exemplified the essayist with a keen interest in cinema in books like *Against Interpretation*. All of these forms of writing have value. This chapter surveys how to research and write a film review or a critical essay, and includes additional suggestions for giving an oral presentation.

The Film Review as a Decision-Making Aid for Moviegoers

Film reviews serve the same general purpose whether they appear in the *New York Times* or *Film Quarterly*: to provide a guide to potential filmgoers as to which films merit their attention. Many filmgoers are only familiar with reviews; critical essays are less widely available. It is therefore quite natural to take review writing as the standard model for film commentary. It is, in fact, but one type of commentary. In most but not all film study courses, film criticism rather than reviewing is the expected form of writing. For this reason the distinction between the two needs clarification.

Reviews typically offer summaries or descriptions of a given film and an assessment of its quality. They place the film in a larger context such as a genre, national cinema, or a director's overall oeuvre. The review also conveys the writer's judgment about how well the film succeeds in achieving certain goals or meeting certain criteria. A film's ability to engage or entertain an audience is often an important criterion for reviews of mainstream films.

Most importantly, the reviewer is writing for readers who have not yet seen the film. This is why not giving away the ending is a standard convention of the review. Filmgoers consult reviews to help decide whether to see a particular film or not. Hence contextualizing the film, socially or formally, providing a plot summary, and assessing its merits are staples of the film review. Readers can quickly determine, from where the film falls within a larger context and from whether the reviewer was impressed with it or not, if it might interest them.

The majority of reviews are a form of consumer report. They help potential audiences make intelligent decisions by comparing their own taste in films with that of the reviewer.

Film reviews, like reviews of other art forms (novels, plays, paintings, and so on), may assess the quality of a given work in relation to either its formal or social context, or both. A review may discuss the historical issues that the film raises, for example. A film may offer provocative insights into an historical event, the war in Vietnam, for example, as *Apocalypse Now* (Francis Ford Coppola, 1979) did for many reviewers, or a social issue like the responsibilities of a free press as did *Good Night and Good Luck* (George Clooney, 2005, U.S./France/UK/Japan), about the life of the pioneering radio and television journalist Edward R. Murrow. Similarly, a film may expand or revise the formal conventions of a given genre in important ways, as *Unforgiven* (Clint Eastwood, 1992) did for the western, with its portrayal of the aging, reluctant gunfighter and his African American sidekick. Noting whether a film takes an innovative approach to formal qualities—genre conventions, the use of editing, sound, and so on—and whether it presents social issues in a fresh light or simply repeats familiar perspectives and attitudes is valuable information for the potential viewer.

Film reviewers take great pride in their ability to write accessible, compelling commentaries that are a pleasure to read. This is particularly apparent in the ways in which reviewers express a distinct perspective or point of view. Like the filmmaker whose style reveals a great deal about her social attitude or political perspective, the great reviewer's personal style reveals a great deal about his aesthetic taste and social judgment. This style becomes apparent over the course of many reviews. Some value the no-nonsense storytelling abilities of the movies, as Pauline Kael clearly did in her books of collected writings like *I Lost It at the Movies*. Others value the political acuity of filmmakers who explore their social context astutely, as David Denby does in his reviews for the *New Yorker*. A discernible pattern of preferences and values explains why the collected reviews of writers from James Agee and Graham Greene to Pauline Kael and Roger Ebert are well respected and closely studied by many aspiring reviewers.

Film Criticism as a Dialogue among Viewers

Film criticism, as opposed to reviewing, is usually not aimed at a general public deciding how to spend its entertainment dollars. Film criticism is directed at those who have already seen the film in question. It is more like a conversation about the film with others who share some knowledge of it than an assessment of it for those who do not. For this reason film criticism can dispense with plot summary; the story is familiar to the audience. Falling back into recounting what happens is one of the most common flaws among those who are beginning to write film criticism. It almost always proves redundant.

Similarly, a general assessment of the film's quality carries less importance than it does in a review. That the author devotes an essay to a film normally is a clear indication that she feels the film merits extended comment. Perhaps she was moved by the film or disturbed by it in a way she wants to explore and clarify. It is generally very hard to write an extended essay about a film that has not aroused some form of emotional and intellectual response. Without such an underlying stimulus the criticism is apt to be a dry, mechanical rehearsal of recycled arguments and ideas without a distinctly personal form of engagement between author and film. The best criticism, like the best reviewing, stands as the trace of one person's encounter with the cinema. An awareness that something is at stake for the writer in this encounter often makes the essay as memorable as the actual argument presented.

The Goals of Film Criticism
in College Courses

Since critical essay writing by readers of this book will normally take place in the context of a college course involving cinema, the most obvious goal of writing could be "to get a good grade and pass the course." This is a perfectly understandable goal, and the remainder of this chapter is designed to help the student reader achieve it. Other goals may underlie this immediate one, however. They may, in fact, if pursued, facilitate achieving this immediate goal. Writing about a topic for which the author feels some sense of curiosity, conviction, or insight will typically pay off better than writing about a topic that ignites no particular passion and elicits no particular opinion. The reader will sense that she is in the presence of someone who is actively attempting to express a response to a film that has provoked feeling and thought.

Classical rhetoric's original intent was to enable an orator to persuade and convince others of matters that did not yield to the tidiness of logic. The true orator spoke of what mattered deeply, that raised issues of principle, meaning, and value. These motivating factors take shape by means of style, in writing, and delivery, in speaking, as well as through structure. It is style that most fully expresses the thought and feeling of the author, and it is style, as much as a good argument, that distinguishes the best critical essays. Writing style gives evidence of the idiosyncratic or distinctive perspective of a specific person: you. Writers who have a point of view, a particular concern, a distinct thesis convey this point of view with style as well as with ideas. The idiosyncrasies of style indicate the presence of an individual with a specific perspective; such a style moves away from empty jargon, banal rhetoric, and other types of formulaic writing.

FINDING A VOICE OF ONE'S OWN

In *Walk the Line* (James Mangold, 2005, U.S./Germany) the novice Johnny Cash (Joaquin Phoenix) enters a storefront recording studio in Memphis and asks if he can make a record. The proprietor, Sam Phillips (Dallas Roberts), is somewhat amused by this eager young man who can't wait to record a song. OK, sing something, he says in so many words, and Cash launches into a flat, uninspired cover of a traditional gospel song. Phillips cuts him off and tells him the truth: no one wants to hear a song they've already heard a hundred times before sung by someone who lacks conviction. He asks Cash, in so many words, if he were dying and could only sing one song, this would not be it, would it? Johnny has to agree. So, Phillips continues, is there anything he had that he could sing, really sing, from the heart, something he might sing on his Judgment Day?

Cash ponders and then comes up with a song he wrote himself, "Folsom Prison Blues," a song his two backup friends haven't heard and don't know. As soon as he launches into it, the flat, uninspired gospel singer disappears and, as if from a chrysalis, the Johnny Cash we all know suddenly appears, belting out the song with his deep-throated, straightforward, grainy but poetic voice. Of course, this is a fiction film, and like *Ray* (Taylor Hackford, 2004) or *Dreamgirls* (Bill Condon, 2006), it condenses the process of finding one's voice into a single, breathtaking scene. In reality, the process is slower and more arduous, but the end result is no less gratifying. When you write or speak about film, strive to find your own voice, even as it takes a lot longer than it takes Joaquin Phoenix in a fiction film.

The Search for a Topic

Certain recurrent topics tend to characterize film criticism that links the formal qualities of films to the social issues they raise.

- *Political perspective and social attitude.* What kind of political perspective or social attitude does a film adopt toward its subject? This approach also addresses how a film might support a dominant ideology on some levels and subvert or challenge it on others.
- *The individual and society as represented in the film.* Whether problems are a result of "bad apples" or of basic social conditions offers clues to the political perspective a film takes toward the individual and society. The style of the film also presents clues to the filmmaker's attitude toward conflict (binary oppositions or a web of social conflict, for example) and regarding the place of the individual in creating and resolving conflict (as loner or leader). How does the hero change and why? What does the change reveal about her relation to others or to social values and beliefs? Does the filmmaker endorse or question these values and beliefs?
- *Emotional impact.* How does a film achieve its emotional impact or effect? Films give us a sense of what it feels like to enter into a certain type of world, to experience certain things, and to act in certain ways. What aspects of the film work to make this a memorable or disturbing experience? What are the implications of our emotional investment, intellectual engagement, and ideological involvement with this world? If the film creates ambiguities, what is the effect of this ambiguity? What does it achieve or mask?
- *Structure of the narrative.* How does narrative structure operate? How does an overall pattern emerge, what characterizes the core

or middle of the narrative, and how does the film attempt to resolve its initial conflict or tension?

- *The social function of a film.* A film's social function or the use made of it by the larger culture is another topic ripe for exploration. Some films like *The Rocky Horror Picture Show* (Jim Sharman, 1975, UK) become cult favorites. What does the use of the film as a cult favorite suggest about the kind of experience it offers to its devotees? Some like *Thelma and Louise* (Ridley Scott, 1991) or *Brokeback Mountain* (Ang Lee, 2005, U.S./Canada) spark widespread debate. Why and how does this happen? What does the reception of the film suggest about underlying issues in the culture at large?

- *Audience response.* The response of the audience is an area that can be quite fruitful. Some students of film use quantitative methods such as surveys and statistical analyses, and some use qualitative methods such as interviews or consulting reviews and criticism, to observe how different viewers respond to a certain type of film. Carol Clover's insightful book *Men, Women and Chainsaws,* for example, does the latter, examining the reception of slasher films among their largely adolescent male audience.

- *Omissions, absences, and questions of emphasis.* Sometimes what is not said or addressed about an issue that seems to be part and parcel of a general theme can be of great significance. Displacement and condensation (See Chapter 7) may obscure or repress underlying conflicts and shift the emphasis away from real-life sources of conflict. How these operations work and whether they succeed can be examined in detail.

In all these cases, the author typically explores some aspect of the film that intrigues her, something that puzzles, disturbs, angers, excites, or inspires. The emphasis may be on something that is intellectually puzzling such as the "mystery" of what "Rosebud" represents in *Citizen Kane* (Orson Welles, 1941) and how it works to join together the disparate stories told by people whom Kane knew well. It may be an emotional effect such as the shock of seeing vast numbers of dead bodies treated like so much debris in *Night and Fog* (Alain Resnais, 1955, France), as it addresses the extermination of millions in Nazi concentration camps during World War II.

If film criticism addresses very large social issues it does so through a sharply focused lens. It is not man's inhumanity to man in general that should be the theme in a paper on *Night and Fog*, for example, but the *representation* of such a theme in this particular film. The focus must be on films more than issues, and on the ways in which the worlds these films construct provide a distinct view of topics and issues that innumerable other films, novels, nonfiction essays, and books also address.

Attending to a specific film is a vital part of addressing larger topics that could be approached from any number of angles. In the introduction to his translation of Pushkin's poem *Eugene Onegin*, Vladimir Nabokov remarks, "all 'general ideas' (so easily acquired, so profitably resold) must necessarily remain but worn passports allowing their bearers short cuts from one area of ignorance to another." Such a vivid denunciation of "general ideas" is a warning against repeating commonsensical "what everybody knows" generalities that pass for knowledge. Such knowledge runs the risk of turning a deaf ear to particulars, to the specific issues and formal qualities that arise in a concrete context.

One popular "general idea" of this sort is that Hollywood films, or all mass entertainment, are necessarily mindless, empty, unsatisfying, or hollow, or that all art cinema is effete and boring. Such views crop up across the political spectrum. This book urges the reader to attend to the particulars of each film before coming to a final judgment. These particulars amount to a set of differences that make a difference. They amount to the difference between a progressive and a conservative work, an innovative or conventional one, a subversive or conformist film, and between a monolithic view of film types and one attuned to complex variations within a given set of formal or social constraints. This means that writing about film requires some preparation and care lest it become an excuse for promoting predetermined values and beliefs, often in the form of opinion.

Viewing, Re-Viewing, and Remembering Movies

A major step toward writing thoughtfully involves gaining more familiarity with a film than a single viewing allows. This also involves having a written record of what you have seen and your response to it. The average film will have hundreds of edits and run for ninety or more minutes. It is impossible to remember everything.

Further, things seen at the start may not take on their full significance until much later in the film, by which time, because they were not immediately significant, they may have been forgotten. For example, in the very first scene of *Citizen Kane*, Kane drops a glass paperweight from his hand as he dies. White flakes drift through the liquid interior of the paperweight, but it seems a minor detail compared to the fact of his death. Later, this same paperweight appears on a dressing table in the room where Susan Alexander lives, and, later still, the paperweight turns up in her bedroom when Kane goes on a rampage after she leaves him. The links between the paperweight, the snowy scene it depicts, and Susan Alexander as a partial and unsuccessful substitute for his lost mother will not be fully clear unless the viewer notes these appearances, and connects them to the flashbacks to Kane's childhood. This is seldom possible on first viewing.

The first step in interpreting a film is to keep a record of what one sees. The most useful way to do this is by taking notes. Students grow accustomed to doing this for lectures, but the normal practices of viewing movies make this task an uphill struggle in the beginning. It seems to distract from the actual experience of the film. It often causes the viewer to glance away from the screen as she makes a note. It can be difficult to write in the dark. For these reasons it may be best to start modestly and make only some basic notes as reminders: names of characters, the plot in terms of the sequence of scenes, particularly striking dramatic moments, lines of dialogue or stylistic effects, motifs or patterns as they emerge, and, when possible, indications of when a given event occurs in the film's running time to make future reference to a particular scene easier. This is particularly easy when watching a DVD or videocassette, which can be stopped or started. Some basic notes can also be written right after seeing the film while it is still fresh in the mind.

Abbreviations can be very helpful to note taking. Table 12.1 gives some examples of convenient abbreviations.

Table 12.1 Abbreviations for Note Taking

/ = a cut or edit	ECU = extreme close-up
~ = dissolve or fade	ES = establishing shot
→ = leads to or causes	FTB = fade to black
> = more or greater than	Hw = Hollywood
Ca = camera	LS = long shot
char = character(s)	LT = a long take
CU = close-up	MS = medium shot
Dir = director	vo = voice-over

As the practice of taking notes becomes more habitual, a question such as "How does the film achieve its effect on me?" or "How does the film convey its meaning cinematically?" might guide the note-taking process. Instead of noting the progression of the plot, the primary emphasis can fall on identifying the techniques and qualities that make the film distinctive. The camera movement toward and then into the open hotel room window at the very start of *Psycho* (Alfred Hitchcock, 1960), for example, produces a strong sense of voyeurism and omnipotence: the camera acts as if it can single out anyone, enter any space, watch and listen to what anyone has to say, as it takes us into this room where Sam and Marion discuss their frustration with furtive lunchtime trysts. Your note, though, may simply say, "Ca enters room; 2 char, sense of prying." This can be elaborated into a critical comment later.

Reference to the basic narrative principles of selection and arrangement, discussed in Chapter 1, also assist note taking. The filmmaker is constantly selecting one particular way to organize a shot or scene over alternatives. This act of selection yields the image or scene that we see, but it implicitly means that the filmmaker rejected other choices. Noting the use of a close-up is partly a reminder that the director has opted not to use a long or medium shot, for example. When do close-ups or tracking shots appear? Is there something unusual about their use in the film? The selective process that lies behind the appearance of an image may not be as obvious as it appears to be.

Similarly, the arrangement of shots into scenes involves another form of choice. Are events told chronologically? Does the film show us characters as they speak or does it prefer to show the face of characters listening to someone else? Are sounds that occur off-screen a cue to cut to reveal the source of the sound, or are the sounds allowed to remain out of view? For what reason? Do flashbacks occur, and how do they alter our understanding of events? Why do they occur in the pattern they do?

The sum total of these decisions constitutes a film's style, and style, as we've seen, is crucial to a film's overall meaning. The notes made up to this point are part of building up a general knowledge of the film and are not, in most cases, directed toward addressing a particular issue or topic in depth. For film reviewing, this would normally be an adequate amount of preparation for writing a review. For a critical essay, additional notes addressing the specific topic chosen for the essay are often needed. This often means reviewing specific scenes more than once.

Writing the Film Review

Writing a review normally requires additional preparation after taking notes. First, spend some time reflecting on the film's impact. Many films hold our attention for their duration, and it is only later, on reflection, that their derivative or distinctive quality becomes apparent. Rather than focusing on a thematic topic, so essential for the critical essay, the review normally concentrates on describing the look and feel of a given film and assessing its distinctive quality or lack thereof.

Second, make an outline. An outline provides scaffolding for the final review. It will help keep you on track within predetermined limits (of time, for spoken reviews, of space, for written ones). The hierarchical structure of an outline, with points nested inside larger topics, makes it easier to visualize the overall structure of the review and ensures that the flow of the argument moves smoothly and logically from one point to the next.

A simple outline of a review of Martin Scorsese's *Cape Fear* (1991) is shown below. Using this outline, the following review of *Cape Fear* might result. The marginal comments offer additional information about how the review works and how it might be strengthened.

OUTLINE FOR A REVIEW OF *CAPE FEAR*

I. Intro: The eagle at the film's start as a memorable image
   A. How it's shot
   B. What the eagle might symbolize
II. The remake question
   A. The original *Cape Fear*
      1. strengths
      2. weaknesses (industry context and constraints)
III. Scorsese's work and *Cape Fear*'s fit within it
   A. *Goodfellas* (1990), the family and violence
   B. *Taxi Driver* (1976) and the obsessive personality
IV. Assessment of *Cape Fear*

SAMPLE FILM REVIEW: *CAPE FEAR*

① The very first image in *Cape Fear* tells you this will not be a run-of-the-mill experience: the camera gazes at the still, reflective surface of a body of water. Trees and sky shimmer softly across the screen. Then, ② suddenly, with a mysterious and potently ominous jolt, the image of ③ a predatory eagle swoops forward, seemingly out of the azure blue ④ of the sky itself, without origin or explanation.

⑤ Inexplicable evil—this could be the theme of the entire film. Mar-⑥ tin Scorsese has clearly turned the tables on the remake tradition in which floundering directors and hack writers imitate something already done well in the hopes that former glory will now accrue to ⑦ them. Instead, Scorsese has chosen a work that, although powerful, suffered from the limitations and constraints of both star casting and the Production Code. Gregory Peck plays the lawyer whose life is ⑧ turned upside down by a malevolent, vindictive Robert Mitchum. The issue is a clear-cut case of '50s paranoia. Evil, in the form of a venge-ful convict, besieges the white picket fence, Wonder Bread whole-someness of all-American honor and virtue. This, of course, was myth, and the same myths play out today, but in a more realistic vein. We may have it all over many other countries, but we also have our internal failures and corruption, our violence and crime, feuds and vendettas.

(9) Innocence can't pretend to the purity it used to claim.

(10) ————Scorsese's *Goodfellas* was as unrelenting a look at the collapse of human decency as anything made in the ten years prior to its release. It was so insistent on probing and recording the sadistic violence of its gangster family that it turned some viewers off. Scorsese hits the

(11) viewer in the emotional solar plexus. *Cape Fear* is in a similar vein but

(12) with a much tighter, more fully nuanced appreciation for the viewer's willingness to experience fright if also allowed to hold onto some sort of moral and human center. Scorsese provides that for us here with each character. Nick Nolte's Sam Bowden, the lawyer hero, is not the icon of propriety that Peck was; he is fallible but well-intentioned, bending the law and his ethical responsibilities for a higher good. His wife, Leigh, played by Jessica Lange, is both long-suffering in her awareness of her husband's lack of total fidelity and immensely compelling in her determination to maintain her dignity. Their daughter, Danielle Bowden (Juliette Lewis), provides an extremely rich role—at 15 she is on the cusp of maturity, yearning for the personal freedom and sexual liberation that will move her beyond the less than idyllic family life of parental discord she must passively endure. And Robert De Niro, as Max Katy, is, if possible, even closer to the border between lucidity and madness than he was in Scorsese's *Taxi Driver*. Katy is not a *Halloween* (John Carpenter, 1978) type stalker whom we never get to know or care about. He is a complex, warped individual for whom 14 years in jail is one long rehearsal for the punishment he plans to wreak on the lawyer assigned to defend him who didn't do enough,

(13) Sam Bowden. Before he's done, he's drawn the daughter closer to him than to her own father, exposed the ugly underside of desperation, denial, and latent criminality in the initially blasé Nolte, and given

(14) new meaning to the phrase "the man you love to hate." Visceral and compelling, this is Scorsese-style filmmaking at its best.

ANNOTATIONS

① The author assumes a conversational tone that is appropriate for an informal style but could be replaced by a more formal one: "The very first image in *Cape Fear* announces that this will not be a run-of-the-mill experience."

② This word might be deleted: "jolt" itself suggests something "potent."

③ This might be rewritten as "a predatory eagle," or "a powerful eagle" since the fact that it is an image can be taken for granted. It detracts from the stress on the impact of the shot.

④ The first paragraph tries to draw the viewer in by evoking some of the beauty and threat of an image rather than by giving a plot summary. It is a more novelistic approach that helps the viewer grasp what it feels like to watch the film.

⑤ After an evocative opening, the review suggests a more abstract theme that underlies the entire film to help the reader see the film as a whole.

⑥ The name of the director, who is well-known to many viewers, helps them place the film within a formal context (Scorsese's overall work).

⑦ An implicit assessment that this film is superior to the average remake leads off the paragraph. It indicates the writer's high regard for the film.

⑧ The author suggests the actors are a limitation but does not say why. An additional sentence would be helpful: "Peck's image as a decent, upright gentleman exonerates him of any complicity, while Mitchum's idea of evil is a lot of silent menace scrubbed clean of sadistic intent." This last reference to sadism might then allow for a remark about the Production Code: ". . . sadistic intent, which the Production Code would not countenance in any case."

⑨ The author is suggesting that the original film suffered from a black/white idea of good and evil that is not seen as simplistically today. A final sentence might make the link more clear: "And Nick Nolte's Sam Bowden is far from the stalwart innocence of Gregory Peck's original version of the honorable family patriarch."

⑩ This paragraph explores the film's relationship to other films by Scorsese. It will be less helpful to those who have not seen them; it assumes that the readership is fairly film-literate.

⑪ For those who haven't seen the other films, this sentence serves as a caution that his films feature violence and that this can be highly upsetting to some.

⑫ This sentence reinforces the positive assessment and gives a reason for it in the film's mixture of suspense with the desire for moral certainty. By extension, the author is implying that the central character of *Goodfellas*, Henry Hill, presents the viewer with a weaker version of this tension between suspense and morality.

⑬ The discussion of the characters' makeup avoids the risk of giving away too much of the suspense plot and also allows the author to back up his claim that the remake has a more complex view of good and evil.

⑭ The final section, IV. Assessment, is reduced to a phrase, but earlier comments have made it clear that author has high regard for the film.

A review of a foreign film calls for more social context, given the dearth of foreign films on American screens. This sample review is of Zhang Yimou's 1991 film, *Raise the Red Lantern* (China/Hong Kong).

After viewing, making notes, and reflecting on the film, your outline might appear as shown below. Using this outline, the following review of *Raise the Red Lantern* might result. The marginal comments offer additional information about how the review works and how it might be strengthened.

> ## OUTLINE FOR A REVIEW OF *RAISE THE RED LANTERN*
>
> I. Oscar hopes for Chinese film
> II. The basic plot and film type
> III. Visual style
>   A. Framing
>   B. Character/acting
> IV. Overall assessment

SAMPLE REVIEW OF A FOREIGN FILM: *RAISE THE RED LANTERN*

①
② Viewers now have a chance to see one of the five films nominated for Best Foreign Picture last year, *Raise the Red Lantern*. It is, without question, a winner. Zhang Yimou, the director, began as cinematographer on the stunning *Yellow Earth* (Chen Kaige, 1984, China), one of the first Chinese films to break onto the international scene. He has gone on to direct *Red Sorghum* (1987, China), *Ju Dou*
③ (1990, Japan/China), and, now, *Raise the Red Lantern,* each time
④ featuring the remarkably expressive Gong Li as his principal actress.

Raise the Red Lantern, like *Ju Dou,* takes places in the 1920s. And once again, it is sexual politics that provides the metaphor for other, equally contemporary issues. Gong Li plays the new fourth wife of Chen, a much older feudal lord. Soon she finds herself caught up in the rivalry and maneuvering designed to win the master's favor. Chen divides his nights among the four wives. He announces his choice by having a series of red lanterns lit in the courtyard of his partner-to-
⑤ be. Every evening this ritual repeats itself, leaving three wives with nothing to do but brood and plot on how to draw their common master away from their favored rival.

⑥ Each wife has a sharply distinct personality as do many of the family servants, especially Gong Li's personal maid, who harbors dreams of becoming a wife herself. Gong Li, who excels at playing women of pride and determination, quickly learns to use the clan's ancient codes and traditions against her rivals, but with disastrous results. The fractious plotting only divides those who should be natural allies. The women are at the center of the film emotionally and dramatically, but an omnipresent force field of patriarchal and feudalistic power pushes their frustration onto each other.

Raise the Red Lantern, like *Ju Dou,* is a visual masterpiece. Shot with a precise formality, it juxtaposes the opulence of the feudal castle's furnishings with the cold, rigid divisions of its spaces. Time after time, Gong Li's character appears dead center in the frame, ⑦ with a perfectly symmetrical backdrop of windows and walls. Rather than conferring power on her by placing her at the center of things, the effect is to lock her within a vise. Similarly, each wife's courtyard is frequently shot from the tile roof line above. The glowing warmth of the red lanterns remains enclosed by the solid, coffin-like grey ⑧ walls of the buildings. Rather than celebrating the women's sexual power over their master, the composition stresses how thoroughly their power and privilege remain completely contained by the very trappings of feudalism itself.

Master Chen remains a faceless entity throughout the film, shown primarily in long shots and from the rear. Like the contemporary Chinese leadership, Chen benefits from the power of his position far more than from the quality of his character. He is but one more cog in the generations-old succession of rulers who may understand some of the human costs this feudal system entails but have no motivation whatsoever to change it (he is not an evil man, and often seems more compassionate than the wives themselves, being ⑨ able, of course, to afford compassion more easily). *Raise the Red Lantern* is a film of remarkable power.

ANNOTATIONS

① The reviewer is indicating that the film's local release has been delayed but that the film itself has already gained attention. Along with the next sentence it points toward a positive assessment.

②   The reviewer helps contextualize the film by saying something about the director's previous work.

③   The use of adjectives in a review is a practical way to convey an evaluation and offer descriptive hints economically.

④   In a longer review, the importance of metaphors and allegory in films from countries where censorship is an issue might be discussed at greater length.

⑤   The paragraph summarizes the *conflict* embedded in the plot without indicating how the conflict is resolved. This helps the reader gain a sense of what it might feel like to enter into this particular world without knowing how it will conclude.

⑥   This paragraph elaborates on the texture or feel of the film in terms of its basic conflict. The reference to a "force field" also sets up the next paragraph, which describes the stylistic devices used to represent it.

⑦   The author gives a concrete, vivid description of what it feels like to view the character in this way. A longer review could explore further how the sense of vise-like entrapment versus empowerment is achieved.

⑧   The reviewer gives a concrete example of how the force field of patriarchal power is represented in the shots of the architecture of the buildings themselves.

⑨   The final assessment boils down to a sentence, but the previous paragraphs have given a clear sense of why the film merits praise.

Research and Planning for the Critical Essay: *Metropolis*

FINDING BOOKS ABOUT THE ESSAY TOPIC

More than the film review, the critical essay requires finding a topic or issue that interests the writer and engages the reader. The actual mechanics of writing a critical essay are illustrated through an example: an essay on Fritz Lang's classic German film, *Metropolis* (1927). After viewing the film and making notes on it, the next step is to find a specific topic. Two possible topics are

1) "Vision and Power in *Metropolis*." How the film uses light, sight, and space to develop its ultimate theme of social harmony.
2) "The Resolution of Conflict in *Metropolis*." Is the seemingly simple-minded ending only that, or does it have a more complex rationale?

The first topic arises from noticing the importance of lighting, characters looking at other characters, and spatial relationships in the film, the second from thinking about the ending, in which the boss's son gets a worker and his father to shake hands in accord with the film's maxim, "The mediator between head and hands must be the heart."

After identifying a topic, the next two tasks can occur simultaneously: watching the film again, or watching selected portions of it repeatedly, and doing research to develop the topic. These tasks focus on the two main sources of information: **primary source material** and **secondary source material**. **Primary source material** includes the object itself, in this case, the film. Material that provides direct access to the thoughts and actions of those involved in the film such as diaries, oral histories, and autobiographies also counts as **primary source material**. Such material has not undergone a process of analysis and interpretation.

Secondary source material is the body of writing that has accumulated about the primary source material; it represents the process of interpreting the primary material from different perspectives: books, articles, reviews, and so forth about *Metropolis* would all be secondary source material. (**Tertiary source material** is information derived from secondary sources that synthesizes, summarizes, or popularizes this material, such as encyclopedia entries. It may provide helpful background but seldom plays a central role in the actual paper.)

A focused sense of curiosity guides engagement with the primary and secondary source material: the writer views or reads with the idea of gaining additional information or insight for her specific essay. What are the principal spaces in the film and how does Lang use lighting in each? Who looks or gazes at whom and what is the result? How are the "head" and the "hands" represented? What do these body parts stand for as metaphors of the social order? How does the idea of the "heart" shift from Maria as a visionary and mediator to Freder, the boss's son? More questions and ideas will arise, but these give an indication of how the re-viewing process is more sharply motivated than the initial viewing.

The amount of research needed will vary. Some instructors prefer for beginning film students to rely on their powers of observation rather than derive ideas and arguments from others. Research may be discouraged or may be subordinated to developing a direct appreciation for how form and content go together. This is not unusual in introductory courses. In this case, re-viewing and planning the essay will take priority. In other cases, the instructor does expect research. Learning how to do research and contribute to the ongoing critical dialogue is a normal part of any academic discipline, including film study.

Libraries are an invaluable source of information. Getting information about what is available requires searching through online catalogues. Once the extent of the available material is known, what looks most useful can be gathered and read. The most physically available library would be the best place to start, but, with Internet access, preliminary research need not be limited to local libraries. The University of California catalogue, accessible at *http://melvyl.cdlib.org/*, for example, lists books in the entire system of ten campuses, which amounts to one of the largest libraries in the world. Melvyl lists films, videotapes, and DVDs held by all the libraries, including the vast collection of primary source material in the UCLA Film Archives. The Pacific Film Archive, affiliated with the University of California at Berkeley, also has a large number of films, plus program notes and other material related to films held by the archive or shown there. Film information and film notes are accessible through the PFA website: *www.bampfa.berkeley.edu/*.

For some topics, gaining a general sense of the formal or social context in which the film was made may be a useful first step. In this case, tertiary source materials such as film history textbooks or encyclopedia articles are a good place to start. Film history texts such as Kristin Thompson and David Bordwell's *Film History* or David A. Cook's *A History of Narrative Film* cover the German expressionist cinema or silent German cinema and give an overview of this period of film history. Twentieth-century history books such as *The Oxford History of the Twentieth Century* will locate the history of the Weimar Republic in the context of world historical developments. Film encyclopedia's like Ephraim Katz's *The Film Encyclopedia* has useful entries on "Fritz Lang," "Germany," and "Expressionism." This level of information provides useful background; it is not likely to be detailed enough to be quoted or used to develop specific points. For this, secondary source material is needed.

Libraries are particularly valuable for secondary source material, and once a search begins, it often snowballs. Finding one title in a library database can lead to other titles, either through subject categories, or by searching for other work by the same author. Here, for example, is a book listed under the subject *"Metropolis"* in the Melvyl system (this book is likely to be in many other libraries as well, since it is part of a well-received series of short books on important films from the British Film Institute):

Author   Elsaesser, Thomas
Title   Metropolis
Publisher   London : British Film Institute, 2000
Description   87 p.: ill. ; 19 cm
Series   BFI film classics
ISBN   0851707777
Language   English
Subject   Metropolis (Motion picture)
Motion picture plays -- History and criticism
Format   Book

Further searching for books by the same author will lead to Elsaesser's *Weimar Cinema and After*. It is also possible to search through subject headings such as the two given in the Elsaesser entry above ("Metropolis" and "Motion Picture Plays—History and Criticism") or others like "Motion Pictures—Germany." "Motion Pictures—Germany" yielded 758 items on one search, but this can be reduced to 144 by modifying the search to "Motion Pictures—Germany—History." Skimming through these brings up the following title as an example:

Title   A culture of light: cinema and technology in 1920s Germany / Frances Guerin.
Author   Guerin, Frances.
Place/Publisher   Minneapolis : University of Minnesota Press,
Date   c2005.
Description   xxxiv, 314 p. : ill. ; 23 cm.
Notes   Includes bibliographical references (p. 243-305) and index.
Subject Headings   Motion pictures -- Germany -- History.
Cinematography -- Lighting.
Electronic Access   • Contributor biographical information
http://www.loc.gov/catdir/bios/cdc051/2004022373.html
• *Table of contents*
http://www.loc.gov/catdir/toc/ecip051/2004022373.html

The subject heading "Cinematography—Lighting" opens new pos-sibilities, and going to the last website listed, which provides a copy of the table of contents, is a quick way to see if this particular title looks promising. At this website the following information is available:

Contents

Acknowledgments

Introduction

    1. The Electrification of Life, Cinema, and Art

    2. Bringing Cinema to Life through Light: German Film to World War I

    3. Legends of Light and Shadow: The Mythical Past in Algol and Schatten

    4. The Spell of Light: Cinema as Modern Magic in Faust, Der Golem, Siegfried, and Metropolis

    5. Reformulations of Space through Light in Die Strasse, Jenseits der Strasse, and Am Rande der Welt

    6. Dazzled by the Profusion of Lights: Technological Entertainment in Varieté and Sylvester

Conclusion

Notes

Index

Library of Congress Subject Headings for this publication:

Motion pictures -- Germany -- History.

Cinematography -- Lighting.

There is direct reference to *Metropolis* in Chapter 4 of the table of contents. By all indications, this is a book to locate and at least skim.

Each book's footnotes and bibliography will lead to yet other books and articles. Elsaesser's book *Weimar Cinema and After*, for example, not only cites Siegfried Kracauer's *From Caligari to Hitler*, which includes some discussion of *Metropolis* in relation to larger socio-political tendencies during the Weimar Republic (1918-1933), but describes Kracauer's book as the key work with which all future books, including his own, must be in dialogue. This would be a strong recommendation to look at *From Caligari to Hitler* (Princeton University Press, originally published in 1947 and reprinted in more recent editions), to see what it has to say about *Metropolis* and the context in which it locates the film. (The chapter in which Kracauer devotes two pages to the film is entitled, "The Prostitute and the Adolescent," a provocative title, to be sure.) In this way a toehold on the research topic can grow to a firm grounding including more and more information, limited primarily by the needs of the researcher.

FINDING JOURNAL AND MAGAZINE ARTICLES ABOUT THE ESSAY TOPIC

To find information in magazines and journals rather than books, turn to the various indexes available in libraries and online. Indexes provide a list or database of all the articles in a given set of sources. They usually allow searches by author, title, and subject matter. Some allow direct access to the full text of articles; others provide the complete bibliographic reference so that the researcher can more easily locate the material in its original source.

Several indexes are import for film research. The FIAF index, compiled by the International Federation of Film Archives, is a compilation devoted to well-regarded film journals and magazines from around the world. It includes journals such as *Camera Obscura*, *The Velvet Light Trap*, *Iris*, *Film Quarterly*, *Sight and Sound*, *Cineaste*, *Jump Cut*, and many others. (See the box with results from the FIAF search on "Metropolis" below.) It is very comprehensive but will not give information about journals in other disciplines or about popular magazines. For these, indexes such as the Humanities Full Text index, the Humanities Index, and the MLA (Modern Language Association)

International Bibliography are useful. JSTOR, an online search engine, covers most of the humanities. It provides access to numerous topics in a wide range of journals. the *Reader's Guide to Periodical Literature* covers many popular or general-interest magazines such as the *New Yorker*, the *Nation*, and *Atlantic Monthly*. A reference librarian can help point researchers toward particular indexes or search engines, depending on the topic; they often have prepared guide sheets to help the research get started as well.

PARTIAL RESULT OF A SEARCH USING THE FIAF INDEX TO FIND ARTICLES

SO: Literature/Film Quarterly Vol VI nr 4 (Fall 1978); p 342-346.

AU: Roth, Laurent, TI: *Metropolis,* the lights fantastic: semiotic analysis of lighting codes in relation to character and theme;.AT: Article; Illustrations.

SO: Enclitic Vol V nr 1 (Spring 1981); p 20-42.
AU: Mellencamp, Patricia

TI: Oedipus and the robot in *Metropolis.* AB: Discusses *"Metropolis"* with reference to Kracauer, Paul Jensen and others, and woman and special effects. AT: Article; Illustrations.

AB: Abstract, a brief summary of the article's contents

For a film like *Metropolis,* decades of critical response exist. The earliest writings, from the 1920s and '30s, including reviews, are less easily located, and many of these sources are not yet catalogued in online databases; the printed version of these reference sources may have to be consulted in the library. The books and articles indicated above would provide a very useful start for tracking down such material. Indexes for newspapers like the *New York Times* will help locate reviews at the time of the original release. Since *Metropolis* was reedited for its U.S. release, reducing its length considerably and eliminating some subplots almost entirely, reviews from the United States respond to a noticeably different film from the one initially shown in Germany.

Information about contemporary films is more readily available. Periodical indexes of the sort already discussed cover recent issues of journals and magazines. Many recent releases have their own websites, which are easy to find by searching for the film title on the Web. Such sites are usually sponsored by the producer or distributor and will not typically include scholarly discussions or negative reviews. Useful for basic information (cast and crew credits, awards, availability on DVD) and various forms of critical commentary is the International Movie Database (IMDB) website: *www.imdb.com/*. The International Movie Database includes "external reviews" by established film critics and "user comments" by anyone who chooses to submit comments to the site. The external reviewers do not include all the major film critics in the United States by any stretch of the imagination, but IMDB is a helpful place to start.

ASSESSING THE VALUE OF SOURCES, INCLUDING WEB-BASED INFORMATION

The actual source of Web-based material is often unclear. It may be inaccurate, unverified, or linked to a vested interest that is not immediately obvious. A published book undergoes editorial review and, often, peer review (independent scholars or academics assess a manuscript's accuracy and cogency; deficiencies require correction prior to publication). By contrast, a Web posting may have received no editorial review at all. People can post items under pseudonyms, create websites at will, and say what they wish, with no editorial process to uphold a predetermined standard. (The makers of *The Blair Witch Project* [Daniel Myrick and Eduardo Sánchez, 1999] used this quality to advantage when they created a website promoting their fictional film as the freshly discovered video diary of the making of a film about the Blair Witch. It was convincing enough to have some early reviews of the film treat it as a documentary.) A "user comment" on IMDB may have been written by a ten-year-old, perhaps a precocious ten-year-old, but nonetheless someone with a radically different level of experience and knowledge from Robert Ebert (at the *Chicago Sun-Times*), A. O. Scott (at the *New York Times*), or David Denby (at the *New Yorker*).

Even more complicated is the potential for conflicts of interest and political perspectives that color writing that at first glance appears objective. That is to say, all commentary, like all films, conveys something of the author's social attitude or political perspective. What is the author's general orientation? Within what institutional framework was the piece written? The National Rifle Association website contains a wealth of critical commentary on Michael Moore's *Bowling for Columbine* (2002, Canada/U.S./Germany), a film that examines the shooting of students and a teacher at Columbine High School. The commentary is highly critical of Moore's anti-gun, anti-violence position, even caustic, but it can still be useful if the reader is aware of the NRA's policy of staunchly defending the constitutional right to bear arms regardless of tragedies like Columbine. Similarly, the Catholic Legion of Decency will look for and value different things in a film than *Rolling Stone* or the *New York Times*.

Writing the Critical Essay

If the chosen topic is "Vision and Power in *Metropolis*"—how the film uses light, sight, and space to develop its ultimate theme of social harmony—the author would first go through the steps described above, review her notes, and make an outline. A sample outline for a term paper is shown below.

STUDENT OUTLINE FOR A CRITICAL ESSAY ON *METROPOLIS*

I. Power, Vision, and the Gaze
   A. Lighting in Silent German Cinema
   B. Technology
      1. Joh's technology of surveillance and the role of the informer (Grot)
      2. Rotwang's technology of subversion and the role of the robot
   C. The True and False Marias: Vision and Power
      1. True Maria
         a. Visionary
         b. No place of her own
         c. Guiding force for the ultimate mediator (Freder)
         d. Self-effacing and chaste
      2. False Maria
         a. Provocateur
         b. No soul of her own
         c. Instigator of discord among sons of the rulers and between workers and their families
         d. Seductive and erotic
   D. Freder as the Mediator
      1. What his eyes tell him
         a. Maria in the Garden (provokes him to search for her)
            1) His first visit to the machines
            2) His second visit and Worker 11811
         b. His father's helper (Josaphat: fired, Freder befriends the despairing man)
         c. The catacombs and Maria
      2. What his visions tell him
         a. The machines as Moloch (tie to Maria's parable)
         b. The vision of Death (tie to False Maria's incitements)
II. The Ending as Resolution
   A. Maria's role as mediator and the space of the frame (she "sees" what needs to be done; others are paralyzed)
   B. What the viewer "sees" (who's in and out of frame)

This ambitious outline reflects the scope of research, and could support an extended essay; it clearly covers too much territory for a short essay. For a short paper, it should be reduced (perhaps focusing on one subsection) so that the essay is not superficial.

A writer who prefers to think through ideas in advance might add annotations to the outline that spell out what each section will cover in greater detail. For example, under I.C.1.b., "No place of her own," the author might note,

> Maria has no home; unlike Freder and his father, the workers, or, most vividly, Rotwang, Maria moves freely through space—from the garden at the top of the city to the catacombs in its bowels— but has no private space of her own. Not a feminist statement referring to Virginia Woolf's call for women to have "a room of their own," her lack of a special space supports the idea of her as a spiritual figure, a visionary or prophet, someone not entirely *of* this world.

These notes might then be transferred in whole or in part to the written paper.

Here are some general guidelines for the actual writing: (1) refer to the outline regularly and note down any changes in structure that come to mind; (2) when pausing to continue at a later time, make a brief note about what the next point will be; (3) before revising a draft or proofreading a final draft, set the essay aside for a day or two, to allow for more detachment from what has already been written. Necessary changes will thus be easier to spot and make. Use the spelling and grammar checkers that are embedded in your word processing software, but keep in mind that such programs will not find all the errors, and they are of little help in determining if the paragraphs are in the optimal order, open with effective lead sentences, and other questions of style; so finally, (4) proofread your essay personally.

Here is what a draft of a short essay that limits itself to a discussion of the True Maria's qualities, and part of II, "The Ending as Resolution," might look like. The comments that follow this thousand-word essay give additional tips about writing.

SAMPLE CRITICAL ESSAY: "VISION AND POWER IN *METROPOLIS*: LIGHT, SIGHT, SPACE, AND THE PURSUIT OF HARMONY"

(1) "Seeing is believing," but seeing can also be a source of knowledge and power. It can not only confirm what is the case but also suggest how things might be different, if we can just "see" an alternative to what stands before us. Maria's way of seeing sets her apart from the other characters. She is a visionary. She sees something not physically present, and Fritz Lang manages to convey this difference not (2) only through acting but also through his use of light and space. In a city sharply divided into socioeconomic zones, where near slavery is the fate of the workers and the sons of the rulers do nothing but (3) play, Maria enters not as a social activist but as the one who can bring harmony to a hierarchical but unstable social order.

We first meet Maria in the Eternal Gardens, where her entry interrupts Freder just as he is about to kiss a woman assigned to entertain him that day. This interruption will be resolved in the catacombs when he concludes the kiss, but with Maria instead of the anonymous (4) woman. Already, Lang suggests that the sight of Maria has the power to change others, namely Freder. The children accompanying Maria seem nervous, as if they know they are trespassing and seeing things not meant for them, but Maria is a calm guide and urges them to see the occupants of the Gardens as their "brothers." One shot shows them entering in a wedge-like shape, with Maria in the lead; it would seem to foreshadow the final resolution when the wedge-like mass of (5) workers confronts Freder's father, Joh, at the cathedral. Both times, it will be Freder's actions that prove crucial.

Unlike the workers, who occupy drab, box-like houses underground, and the rulers, who command palatial suites at the top of ⑥ the city; unlike Rotwang, who has his own bizarre, almost medieval cottage, and Freder, who has a nicely decorated room of his own, Maria has no place of her own. She seems to float from space to ⑦ space. She transcends physical space. In Lang's universe, this does not make her an early feminist, leaving home and doing the things reserved for men, so much as a spiritual presence, inspiring others by what she "sees" in store for them (a mediator who will bring head ⑧ and hands together). Tellingly, it is when she is trapped, in the beam of light Rotwang uses to corner her, and pinned down, on his laboratory table, as he transfers her appearance to his robot, that Maria ⑨ has the least power. She needs to be able to move through space freely so that she can bring together that which is kept apart. Joh can do the same thing with his surveillance technology (he can see what is happening with the machines without leaving his office). ⑩ Here Lang shows technology in the service of power and control; Maria's visionary spirit is of a different order.

⑪ Maria, in sharp contrast with the False Maria, is also a chaste, ⑫ self-effacing figure. She does not think of herself. She has a sacrificial air about her. After she tells the story of Babel, which is rendered as a "vision" that we are able to see as she speaks, similar to Freder's vision of the machines as Moloch, she utters her fundamental maxim that the heart must mediate between head and hands. She is more curious whether Freder is "the One," the medi- ⑬ ator, than attracted to him as a lover. She asks, "Oh, mediator, have you finally come?" but Freder responds more personally, as someone in love rather than as a potential mediator, "You called me and here I am." Their first kiss is very chaste; Freder seems eager to ⑭ extent it, but Maria is happy to move on to more important things ⑮ like convincing Freder of his destiny. Just as she moves through space with ease, she sacrifices personal happiness, and love, for a higher cause.

16 The ending brings her mission to a conclusion. As Grot, the
worker (and, ironically, Joh's informant among the workers), and Joh
stand frozen to their respective spots, unable to cross the space
17 between them, Maria looks on and "sees" the impasse (Freder is out
of focus in the far right-hand corner of the shot; Maria is also out of
focus but between Grot and Joh). In the next shot, Maria is in focus
and between the two men; Freder is off-screen to the right. Maria
exits screen right and, in the next shot, beseeches Freder to show
them the "heart" they need in order to shake hands. The mediator
18 has arrived and all is well. The spirit of Maria is now in Freder's heart
and she, now off-screen, can exit the scene, having achieved her
goal.

19 Is this ending an example of the "radical naïveté of mythic
clichés" that Elsaesser thinks it is?[1] Corny, yes, but it also seems a
sophisticated expression of a specific political perspective, namely
20 one in which Maria "sees" a world others don't. Rather than alienated workers and isolated rulers, she sees these parts forming a single whole. If there is but one body there can only be one head.
Hands that know they serve a specialized function cannot rebel: a
21 hand cannot exist on its own. Once the workers "see" that they are
not exploited for their labor but are actually part of one harmonious
whole, their discontent will be over. Lang's "mythic cliché" is actu-
22 ally a sales job for spiritual unity based on the benevolent despotism of a strong leader (Joh, the head), willing hands (the workers),
23 and the caring "heart" (Freder). Maria's visions help make this a
believable way to resolve conflict. It represents a conservative political perspective that transcends class division with good feelings.
24 Perhaps this is why Kracauer argues that "Maria's demand that the
heart mediate between hand and brain could well have been formulated by Goebbels."[2]

1. Thomas Elsaesser, *Metropolis* (London: British Film Institute, 2000), p. 17.
2. Siegfried Kracauer, *From Caligari to Hitler: A Psychological History of the German Film*
(Princeton: Princeton University Press, 1946), pp. 163–64.

ANNOTATIONS

① The first sentence is somewhat catchy; it modifies a common saying to suggest a different linkage between sight and power.

② We will expect the paper to substantiate this claim in due course.

③ The first paragraph sets out the paper's theme—Maria stabilizes the existing social order and does so by seeing things differently.

④ This comment is only possible after reviewing the film and seeing how later events are tied to earlier ones.

⑤ This discussion of the wedge and Freder's role is also made possible by reviewing the film and thinking about its internal structure. It serves as an example, or evidence, to support the thesis. Evidence is essential to making a convincing case. Examples taken from the film are a key form of evidence.

⑥ This observation notices something *absent* from the film: Maria has no home. Noticing absences like this one can be as important as noticing what is shown.

⑦ This sentence nearly repeats the previous one; it could be dropped or the two sentences revised into one.

⑧ A reference to the use of light. Maria is one who "sees" things, but excess light seems to be a threat to her powers. This might be pursued.

⑨ Being seen is contrasted with mobility. The author is indirectly contrasting the spotlight as a fixing agent and space as something Maria can transcend.

⑩ A different paper might expand this point to argue that, if utopian, *Metropolis* seems to have a very ambivalent attitude toward technology.

⑪ The lead sentence nicely introduces the main point of the paragraph, which comes almost directly from the outline.

⑫ This and the previous sentence nearly repeat each other. Useful for emphasis, the two might also be combined.

⑬   A good point but a long sentence. It could be broken into two or three separate sentences when the essay is rewritten as a final draft.

⑭   The author meant "extend:" this is a typo but because "extent" is a word, a spell check program will not catch it. Proofreading is necessary to eliminate errors like this.

⑮   The author returns to the theme of space and suggests that getting "tied down" to a partner is contrary to her mission.

⑯   A good point but not necessarily relevant to this paper; it could be deleted.

⑰   The author employs close analysis of the last shots, no doubt achieved by pausing a tape or DVD to make careful notes.

⑱   Although she is "squeezed out" of the final reconciliation, the author sees Maria's spiritual mission accomplished. From a feminist point of view, she might be seen as excluded from the "boy's club," but the latter reading would take the paper in a different direction. Such a paper might see Maria as a fetish object that is spiritualized to deny it effective agency in confronting class conflict and gender hierarchy.

⑲   The last paragraph refers to two books and argues in support of Kracauer over Elsaesser. This involves research of the sort that may not be expected for all papers, but, if it is, this is a good example of making critical use of the source material.

⑳   Formal writing usually avoids contractions and colloquialisms such as "blow away," "spaced out," "sketchy," etc.

㉑   These comments take up questions of ideology without making ideology the central topic; the essay stays focused on the film.

㉒   "Sales job" is a bit colloquial; "an illusory form" might be preferable in a formal context.

㉓   This returns to the opening sentence and shows how power can be linked to seeing.

㉔   A good ending that positions the "social harmony" achieved as
one the Nazis could exploit. Generally, it is preferable not to end
a paper with a quotation, since it deflects from the author's own
voice. One more sentence could be added; but, by shifting consideration to a larger frame, the quote works well in this case. It
assumes knowledge of who Joseph Goebbels was (Hitler's Minister for Propaganda), but this is reasonable for a course that takes
up German cinema.

Giving Credit Where Credit Is Due

Giving credit to ideas or statements that belong to others holds as
much importance in film studies as it does in other areas. Other writers deserve credit for their point of view and their way of saying
things. This is true even if the gist of someone else's thought is para-
phrased: if the summary or paraphrase represents the original thoughts
of someone else, this indebtedness must be formally acknowledged.
Failing to honor this principle amounts to **plagiarism**. **Plagiarism** is,
in essence, intellectual fraud: the author claims the ideas of someone
else as his own. The result gives a fraudulent impression. This activity clouds the core goal of speaking in a voice of one's own. Plagiarism,
like the deliberate misrepresentation of facts, is an extremely serious
offense; it can lead to substantial penalties.

  How can credit be given where credit is due? Several systems of
formal acknowledgment exist. This section offers a brief overview of
the key components of two widely used systems. Various reference
books provide details on how to use these systems. These longer
works explain how to handle any eventuality and give the proper
credit (See Further Reading below).

The humanities use two main systems for giving credit.

- The Note system involves the use of numerical superscripts in the text, such as the two in the sample essay above, and then footnotes, on the same page, or endnotes, at the end of the essay, which provide bibliographic detail. Most software programs arrange notes in numerical order automatically. Endnotes are generally preferred to footnotes.
- The Works Cited system involves the use of a "key" in the text to identify each source in minimal fashion, usually with the author of the source and the page number cited, or just the page number if the author's name already appears in the text. The essay writer generates an alphabetical list of "Works Cited" that spells out the bibliographic details and places it at the end of the essay. This system puts names and page numbers in the text rather than just superscripts, but, by listing all the references in one alphabetical list, it makes referring to these works easier for the reader.

USING THE NOTE SYSTEM FOR GIVING CREDIT

The sample essay demonstrates how to use this system. The superscript numbers are entered in the text by the software system, and the author then enters the bibliographic information in the endnote. An example would be:

If, in an article, the author said about *Metropolis*,

Martin Koerber states that "It is impossible to imagine a retrospective of classic German silent films, science fiction films, or cinematic architecture films (the series of possible topics could go on and on) without this film." [1]

1. Martin Koerber, "Notes on the Proliferation of Metropolis," *The Moving Image* 2, no. 1 (Spring 2002): 74.

With this system a list of works cited is not necessary, since all the cited works appear in the endnotes. Reference books give full information about how to cite other sources including films, television shows, documents, unpublished material, interviews, newspaper reviews or articles, and material from the Web.

USING THE WORKS CITED SYSTEM FOR GIVING CREDIT

Taking the citations in the sample essay, they would appear like this in the "Works Cited" system:

> . . . Is this ending an example of the "radical naïveté of mythic clichés" that Elsaesser thinks it is (17)? . . .
>
> . . . Perhaps this is why Kracauer argues that "Maria's demand that the heart mediate between hand and brain could well have been formulated by Goebbels" (163-64).

On a new page at the end of the essay:

Works Cited (listed alphabetically)

Elsaesser, Thomas. *Metropolis*. London: British Film Institute, 2000.

Kracauer, Siegfried. *From Caligari to Hitler: A Psychological History of the German Film*. Princeton: Princeton University Press, 1946.

Note that the format of the citations is somewhat different in the list of "Works Cited" than it was in the endnotes, but they both provide the same information. To determine format, refer to a style reference book (often a professor will let you know what book to use), but note that it is always better to provide an acknowledgment in a somewhat incorrect format than to omit an acknowledgment altogether.

Making Oral Presentations

Oral presentations typically involve classroom presentations in groups or individually, but they also include presentations at conferences or before community groups, as well as radio and television commentary, especially reviews. Most commentary is written out in advance, even if it is designed to appear spontaneous. Delivery—how the text is actually spoken, with what expressivity, rhythm, volume, tone, gesture, expression, and so on—is important and should always take into consideration the nature of the audience. (A classroom presentation does not call for the same degree of emphasis as a political campaign speech.) Delivery is a public speaking skill that involves shifting from reading a text dryly to presenting a prepared text expressively. It does not require assuming a role as acting does, but it does call for speaking in an engaging, affective way.

Classroom presentations are usually more informal than other spoken formats. A fully written text may not be necessary and may, in fact, be difficult to deliver as effectively as an outline of points or ideas, where the speaker finds the exact words to express the basic ideas on the spot. This latter strategy ensures some of the naturalness that a more experienced speaker may perfect by mastering public speaking techniques.

Oral presentations involve the same forms of research and preparation as written papers. In addition to researching the topic and preparing an outline, or, in some cases, a written text to deliver, here are some other guidelines for preparing a presentation:

- Have a clear, distinct focus and convey it at the start. Presentations are normally brief (even papers delivered at professional societies are seldom more than twenty minutes). Be clear what the point of the overall presentation is. Make the progression through the material as clear as possible, since the audience does not have the benefit of a written text they can reread or read at different speeds. Avoid description, plot summary, or skimming over large amounts of material. A specific, well-made point is usually better than generalizations.

- Develop no more than three to four main points in a ten-minute presentation, where each point is the equivalent of a well-developed paragraph. Longer presentations can include a larger number of points, but should still build around a single focus or theme. Be sure to back up general claims with concrete reference to the film or films. Examples, whether they involve clips or not, link the general argument to the specific work in question.

- Clips, selected portions from films, are often very useful supporting material, but there are pitfalls in showing clips. Be sure in advance that the equipment is familiar to you and functioning properly. Have someone else start and stop clips for you if possible. Select clips with great care. If the audience has not seen the entire film some background or context may be necessary. If the audience has seen the film, be sure to indicate, explicitly, what specific point you wish to make with the clip. Avoid showing the clip and assuming the audience will see what you wish them to see. Don't let the clip "speak for itself."

  The clip can be run backwards or in slow motion or paused; the volume can be turned down: all these techniques allow you to point out specific qualities that you find significant in the clip or to point to the filmmaker's use of techniques such as lighting, composition, or editing. If there are multiple clips, transferring them all to one DVD can simplify the playback process. PowerPoint presentations achieve a similar result.

- Rehearse the presentation out loud, preferably with someone who can provide feedback. This will help you find the right words if the text is not fully written. It will also help identify weak points or faulty transitions, which often become more apparent when rehearsing. Work on delivery and make sure the clips come at appropriate points in the talk. This exercise will also help give a realistic sense of how long the presentation will take. A common mistake is to underestimate the time it takes to deliver an oral presentation. Running out of time is a stressful experience; rehearsal will help avoid it. Come prepared, with a plan in mind for how to jump to the final point and to state it briefly if time runs short.

These are general guidelines. Other more specific requirements may arise from the particular circumstances in which the presentation is made.

Further Reading

Chapter 1 Film as a Language

Many concepts treated in this book involve elaborations of ideas discussed in the works mentioned here. The language of film is the core topic of every other introductory film textbook. Just about any of them will provide more examples and detail about the formal dimensions of cinema, but they lack extended discussion of the social context for film. Many of them have a strong emphasis on the fiction film. The works listed on avant-garde and documentary film below will compensate for this deficiency. Introductory texts come out with a new edition every three or so years. Newer editions will cover more recent films and sometimes include new topics as well. For that reason the most recent edition of these textbooks is recommended.

A useful introduction to film language that does take note of the social context to a greater degree than many others is Timothy Corrigan and Patricia White, *The Film Experience: An Introduction* (Boston: Bedford/St. Martin's, 2004). More focused on aesthetic qualities is Richard Barsam, *Looking at Movies* (New York: 3d ed. Norton, 2009). Widely used, with a style that some find dry but that covers less well-known formal qualities, is David Bordwell and Kristin Thompson, *Film Art: An Introduction* (Boston: McGraw-Hill, 2008). At least a few dozen other textbooks exist; any of them will provide coverage of the basic concepts.

A classic introduction to the general topic of semiotics is Ferdinand de Saussure's *Course in General Linguistics* (New York: McGraw-Hill, 1966). Christian Metz's *Film Language* (New York: Oxford University Press, 1974) was an early application of semiotics to film. His several books pioneered an understanding of film as a semiotic system. Over time he shifted from an empirical view of semiotics as the language of films to a psychoanalytic view of the relationship between spectators and text. His *The Imaginary Signifier: Psychoanalysis and the Cinema* (Bloomington: Indiana University Press, 1982) demonstrates this shift. Kaja Silverman's excellent book, *The Subject of Semiotics* (New York: Oxford University Press, 1983), provides a very comprehensive discussion of the value of semiotics in the analysis of films.

Chapter 2 Forms of Cinematic Engagement and the Avant-Garde Film

The idea of cinematic worlds derives from Nelson Goodman's suggestive book *Ways of Worldmaking* (Indianapolis: Hackett, 1978). A good exploration of how films generate an affective sense of what it feels like to inhabit a particular world is Richard Dyer's essay, "Entertainment and Utopia," in Bill Nichols, ed., *Movies and Methods*, vol. 2 (Berkeley: University of California Press, 1985). Further reading suggested for chapters 3 and 4 includes some additional material on rhetoric and narrative discourse. Poetic discourse, in relation to the avant-garde, receives treatment in Bordwell and Thompson's *Film Art: An Introduction*.

Among the most useful books on the avant-garde are Scott MacDonald's series of volumes devoted to interviews with different directors: *A Critical Cinema: Interviews with Independent Filmmakers*, vols. 1–5 (Berkeley: University of California Press, 1988-2006), as well as his *Avant-Garde Film: Motion Studies* (New York: Cambridge University Press, 1993). A classic, formally oriented study of the American avant-garde is P. Adams Sitney's *Visionary Film: The American Avant-Garde* (New York: Oxford University Press, 1974). More recent works that take up political aspects of avant-garde filmmaking include Lauren Rabinowitz, *Points of Resistance: Women, Power and Politics in the New York Avant-Garde Cinema, 1943-71* (Urbana: University of Illinois, 1991), Bill Nichols, *Maya Deren and the American Avant-Garde* (Berkeley: University of California Press, 2001), and Jeffrey Skoller, *Shadows, Specters, Shards: Making Meaning in Avant-Garde Film* (Minneapolis: University of Minnesota Press, 2005). A great deal of additional information on individual films and directors can be found using the research tools (databases and indexes) discussed in Chapter 12.

Chapter 3 Documentary Film

The field of documentary film study has blossomed in the last fifteen years. Of particular value as a starting point is Erik Barnouw's *Documentary: A History of the Non-Fiction Film* (New York: Oxford University Press, 1992). This book is somewhat dated, but it provides an excellent overview of the development of documentary film around the world from its beginnings until the 1980s. Among more recent work, Bill Nichols's *Introduction to Documentary* (Bloomington: Indiana University Press, 2001) provides a comprehensive conceptual overview of the many forms and strategies of documentary film, while Barry Keith Grant and Jeannette Sloniowski's edited volume *Documenting the Documentary* (Detroit: Wayne State University Press, 1998) gathers together insightful essays on over two dozen important documentary films.

On a more advanced level, Michael Renov's edited collection *Theorizing Documentary* (New York: Routledge, 1993) and Bill Nichols's *Representing Reality* (Bloomington: Indiana University Press, 1991) take up a wide range of issues. Both articles and books also abound on individual films, directors, and more specialized topics like the mockumentary and docudrama.

Chapter 4 Storytelling and Narrative Fiction Film

This is a vast topic, and there is only room here to highlight a few works that provide further orientation to the chapter's specific topics. Most other introductory film textbooks elaborate on the formal qualities of narrative film in considerable detail. Many also discuss different interpretative strategies and offer sample essays. These can supplement the discussion here. Film histories such as David Cook's *A History of Narrative Film* (New York: Norton, 1996) and Kristin Thompson and David Bordwell's *Film History: An Introduction*

(Boston: McGraw-Hill, 2003) supply more comprehensive accounts of the history of narrative film's development around the world.

Many of the basic principles of narrative structure first arise in Aristotle's *Poetics*. With regard to film specifically, Robert Kolker's *The Altering Eye* (Oxford: Oxford University Press, 1983) discusses European and Third World cinemas as clear alternatives to mainstream Hollywood. It combines a keen eye for form with sensitivity to underlying social issues. The text is available online at *http://otal.umd.edu/~rkolker/AlteringEye*. David Bordwell's *Narration and the Fiction Film* (Madison: University of Wisconsin Press, 1985) offers considerable detail on the differences between mainstream or Hollywood cinema and art cinema from a more strictly formal perspective. Anthologies such as those edited by Leo Braudy and Marshall Cohen (*Film Theory and Criticism* [New York: Oxford University Press, 2009]), Bill Nichols (*Movies and Methods* [Berkeley: University of California Press, vol. 1, 1976; vol. 2, 1985]), and Robert Stam and Toby Miller (*Film and Theory* [Malden, MA: Blackwell, 2000]) all include numerous essays that deal with narrative principles and with individual films or directors.

Laura Mulvey's *Citizen Kane* (London: BFI, 1992) provides a valuable critical analysis and can lead to further work on the film. It is part of a series from the BFI (British Film Institute) that covers numerous films in short, very readable books that are, unfortunately, of uneven quality. Robin Wood's *Hitchcock's Films Revisited* (New York: Columbia University Press, 2002) offers insightful analyses of *Psycho* (1960), *Vertigo* (1958), and other films, as well as a valuable overview of his work. Mark Shiel's *Italian Neorealism: Rebuilding the Cinematic City* (London: Wallflower Press, 2006) sketches out a useful overview of this important film movement and its relation to Italian social history. The classic but also dated English-language work on auteur theory is Andrew Sarris's *The American Cinema: Directors and Directions 1929-1968* (New York: Da Capo Press, 1996). Books by Robin Wood such as *Hitchcock's Films Revisited* (New York: Columbia University Press, 1989) and *Howard Hawks* (Detroit: Wayne State University Press, 2006) are models of auteur analysis, as is Jim Kitses's *Horizons West: Directing the Western from John Ford to Clint Eastwood* (London: BFI, 2004), which skillfully combines genre analysis with auteur study.

Mentioned also in the chapter on writing about film, Timothy Corrigan's *A Short Guide to Writing about Film* (New York: Pearson/Longman, 2007) offers many valuable suggestions for viewing and writing about narrative films.

Chapter 5 Three Fundamental Styles: Realism, Modernism, and Postmodernism

These three styles receive considerable attention in related disciplines such as art history and literature; the suggestions here focus on film study. Most introductory textbooks on film address realism well, especially in terms of how it relates to continuity editing, but they usually oppose it to fantasy, a somewhat limited dichotomy. Roy Armes, *Patterns of Realism* (New York: Garland, 1986), and Christopher Williams, editor, *Realism and the Cinema* (London: Routledge and Kegan Paul, 1980), provide helpful overviews of realism and some of the larger issues it raises; they also refer the reader to other references. Plato's Allegory of the Cave occurs in Book VII of *The Republic*. Roland Barthes takes up the difference between the mythic and historical, or the ideological and analytical, in his book *Mythologies* (New York: Hill and Wang, 1972), an entertaining early work whose premises he later modified. His *Image, Music, Text* (New York: Noonday Press, 1988) includes several insightful essays on the cinema and the effects of realism, and his close analysis of narrative in a novella by Balzac, *S/Z* (London: Jonathan Cape, 1975), develops the idea that "readerly" works offer the accessibility of realism and that "writerly" works present the challenges of modernism. These writings have been quite influential in film studies.

Discussions of Soviet silent cinema in introductory film textbooks elaborate on the concept of montage and sometimes link it to the larger movements of modernism, internationally, and constructivism, in the Soviet Union. Each of the various movements within modernism—surrealism, German expressionism, Dada, and so on—have numerous works devoted to them. Of particular value in film study is Thomas Elsaesser's study of German cinema, *Weimar Cinema and After: Germany's Historical Imaginary* (New York: Routledge, 2000). Though focused on literature, *The Cambridge Introduction to*

Modernism (Cambridge: Cambridge University Press, 2007) covers most of the key topics that also pertain to film such as issues of interpretation, the rise of an avant-garde, and the diversity of modernist movements. Walter Benjamin's collected essays, *Illuminations* (New York: Schocken Press, 2007), contains a rich variety of essays that have found wide use among film scholars. Sergei Eisenstein wrote several books that offer valuable insights into his filmmaking theory and practice. *Film Form*, edited by Jay Leyda (New York: Harcourt, Brace, 1969), provides an excellent point of entry.

The Cambridge Companion to Postmodernism (Cambridge: Cambridge University Press, 2004) includes an essay on postmodernism and film, as does *The Routledge Companion to Postmodernism* (London: Routledge, 2005). Nicholas Mirzoeff's *An Introduction to Visual Culture* (London: Routledge, 1999) gives a useful overview of postmodernism but, like most work in cultural studies, tends to neglect film study in favor of television, advertising, and other media. Jeffrey Dawson's *The Cinema of Cool* (New York: Applause Press, 1995) offers valuable insights into Quentin Tarantino's relationship to postmodernism. Fredric Jameson's *Postmodernism, or, the Logic of Late Capitalism* (Durham, NC: Duke University Press, 1991) is an advanced text that sets out the key elements of postmodernism in its early pages before turning to more specific issues. Hal Foster's work, especially *The Return of the Real* (Cambridge, MA: M.I.T. Press, 1996), examines postmodernism and politics extensively.

Chapter 6 The Institutional and National Contexts:
Hollywood and Beyond

Hollywood and other national film industries have attracted many to write about them. Commentary ranges from fan gossip to highly sophisticated financial analysis. Further readings here generally place the motion picture industry in a social context but also give attention to the formal qualities that distinguish mainstream, studio-based filmmaking. David Cook's *A History of Narrative Film* is only one among many introductory film history textbooks that provide a valuable introduction to narrative storytelling in Hollywood and elsewhere. Kristin Thompson and David Bordwell's *Film History: An Introductory* is more exhaustive and gives useful surveys of many national cinemas as well as of the Hollywood studio system. These books will point to other books that cover individual national cinemas in greater detail.

Thomas Schatz's *The Genius of the System: Hollywood Filmmaking in the Studio Era* (New York: Henry Holt and Company, 1996) is a lively overview of the studio filmmaking process. Robert Sklar's *Movie-Made America: A Cultural History of American Movies* (New York: Vintage Books, 1994) is somewhat dated but provides a socially oriented look at Hollywood film production. David Bordwell, Janet Staiger, and Kristin Thompson's *The Classical Hollywood Cinema: Film Style and Mode of Production to 1960* (New York: Columbia University Press, 1985), an advanced text, is the inspiration for the discussion here of standardization and differentiation in Hollywood filmmaking. Two books on the production code are Thomas Doherty's *Hollywood's Censor: Joseph I. Breen and the Production Code Administration* (New York: Columbia University Press, 2007) and Leonard Leff and Jerold Simmons's *The Dame in the Kimono: Hollywood Censorship and the Production Code* (Lexington: University Press of Kentucky, 2001). The historical background for current issues involving the Hollywood rating system are well covered in Stephen Vaughn's *Freedom and Entertainment: Rating the Movies in an Age of New Media* (New York: Cambridge University Press, 2006).

The story of the Hollywood blacklist is told comprehensively in Larry Ceplair and Steve Englund's *The Inquisition in Hollywood: Politics in the Film Community, 1930-1960* (Urbana: University of Illinois Press, 2003). Another account, focused more precisely on the moral implications and political consequences of informing on others or refusing to inform, is Victor Navasky's *Naming Names* (New York: Penguin, 1981). Paul Lazarus's *The Film Producer: A Handbook for Producing* (New York: St. Martin's Press, 1992) gives a nuts-and-bolts view of what a producer does, including questions of budget.

Chapter 7 Genre Films and the Resolution of Social Conflict

A considerable literature exists on specific genres and on genre films in general. Thomas Schatz's *Hollywood Genres: Formulas, Filmmaking, and the Studio System* (New York: McGraw-Hill, 1981) examines the major genres and how they relate to basic principles of Hollywood filmmaking. Peter Biskind's *Seeing*

Is Believing: How Hollywood Taught Us to Stop Worrying and Love the Fifties (New York: Henry Holt, 2000) is a lively and witty book that explores how fifties genre films adopted both conservative and progressive views of major issues such as race, class, technology, and hierarchy. My discussion in Chapter 7 is strongly indebted to Biskind's work.

Robin Wood, in his writings on Hollywood films, including *Hollywood from Vietnam to Reagan . . . and Beyond* (New York: Columbia University Press, 2003) and *Hitchcock's Films Revisited*, explores the tensions between the vision of individual directors and the genre system, as well as the social implications of different genres. He is particularly insightful on the horror film in his essay, "An Introduction to the American Horror Film," in Nichols, ed., *Movies and Methods*, vol. 2. Nick Browne has edited *Refiguring American Film Genres: History and Theory* (Berkeley: University of California Press, 1998), which includes an excellent assortment of articles on different topics and genres.

Jim Kitses's *Horizons West: Directing the Western from John Ford to Clint Eastwood* is a superb study of this central genre. He describes many of the binary oppositions that inform the genre and gives astute interpretations of the distinctive style of some of the genre's most important directors. Vivian Sobchack's *Screening Space: The American Science-Fiction Film* (New Brunswick, NJ: Rutgers University Press, 1997) provides an excellent introduction to this important genre, and Carol Clover's *Men, Women and Chainsaws: Gender in the Modern Horror Film* (Princeton, NJ: Princeton University Press, 1992) incisively examines horror films in relation to the gender identity of both characters and audience. Paul Feyerabend's *Against Method* (London, New York: Verso: 1988) does not address genre films directly. It is a far-ranging study of scientific method but his comments have applicability to the arts and to a consideration of genre films in particular.

The concepts of condensation and displacement derive from the work of Sigmund Freud but are not used here as psychoanalytic tools as much as interpretative ones. His discussion of these two processes as key elements of dreams occurs in *The Interpretation of Dreams* (Oxford: Oxford University Press, 1999). An early and extremely stimulating use of these ideas occurs in Charles Eckert's essay, "The Anatomy of a Proletarian Film: Warner's *Marked Woman*," in Nichols, ed., *Movies and Methods*, vol. 2.

Chapter 8 Ideology and the Cinema

Discussion of ideology shifted markedly in the 1970s as the older notions of ideology as false beliefs and the existence of an ideology-free zone of reason and truth gave way to the idea of ideology as a necessary social condition. Freed from its essentially negative connotations, ideology became understood as a form of social glue that guided customary or habitual forms of exchange. Crucial to this shift from Karl Marx and Frederick Engel's treatment of the concept in *The German Ideology* (Amherst, NY: Prometheus Books, 1998) was Louis Althusser's essay, "Ideology and the Ideological State Apparatuses," in *Lenin and Philosophy* (New York: Monthly Review Press, 2001). Althusser sketched out the key elements of a theory of ideology as something more unconscious than conscious, habitual rather than chosen. Slavoj Žižek has edited a valuable series of more recent essays that further develop, and debate, Althusser's ideas, in *Mapping Ideology* (London: Verso, 1994). Antonio Gramsci did the most to develop the idea of hegemony. A collection of writings from the time he spent in prison in the 1920s, *Prison Notebooks* (New York: Columbia University Press, 1992), show how he developed this concept to account for the phenomenon that an apparently oppressive social system (for him, capitalism) could gain the loyalty of those it oppressed.

An early application of ideological analysis to film, coupled to elements of psychoanalysis, was a joint essay by editors at the French journal, *Cahiers du Cinema*: "John Ford's *Young Mr. Lincoln*" (collected in Bill Nichols, ed., *Movies and Methods*, vol. 1). In it, the authors adopt traces of an auteur analysis of Ford's work but focus on the relations of power within the film and how these relations expose contradictions in the social fabric. Jean-Louis Comolli and Jean Narboni's "Cinema/Ideology/Criticism," also in *Movies and Methods*, vol. 1, sketched out various possible relationships between film form and political content. It served as the basis for the similar sketch provided in Chapter 8 on "Possible Relationships between Aesthetic Form and Social Impact." Other important essays that developed the concept of ideology in relation to film include Jean-Louis Baudry, "Ideological Effects of the Cinematographic Apparatus," Stephen Heath, "*Jaws*, Ideology and Film Theory," and Dana Polan, "A Brechtian Cinema? Toward a Politics of Self-Reflexive Cinema," all in *Movies and Methods*, vol. 2. These are relatively advanced texts and are often discussed in courses devoted to film theory.

John Willett gathered together many of the core writings of Brecht in his *Brecht on Theatre* (ed. and trans. by Willett, New York: Hill and Wang, 1966). Table 9.1 makes use of some of the elaboration Brecht provides in his essays. All quotations from Brecht come from this book.

Although it may not be specifically addressed, a great deal of film criticism that examines ethnicity, gender, or class in film assumes an understanding of ideology of the sort discussed in this chapter.

Chapter 9 Race and Ethnicity in Film

W. E. B. Du Bois's *The Souls of Black Folk* (New York: Signet, 1995) is a classic study in race relations and has had tremendous influence since it was first published in 1903. Important discussions of race and ethnicity dominate a number of recent books. Robert Stam and Ella Shohat's *Unthinking Eurocentrism: Multiculturalism and the Media* (London: Routledge, 1994) looks at mainstream Hollywood film, independent cinema, and Third World film to expose underlying tensions and contradictions surrounding race, ethnicity, and the postcolonial legacy of imperialism. A bit overwhelming in its numerous references, it nonetheless provides a superb orientation to the basic issues of ethnic representation.

Donald Bogle's *Toms, Coons, Mulattoes, Mammies, and Bucks: An Interpretive History of Blacks in American Films* (New York: Continuum, 2001) was a pioneering work in the field of racial stereotypes in film. The 2001 fourth edition surveys this issue across the entire twentieth century. Mark Reid's *Black Lenses, Black Voices: African American Film Now* (Lanham, MD: Rowman & Littlefield, 2005) brings a contemporary perspective to the discussion of race, while the essays in Lester Friedman's edited volume, *Unspeakable Images: Ethnicity and the American Cinema* (Urbana: University of Illinois Press, 1991), take up with insight questions of ethnic representation among different groups and from different perspectives. Jane Gaines's "White Privilege and Looking Relations: Race and Gender in Feminist Film Theory" (*Screen* 29.4 [Fall 1988]: 12–27) is a groundbreaking article that introduced questions of race to feminist film theory at a time when its focus was almost entirely on gender. Richard Dyer's *White* (London: Routledge, 1997) explores the representation of race in cinema brilliantly; he does not limit his exploration to stereotypes and the representation of minorities, but expands his study to take on the idea of whiteness and the role it plays in film as well.

The idea of the Other comes from philosophical investigations and has taken on more politically loaded significance in the work of Louis Althusser and Slavoj Žižek, among others. In a highly accessible publication, *Anti-Semite and Jew* (New York: Schocken Books, 1995), written at the close of World War II, Jean-Paul Sartre explored the concept of the Other and the ambivalence of attraction/repulsion characteristic of the bigot. Sartre includes a discussion of the liberal's treatment of Jews. It is an early look at the distribution of prejudice across the political spectrum. Roland Barthes extends Sartre's discussion to take on the universalizing tendency of liberalism in general in his essay on the "Family of Man" photographic exhibit in his book *Mythologies* (New York: Hill and Wang, 1972). The book consists of numerous, very short, trenchant essays on topics from wrestling to wine, including one on Barthes's response to this photography exhibit. Sartre's work was also one of the catalysts for the pointedly anti-colonial writing of Frantz Fanon. His *Black Skin, White Masks* (New York: Grove Press, 1967) and *The Wretched of the Earth* (New York: Grove Press, 1963) have had considerable influence on the study of racial representation in the cinema.

The web of conflict derives from the work of Georg Simmel, a nineteenth-century German sociologist who wrote *Conflict: the Web of Group Affiliations* (New York: Free Press, 1964), an important corrective to Marx's binary opposition between two inevitably opposed classes, the workers and owners, most vividly expressed in his and Friedrich Engel's *The Communist Manifesto* (New York: Russell & Russell, 1963). The study of binary oppositions, however, has played a significant role in genre study where such oppositions often provide the main source of dramatic conflict. *Horizons West*, mentioned above in the readings for chapters 4 and 7, exemplifies the careful use of oppositions.

The alternative to conflict, the social symbolic, receives deft treatment in Richard Dyer's illuminating article, "Entertainment and Utopia," collected in Nichols, ed., *Movies and Methods*, vol. 2. Using the term utopia rather than social symbolic, Dyer discusses how a variety of entertainment forms, most notably musicals, create a strong sense of what it might feel like to enter into a utopian domain of harmony, happiness, and community.

Chapter 10 Gender and Masculinity

Many of the concepts discussed here, especially the so-called perversions such as voyeurism, have received considerable attention in feminist film criticism and theory. Some of these works are mentioned below, and the Further Readings for Chapter 11 provide additional reference to some of the key works in this area.

The understanding of individual identity as an amalgam of biological sex, sexual identity or orientation, and gender identity goes back to the work of Sigmund Freud. His *Introductory Lectures to Psychoanalysis* (New York: Liveright, 1977), *Civilization and Its Discontents* (New York: Norton, 1962), *The Ego and the Id* (New York: Norton, 1962), *Three Essays on the Theory of Sexuality* (New York: Basic Books, 1962), and *Beyond the Pleasure Principle* (New York, Liveright, 1950) all offer valuable insights. His models of mental functioning and therapeutic treatment have been modified or rejected by many in the mental health field but his basic concepts continue to find application in the humanities, including film study. A useful survey of assumptions about gender through western European history is Thomas Laqueur, *Making Sex: Body and Gender from the Greeks to Freud* (Cambridge, MA: Harvard University Press, 1992), and an incisive treatment of contemporary debate is Judith Butler, *Undoing Gender* (New York: Routledge, 2004).

The *performance* and *pleasure principles* were terms made popular by Herbert Marcuse in *Eros and Civilization* (Boston: Beacon, 1974); he adapted aspects of Freud's thoughts to a less individualistic and more socially rooted context. A look at recent films from a comparable perspective is Susan Jeffords's *Hard Bodies: Hollywood Masculinity in the Reagan Era* (New Brunswick, NJ: Rutgers University Press, 1994). She examines box-office hits such as the *Rambo* (Ted Kotcheff, George P. Cosmatos, and Peter MacDonald, 1982–1988) and *Star Wars* (George Lucas, Irvin Kershner, and Richard Marquand, 1977–1983) in relation to gender, politics, and American culture generally.

The relevance of voyeurism and fetishism to cinema was first analyzed closely in Laura Mulvey's essay, "Visual Pleasure and Narrative Cinema" (in

Nichols, ed., *Movies and Methods*, vol. 2, and a number of other anthologies). A comparable essay plumbing the depths of masochism and its relation to the cinema is Gaylyn Studlar's "Masochism and the Perverse Pleasures of the Cinema," also in *Movies and Methods*, vol. 2. Studlar's book *In the Realm of Pleasure: Von Sternberg, Dietrich and the Masochistic Aesthetic* (New York: Columbia University Press, 1988) examines masochism in greater detail. A wide-ranging study of sexual identity and gender in relation to the horror film is Barry Keith Grant, ed., *The Dread of Difference: Gender and the Horror Film* (Austin: University of Texas Press, 1996).

The discussion of adolescence and masculinity in this chapter derives from my article, "Sons at the Brink of Manhood: Utopian Moments in Male Subjectivity" (*East-West Journal* 4.1 [1989]: 27–43). Phillip Harper's *Are We Not Men? Masculine Anxiety and the Problem of African-American Identity* (New York: Oxford University Press, 1996) complicates questions of sexuality and gender by addressing them in relation to racism and race.

An excellent survey of gay representation in Hollywood cinema occurs in the pioneering book by Vito Russo, *The Celluloid Closet: Homosexuality in the Movies* (New York: Harper & Row, 1987). The book formed the basis for Rob Epstein and Jeffrey Friedman's documentary film of the same name. Thomas Waugh, *The Fruit Machine: Twenty Years of Writing on Queer Cinema* (Durham, NC: Duke University Press, 2000) gathers together a prominent gay film critic's commentaries on a wide range of films. Richard Dyer's *Now You See It: Studies on Lesbian and Gay Film* (London: Routledge, 2003) provides thoughtful analyses of a considerable number of films, both classic and contemporary, from a gay perspective. *Jump Cut* magazine, whose back issues are all available online, has consistently published provocative, informed reviews and commentaries on films that raise issues of gender as well as of gay and lesbian representation.

Chapter 11 Feminism and Film

Several books initially published some time ago provide valuable surveys of the representation of women in films and address the function of stereotypes. Molly Haskell's *From Reverence to Rape: The Treatment of Women in the Movies* (New York: Holt, Rinehart and Winston, 1974) was an early, journalistic-style account of women in film and has been updated to include recent work. Janice R.

Welsch's *Film Archetypes: Sisters, Mistresses, Mothers and Daughters* (New York: Arno Press, 1978) was another early contribution to the study of the representation of women. Patricia Erens collects a number of valuable essays in *Issues in Feminist Film Criticism* (Bloomington: Indiana University Press, 1990), and E. Ann Kaplan has edited a very solid collection of essays on the representation of women, *Feminism and Film* (Oxford: Oxford University Press, 2000).

Gayle Rubin's essay "The Traffic in Women" can be found in Rayna Reiter, ed., *Toward an Anthropology of Women* (New York: Monthly Review Press, 1975). The essay draws on anthropology, psychoanalysis, and Marxism but is a reasonably accessible account of a complex subject.

Laura Mulvey's "Visual Pleasure and Narrative Cinema" exists in a number of different film studies anthologies as well as in Mulvey's book *Visual and Other Pleasures* (Bloomington: Indiana University Press, 1989). Her stress on voyeurism, sadism, and fetishism finds its complement in Studlar's emphasis on masochism, mentioned in Chapter 10. *Women in Film Noir* (London: BFI, 1998), edited by E. Ann Kaplan, is an excellent collection of essays on the representation of women in this classic cycle of films. A comparable but somewhat more advanced book for the horror film is Barbara Creed's *The Monstrous-Feminine: Film, Feminism, Psychoanalysis* (London: Routledge, 1993).

Many early women directors have received book-length treatment. Alison McMahan, for example, has given us *Alice Guy Blaché: Lost Visionary of the Cinema* (New York: Continuum, 2003); Judith Mayne has written an incisive study, *Directed by Dorothy Arzner* (Bloomington: Indiana University Press, 1994), and Anthony Slide's *Lois Weber: The Director Who Lost Her Way in History* (Westport, CT: Greenwood Press, 1996) provides an informative look at Weber's career. Maya Deren, discussed in the avant-garde chapter, is the subject of an anthology, *Maya Deren and the American Avant-Garde* (Berkeley: University of California Press, 2001), edited by Bill Nichols.

Just as there are books about *Do the Right Thing* and *JFK* that include commentary and the screenplay, there is a comparable book, edited and written by Julie Dash, Toni Cade Bambara, and bell hooks, *Daughters of the Dust: The Making of an African American Woman's Film* (New York: New Press, 1992). The subject of documentary film and women is well represented by the essays collected by Chris Holmlund and Cynthia Fuchs in *Between the Sheets, In the Streets: Queer, Lesbian, Gay Documentary* (Minneapolis: University of Minnesota Press, 1997).

The writings of prominent critic B. Ruby Rich in her *Chick Flicks: Theories and Memories of the Feminist Film Movement* (Durham, NC: Duke University Press, 1998) include a number of essays on lesbian cinema. Teresa de Lauretis's *Alice Doesn't: Feminism, Semiotics, Cinema* (Bloomington: Indiana University Press, 1984) is an early, theoretical introduction to feminist film analysis. De Lauretis has written several other books that pursue related issues in depth. Richard Dyer edited *Now You See It: Studies on Lesbian and Gay Film*, a valuable collection of essays.

Chapter 12 Writing and Speaking about Film

Among the most useful books are Joseph Gibaldi, *MLA Handbook for Writers of Research Papers*, 6th edition (New York: Modern Language Association of America, 2009) and *Chicago Manual of Style*, 15th edition (Chicago: University of Chicago Press, 2003). These later editions include much more information about citing electronic (Web-based) sources than earlier editions. The *Chicago Manual of Style* is an invaluable resource for anyone planning to continue studies in the humanities, since it provides a comprehensive treatment of research methods and the accepted forms of citation.

Of particular value to the film student is Timothy Corrigan's *A Short Guide to Writing about Film*, since it includes chapters on watching movies and making notes and is entirely devoted to writing about film. Bill Nichols's *Introduction to Documentary* includes a chapter on how to write essays on documentary. Almost all introductory film textbooks also cover essay writing. Corrigan and White's *The Film Experience* is particularly helpful. It recaps many of the points in *A Short Guide to Writing about Film* and includes a discussion of how to go about exploring film theory and film analysis further. Bordwell and Thompson's *Film Art* may be somewhat overwhelming in the number of films analyzed and in the emphasis on formal detail but it, too, guides the reader toward alternative approaches and covers the specific mechanics of essay writing. Richard Barsam's *Looking at Movies* is another good choice for help with the basics of writing essays on film topics. None of these other introductory texts provide guidance for film reviewing or oral presentations, but they do cover essay writing in considerable detail.

GLOSSARY

180-degree rule This rule, actually a convention that can be violated, states that if an imaginary line is drawn between the two characters and treated as if it were the diameter of a circle surrounding the two characters, all of the shots should be taken from one side of that line. This allows each character to remain on the same side of the screen, which, in turn, minimizes any possible confusion on the part of the audience as cuts occur.

above-the-line Expenses for personnel that exercise a significant degree of creative control over the entire project.

A-budget films Films that, while not necessarily blockbusters, have enough funding to utilize a studio's best above-the-line talent.

ADR (additional dialogue recording) The replacement of sync sound recorded on the set or location with more carefully controlled recording done on a sound stage as the original scene is projected on a screen in front of the actors.

alienation effect The Brechtian strategy of distancing viewers from emotional **identification** with characters while heightening engagement with a broader social perspective. Also referred to as **distanciation**.

allegory A sustained narrative in which the characters and situations stand for more general qualities or states.

alternative ideologies Ideologies that resist, challenge, or subvert the **dominant ideology**. Alternate ideologies are the belief systems of individuals who feel that the dominant ideology does not meet their needs.

ancillary markets Markets that comprise all the ways a film can be distributed outside of U.S. movie theaters: foreign theater distribution, foreign and domestic television, cable, satellite, and online, as well as videotape and DVD rental and sales.

aperture The camera opening through which light passes. Most film cameras, be they film-based or digital, use a variable aperture lens: the amount of light admitted through the lens can be adjusted to take account of different lighting conditions. The aperture is made smaller in bright light and larger in dim light to achieve a well-exposed image. The size of the aperture is usually measured in **f-stops**.

apparent motion The phenomenon that every frame of a film strip is a still image, but when these frames are projected successively, at 24 frames per second, the eye perceives movement rather than slight shifts or jumps in position from one frame to the next.

art cinema A cinema of interiority (mental states) and style more than of exteriority (physical action) and plot. Often associated with European cinema, but these qualities appear in some films from many nations, including the United States.

artisanal production Production that occurs outside the context of a full-blown film industry. A filmmaker or the producer of a film marshals the resources to make one film and then does the same thing again for the next film, using a mix of funding sources. The individual artists retain a high degree of control over the final outcome.

aural cue A sound that activates the viewer's awareness of the space beyond the frame.

auteur theory More a matter of emphasis than a true theory, auteur theory began with French critics who saw recurrent patterns and themes in the work of Hollywood directors whom other critics regarded as highly competent journeymen carrying out a wide variety of assignments in different genres. The discovery of underlying themes and consistent stylistic tendencies among films in different genres by the same director became evidence that some studio directors qualified as artists: they pursued personal preoccupations and developed an individual **style**.

background The area of the frame farthest from the camera in distinction to objects, actions or individuals who occupy the **foreground**.

back light A light placed behind the main characters, out of view, which serves to cast something of a halo around the head or figure of the character. It differentiates the character from her surroundings and makes her stand out in the frame.

B-budget films Studio-sponsored films that have more limited budgets than **A-budget films** and were, historically, the standard genre films that filled double bills as the second feature. Some are very pedestrian and others possess strikingly unusual qualities, partly because more artistic risk is possible with a smaller budget.

below-the-line Expenses for personnel that perform tasks at the behest of the **above-the-line** personnel, but nonetheless possess distinct talents and skills of considerable value.

between pictures A term used during the era of the Hollywood studio system to indicate that a producer, director, star, or other film personnel under contract was not productively employed in making a film at that particular moment.

binary oppositions Either/or categories such as us/them, black/white, good/evil, and so on. These oppositions are often based on fixed images of others, and govern **hegemonic** relations in the **social imaginary**.

biological sex The anatomical sex characteristics of an individual.

blaxploitation films Films that featured African American males in the role of the heroic tough guy who defeats an assortment of villains, usually drug dealers, pimps, and mobsters.

bricoleur Someone who "makes do" with what's available.

Buck A stereotype that represents a black variation on the stereotype of the **Greaser**. Sometimes brutal, often ruthless, and almost always oversexed, the buck stereotype represents a hyper-masculine image of the African American as a powerful, magnetic physical force. Whereas the **Coon** forfeits intelligence for buffoonery, the buck subordinates intelligence to physical and, often, sexual prowess.

carnivalesque An occasion when for a limited time and in a specified place, the normal order of things is suspended and a festive, defiant, subversive spirit breaks loose.

CGI (computer-generated images) A technique for generating images that does not photograph objects but creates them from software. CGI offers a huge range of options for creating entirely fabricated images, or altering images that have real-world **referents**.

charisma A form of personal magnetism that draws people to those who possess it.

choker close-up A shot that presents only part of the face or an object. Also known as **extreme close-up**.

closed frame A shot that gives the sense that it is entirely self-sufficient. This type of framing creates the sense of a world where action takes place inside the boundaries of the shot.

closeted Refers to individuals who mask their **sexual identity**.

close-up A shot that fills the screen with an object or figure of significance, typically the face, but the shot is also used for important objects such as a key, knife or letter.

collage A favorite device of many **modernist** artists, it involves mixing together various elements from different sources or media to create a new effect. Photo-collage involves combining different photographic images into a single new image.

coming out Making an open acknowledgment of a non-heterosexual identity.

computer-generated images See **CGI**.

condensation The process of loading something with more meaning or importance than it would normally receive. Condensation usually packs a variety of values and meanings into a single signifier or image.

consciousness-raising The process of arriving at a state of greater awareness about something. Through this process individuals or groups see things in a fresh way.

constructivism A movement peculiar to the Soviet Union. It began before the revolution of 1917 and continued, in different forms, after. Constructivism helped pave the way for the great silent films of the Soviet cinema by breaking with realist representation. Form and the physical materiality of objects received prominent attention.

continuity editing, continuity The standard form of editing. Continuity includes all the ways of organizing shots so that the transition from one shot to the next does not jar the viewer. It creates a smooth sense of flow so that the story takes priority over the mechanics of storytelling.

contrapuntal sound Sound that adds informational or emotional qualities that comment on the visual image rather than simply reinforce it.

conventions The patterns of organization that operate most frequently in films and that viewers expect to encounter. Conventions are a customary way of doing things, rather than strict rules.

Coon A comic stereotype of African American males. The Coon condenses all of the assumptions of intellectual inferiority assigned to blacks. Fumbling, full of comic malapropisms and antic gestures, he is invariably made into the butt of jokes.

coping behavior Behavior that may not consciously endorse or reaffirm the **dominant ideology** but nonetheless conforms to it.

coverage A practice of shooting designed to give the editor options in case more specific shots do not work out.

crosscutting An editing pattern in which the film cuts back and forth between two different actions: one person fleeing and another in pursuit, for example. Also known as **parallel editing**.

cultural capital Non-monetary benefits from the arts that accrue to a country as a whole in terms of prestige, status, and international reputation.

cultural ideals Ideals that give utopian, or ideal, embodiment to the values and beliefs that lie behind day-to-day activities, social policies, and institutional functions. Values and beliefs are typically intangible concepts that give more specific meaning to qualities such as love, status, or power.

cut-aways Separate shots that are inserted into scenes, normally shots of objects that can be made at an entirely different time or place, and then inserted or cut into the scene at the appropriate point. Also known as **inserts**.

Dada A small but influential movement at the start of the twentieth century that used shock, strange juxtapositions, and **collage** to create work that often had a political, confrontational tone.

decorum The choice of behavior most fitting to a particular occasion. In terms of rhetoric, the choice of style that is fitting for the subject and purpose.

deep focus cinematography A form of cinematography that keeps objects at different distances from the camera clearly in focus.

depth of field The span of distance from the camera over which the image remains in sharp focus.

diegesis The story world occupied by the film's characters.

diegetic sound Sound that appears to originate in the story world or **diegesis** such as sound from a radio playing in the scene.

differentiation All those innovations to narrative convention, variations on familiar plots, stylistic idiosyncrasies, distinctive forms of character development, and specific choices of selection and arrangement that mark any given film as unique.

director's cut A new release of a film that has the full approval of the director.

discontinuity editing A form of editing that violates the rules or conventions that make **continuity** a relatively invisible or unnoticed form of editing.

displacement A process that shifts tension, conflict, and emotional energy from its primary source to a secondary, less inflammatory focus.

distanciation See **alienation effect**.

dolly A wheeled platform that rolls the camera to a new location. A dolly shot is a form of **tracking shot**.

dominant ideology The view of the world that tends to prevail in a given time and place, upholding the existing relations of power and hierarchy.

double consciousness African American scholar W. E. B. Du Bois's term for the acute awareness a victim of discrimination must have of the intentions and dispositions of those who wield social power over him or her. The victim must be highly vigilant: misjudging the meaning or intention of someone who has the power to cause harm, emotionally or physically, can have dire, even deadly consequences.

dumb blonde The stereotype of a woman who may not actually be a **virgin** but whose innocence combines with apparent ignorance of common knowledge and obliviousness regarding her erotic effect on others.

Dutch tilt A shift of the entire camera off its horizontal axis so that it tilts to the left or right, producing an image no longer perpendicular to the ground.

dystopia An imagined world gone awry. Instead of a Shangri-La of dreamed perfection, a dystopia presents a world where balance is lost, hierarchy prevails, technology runs amok, aliens scourge the land, and so on.

establishing shot A shot that provides an overview of the scene, often locating the action in a larger context.

ethnocentrism The tendency to rank one's own cultural values over those of another culture.

ethnography That part of anthropology devoted to the descriptive study of other cultures; ethnographic film is the visual version of written ethnographic accounts.

evidentiary editing Presenting the best possible visible evidence rather than giving the appearance of a smooth continuum of time and space between shots. A distinctive feature in many documentaries as an alternative to **continuity editing**.

expressionism A movement that arose in Germany and spread to many countries, and gave visual expression to inner, typically conflicted or disturbed states of mind. It emphasized what it feels like to experience emotional turmoil more than it sought out the social causes for this turmoil.

extra-diegetic inserts Shots that don't belong to the same world that the characters belong to. They inform the audience of a value judgment by the filmmaker about a character or his world.

extra-diegetic sound Sound that comments on the story world and belongs to the narration (the process of storytelling) rather than the narrative (the story that is told).

extreme close-up See **choker close-up**.

eyeline match A form of **match editing** that involves having one character look in the direction of another character even if the other character is not in the shot. To match, the second character must look back in the direction of the first character.

fade A gradual elimination of light from a shot so that the image becomes darker.

fade to black A gradual elimination of all light from a shot so that the screen becomes black.

family romance A term of Sigmund Freud's for the various emotional currents that play out within family relationships.

fellow travelers Individuals who are not members of the Communist Party but support many of the same causes as those who are.

fetish A person or object that is overvalued because of meanings or needs projected onto it. In cinema, the fetish often serves as a projection of the male's fantasy of female perfection. As an idealization, the fetish also denies women's real limitations and needs in order to fabricate an image devoted entirely to the fulfillment of male needs.

field of view The amount of the scene before the camera that is actually visible through the camera. A **telephoto lens** narrows the field of view and flattens the sense of depth within the image, but also magnifies that limited field so that much more detail can be seen. A **wide-angle lens** broadens the field of view and increases the sense of depth within the image.

fill light A light typically placed lower than the **key light** and to the opposite side of the main characters. It is a weaker light but is adequate to fill in most or all of the key light's shadows.

film noir ("black film") A cycle of postwar films that employed **low key lighting** and were literally dark. They were, in fact, often shot at night with only enough **key light** to identify the main characters. Their tone was also dark, exploring themes of seduction, betrayal, and murder.

final cut The power to make the ultimate decision about the final shape of a film.

flashback or **flash forward** An editing pattern in which the disparity between shots is not accidental but is a result of jumping back or forward in time; the director normally goes to some pains to make the jump in time and space intelligible, motivated by memory or anticipation on the part of a character.

floodlight A light that covers a larger area diffusely.

focal length The distance from the lens to the recording material in the camera (the film strip, for example) needed to bring the image to a focus, measured in millimeters. A 50mm focal length lens, for 35mm film, produces an image similar to that of the human eye. Shorter focal lengths produce **wide-angle** shots and longer ones **telephoto** shots.

foreground The area of the frame closest to the camera, usually populated by the main characters or crucial pieces of action.

formalism A self-referential quality in **modernist** art that often engages in a dialogue with its medium, making the brushstrokes of a painting, the flatness of a canvas, the concrete and steel of a building, the presence of words on a page, or disruptions in time and space produced by film editing the subject of the work as much as the external world to which the work refers.

found footage Footage that was originally shot for another purpose. It can be footage that was never used in a film (outtakes), or portions of a finished film.

free speech The principle by which individuals, or filmmakers, can say and do what they choose. It is then only after they have done so that courts may become involved in cases that question whether the utterance or film violated certain standards, such as those of obscenity, slander, or libel.

French New Wave A movement that took shape at the end of the 1950s and beginning of the 1960s with the first films of Jean-Luc Godard, François Truffaut, Claude Chabrol, and others. Their films broke sharply with the poetic and literary traditions in French cinema to celebrate a raw immediacy and to pay overt tribute to American genre films by largely neglected directors like Sam Fuller, Nicholas Ray, and Phil Karlson. Godard's *Breathless* is often considered the quintessential New Wave film.

fronts Intermediaries who sold screenplays on behalf of blacklisted writers. The front, usually a writer and member of the screenwriter's guild, would represent the work as his own and then pass along payment to the blacklisted writer.

f-stop A measure of the lens **aperture**, or opening, that admits light.

gender identity How individuals act in relation to norms of masculinity and femininity in a given culture; the display of traits, mannerisms, and general behavior that falls somewhere along a spectrum from very masculine (rational, independent, self-sufficient, stoic, "tough") to very feminine (emotional, relational, dependent, vulnerable, "soft").

genre films Films that share thematic and stylistic features that become known as conventions, such as shoot-outs in westerns, betrayal in **film noir**, or episodes of song and dance in musicals. These conventions establish a set of constraints, and opportunities, that individual films explore in distinct ways.

good-bad girl The stereotype of the vamp who proves to have a heart of gold.

graphic match A form of **match editing** that tries to guide the viewer through the transition from one shot to the next by making the two images similar in appearance.

Greaser Stereotype of Mexicans as scheming, deceptive, and murderous, dating from the early days of cinema, when films first portrayed Mexican characters as thieves, drunks, or killers.

green-light To approve and fund a film.

hegemonic order A particular distribution of power and hierarchy that results from the work of **hegemony** in practice.

hegemony The process by which a given social system wins the voluntary consent of its members to accept their place within a hierarchical structure.

High art Refers to the traditional arts (painting, sculpture, ballet, opera, literature, and theater), especially as they flourished during the

Renaissance and after. High art served the interests of a largely bourgeois and aristocratic audience and received patronage and support from these classes. Modernism often drew on this tradition to distinguish itself from popular culture and the generally middle-class audience it served, at least in the nineteenth and early twentieth centuries.

high definition (HD) A digital television broadcast system that more than doubles the **resolution** of traditional television sets. High definition produces images with almost as much detail as 35mm film.

high key lighting The predominant form of lighting, in which available natural light is supplemented to ensure a uniformly well-lit image. The light is bright throughout the frame, with few shadows, and a minimum of contrast in the lighting values throughout the scene.

homoerotic Involving same-sex attraction, whether associated with sexual activity or involving the indirect expression of sexually charged feelings.

homosociality Those **sublimated** forms of shared endeavor among men, from cattle drives and bank capers to putting on a show or fighting a war. These sublimated but emotionally charged forms of male bonding channel energies to nonsexual ends that might have otherwise taken a more overtly sexual turn. They provide some of the gratifications of sexual intimacy with none of the risks.

humanism An attitude that stresses the common bonds of love, trust, labor, hopes and dreams that can bind people of diverse backgrounds to a common destiny.

identification The emotional and psychological involvement with characters and the stars who play them.

ideologues Those who proselytize for a given way of seeing things.

ideology The ways in which a certain image of one's place in the world becomes internalized and then functions as a guide to proper conduct in a given social context.

indexes Available in libraries and online, indexes provide a list or database of all the articles in a given set of sources. They usually allow searches by author, title, and subject matter.

indexical relationship The relationship of the photographic image to its **referent**. The photographic image commonly bears a strict correspondence to what it represents. That is to say, normal photographic lenses and film or digital storage devices preserve the appearance and proportions of what they photograph in extremely precise ways. This quality is what made photography, and later film, seem revolutionary: painting and sculpture possessed great beauty but they did not present a precise duplication of what the artist used as a model. The indexical relation of the photograph to its referent meant that artistry had to lie elsewhere: in composition, lighting, choice of lens, and so on, rather than in how the original referent became the springboard for artistic license.

individual racism Racism or prejudice in which individuals regard others as inferior to themselves.

infrastructure A basic system of organization that exists to achieve particular goals such as the transportation of goods or the production of films.

inserts See **cut-aways**.

institutional racism Racism or prejudice in which the social practices of an institution embody discriminatory patterns. Institutional racism involves forms of discrimination built into the legalized, everyday activities of institutions.

irony A mode of expression where what is said is not necessarily what is meant, or where what is said is said as if in quotes, as if it didn't quite mean what it appears to mean.

jump cut A form of **mismatch** in which the shift from one shot to the next fails to maintain smooth **continuity** in space or time.

key light A light typically placed above and to the side of the main character(s). It is the strongest source of light on the set and casts some shadows.

kick light A light that casts a harsh, silhouetting light that catches only part of a face or figure. Also known as a **rim light**.

legs The ability of a film to continue to bring in appreciable revenue over time.

long shot A shot that renders the central characters as small figures relative to their surroundings.

long take Shot that is noticeably more extended than usual: the viewer gains the most obvious plot information from the shot but the shot lingers, or things continue to happen without a cut occurring.

looking relations The relationships between what the camera sees, what characters see, and what the audience sees.

low key lighting A dramatic way of lighting in which only parts of the frame, if any, are well lit, shadows are plentiful, contrasts vivid, and the human figure may blend into the surrounding darkness and shadow (little or no **backlighting**).

male chauvinism, masculinism, and **machismo** Terms adopted by the women's movement to describe male behavior that derives from an assumption of male superiority such as deciding whether a wife should work and under what conditions or having the right to make crude passes at women.

Mammy A stereotypical representation of African American women. The large, cantankerous Mammy speaks her mind but is basically ineffectual. She is like the Greek chorus of old, speaking truths, but with a comic manner that makes her more laughable than forbidding.

master shot A shot that positions the camera at sufficient distance from the actors to cover all their movements and gestures.

match action One of the most common forms of **match editing**, in which movement is the element carried over from one shot to the next.

match editing A form of **continuity editing** in which some element of one shot is carried over to the next shot to smooth the transition.

medium close shot A shot that presents the human figure from mid-chest up.

medium long shot A shot in which a character is visible from the ankles or knees up. Also known as a *plan américain*.

medium shot A shot that presents the human figure from the waist up.

medium two shot A shot that shows two people from the waist up.

metaphor A figure of speech where one thing stands for another.

method acting An approach to acting that heightens emotional investment through **identification** with the character's state of mind.

miscegenation Mixed-race sexual relationships, especially between blacks and whites.

mise-en-scène The arrangement of what appears in front of the camera. It can include set design, lighting, costumes, props, character placement, and movement.

mismatch Result of a lack of continuity between shots. A mismatch is treated as a violation of **continuity** but may be valued in **montage editing**.

modernism A reaction against both the apparent sacrifice of a high art tradition to commercialism and the collapse of civilization and the social order signaled by the horrific carnage of World War I. Modernism exhibits two alternative characteristics to the tenets of **realism**: (1) a very noticeable storytelling process, replacing the effort to make it seem as if the story world possesses an existence of its own; (2) an exploration of the interior, subjective life of characters, in which characters drift into their own imagined worlds regardless of their surroundings.

modernity The conditions of life in the period of twentieth-century capitalism, especially in the urban centers of industrialized nations. Modernity referred to the consolidation of capitalism into large, corporate, often international or colonial forms and to the ascendancy of finance capital as a way to control development at one remove from actual production.

montage editing A form of **discontinuity editing** that brings individual shots together to generate a shock, strange juxtaposition, or new idea. These editing techniques were advanced by the Soviet silent cinema and by Sergei Eisenstein in particular.

montage sequence Within the conventions of Hollywood cinema, an assembly of shots that mark the passage of time or the unfolding of a process.

neo-noir A film made after the heyday of **film noir** in the late 1940s to late 1950s but in the same spirit and style.

neorealism A movement that arose from the historical ashes of Italy's defeat at the end of World War II, but also from the desire to construct a different kind of narrative, one that focused on everyday life and "little people" who endured hardship outside the spotlight reserved for public figures and historic events.

normal lens A lens that renders the relationships between figures in depth much as they appear to the human eye, typically a 50mm lens in 35mm film production or a 25mm lens in 16mm.

novelization A novel based on a film that closely follow the same plot.

objectivity A term in the sciences for the detachment of the experimenter from the experiment and the replicable, verifiable nature of the results; it is a more complicated term in the humanities, since the subject of study is human society itself.

off-screen look A technique for activating **off-screen space** that produces a sense of asymmetry or imbalance to the image as if more space should be included.

off-screen space The space outside the frame.

one shot A shot showing only one character in the frame.

open frame A shot that gives the sense that what occurs inside the frame is part of a much wider field of potential action rather than an enclosed, self-contained composition.

Other The Other, with a capital O, is often used to signify an abstract other that is the product of **hegemonie** processes. It is what becomes of others when they are subordinated, demeaned, and reduced to a stereotype. A hierarchy comes into existence. One group dominates by making another group subordinate.

over-the-shoulder shot A shot or editing pattern that locates the two principal characters in relation to each other by filming over each character's shoulder in succession.

packaging The practice of assembling many of the **above-the-line** personnel as a single package to market to a studio for funding.

pan A horizontal movement of the camera.

pan and scan An electronic process that selects what appears to be the most important part of an image (bodies and faces, for example) and crops or eliminates the rest in order to cut down wide-screen film images to fit the narrower television screen.

paradigmatic axis All the choices that work in a given context, out of which one is chosen; sometimes referred to as the metaphoric axis.

parallel editing See **crosscutting**.

patriarchy A social system in which public and domestic power resides with males, notably with the senior male member of a family group, the patriarch.

performance anxiety Strong visceral feelings of self-doubt, feelings of inadequacy, and fear of rejection, humiliation, or failure that for some men accompany the demands of the **performance principle**.

performance principle In writings of Herbert Marcuse, the principle that revolves around work, toil, sacrifice, discipline, and obedience. The performance principle and the **pleasure principle** can be considered as different points on the spectrum of **gender identity**, from highly masculine to strongly feminine.

periodization An analytic tool that involves identifying specific time spans during which consistencies prevail and between which differences emerge or transformations occur.

plagiarism In essence, intellectual fraud: the author claims the ideas of someone else as his own. Plagiarism, like the deliberate misrepresentation of facts, is an extremely serious offense; it can lead to substantial penalties.

plan américain See **medium long shot**.

pleasure principle In writings of Herbert Marcuse, the principle that centers on play, pleasure, spontaneity, creativity, and joy.

plot The sequence of situations and events as they unfold chronologically on the screen. The plot is what is most often summarized or distilled as the content of a film.

point-of-view shot Shot that shows what a character sees, usually to produce subjective **identification** with the character. Point-of-view shots normally use **eyeline matches**.

postmodernism The most recent of the three grand styles, postmodernism presents two alternative characteristics to those of **realism** and **modernism**: (1) the storytelling process draws attention to itself through a high degree of quotation, homage, borrowing, copying, and otherwise recycling previous work; (2) postmodernism emphasizes how any one imagined world is more like other imagined worlds than like reality itself.

post-production The editing of sound and image, and **special effects**.

pre-production The preparation to shoot a film, such as screenplay development.

presence-in-absence The phenomenon by which the photographic image represents in a realistic way a **referent**, an object or person, that is no longer physically present. The spectator knows that the image's referent is no longer present, but it appears to be.

primary source material The object itself, in this case, the film, as well as sources that provide direct access to the thoughts and actions of those involved in the film such as diaries, oral histories, and autobiographies.

principal photography The portion of shooting that involves the main characters themselves.

prior censorship The determination of what can and cannot be said or done prior to the saying or doing of it. It often involves lists of prohibitions, along with penalties for violations. Prior censorship contrasts with the principle of **free speech**.

prior restraint The banning of certain forms of expression before they reach the public; as exemplified by the Hollywood Production Code, usually by reviewing screenplay proposals or by examining a finished film and demanding the elimination of objectionable material.

production The actual shooting of a film.

prop An object provided for use in a film such as a gun, photograph, or piece of clothing.

prototype In the film industry, a film similar to but distinct from previous films that is also a possible model for future films.

psychological realism A form of **realism** that stresses the plausible, lifelike traits, mannerisms, feelings, and behavior of characters. This form tends to draw the viewer into patterns of **identification** with characters.

racism See **individual racism, institutional racism.**

rack focus The practice of shifting from one plane of focus to another rapidly during a shot.

realism The construction of a cinematic world that bears strong resemblance to the world with which viewers are already familiar. Realism also involves a process of storytelling that typically passes unnoticed by means of techniques such as **continuity editing**.

referent What a sign refers to outside the language in which it appears. The word "computer" is just a set of letters, but its **referent** is a real-world device.

reflexive film A film that uses various means to draw attention to what would otherwise be taken for granted as conventions. A reflexive documentary, for example, might draw attention to the efforts made to give an interview the appearance of being entirely spontaneous when it was, in fact, rehearsed by showing some of the rehearsal. Reflexive films usually encourage the audience to be more aware of the viewing process itself and the conventions that typically operate in a given genre or type of film.

repression The denial of the existence of certain thoughts or feelings, or the stifling of alternative **gender identities** or **sexual orientations**. Repression can be external, in the form of social pressures that encourage individuals to conform to the status quo, or internal, in the form of a psychic process that removes some thoughts and desires from consciousness by pushing them into the unconscious.

resolution In cinematography, the maximum degree of detail captured by the medium.

reverse shot A shot that shows what could be seen if the camera angle were reversed 180 degrees, usually showing another part of the story world or **diegesis**.

rim light See **kick light**.

saturation booking The practice of filling as many theaters with as many people as quickly as possible.

Schüfftan process A **special effect** that allowed filmmakers to shoot a miniature model of a set through a mirror and superimpose this shot onto the same strip of film that recorded the principal actors. The actors would now appear to stand before a vast, possibly fantastical set.

screen direction Onscreen direction in which characters are looking. In **match editing**, screen direction is quite important. If a first character looks to the right as she talks to another character, the second character needs to look to the left to achieve match. If both characters look off screen to the right, they will appear to be looking at someone or something else and not at each other.

screen left The area of space to the left side of the screen from the audience's perspective.

screen right The area of space to the right side of the screen.

secondary source material The body of writing that has accumulated about the **primary source material**; it represents the process of interpreting the primary material from different perspectives.

semiotics The study of communication, whether verbal or non-verbal, visual or aural.

sex-gender system The ways in which the biological male and female sexes turn into a socially constructed and ideologically loaded range of **sexual** and **gender identities**, some of which may be treated as normal and others as deviant.

sexual identity, sexual orientation Sometimes used interchangeably with biological **sex**, sexual identity also refers to whether a person is attracted to the same sex or the opposite sex. Same-sex attraction goes by terms such as homosexual, gay, or lesbian, while opposite-sex attraction is commonly known as a heterosexual and straight orientation. The word "orientation" is often used to indicate that sexual attraction is not primarily a matter of conscious choice and usually originates in childhood.

sexual perversions Forms of sexual behavior that strikes many as strange, aberrant, unpleasant, or distasteful partly because they are typically uncoupled from any reproductive goal.

shot/reverse shot An editing pattern in which one of the characters talks to the other person, who is off-screen. The next shot reverses the view and shows the other person talking to the first person, who is now off-screen.

sign The smallest meaningful unit of communication. The sign is made up of the **signifier** and the **signified**.

signified The meaning of a given image, or the meaning the viewer supplies to it.

signifier The thing seen or heard, or what is materially presented to the viewer.

social gests A Brechtian term referring to **ideological** action and behavior such as treating a subordinate discourteously and a superior obsequiously.

social imaginary The collection of prejudicial images assigned to different groups within the social dynamics related to power and hierarchy. It is the arena within which members of one group picture members of another group in terms of stereotypes and clichés.

social practices The speech, behavior, and actions that individuals exhibit and institutions adopt in day to day activity.

social problem genre A genre of film that draws public attention to a serious public issue.

social symbolic A distinct realm comprised of symbolic acts of understanding and empathy that shine a light on cultural ideals, which otherwise often disappear within the darkness of prejudicial social practices.

soft-focus cinematography The use of a special lens, gauze, or filmy substance (like Vaseline) to produce a slightly out-of-focus or soft, diffuse look to the image. Frequently used for close-ups of female stars.

sound mixing The careful blending of as many as 48 different soundtracks into one master soundtrack. See also **subjective sound**.

special effects A way to do things in cinema that can not be done in reality. Special effects produce images or scenes that supplement what a camera can record on its own.

spotlight A light that is sharply focused on a limited area.

standardization A process involving all those narrative conventions, filmmaking techniques, skills, and facilities that can be carried over from one film to another.

steadicam A harness, used during **tracking shots**, that absorbs the jerkiness of human movement.

studio cut The version of a film whose final form was determined by executives at the film studio that funded or distributed the film.

style The particular way a filmmaker makes use of cinematic **signifiers**. Style also refers to broad categories like **realism** to which many works belong. Unlike plot, style is always medium-specific. Film style involves the way a filmmaker selects and arranges images, together with any accompanying sounds.

subculture A distinct cultural group living within a larger society.

subjective sound The rendering of sound or images in films as a character would hear or see them, rather than how an objective auditor would hear or see them.

sublimation The conversion of a basic drive, such as sexual desire, into a non-overtly sexual form. It is a form of **displacement** from a physical urge to a more creative or spiritual activity.

subtext An unstated or implicit theme or message that is not readily apparent but that may nonetheless register and have an impact on a viewer.

superimposition A **special effect** created by placing one shot on top of another so that the two images are seen at the same time.

surrealism A movement that took **collage** principles in the direction of the unconscious by rejecting **realism** and substituting the more bizarre and fantastic principles of dreams.

suspense Uncertainty about the outcome of a situation. Suspense is a key difference between storytelling and logical discourse: reason seeks the simplest, clearest, shortest path to the solution of a problem, while narration looks for ways to postpone or delay the resolution so that the psychology of characters, the complexity of situations, and the suspense of not knowing what will happen next gain intensity.

syllogism A way to state premises and draw a conclusion. Some syllogisms are valid, but some only appear valid. "Dogs have four legs; Fido is a dog; therefore he has four legs" is valid, but "Fido is a dog; Fido has spots on his legs; therefore all dogs have spots on their legs" is faulty. A characteristic of one dog may not be true of all dogs.

synchronous sound, sync sound Spoken dialogue or other sounds that are synchronized to a shot of the characters speaking or to any other source, such as a gun shot or a car starting up.

syntagmatic axis As opposed to the **paradigmatic axis**, the actual arrangement of the chosen signs; sometimes referred to as the metonymic axis. This axis unfolds over time.

taboos Prohibitions that carry a strong emotional charge. Violating them may jeopardize one's social status. Incest is often cited as the most fundamental social taboo, since the taboo guarantees that individuals will seek sexual partners outside the family unit and thereby create a network of kinship relations that can broaden into an entire social order.

telephoto lens A lens with a long focal length that brings a narrow slice of the field of vision in front of the camera into close, detailed view.

tertiary source material Information derived from **secondary sources** that synthesizes, summarizes, or popularizes this material such as encyclopedia entries. It may provide helpful background but seldom plays a central role in research, since **primary** and **secondary source material** are more reliable.

Third Cinema Films made in underdeveloped countries that actively seek alternatives to the characteristics of mainstream, Hollywood-style cinema. The alternatives may involve more leisurely pacing, less stress on actions and deadlines, an emphasis on groups more than heroes, deeper explorations of situations or states rather than challenges and obstacles, and the use of modernist or postmodernist techniques.

Third World cinema Films from what have been identified as Third World countries. The term arose during the Cold War for those nations that were neither part of the communist bloc nor of the advanced capitalist nations. Third World cinema is a more inclusive term than **Third Cinema**, since it represents any form of film production from these countries.

tie-ins Products, such as **novelizations**, clothing, toys, or video games associated with an original film, that provide additional income.

tilt A vertical movement of the camera.

tracking shot A shot in which the camera is moved from place to place while filming continuously.

tracks Tracks similar to small-gauge railroad tracks, used to mount a **dolly** to assure smoothness of motion.

Tragic Mulatto A stereotype that has historically functioned as a dramatic warning of the perils of miscegenation. The Mulatto is the light-skinned black who often tries to pass for white. Doom awaits. Once the secret of mixed blood gets out, no matter how white the character may not only look but behave, the Tragic Mulatto plummets from the white world back into the African American culture he or she sought to escape.

two shot A shot with two people present in the same frame.

Uncle Tom A stereotype of male blacks that comes from the 1852 novel *Uncle Tom's Cabin*, about a good-hearted slave who aspires to nothing more than fulfilling his master needs. The Tom is benign, innocent, trusting, compliant, obedient, and faithful. Nothing can rouse him to regard his master in a bad light; he remains loyal to the end even when subjected to physical threat or violence.

virgin As a stereotype, a male projection onto women of profound innocence and vulnerability. Men can then play the role of strong, resourceful protector.

visual cue An image or look that activates the viewer's awareness of the space beyond the frame.

voice of authority A visible voice, someone who is both seen and heard, such as a television reporter, anchorperson, or the filmmaker.

voice-off Spoken dialogue that is heard but spoken from beyond the frame, off-screen.

voice of God An unseen voice that delivers commentary on behalf of the film and is external to the events depicted.

voice-over commentary Commentary that arrives from **extra-diegetic** space, that is, from outside the story world.

white skin privilege In terms of race in the United States and other predominantly white countries, white skin privilege is the assumption of rights or privileges for oneself because of the color of one's skin. Elsewhere, other skin colors may be privileged.

wide-angle lens A lens with a short focal length that captures a wide field of vision.

zoom lens A lens that can effectively shift from a **wide-angle lens**, with an exaggerated sense of depth, to a **telephoto lens**, with a diminished sense of depth.

zoom shot A shot that traverses space by changing the focal length of the **zoom lens** rather than by moving the camera.

INDEX OF NAMES AND TITLES

INDEX OF SUBJECTS

defined, 137, 502
differentiation in, 254–57
displacement in, 271–78
distinct world view, 252–53
genres as total system, 258–64
individual and society, 264–67
industrial context and, 218
interpreting, 280–85
power/fascination of, 285–86
realism and, 181–83
representative list of, 249–51
standardization in, 254–57
voyeurism in, 376–77
giving credit where due, 471–73
good-bad girl stereotype, 400–401,
    502
government policy, persuasion and,
    104–6
graphic match, 40, 502
Greaser stereotype
    Buck stereotype and, 495
    defined, 333, 502
green-light, 229, 502

Hays Code, 239
HD (high definition), 66, 503
hegemonic order
    defined, 296, 502
    Other and, 507–8
    social imaginary and, 494
hegemony
    cultural ideals and, 294–95
    defined, 295, 502
    ideology and, 294–97
    meaning/function of, 295–97
heterosexuality, see sexual identity
high art, 176, 502–3
high definition (HD), 66, 503
high key lighting, 57, 503
historical periods, see periodization
Hollywood blacklist, 242–44
Hollywood Production Code, see
    Production Code
Hollywood Ten, 243–44
Home Box Office (HBO), 210
homoeroticism, 82, 503
homosexuality, see sexual identity
homosociality, 389, 503

House Un-American Activities
    Committee (HUAC), 242–
    44
humanism, 157, 503

IDA (International Documentary
    Association), 210
identification
    alienation effect, 492
    defined, 68, 503
    method acting and, 506
    point-of-view shot and, 509
    psychological realism and, 510
ideologues, 291, 503
ideology
    behaviors and, 297–310
    blind adherence to, 291–92
    consciousness-raising and, 293–94
    defined, 9, 503
    dominant, see dominant ideology
    feminist, 187
    film forms challenging, 310–22
    Great Refusal of, 367–68
    hegemony and, 294–97
    narrative films and, 161–62
    prejudice and, 338–39
    as productive force, 287–90
    of realism, 183–84
    as repressive force, 287–90
    social context and, 322–24
    social gests and, 512
IMDB (International Movie
    Database), 462, 463
IMPA (International Motion Picture
    Association), 212–13
indexes
    defined, 504
    of journal/magazine topics, 460–
    62
indexical relationship
    as copy of reality, 106–7
    defined, 86, 106, 504
    question of evidence, 107–8
individual racism
    defined, 326, 504
    social imaginary and, 326–29
*Industrial Commission of Ohio, Mutual
    Film Corporation v.*, 231